COLD WAR COLD PEACE

The United States and Russia since 1945

COLD WAR COLD PEACE

The United States and Russia since 1945

Bernard A. Weisberger

Introduction by HARRISON E. SALISBURY

AMERICAN HERITAGE
New York
Distributed by
HOUGHTON MIFFLIN COMPANY
Boston

Library of Congress Cataloging in Publication Data

Weisberger, Bernard A., 1922–
  Cold war, cold peace.

  Bibliography: p.
  Includes index.
  1. World politics—20th century.   2. United States—
Foreign relations—Soviet Union.   3. Soviet Union—
Foreign relations—United States.   I. Title.
D445.W37   327'.0904   81-20495
ISBN 0-8281-1163-4
ISBN 0-8281-1164-2 (deluxe)

Printed in the United States of America

For Judy

Table of Contents

INTRODUCTION

Ask the ordinary American when the Cold War began and, if he ventures a date, it will almost certainly be March 5, 1946, that historic evening when Winston Churchill appeared on a platform with President Truman at Westminster College, Fulton, Missouri, and declared:

> From Stettin, in the Baltic, to Trieste, in the Adriatic, an Iron Curtain has descended across the continent. . . .

Few, indeed, will recall that four weeks earlier Generalissimo Stalin, in a speech to the Moscow electorate on February 9, sounded an equally somber warning to the Russian people, declaring that the conflict just ended had not driven away the threat of war; World War II had not been accidental; Hitler was not an aberration; so long as imperialism (that is, the United States and Western Europe) remained, so long must Russia arm for battle. He presented to his countrymen the grim prospect of three more five-year industrial plans, fifteen years of struggle and sacrifice to meet the overhanging danger.

Churchill and Stalin, leagues apart in philosophy—one democracy's finest spokesman, the other the cruelest of Marxist dictators—saw the world in the same terms of realism.

Long before Fulton, Churchill had privately warned and publicly prepared for the postwar struggle, the Cold War. So had Stalin. Not so the United States.

Americans have notoriously short historical memory. Each morning we awaken to what seems to us a world made new; crises flare up; our lives are twisted askew by events that seem to us to originate somewhere in the blue—like the Cold War. But the Cold War did not begin with Stalin's speech in Moscow nor Churchill's at Fulton. The two orators simply sought to alert their constituencies to the

1

facts of life, the essential conditions of the world order, the perils that must be expected, and the tasks that must be undertaken.

Wars, cold wars, confrontations, tension in international relations, have deep roots. They do not bound onto the world stage in one dramatic leap. They develop slowly over long periods of time from one phase to another. Tension between the United States and Russia had attained a stubbornly high level long before World War II came to an end. Bad relations had existed before, during, and after World War II. They had been even worse before, during, and after World War I. In fact, relations between the United States and Russia could hardly have been worse than in the decade before 1914. At that time a U.S. trade embargo was in effect, and there was talk of severing diplomatic relations. American sympathy during the 1905 revolution in Russia was with the revolutionaries, as strongly as it has been in recent times with Russian dissidents.

Public hostility in America toward czarist Russia from the 1880s onward matched that of the period we now call the Cold War. It was fueled by many of the same perceptions that fuel it today. Americans saw Russia, Imperial Russia, as they see present-day Soviet Russia—autocratic; despotic; dictatorial; bulwarked by a pervasive system of secret police, informers, provocateurs; its people deprived of human rights, shorn of liberty, without free speech, free press, or freedom of religion. The Russian Orthodox church, the official faith, maintained a monopoly. Protestants and Roman Catholics were barred or subject to severe restrictions. Jews were persecuted.

There was no political democracy. The Russian czar was an all-powerful satrap straight out of the dark ages. Order was maintained by the Okhrana, the czar's political police, the harshest in the world. Mounted Cossack troops rode down demonstrators or strikers, wielding the knout, the short Russian whip, slashing with sabers, firing their carbines.

The exile system swallowed tens of thousands of unfortunates who were marched in chains thousands of miles from European Russia through blizzards and minus-60-degree temperatures to labor and die in Siberian mines, pits, factories, and forests. The system was the foundation on which Stalin was to build his Gulag. The horrors of Siberian prisons were vividly exposed by a prominent American writer, George Frost Kennan (an uncle of the contemporary George Kennan), whose *Siberia and the Exile System,* published in 1958, became a best-seller around the world, much like Aleksandr Solzhenitsyn's *The Gulag Archipelago* has in our time.

When famine swept the Volga region in 1891-92, and Tolstoy and other prominent Russians tried to save the lives of millions of peasants, a group of American midwestern flour millers sent a shipload of flour to Russia. They had to fight violent anti-Russian sentiment in Congress and in the East, where millions of immigrants driven out of Russia by anti-Semitic persecution were now arriving.

American hostility to Russia was matched by Russian hostility to America. The Russian autocrats typically regarded the United States with hatred and loathing. They felt that the American doctrine of democracy threatened their traditional autocracy. The American Revolution seemed as deadly a threat to successive czars as the Bolshevik Revolution would seem to successive American presidents 150 years later.

Even Catherine II, a comparatively enlightened leader who first hailed the democracy of the West, took fright and clamped down on anyone she suspected of sympathy with Washington or Jefferson. The attitude of the czars and their closest advisers changed little as the nineteenth century gave way to the twentieth.

This does not mean that the two states have not occasionally found common ground, but this has not been a product of admiration or friendship but of selfish national interest.

Russia gave some support to the struggling American colonies because the U.S. action weakened her great rival, England. She supported the United States at the time of the War of 1812 for the same reason, and in the Civil War Russian sympathies were with the North, at least in part because English sympathies were for the South. So it went. The United States and Russia made uncomfortable allies in World War I just as they were to be uncomfortable allies in World War II. It was the national interest of each party that dictated the terms of what General John Deane so vividly called the Strange Alliance.

The end of World War II meant a resumption of that "cold war" that, in one fashion or another, had characterized U.S.-Russian relations long before Communism arrived on the scene. What made the hostility different in degree was the newfound status of the two countries. American power, backed by the atom bomb, now dominated the world. Soviet land power now dominated the Eurasian landmass. These simple facts dictated a clash of American and Soviet interests on a global scale, and the long-existing differences in political and social philosophy provided a made-to-order ideological framework in which the conflict might be set. It is beyond the scope of this work to assess the comparative domestic effects of the Cold War in Russia as well as in the United States. But it can be noted that within the Soviet Union there emerged in heightened form a wave of paranoia, xenophobia, and fear of U.S. attack, which produced the resumption on an unparalleled scale of those elements of terror that had been inherent in Stalin's government (and earlier, under czarist rule)—that is, mass repression, executions, prison camps, censorship, all of the instruments embodied in Churchill's Iron Curtain image.

The Cold War has now lasted for more than thirty-five years. At times it has been so acute as to produce surrogate wars or armed conflicts—the Soviet incursion in northern Iran in 1946, the Berlin confrontation of 1948-49, the Korean War, and so on. At other times it has subsided into "détente." But the underlying factors remain and will remain into the future. It is actually a credit to the statesmen of both Washington and Moscow that the tensions have not spilled over into open war.

It is extremely useful to analyze the historical roots of the U.S.-Russian confrontation because the process brings into perspective long-term trends and makes clear that ideology is not the main component; basic power factors are. This analysis suggests that the past pattern may not necessarily regulate the future. Power shifts are now in progress. Japan has risen as a great technological and industrial power but has not yet assumed diplomatic or military responsibility. China is rising to world status. The European community equals in strength the United States or the Soviet Union. The Third World now plays an increasing role in the world balance.

Any or all of these factors will eventually modify and change the Russian-American superpower balance and with it the nature of what we have known as the Cold War.

HARRISON E. SALISBURY

PROLOGUE

I N THE LAST HALF of the year 1983, like the intermittent rumbling of
a volcano that regularly threatened to erupt, the perennial battle
of words and gestures, thrust and parry between Moscow and
Washington began an ominous escalation.

In July, Soviet aircraft shot down a Korean Airlines passenger jet
that had strayed into their airspace, thereby killing some 269
civilians. The President of the United States and the American
ambassador to the United Nations, using the language of war,
denounced the act as calculated, cold-blooded murder, and proof of
the essential barbarism of the Soviet system. From the Russians
there came initially denials, then a charge that the airliner had
actually been on a spying mission, and finally a statement that
Soviet military pilots had mistaken KAL 007 for an American
military reconnaissance plane. But that final admission was un-
apologetic, and strongly implied that any plane crossing Soviet
boundaries without authorization risked destruction.

In September, addressing a session of the United Nations,
President Reagan blamed the Soviet Union for the precarious state
of world peace, due to its policy of fomenting "Marxist-Leninist"
revolutions around the globe as a screen for its own goal of world
domination.

In October, after 241 U.S. Marines, part of a peacekeeping force
in Beirut, were killed by a terrorist bomb set off in their barracks,
Reagan insisted that they were casualties of an essential mission.
Their role was to keep Lebanon free of domination by Moslems who
were controlled from Syria, which was in turn a Soviet client
through which Moscow hoped to penetrate the oil-rich Middle East.
(By the time the Marines were withdrawn to carriers offshore, in
February of 1984, their total of dead had reached 270.)

Only a few days later, United States forces invaded the indepen-

dent Caribbean nation of Grenada, after a splinter faction of its
left-wing government had taken power through a coup. The
short-range justification was the "rescue" of American students
enrolled in a medical college on the island. But the President, the
Secretary of State, and other Administration officials explained the
deeper underlying reason as well. The Soviet Union, Cuba, and
Nicaragua—all "Marxist" dictatorships—were collaborating on a
plan to turn Grenada into a military base threatening American
lifelines to the Panama Canal. We had gotten there "just in time."
And we would continue our "covert" aid to rebels trying to
overthrow the Nicaraguan government. In effect, the President was
saying, our actions were defensive tactics in a war the Soviet Union
was waging against the western hemisphere.

In early December, the first American cruise and Pershing
missiles were installed at European sites—six minutes' flying time
from Moscow. The Americans had announced the move months in
advance, as a retaliation for Soviet emplacement of SS-20 missiles
that were targeted on European cities. Russia's President Yuri
Andropov swept this argument aside. The Americans, he said, were
simply making intolerable threats against the U.S.S.R., but he would
not be intimidated. Soviet delegations walked out of ongoing talks
with the Americans on the control and reduction of strategic
weapons, and said they would not be back until the "provocations"
were ended. And Andropov promised that there would be some
Soviet move forthcoming to match that of the Americans.

The talk was of war—and it was familiar—and it was taking place
thirty-eight years after the spring and summer that saw Hitlerism
crushed, the United Nations founded, and a new era of peace and
freedom from fear solemnly proclaimed. Thirty-eight years! Over a
third of a century. An entire generation had grown up and become
accustomed to the conflict between the United States and the Soviet
Union that was called the Cold War—a stormy drama of denunciations, propaganda, coups, proxy wars, invasions, alliances, and arms
buildups, punctuated by brief episodes of cooperation, but always
veering perilously toward the brink of nuclear holocaust.

Going into its thirty-ninth year, the Cold War was an old story.
Americans were not so much bored with it as numbed by it, or
rather by the constant fear that it generated. It was a bizarre and
unprecedented historical situation, a perennial conflict between two
giant powers in which neither could vanquish the other without
destroying itself. Yet it could not be settled or compromised by
traditional economic or territorial bargains because it was not
merely a struggle for power and influence. Instead it was a battle of
ideologies between two totally different societies—two nations that
lacked any common ground of discourse except mutual fear of

annihilation. In that way it was less like a conventional national rivalry and more like a war of religion, involving fundamental principles that could not be compromised. So the superpowers were locked—and the world was locked with them—into what appeared to be a permanent situation of tension without termination.

This unique and revolutionary historical situation is the underlying story of the decades since 1945. It is also the theme of this book, which aims to provide some perspective on our time. The chapters that follow will show how, step by step—and often without knowing where the next step would lead—we arrived at our present situation. But they deal with far more than broken treaties and civil wars, espionage trials and summit meetings, nor are they profoundly concerned with who was primarily "at fault" in one crisis or another. The point is rather to show how every aspect of American society has been touched by the conflict. The question of "How did we get here?" is important, but so is one that is less frequently asked: "And what has it done to us?"

Consider this book, then, as a *partial* story of a profoundly transformative period in human history—as much so as the revolutions of four and five centuries ago that gave us the modern world with its discoveries, its great nations, its sciences, its intricately webbed economic and political systems, its philosophies. The Cold War is only an element—though perhaps a fatal one—in that larger tale. Think only of a few of those changes: the decline of the power and influence of Europe, once mistress of civilizations and queen of continents; the defeat of the idea of automatic progress in human affairs; the enormous power given to the state (as against the individual or the tribe) by communications and military technology.

We Americans have not only been involved in these shifts but, to our surprise, have played a major role in them—another of the era's big changes. Since we came onto center stage in world affairs along with the Russians (also newcomers), events have swept us into one whirlwind after another. We have known and mourned the dead of undeclared (and unwinnable) wars. We have known witch hunts and missile crises. We have thrilled to the space race, waited eagerly for headlines describing events in places we once never knew existed, and involved our destiny with that of unpronounceable peoples whom our grandparents thought of only as subjects for missionary work. We have accepted a degree of secrecy and authority in our government—and a level of taxation—that would have caused revolutions a century and a half ago. This steady diet of change, born of the Cold War, has affected us all in ways we could not have imagined before the Cold War started. How could it be otherwise?

Erich Maria Remarque dedicated his great antiwar book, *All Quiet on the Western Front,* to a generation of his fellow veterans who, though they might have escaped the bullets and shells of World War I, were nevertheless destroyed by it. This book tells a tale about our generation, and how even those of its members not directly affected by the crises of the Cold War have been changed by it.

A full understanding of what has happened to us, and what it means for the future, can only come slowly. But the beginning of wisdom is simply to tell the story. And so we must go back to the two major contending parties—Russia and America. As Harrison Salisbury notes in his preface, their relationship has always been stormy, though its ups and downs did not mean as much to the whole human race as they do now. Americans were wary of the bear even before it became the Bolshevik bear. And there were some who argued that, once the Communist Revolution had taken place, its very nature meant that Russia must be on an inevitable, fatal collision course with the United States.

But it was not so from 1941 to 1945. It may be a harbinger for good that when confronted with a mutual threat—in this case, Hitler—the closed society of Russia and the open society of America could somehow, in some fashion, collaborate. And it is at the high point of that alliance—which, however temporary, was real—that we begin.

Chapter 1

THE ROOTS OF HOSTILITY

1917-1945

THE BRIDGE OVER THE ELBE RIVER was a technological carcass, its bent metal and blistered paint witnesses to the power of the high explosives that had battered it to death. From a distance the two dots crawling toward each other from opposite banks looked like purposeful insects on a skeleton. When they met, there was a moment of incomprehensible ritual. They hugged, beat each other's shoulders, waved their arms toward the late April sky. A close-up would have showed grins on the stubbled faces of two tired but jubilant men.

They were soldiers—the one an American from General Courtney Hodges's First Army, the other a Russian scout from a tank unit in Marshal Ivan Konev's First Ukrainian Army. It was spring at Torgau in southern Germany, the spring of 1945, a spring of hope and deliverance. Elsewhere along the Elbe advance patrols of Russians and Americans were splashing across the river in commandeered boats, breaking out bottles of "liberated" wine and vodka from backpacks, dancing in their heavy combat boots to handclaps and mouth organs. For their linkup meant that the end of Adolf Hitler's Third Reich was near.

Some of those happy men would die in the next few days, as men had died endlessly in the bloody months that stretched, for the Americans, back to the Normandy landings just over ten months earlier, and for the Russians to a dark time two and a half years in the past when Hitler's armies poured fire from almost point-blank range into Moscow, Leningrad, Stalingrad. But now it was Hitler who was in the jaws of steel, trapped in his bunker beneath the rubble that had been Berlin. From field marshals to privates, the fighting men of the Allied armies knew that they had not only survived the war, but won it.

And won it together. The forces that freed Europe were mainly

Russian and American, with a healthy contingent from Britain and scattered units from other countries subjugated by the Nazis before 1941. There was not only the joy of peace, but of comradeship. President Harry S Truman saluted the collaboration that had brought about the rendezvous "in the heart of Nazi Germany." The Soviet Army newspaper *Red Star* said that the Red Army, like the armies of the Allies, would never forget "the word 'Torgau'—the funeral salute . . . over the grave of Hitlerite Germany." And when, two weeks after the Torgau meeting Germany surrendered, a cheering Moscow crowd gathered in front of the United States embassy there, hailing the officer in charge that day, George F. Kennan, and the American flag draped over the balcony on which he was standing. When he sent a young staff member out to get a Soviet flag and hung it next to the Stars and Stripes, the crowd—in plain sight of the Kremlin—went wild.

But amid the love-feast in the ruins, only a few top-level officials knew that the junction point on the Elbe, which had a strong impact on how much of Germany would be under Soviet occupation, had been chosen after secret arguments between London and Washington over Russian intentions. Or that brooding and angry cables had flashed from Josef Stalin to Franklin D. Roosevelt only days before the latter's death on April 12. Behind the sunny, censor-approved press releases was the fact that the years of Russian-American partnership in combat had also been years of wary sparring and deep suspicion. There was an ambivalence in the relationship, a jarring dissonant chord in the chorus of victory.

On March 28, General Dwight D. Eisenhower's forces had reached the Rhine. From Supreme Headquarters, Allied Expeditionary Forces, he radioed his plans for the immediate future directly to Moscow. His main objective was to encircle and destroy the remaining German armies before they could retire into the mountains of Bavaria, Austria, and Czechoslovakia for a bitter last stand. Accordingly, the Americans would push on as far as the Elbe, then fan out north and south to trap retreating Germans. There would be no drive eastward toward Berlin. The Russians, meanwhile, should hit the Germans hard and simultaneously, keeping the pressure on from all sides.

When copies of this message reached Winston Churchill, the British Prime Minister protested by cable to Roosevelt. "I . . . consider that from a political standpoint we should march as far east into Germany as possible," he said. To Eisenhower he expressed the same desire, consistent with his longstanding view that Allied armies should not leave, in the center of Europe, a vacuum into which Russian power could flow as the enemy crumbled. The more easterly the point at which Red and red-white-and-blue forces should "shake hands," the better.

Eisenhower and his field commanders looked at the map again—on April 11. They operated on the American principle of warfare: Do the job as quickly and efficiently as possible, then go home. The American Ninth Army was only fifty miles from Berlin. But Marshal Georgi Zhukov, on the other side of the city, was even closer and had easier ground in front of him. The decision was swift. Avoid glory-hunting and keep the casualties low. Let Zhukov take Berlin.

Six days later, Churchill wired again, this time to a new American President. He urged that the Americans keep moving eastward until a promise was extracted from Stalin that, in the postwar occupation, food surpluses in Eastern Germany's farmlands would be available to feed the cities of the Western zone. In this he was supported by the American Department of State; like Churchill, its Russian experts wanted the Americans to have more German territory to trade for Soviet promises of one kind or another. But Truman, still in a daze in his first unexpected week in the White House, could only pass the issue on to the Joint Chiefs of Staff, who in turn left it to Eisenhower, who firmly ruled out "any move which I deem militarily unwise." Case closed. Even a final Churchill bid to get "Ike" to race the Russians for Prague failed.

But not all the suspiciousness was on the Allied side. Early In March the commander of the elite German SS (Schutzstaffel) forces in Italy made secret contact with Allied headquarters and said that he might be able to arrange the capitulation of all the forces facing the British and Americans. General Sir Harold Alexander skeptically authorized a clandestine meeting to set up a formal surrender parley. By previous agreement, a Soviet representative would be involved in that final conference; but he saw no need to invite one to help make the initial arrangements, and he so informed London, which approved his plans.

But when Stalin was routinely informed of this, he flew into a rage. No discussions of any kind should take place with Germans in the absence of Soviet spokesmen. London nevertheless held firm, and the American ambassador to the Soviet Union, W. Averell Harriman, urged Roosevelt to stand behind the British. To give in to the Russians on this minor matter now, he said, would guarantee more obstreperous behavior later. While the President digested this counsel, he received a violent message from Stalin, who said that he had trustworthy information from his agents that a sellout was in the making, a deal whereby the Germans would give up to the Americans and British but keep on fighting the Russians, a clear violation of all wartime Allied promises.

FDR elected to be soothing, even though he expressed "bitter

resentment" at the informers who had made such "vile misrepre-
sentations." He simply said it would be tragic for distrust to
overshadow the moment of victory. Fortunately, the peace initiative
collapsed—it was very possibly a ruse to divide the Allies—and
Roosevelt could wind up the exchange with Stalin by hoping there
would be no more such "minor misunderstandings." When Harriman got the message for delivery, he begged Roosevelt to take out
the word "minor." His chief would not do so, however, and on April
12 wired Churchill: "I would minimize the general Soviet problem
as much as possible . . . these problems seem to arise every day, and
most of them straighten out."

Behind the jubilation and the smiles, then, there was an
uneasiness overhanging the relations between Washington and
Moscow. In the light of history, that was no surprise. Ever since the
Bolshevik seizure of power in November of 1917, the two nations
had been involved in a series of confrontations and wary contacts
that could have been called a "cold war" long before anyone
thought of inventing the term.

HISTORICALLY SPEAKING, both nations shared an ambivalent
relationship with Europe. The Soviet Union lay straddled
between Europe and Asia, and had played little part in the
intellectual developments of the Renaissance, the great revolutions
in thought that led to the modern age. Russians swung back and
forth between an ache of cultural inferiority, and a blunt pride in
their uniqueness. Strong czars and czarinas like Peter and Catherine
the Great had sometimes imported Western technology and culture
wholesale—and forced them on subjects whom they ruled without
heed to such niceties as religious and civil liberties. Nineteenth-
century aristocrats like Count Leo Tolstoy learned to speak, dine,
and party in French; but by the time he had written *War and Peace*,
Tolstoy was convinced that the strength that had defeated Napoleon
lay in the unsophisticated Russian peasantry, uncritical in their
Eastern Orthodox Christianity, inseparable from their beloved soil,
their folk traditions.

Americans likewise tended to downplay their European origins
and boast of how their great land frontier had given them special
qualities of independence and optimism. (Alexis de Tocqueville,
writing in 1840, predicted that both Russia and America, these crude
giants outside the central arena of Europe, would one day hold the
fate of the world between them.) But Americans did not, on that
account, feel any identification with Russians. On the eve of World
War I, a few cultivated listeners and readers hummed Tchaikovsky
or enjoyed Chekhov and Turgenev; but the popular impression of
Russia was formed mainly by contact with refugees from the Czar:

Kansas Mennonites, Polish peasants (their country then mostly a Russian province), ghetto Jews with the fear of the pogrom in their drawn faces—all serving to confirm lurid newspaper accounts of Russia as the land of the knout, Siberia, Cossacks, and bomb-throwing terrorists. As a result, American sympathy for French and British claims to be defending freedom in World War I was sharply restricted by the fact that the Czar was on the Allies' side.

Then, to the joy of Allied propagandists, in March of 1917—one month before American entry into the war—the Czar was deposed by a revolt of moderates aiming to create a constitutional government. But this prospect was shattered in November when the Bolsheviks overthrew this provisional regime, in turn, and set up the system of Soviet Communism. That spelled an end to any chance for improved understanding between Russia and the West. The Bolsheviks did nothing by halves. Lenin and Trotsky pulled Russia out of the war against Germany, executed the Czar and his wife and children, exposed the secret treaties that he had made with his allies to divide any postwar spoils, and repudiated his debts. They also called for world revolution and boasted of how they would abolish all repressive "bourgeois" institutions, down to and including the conventional family and religion, not only in the Soviet Union, but as quickly as possible in all other countries groaning under capitalism.

These claims and actions exploded amid an American public opinion already superheated by wartime hyperpatriotism, and ready to billow into hysteria. Almost all Americans were wedded to the idea that capitalism alone guaranteed freedom and progress. They lumped together in rejection all left-wing parties, and in 1917 the federal government used emergency antisedition legislation to smash the overtly anticapitalist and antiwar Industrial Workers of the World, and to jail the three-time Socialist presidential candidate, Eugene V. Debs. That Debs was an ex-locomotive fireman from Terre Haute, and William D. Haywood (head of the IWW) a hard-rock miner from the Rockies, did not allay suspicions that there was something repulsively "foreign" about their ideas. Nor did Americans want to listen to John Reed, another impeccably American-born voice, Harvard-educated, who had gone to the Soviet Union as a reporter and had written sympathetic accounts of the Bolshevik takeover, alive with the raucous sounds and sweaty smells of mobs of soldiers, sailors, workers, and peasants.

Americans wanted, instead, to hear the warnings of someone like Attorney General A. Mitchell Palmer, who was eager to win the 1920 Democratic nomination and succeed Woodrow Wilson. "Like a prairie fire," he wrote, "the blaze of revolution was sweeping over every American institution of law and order. . . . It was eating its way into the homes of the American workman, its sharp tongues of revolutionary heat were licking the altars of the churches, leaping into the belfry of the school bell, crawling into the sacred corners of American homes, seeking to replace marriage vows with libertine laws, burning up the foundations of society." That was more acceptable reading than Reed's news stories, later gathered into a book called *Ten Days That Shook the World*. On New Year's Day of 1920, Palmer struck back at the enemy. Without warning, federal agents swooped down on four thousand "suspicious" aliens of Russian origin in various cities. They were handcuffed, marched through the streets, and held incommunicado in overcrowded detention pens without benefit of arrest warrants or charges. All but a handful were finally freed, the rest deported. Palmer, unabashed, predicted that thousands of Bolsheviks would converge on Washington on May Day, and mini-Palmers echoed his alarm, as what became known as the Red Scare swept the land. Illinois State's Attorney General Hoyte, for example, said that Palmer's raids had thwarted a plot to "seize the businesses, the industries, and the natural resources of the country by direct action." But the only direct action of 1920 consisted of two bombings. In one, a person who was never identified attempted to leave an explosive device at Palmer's front door, but was blown to bits on his lawn when it apparently detonated prematurely. In another, a bomb blew up in Wall Street, causing some casualties and pock-marking the façade of J.P. Morgan and Company. In neither case was any link to Bolsheviks ever established.

But the Red Scare at home made possible partial American support for an anti-Soviet war abroad. The Allied governments had practical motives for trying to replace Lenin with a leader who would keep Russia in the war, diverting Germans. In addition, they were frightened at the possible spread of revolution to their own war-weary capitals. The Bolsheviks themselves fed this anxiety with inconsistent approaches. They tried to establish relations with the West through various informal conferences—the last thing they needed was more enemies—but they also continued to sponsor statements such as that of their creation, the Communist International, urging "common activity by the workers of various countries . . . towards a single aim, the overthrow of capitalism, the establishment of . . . the International Soviet Republic, [and] the complete abolition of classes."

So on what they insisted were high-minded and defensive grounds, France, Great Britain, the United States, and Japan gave various amounts of support to the armies of at least three White Russian generals aiming to reconquer Russia. A small American army contingent shared billets in Vladivostok with over seventy thousand Japanese troops. Two others were sent to Murmansk and Archangel, far northern ports of entry into the country; there they saw little combat but froze through the bitter 1918-19 winter, wondering why they could not go home now that the war in France was over.

The Yanks finally did leave in May of 1919, the British that autumn, the French and Japanese later. By 1920 it was clear that the Reds, despite invasion, counterrevolution, and the Franco-British naval blockade, were going to survive. They even stood off an invasion by Poland in 1920, which they turned around and pushed back to the very gates of Warsaw. But the cost had been beyond calculation. The huge country's transport and industrial systems, primitive to begin with, were in shambles, its farms untended, its populace uprooted. Red and White armies alike had scourged villages, shooting suspected enemies on suspicion, plundering, burning. "Life for all," one historian said in summation, "hung by a thread." Leon Trotsky had brilliantly built a Red Army to fight off enemies in Siberia, the Baltic region, the Crimea, the Ukraine—but his resourcefulness was no match for disease and hunger. Literally millions died of typhus and other plagues incidental to famine (including John Reed, who was buried beneath the Kremlin wall). An American Relief Association was formed, headed by Herbert Hoover, supposedly to feed starving Reds and Whites alike, but it was overwhelmed by the size of the task.

The Soviet Union was born in blood and fire, and its troubles were not over. Lenin died in 1924. Josef Stalin won the power struggle for the succession, exiled Trotsky, and began a process of building a modern nation on collectivist lines through a series of plans for economic development that were forced on the population to the accompaniment of much fresh suffering, more starvation, arrests, and executions. But from the point of view of relations with the rest of the world, the rise of Stalin opened a period of at least temporary accommodation. He needed peace and assistance from the outside. Talk of world revolution was muted. Bolshevik diplomats began to appear, in "reactionary" formal attire, at international gatherings. Treaties were made with old enemies— with Germany; with China's Chiang Kai-shek, who had defeated a Communist army to come to power; with new states like Estonia and Latvia, torn from the body of imperial Russia; with hostile neighbors like Poland and Finland. Genial-looking Maxim Litvinov, the Soviet Foreign Minister, talked disarmament and economic collaboration and laid the groundwork for entry into the League of Nations. And so, by about 1931, most world regimes had accepted the outcasts.

But not the United States of America.

The official American position was first stated in 1920 by

Secretary of State Bainbridge Colby, a man whose very name
reflected establishment propriety and inherited wealth. We would
not, he said, deal with "the present rulers of Russia" because "the
very existence of Bolshevism . . . depends, and must continue to
depend, upon the occurrence of revolutions in all other great
civilized nations." So the door was slammed on over a hundred
million people. Three successive Republican Presidents (including
the humanitarian Hoover) maintained that stance, even when it was
suggested that the United States might benefit from greasing the
wheels of commerce with the Soviets. "I do not propose," said
Calvin Coolidge icily, "to barter away for the privilege of trade any
of the cherished rights of humanity."

All the same, the Department of State needed information on
Russian affairs that a Moscow embassy would have facilitated.
Between Russian secretiveness and censorship on one hand, and
American Red-baiting on the other, the press contributed no help in
solving the enigma of Kremlin behavior. Rather, it specialized in
dramatic headlines like those of the Chicago *Tribune* in the
1920s—SECRET REPORT SHOWS RUSSIA NEAR COLLAPSE, or INDUSTRY
FACES SWIFT DISASTER IN RED RUSSIA, or ODESSA TROOPS MUTINY AGAINST
MOSCOW REGIME. In order to obtain more accurate perceptions, a
Soviet Service was created within the Department of State, and
its members were assigned posts in the American mission to
Riga, capital of Lithuania, the third small Baltic state created after
1918.

The young men of the Riga group were well trained in Russian
language, culture, and history. Though they were meticulous and
objective in compiling reports on conditions inside the Soviet
Union, they were united in an upper-class sympathy for the cultural
aspects of the czarist past. At one time or another their ranks
included Loy Henderson, a one-time Red Cross official; George
Kennan, a brilliant Princeton graduate whose powerful intellect had
early on impressed superiors; Charles Bohlen, Harvard '27, an
affluent and well-traveled young man who was precisely the type
that the Foreign Service liked to recruit. They all would live to
become important figures in Soviet-American relations, and they all
were influenced by their chief, Robert F. Kelley, the head of the
Eastern Europe Division of the State Department. He was a
graduate of Harvard and the Sorbonne, a believer in the dispassion-
ate collection of as much solid economic and social information as
possible—his "boys" in Riga became, in effect, professorial experts
in their field—and a man with a hearty distaste for the "Boles," his
nickname for the Bolsheviks. He thought that their "world revolutionary aims and practices" precluded recognition, and the "boys"
agreed with him, much as an opening of relations would have

helped their work. "Neither then nor at any later date," Kennan recalled, "did I consider the Soviet Union a fit ally or associate, actual or potential, for this country."

But the diplomatic chill on dealings with Moscow was offset by the warming breezes of commercial interest. Profit had its own logic. American businessmen who choked with rage at any expression of Communist economic theory were nonetheless willing to listen when Soviet trade organizations, laying aside their own revulsion at capitalism, made bids for desperately needed machinery, raw materials, and technical expertise. And so, in the 1920s, the Russians began to see (and keep under surveillance) a new breed of visitors from the United States. Not left-wing pilgrims to the motherland of socialism, but emissaries from the corporations that were the backbone of American power: Ford, Du Pont, General Electric, RCA. They came to sell tractors, dyestuffs, chemicals, machine tools, and communications gear—or else to build, on contract, the sinews of Soviet industry. Soviet labor under American engineering supervision built a hydroelectric dam on the Dnieper, opened coal mines, raised steel mills in the Urals. It was a nice touch that Albert Kahn and Associates, architects of both the General Motors building in Detroit and Ford's great River Rouge factory, put up a number of Soviet auto-assembly plants. Individual initiative had its place, too. A young doctor named Armand Hammer went to Russia to minister to the famine-stricken and stayed on to become wealthy running an asbestos mine and a pencil factory.

There were also small groups of workers who went to Russia at the start of the Great Depression in search of what they heard were good jobs in Russian factories. (One of them was Walter Reuther, future head of the United Auto Workers, who worked for a short time in the Gorky vehicle plant.) Most who went returned to the United States quickly, sharing the opinion of an American vice-consul in Moscow who reflected, years later, that "once you went there and . . . saw what the hell it was like, it confirmed your worst fears."

Soviet imports from the United States in this period ranged from as little as $9 million to as high as $114 million annually; but they were highly concentrated, furnishing up to two-thirds of all United States exports of agricultural and metalworking machinery in some years. Small as it was, the economic exchange did help to modify the climate. It proved that both parties could profit by dealing with each other, and that even Soviet Russians, under the right incentives, would fulfill contracts and keep agreements. The stage was set for the first of a series of relaxations in the tension between Moscow and Washington, the first period of what in later years would be labeled détente.

WAR AND DEPRESSION PROVIDED the backdrop. The Japanese seizure of Manchuria in 1931 gave both Russia and America the feeling that they had something of a common source of worry in Tokyo. And when Roosevelt was inaugurated two years later, the hope of stimulating even more trade loomed large in his recovery program. So nonrecognition was dropped, in exchange for Russian promises to negotiate on the still-hanging question of the honoring of pre-1918 debts, and (as a concession to American public opinion) to refrain from support of any subversive movements in the United States. To Washington came Maxim Litvinov as ambassador, and in exchange the State Department sent William Bullitt, a stormy figure, to the Kremlin. Bullitt had gone on an unofficial and secret journey to Russia in 1919 and had come back with peace proposals from the Red leaders; but Woodrow Wilson had pulled the rug from under him, creating a lifelong hostility. (Bullitt's revenge was later to write a book with Sigmund Freud in which, using Wilson's published correspondence, they psychoanalyzed him as an infantile, father-dominated figure.)

Bullitt arrived in Moscow in December of 1933, where, by coincidence, Harpo Marx was convulsing Russian audiences. He found Stalin, whom he described as a "wiry Gipsy," in a genial mood. "I want you to understand that if you want to see me at any time, day or night, you have only to let me know," the dictator promised. The staff members of the new embassy were mostly trained in the Soviet Service of the State Department, and were highly skeptical. But even they enjoyed the sudden springtime of open doors, vodka toasts, and smiling dinner parties.

It did not last long. Negotiations began, looking toward a deal in which the Russians would pay off American owners of old czarist bonds (which Moscow had repudiated early in the Revolution) and in return would get a loan from the United States. But the talks soon collapsed.

Bullitt became outspokenly hostile, was relieved at his own request in 1936, and returned home convinced for life that Communism was "a militant faith" hoping for "world revolution and the 'liquidation' of all nonbelievers." Bullitt's successor, Joseph Davies, resumed the cordial tempo. He was a Wisconsin lawyer who combined corporate practice with progressive politics and had given generously to Roosevelt's campaigns. The career Foreign Service men resented him as the embodiment of the uninformed rich-man appointee to high diplomatic office, and their contempt deepened when Davies made it a point to speak publicly of Stalin in the most flattering terms. Ambassador Davies was not entirely naïve. He simply saw his mandate from Roosevelt as one of winning Stalin's goodwill in the worsening international situation of the late 1930s, and he did this by keeping to himself his private judgment that the Soviet Union was a "tyranny, without any protection whatever to the Proletariat of 'life, liberty and the pursuit of happiness.' " Later on, during the war, he would nonetheless say even kinder things about Russia in his memoir, *Mission to Moscow*—this time to assist in the Allied propaganda campaign.

The Soviet leaders, for their part, also downplayed past quarrels, as they groped for a united front against the rising threat of Hitler and international Fascism. Delegates to the Seventh World Congress of the Comintern at Moscow in 1935 were told to soften their warfare against other left-wing parties. American comrades were bidden to form a "workers' and farmers' party" that would speak a "common language with the broadest masses." The American Communist leader Earl Browder, returning home from the Comintern meeting, could not get the proposed new movement off the ground; but the Communist Party convention, which nominated him for President in 1936, tried hard to speak that common tongue. "Communism is Twentieth Century Americanism," read the banners that hung in the convention hall along with portraits of Jefferson and Lincoln. "We love our country," proclaimed the Kansas-born Browder, who was also called, by a delegate, "the new John Brown from Osawatomie."

But the honeymoon was not long-lasting. Suspicion of Reds remained a strong and politically useful force in the United States. A widely discussed book of 1934, *The Red Network*, charged that at least 1,300 named individuals were tunneling under the foundations of American life; a Texas congressman, Martin Dies, chaired a special House Un-American Activities Committee in 1938, which began a long career of headline-grabbing by accusing various celebrities of being Communist sympathizers or dupes. Even liberals and leftists not already disillusioned by Stalin, moreover, were shaken by the great purge trials of 1936, in which he wiped out more potential rivals. One by one, tough old Bolsheviks who had outlasted czarist jails, White terror, and assassination plots somehow stood up in open court in the Soviet Union to confess "errors" and "crimes against the state" for which they deserved execution. If there was mystery about how the performance was achieved, there was none about its underlying savagery.

The Spanish Civil War also put strains on the tenuous new friendship of America and the Soviet Union. Erupting in the summer of 1936 and lasting until early 1939, it was widely seen as a dress rehearsal for World War II, especially by the German and Italian "volunteers" who supported General Francisco Franco's conservative insurgency against the recently established Spanish Republic. But Franco had the strong backing of the Spanish Church, and this meant that millions of Americans, Catholics in particular, were inclined to accept uncritically his claim of fighting to free Spain from Moscow-dominated Reds, and likewise to believe many stories of alleged Loyalist atrocities against priests, nuns, and believers. In fact, the Loyalist government was a coalition whose radical and democratic factions savaged each other, and got only erratic support from Russia. Both sides were guilty of the cruelties that seem reserved for civil wars. Yet somehow the notion that the struggle was a proxy battle between the Soviets and their enemies only intensified American distaste for Stalin's policies. Anti-Communist feelings hardened majority opinion behind United States neutrality laws conceived in an early 1930s mood of isolationism. These banned trade with, or loans to, any belligerent power as a means of avoiding entanglement in "foreign quarrels." Their practical effects in Spain's civil war was to weaken the Loyalists, since under them the Republic was unable to buy American weapons and supplies to match those freely furnished to the insurgents by Hitler and Mussolini. There were pro-Loyalist Americans who protested bitterly that our policies were effectually helping the general Fascist assault on democracy, but their attacks on the neutrality laws were in vain. So were the sacrifices of a handful of American volunteers who actually fought with the International Brigades in the Loyalist army. In all, it was a time of high passion, and the storms aroused helped to beat to pieces the idea of a united front against aggressions.

Moreover, the attempted anti-Fascist coalition splintered on mutual distrust between Moscow and the governments of France and Great Britain. The significant climax came in the Munich crisis of 1938, whose echoes were to reverberate for the next forty years. All three nations had mutual assistance pacts with Czechoslovakia. When Hitler demanded that the small country yield up "German-speaking" areas to him that contained key defensive fortifications, the French and British collapsed before the threat of war, refused to honor their alliance, and left the Czechs no choice but surrender. The Russians were not consulted. British Prime Minister Neville Chamberlain made a humiliating airborne pilgrimage to Hitler's Bavarian mountain retreat, and came back to assure welcoming London crowds that he had brought "peace in our time"—that Herr Hitler had no further territorial ambitions in Europe. Six months later, Herr Hitler's troops rolled into the rest of Czechoslovakia, and in Prague Nazi band music and orders brayed harshly from loudspeakers that freedom was dead there.

The Munich agreement—the formal pact to give Germany Czechoslovakia's Sudetenland border region—was a profoundly tragic, moving, and meaning-packed experience for the world.

Americans were by and large sickened by the sellout in which two supposedly great democratic powers had cravenly tried to "appease" Germany's aggressive appetite. And "appeasement" became a code word standing for a disastrous policy of giving in to threats. In time, the Munich analogy would be repeatedly invoked to bar tactical compromises or strategic retreats of any kind.

Munich was a turning point for the Russians, too; they knew that Chamberlain and French Premier Edouard Daladier were deeply conservative, and they believed that French and British reactionaries had decided to turn the frenetically anti-Bolshevik Hitler eastward. To them, a Balkan peninsula of Nazi satellites (at least so Stalin interpreted British and French reasoning) was a better bargain than a deal with Communism. If the word Munich thereafter rang "appeasement" in American ears, it deafeningly shouted "encirclement" to the Kremlin. In point of fact, through the spring of 1939, French, British, and Soviet diplomats struggled vainly to build a new common front against what even Chamberlain and Daladier realized by then was inevitable—a German stab at Poland, already being denounced in ominously familiar terms by Hitler for its anti-Reich "atrocities." The effort stalled on the question of how to involve Russia in a war against the Nazis without inviting her into Poland and the other borderlands that Moscow still claimed.

Then Stalin took matters into his own hands.

As the summer of 1939 ended, and harvests were gathered in, and German divisions and air wings secretly filled their supply depots and moved into jump-off positions, a shattering announcement hit the airwaves, on August 23. The foreign ministers of the Third Reich and the Soviet Union had signed a twenty-five-year nonaggression pact. The Molotov-Ribbentrop agreement signed Poland's death warrant, turned diplomacy on its head, and stunned the world. For Hitler it lifted the immediate threat of a two-front war. For Stalin it bought territory and time. And for the American people it brought confirmation of their deep distrust of the Russians, plus a curious ease of mind for all but the most self-deluding Communists. With both tyrants in the same camp it was easier to see the war that began September 3 as a contrast in stark black and white.

Three weeks after the German onslaught, Russia seized the eastern portion of Poland, and Collier's magazine thanked Hitler and Stalin for "dropping the pretense of hating each other's gizzards" and removing "all doubt . . . that there is any real difference between Communism and Fascism." The Russians attacked Finland in December of 1939, and American public opinion cheered the Finns' successful resistance through the bitter winter, ignoring the right-wing sympathies of their leader, Baron

Carl Mannerheim. The Russians seized the provinces of Bukovina and Bessarabia from Rumania, as well as Estonia, Latvia, and Lithuania, while German Stukas and armored columns stamped out the independence of Denmark, Norway, the Netherlands, Belgium, France, Yugoslavia, Albania, and Greece—and the American people agreed with liberal clergyman John Haynes Holmes that "the leopard has the same spots in every jungle." Russia kept her word to provide the German war machine with raw materials, and the popular mind in the United States agreed with the *Wall Street Journal* that "the principal difference between Mr. Hitler and Mr. Stalin is the size of their respective mustaches."

But neither dictator desired or expected the truce between them to last. And it was Hilter who struck first.

On the Sunday morning of June 22, 1941, Panzer units burst through the Soviet-German frontier, racing for their first-phase objectives. By nightfall, columns of smoke from Russian villages marked their trail of progress. And still another episode in Soviet-American relations had begun.

AT FIRST SOME HAILED what seemed to be a falling-out among thieves. A contest between Satan and Lucifer, William Bullitt called it. A little-known Missouri Senator, Harry S Truman, delivered it as his opinion that the two dictatorships should be allowed to claw each other into mutual exhaustion, with the United States helping whichever side was losing whenever the pace slackened.

But that attitude did not long prevail, and had no footing whatever in the White House. Franklin D. Roosevelt had no misapprehensions about Russia. Only a year earlier he had told an audience of heckling left-wing students that the Soviet Union was "a dictatorship as absolute as any other dictatorship in the world." He dismissed accounts of Soviet progress that did not take into account the "costs in hunger, death, and bitterness."

But in June of 1941, Roosevelt saw America's indispensable first priority, the key to her own safety, to be the defeat of Hitler. Whoever was his enemy would have to be sustained. In this view Roosevelt did not differ from the even more vigorously anti-Communist Winston Churchill, who had immediately offered British support to Moscow, while explaining to his private secretary: "If Hitler invaded Hell I would make at least a favourable reference to the Devil in the House of Commons." Roosevelt saw that the Fuehrer had blundered in tackling the vast manpower reserves, the aching distances, the uncertain seasons of Russia. "It will mean the liberation of Europe," he told his military aide, Admiral William D. Leahy. "I do not think we need worry about any possibility of

Russian domination." That curious afterthought was not an apprais-
al of Russia's intentions, but of her weakness. Given the woeful Red
Army performance at the start of the Russo-Finnish War, and the
Germans' extraordinary military achievements, the question was:
Could the Reds contain the first onslaught or would they, too, fall in
a matter of weeks?

To find out, a man described by British Ambassador Lord Halifax
as an "odd creature" climbed aboard a seaplane in Scotland one
July day in 1941, Moscow-bound, wearing a homburg borrowed
from Churchill. This was Harry Hopkins, Roosevelt's friend and
confidant. His qualifications for diplomacy were bizarre. He had
been a social worker, then administrator of New Deal relief
programs, and was known for a total impatience with bureaucratic
routine. He was high-living, sharp-tongued, unimpressed by rank,
and quick to get to the heart of a question. ("Lord Root-
of-the-Matter" was Churchill's nickname for him.) If he had ever
held political ambitions, he abandoned them after 1937, when he
survived an operation for stomach cancer but began to die by inches
from a series of complications. Thereafter his whole life was
wrapped up in loyalty to Roosevelt, which made him precisely the
kind of alter ego that a man in power needed. This frail man,
looking "like Death on the way to a frolic," handed Stalin a note
from the President that said: "I ask you to treat him with the
identical confidence you would feel if you were talking directly to
me."

Hopkins put the question of holding out to Stalin, and Stalin
answered bluntly that the Russians could do so if they received
massive material aid and eventually some military action to draw
away the German forces from their front. Hopkins went back to
Washington with this word, and added what Roosevelt was
perfectly willing to hear. The best way to deal with Stalin was in
direct give-and-take, leader to leader, bypassing the State Department, whose personnel in the embassy in Moscow inspired no
confidence among Soviet brass. The policy was followed, and it
meant that the negotiations would be controlled, not by the wary
views of the Riga-trained professionals, but by the quite different
ones of FDR.

The shape of summit diplomacy would emerge later. In the
autumn of 1941 the first task was to lay the groundwork for
shipments, under the young Lend-Lease Act, of the guns, trucks,
tanks, scout cars, planes, medicines, radios, telephones, rubber,
leather, cloth, and grain that Russia needed as her economy
hemorrhaged from the wounds of the invasion. There might have
been long-run problems with congressional resistance, but Hitler
came to the rescue on the day after Pearl Harbor. Uncharacteristi-

cally, he honored a treaty (with Japan), declared war on the United States, and thus made Russia more than a nation receiving grudging American help—in fact, an ally.

It was, in the words of General John R. Deane, who headed the U.S. military mission to Moscow, a "strange alliance." The mills of wartime "public information" promptly ground out new images of the Russians, tailored to the American habit of seeing all international confrontations in terms of shootouts between the rustlers and the posse. Now the Soviet leaders were wearing the white hats. Suddenly it appeared that they were not only brave anti-Fascists, but virtually undistinguishable from next-door neighbors. *Life*, in 1943, labeled the Russians "one hell of a people" who "to a remarkable degree . . . look like Americans, dress like Americans, and think like Americans." A movie version of Ambassador Davies's book almost made Stalin a cuddly bear of a man. The *New York Times* informed its readers in April of 1944 that "Marxian thinking in Soviet Russia is out. The . . . competitive system is back." Wendell Willkie, defeated Republican presidential candidate in 1940, said after a globe-trotting tour that he thought the two nations would be able later to "work together for the economic peace and freedom of the world." Stalin's contribution to the euphoric mood was to abolish the Comintern in 1943. Not all Americans were totally convinced of Soviet benevolence, but the propaganda war, which inflated a few small truths with a great deal of hot air, created expectations that were cruelly disappointed afterwards, leading to overreaction in the opposite direction.

In reality, the partnership was never placid. The Russians, for example, never relaxing their suspicions of foreigners, demanded gigantic quantities of matériel without condescending to show Americans the precise figures justifying the requisitions. In asking for foodstuffs, Russian emissaries in Washington would approach Secretary of Agriculture Claude Wickard "sober-faced, never cracked a smile, smart as they could be . . . said, 'Here is what we want.' . . . There wasn't much negotiation to it." Moreover, while expecting much, the Russians gave little in return. As General Deane wryly put it: "After the banquets we send the Soviets another thousand airplanes, and they approve a visa that has been hanging fire for months."

Moscow also assumed that the British and Americans would readily divert crucial merchant shipping from other areas in order to deliver supplies for Russia, even though the only available route in 1943 was around the northern cape of Norway to Murmansk, and the losses were inconceivable. (In the summer of 1942, two convoys lost two-thirds of their ships before getting through.) Temporary suspensions of the convoys brought outraged protest. Over the years from June 1941 to April 1944, Allied sailors froze and drowned to bring the Russians an enormous rescue sealift—some 8,800 aircraft, over 3,700 tanks and 3,000 antiaircraft guns, nearly 207,000 trucks, 5.5 million pairs of army boots, over 2 million tons of food—without much public gratitude.

But the Russians argued, on their side, that they had the brunt of the land fighting and the casualties, that the capitalist allies furnished only munitions and supplies (manufactured at a profit), while the Russians poured blood. And throughout 1942 and 1943 they hammered ungraciously at Britain and America with demands for an invasion of northern Europe, a second front to absorb a stiff percentage of the two hundred German divisions chewing and tearing inside the guts of the Soviet Union. When—largely at British insistence—plans for cross-Channel attacks in those years were shifted, first to the landings in North Africa and then to those in Italy, the Russians did not disguise their bitterness behind pleasantries. A cartoon in Pravda in October of 1942 showed a military conference, with two young Red Army officers, Generals Determination and Courage, appealing for help to three fat, elderly Allied officers, Generals They Will Beat Us, No Need to Hurry, and Something Might Go Wrong.

The ridicule—and the easy dismissal of American sacrifices in the Pacific, or British casualties under Nazi bombs at home—did not trouble London and Washington so much as the unvoiced anxiety that the Russians, if desperate enough, might hit off another deal with Germany. And, for a man of Stalin's paranoid disposition, all the vodka toasts to unity could not drown his fear that the Allies might sit on their hands, wait for Russia's destruction, then deal with a fresh deck. In the end, both sides recognized that the struggle was truly to the death, and neither could afford a separate peace; but subterranean rumbles of suspicion always made it clear to those in the know that the alliance was one of mutual necessity rather than mutual admiration.

Until the autumn of 1943, the issues that topped the agenda of wartime conferences had largely to do with defense and survival, with turning the tide. But by then, the miracle had been achieved: Stalingrad, El Alamein, and Guadalcanal were all behind the Allies; the Germans were out of Africa and retreating in Italy, backpedaling in Russia, too; and the Japanese seaborne empire was being hammered by air and sea, strangling under submarine blockade. It was inevitable that thereafter discussions would turn to postwar problems. When Churchill, Roosevelt, and Stalin met face to face in Teheran, in November of 1943, and in Yalta, fifteen months later, critical questions and overt disagreements surfaced, though few of them were visible through the curtains of censored press releases that surrounded the meetings.

The questions seemed deceptively elementary, yet all tentative answers contained fearsomely complicated future possibilities. What should be done with Germany? What kinds of governments should be created in Eastern Europe after liberation? (It was assumed that the Western countries subdued by Hitler had stable enough political traditions and boundaries to take charge of their own restoration.) Finally, what kind of security arrangements would be created to make sure that a new war would not break out? The difficulties in reaching harmony stemmed from the differing perceptions of each of the Big Three leaders, each one expressing his sense of his country's needs in a characteristically personal style.

Franklin D. Roosevelt, just under sixty when Pearl Harbor's explosions made him a war chieftain, was at the peak of his considerable powers as a pragmatic and engaging democratic statesman. Coming back from a crippling disease, he had won the Presidency of a prostrate and dazed nation, and in seven years infused it with a sense of movement and direction. He started with no strongly articulated program, but as he went along evolved a combination of short-term relief measures and major new steps in government management of the economy. Then, with profound competence in using the press and the new medium of radio, he sold the New Deal to an unlikely aggregation of small farmers, laborers, urban blacks, college liberals, native-white Southerners, and immigrants' children. He convinced them of his sympathy for them as underdogs without appearing to condescend to them, and won huge electoral majorities through his homely illustrations, high good humor, and evident enjoyment of a good fight. The same qualities kept subordinates loyally working for him in spite of a maddening administrative sloppiness, which consisted in allowing some of them to work unwittingly at cross-purposes until he decided what would be most acceptable. Some did stamp off in outrage.

But above all, Roosevelt knew real opposition when he saw it, and was, with rare exceptions, acutely aware of the impossibility of securing any legislation that flouted public or congressional majority opinion. He became a master of delay, of opportune evasion, of statements that did not quite match policy, and of tactics that gave him time to orchestrate a popular chorus in favor of what he wanted. Opponents branded this as deviousness and supporters as simple realism, but both would have seen, in Roosevelt's foreign policy, a stellar illustration of his approach.

From 1933 onward, Roosevelt was a convinced anti-Fascist, certain that the security of the United States lay in making common cause with the other democracies against the disruptive redrawing of the world map by streams of bullets. Yet he spent the 1930s hobbled by public reluctance to become involved once more in "Europe's quarrels." The majority of voters wanted neutrality, though they also disliked aggression. This last was Roosevelt's only lever. Playing on the general revulsion against Hitler and Japan, and skillfully combining appeals to it with executive power, he managed a series of improvisations to keep Britain in the war after the disasters of 1940. Among them were the swapping of "over-age" destroyers for Caribbean island bases, then Lend-Lease (like lending one's neighbor a garden hose to fight a fire, he argued with apparent ingenuousness), then convoying Lend-Lease supplies halfway across the Atlantic, then firing on submarines that threatened them. But until December 7, 1941, he had been unable to confront Americans directly with the truth that their desire to see Hitler beaten was impossible without giving up their equally strong desire to stay officially out of the war. Then Hitler and the Japanese solved the problem for him.

But new dilemmas faced him in 1943. American thought still tended to embrace conflicting ideals in an illogical hug. Public opinion polls showed a decline in isolationism. There was willingness, now, to help guarantee peace. But it must be a just and high-minded peace, without secret treaties, the trading of territory, the reassignment of nationality groups against their will, the maintenance of mighty armies—a peace guaranteed by a new and tough international organization. In effect, Americans appeared eager to rewrite the history of 1919, this time without turning their backs on Woodrow Wilson's vision of a near-perfect world.

The trouble was that such an international order was still a pie-in-the-sky impossibility, as Roosevelt knew. Old colonial ties, old rivalries, old economic interests, were too strong to be wiped out instantly and replaced with a world parliament of democracies (whose sovereignty the American Congress would not have accepted anyway). Conventional arrangements would have to last for a while—especially with the Russians, who were moving steadily into the center of Europe as they went about the job of beating Nazi legions. They "had the power in the areas where their arms were present," Roosevelt explained to a group of Senators toward the war's end; all the United States could do was "use what influence we had to ameliorate the situation."

The battle lines, it turned out, were dividing the Continent into spheres of influence. Peace could be arranged between spheres of influence, but the concept unfortunately had a dirty, antiquated sound. It echoed of old men in back rooms dealing with the hopes of enslaved peoples, thwarting young rebels, muzzling voices of change. It was much easier for Roosevelt to stress, for the voters, such fine documents as the Atlantic Charter of 1941, and its promise of freedom and self-determination to all captive peoples, or the Declaration on Liberated Europe that emerged from Yalta, reaffirming the intention of the victors to let Europeans "solve by democratic means their pressing political problems." The drawback lay in encouraging the impression that these were immediate possibilities instead of remote ideal goals.

Nonetheless, Roosevelt hoped that he could keep the American sense of international responsibility alive by promising a noble future, while at the same time hammering out a peace with Stalin and Churchill that was adapted to the grimy realities of the mid-1940s. He would use the old-fashioned process of day-to-day accommodation that worked so well on Capitol Hill, and the same magical powers of invocation that had such splendid results on election days.

Churchill's role in the triad of power was a difficult one. Born in the 1870s at the high noon of the British empire and Victorian security, he had lived a full life as soldier, journalist, politician, aristocrat, and artist with language as well as brush and palette. His problem as an aging warrior was to do the best he could for a Britain that his Tory realism told him was in decline. His bulldog courage had kept the English afloat (and thrilled Americans) in 1940, but only U.S. intervention had saved Britain in the long run. After two massive wars inside of thirty years, her people, her resources, and her treasury were nearly exhausted. She was a junior partner to America in the alliance. Churchill's difficult task—well performed—was to save as much of Britain's overseas realm and influence as he could.

Where Europe was concerned that meant having as strong a military and diplomatic position as possible, and salvaging what he could of the pre-1939 Franco-British network of dependents in the Balkans. Churchill could reel off the rhetoric of idealism as well as any American, but he also had fewer inhibitions than Roosevelt about carving up territories. In October of 1944 he saw Stalin alone in Moscow, and scribbled on a sheet of paper a hard-boiled proposal for dividing influence between Russia and the British-American partnership: 90 percent for the West in Greece; 90 percent for Russia in Rumania; 75 percent for Russia in Bulgaria; in Hungary and Yugoslavia, 50–50. Stalin studied the numbers for a moment, then made an "OK" check mark with a blue pencil. "Let us burn the paper," said Churchill. "No," Stalin answered, "you keep it." Later, Churchill summarized the conversation by cable for Roosevelt, who promptly made it clear that no arrangements were valid without American participation, and that there would be time for such discussions later. The mere knowledge of even theoretical consideration of such deals would have been political TNT, but the President's response did not entirely foreclose the possibility of future explorations.

Stalin himself was then and remains still (until Soviet archives are opened, if ever) a mystery. His power was absolute, though he would occasionally parry an American or British suggestion with a hint that some things were impossible for him. The world would later learn of his campaign of terror against all potential challengers, which, as someone said, "killed more good Communists than the bourgeoisie of the whole world put together," and filled the prison camps. But Stalin had legitimate fears, too—chief among which was the spectre of a resurgent Germany. Twice in thirty years, armies commanded from Berlin had swept over Russia like gray-green locusts. Then there were Russia's neighbors, all of them supporters of counterrevolution in 1918, and all of them—not entirely involuntarily—Axis partners after 1941. Even if the concept of world revolution had never existed, it was likely that Stalin would have desired friendly, that is to say Communist, regimes in Rumania, Hungary, and Finland, to say nothing of Poland, which had every reason to be hostile.

Stalin's basic demands, therefore, were always for a helpless Germany and a subservient border zone. On other points he seemed open to compromise, and later on, when his darkest side was revealed, it was forgotten that he had an amiable aspect that was appreciated even more by foreigners than by his own frightened entourage. American journalists found him "acute" and "tenacious." At Yalta the Director of the United States Office of War Mobilization, James Byrnes, declared: "Joe was the life of the party," an opinion that might have been credited to American innocence except that it was almost echoed by Alexander Cadogan, the permanent under secretary of the British Foreign Office. "Uncle Joe," Cadogan wrote to his wife, "just sat taking it all in and being rather amused" while Roosevelt "flapped about" and Churchill "boomed." Stalin had even learned some English phrases such as "So what" and "You said it," and once stunned Roosevelt and Churchill by springing on them with "What the hell goes on here?"

They seemed able to get along together, the odd trio—the Hudson River squire in his business suits, the cigar-waving and bibulous descendant of the Duke of Marlborough, and the chunky ex-seminarian from Russian Georgia, the latter two enjoying natty uniforms. They smiled their way through the two great conferences, kindling premature optimism. Yalta seemed to go especially easily. The military decisions were quickly made. The Russians were to come into action against the Japanese ninety days after the war in

Europe ended, and it was the military chiefs who pressed vigorously for whatever concessions were necessary to hold them to this bargain. Stalin asked for, and got, the Kurile Islands and the northern half of Sakhalin (to be taken from Japan), and economic concessions in Chiang's Manchuria.

The political problems were tougher, but progress was made. Joint occupation of Germany was agreed to. At first, at Teheran, there had been talk of "pastoralizing" Germany after her unconditional surrender. But they backed away from that, knowing that it would be foolish to destroy the productive capacity of an industrial people in the heart of Europe, which would need every ounce of strength to rebuild. The Russians insisted on reparations from Germany for the vast damage done by the invaders. There were some reservations, especially from the British, who did not want to support a Germany bled white; but after a time the principle was accepted and a tentative sum of $20 billion fixed, the details and division of which were to be left for later pinpointing.

As for peacekeeping machinery, the outlines of the future United Nations Organization were lightly penciled in. The new body would be a compromise between a Wilsonian League and an old-fashioned "concert of Great Powers." The General Assembly would be the forum and court of world moral judgment. The Security Council, with permanent places for the Big Three and (at Roosevelt's insistence) China, would be the group with power to take police action. But there would have to be unanimity for that; in short, any Great Power could veto a move. This was supposedly a concession to the Russians, who feared being outnumbered by clients and friends of the United States; but it was equally deferential to the United States Senate, which was unlikely to give up American sovereignty, even though the majority and minority leaders, Senators Tom Connally and Arthur Vandenberg, were on record as favoring the organization. (Roosevelt had won them over, fully aware of Wilson's mistake a quarter of a century earlier in ignoring the Senate until too late in his peacemaking process.)

With the veto, the Security Council could act to keep international order whenever all the major powers agreed on what that was and what to do about it—a statement akin to saying that water would boil if heated to 212 degrees Fahrenheit. But what of the obvious question? What would happen if they disagreed?

Warmed by approaching victory, Roosevelt appeared to believe that disagreements could be worked through one at a time. He would have until January of 1949. In four years, he might bring Russia around to having some confidence in a genuinely international system of security, or he might induce the American people to accept, temporarily, some balance-of-power arrangements. In either case Russia would play a new role. She would no longer be merely a customer, or a pariah, or some happy Never-Never Land of radical dreams. She would simply be a major world power with a totalitarian government and Communist supporters around the globe—but like any nation, she would have a self-interested stake in maintaining peace, freeing resources for her internal growth, lifting the burden of arms, and letting her people share in the world's progress. At least such expectations could be inferred from the President's post-Yalta comments.

SHADOWS ALREADY OVERHUNG this prospect, however, the biggest of them in the indefinite shape of the future state of Poland. Stalin had agreed to the restoration of the ruined and occupied country, the war's first victim, but not with its pre-1939 borders. He wanted to keep what he had seized, both on grounds of security and because he claimed the territory was unfairly detached from the Soviet Union in 1920. Roosevelt and Churchill accepted the idea with the understanding that the Poles could, in good nineteenth-century fashion, compensate themselves by taking "Polish" territory from Germany. In effect, Poland was to be shoved some distance westward.

There was a Polish government-in-exile in London, made up of escapees from the German Juggernaut of 1939. Its members resolutely rejected the new border arrangements, and almost any kind of accommodation with the Russians, whom they still regarded as enemies even after June of 1941. They accused the Soviet Union, in 1944, of the deliberate massacre of thousands of Polish officer-prisoners in the Katyn Forest, part of a presumed plot to wipe out prewar Polish leadership. Moscow broke off relations with them as a result. Then, in October of 1944, as Red units neared Warsaw, Polish underground forces in the city rose up against the Germans. The Russians halted at the Vistula River and waited until the Germans had wiped out the guerrillas. They claimed that German resistance had slowed them down, but the London Poles insisted that it was a deliberate plot to decimate further the ranks of Polish patriots. Finally, the Russians set up a "provisional government" of their own in the city of Lublin, and began to deal with it in matters relating to Poland's future. They insisted that it was truly represent-ative of the Polish people, unlike the London government, which, Moscow said, was drawn from Poland's prewar reactionary upper class.

Neither Churchill nor Roosevelt relished involvement in the battle between the Lublin Poles and the London Poles, but each found it impossible to accept openly the Soviet transformation of Poland into a puppet state. Roosevelt pointed out that, other considerations aside, there were 6 million voters of Polish descent in the United States with whom he had to deal, and at Yalta he told Stalin that it would be helpful to him if the Russian ruler could "give something to Poland." Churchill's position was that Great Britain had gone to war to guarantee an independent Poland, and could hardly change its mind after all that the struggle had cost.

The compromise reached at Yalta was, in essence, to let the issue dangle. On the surface, the Russians did some yielding. It was agreed that they would "reorganize" the Lublin government by adding to it some mutually acceptable recruits from the London group and the Polish underground. Then this "government of national unity" would, "as soon as possible," hold "free and unfettered elections." But the loopholes were obvious: Such terms as "unfettered" and "as soon as possible" were open to definition, and definition was most likely to come from Poland's Soviet occupiers. Admiral Leahy pointed out the elasticity of the communiqué on the subject to Roosevelt. "I know, Bill," was the answer. "I know it—but it's the best I can do for Poland at this time."

The Polish issue was a concentrated sample of the real difficulties that lay ahead, of dilemmas that could not be solved by slogans and victory salutes. In genuinely free elections, the conservative, Catholic, and nationalistic Poles would almost surely return a government committed to ousting the Russians; and just as surely, the Moscow regime of 1945, which had barely escaped from the abyss itself, would not allow that. Only some miracle, some entirely new development, could change things. Until then, only patience and negotiation could keep the wartime grand alliance alive.

Roosevelt returned from Yalta ready to work hard on the postwar blueprints and use his formidable assets as a politician to advance the cause. But he was not quite himself. "I'm a bit exhausted, but really all right," he wrote to Eleanor on the last day of the conference. But no, he was not "really all right." Uncharacteristically, he reported to Congress on his trip from a seated position, admitting as he had never done before what an effort it was for him to drag around the steel braces that kept his wasted legs from collapsing under him. Then, soon after, he was off to Warm Springs for a rest. In that relaxing atmosphere, perhaps his natural optimism fought its way through fatigue. Perhaps that was why he cabled Churchill on April 12, just after the flap over the abortive surrender proposal in Italy, advising him to minimize the general Soviet problem as much as possible. He added a sentence that would tease historians as to his future intentions: "We must be firm, however."

No one would ever know if this was a casual afterthought or the signal for a change of stance. A few hours later, he was dead of a massive stroke. His plans went with him into the grave. Inside of another four weeks Hitler, too, was gone, and the swastika trampled into the ashes of the Reich. Not quite four months afterwards, in the searing fireball over Hiroshima, World War II ended, and with it an era when weapons seemed to guarantee the security of nations— and not to threaten victor and vanquished alike with annihilation.

Wilson and Lenin, the Palmer raids and the Comintern, Bullitt and Litvinov, the Murmansk convoys and the drive to the Elbe were all part of that past. The prelude to Russian-American confrontation was over. Its themes might be repeated, like those of any overture. But there would be a difference. The two nations were now at the center of things, their influences radiating out to the limits of the earth and even beyond, into space. After 1945 the spotlight of history shone relentlessly on the two peoples who had stood somewhat outside of four centuries of European development, and whose soldiers had touched hands in peace over the wreckage of a bridge in Germany at the start of a new age.

Chapter 2
THE POLITICS OF VACUUM
1946-1947

IT WAS THE TWO MEN representing the Navy viewpoint who were dishing out the toughest advice. In effect, they were telling the new President to stand fast—to let the Soviet Foreign Minister know, when he showed up at the White House that Monday afternoon of April 23, 1945, that the United States would not be pushed around, and that we were plainly annoyed at Russia's dragging her feet on her Yalta promises of free Polish elections. The exact words of Secretary of the Navy James Forrestal were: "We had better have a showdown with them now than later."

Being hard-boiled with "them" was entirely in character for Forrestal. He was a lean, piercing-eyed fifty-five-year-old, a successful contractor's son from Beacon, New York, who had gone to Princeton, flown for the Navy in 1918, and then had come to Wall Street, working for the brokerage house of Dillon, Read. He was tireless, smart, pushy, and had become company president by 1937. In 1940 Roosevelt brought him to Washington as an administrative assistant, a businessman-Democrat who could help rearm America in a world that was suddenly a jungle. He earned his way up to the top Navy post by continuing his driving, workaholic ways. In rare moments of relaxation he read books on history and world affairs, and deepened his conviction that Communism was a malign force with which there could be no long-term truce. He looked more like a pugilist than a thinker or an executive, thanks to a nose broken in a recreational boxing bout—and he liked that.

Forrestal's attitude meshed with that of Admiral William D. Leahy, the old salt who was there as "Chief of Staff to the Commander-in-Chief." Leahy was graduated from Annapolis when Jim Forrestal was five years old. He served in the waters around Cuba, the Philippines, China, Nicaragua, Haiti—wherever the flag and sixteen-inch rifled guns made it clear who was boss. He worked his way up to Chief of Naval Operations and then retired; but sea-loving FDR, who admired him, first made him governor of Puerto Rico, then ambassador to Vichy France, and, finally, his personal military adviser.

But there was conflicting counsel, too. The Secretary of War, Henry L. Stimson, was urging an easier stance. He was the oldest man in the room—seventy-seven—and an old-fashioned gentleman, who had held the same post under William Howard Taft in 1910—only thirty-five years ago but a whole historical era away. As Secretary of State in 1931 he had sounded the alarm when the Japanese punched into Manchuria: There must be unity against aggression! But now he saw no reason for strong words to the Russians. Their orbit did not clash with ours, and we should avoid any part of what he privately called "the Balkan mess."

And on Stimson's side was the man whom the new President most admired of all those present—General George Catlett Marshall, the Army's Chief of Staff, the architect of victory, the universally respected model of integrity, reserve, and intellectual grasp. Marshall's reason was simple. A fight with the Russians might let them back out of their promise to enter the war against Japan within three months of Germany's surrender, leaving Americans to "do all the dirty work."

Harry S Truman listened and pondered what course to take. The decision would be his, of course. He would later express that notion with a sign on his desk, "The Buck Stops Here." That was what being President meant. It was never easy, but it was harder than ever for Truman, catapulted into office by Roosevelt's fatal brain hemorrhage, and woefully unprepared for leadership by a tradition of do-nothing, Throttlebottom Vice Presidents who were expected to preside over the Senate and remain untroubled by any knowledge of what was going on at 1600 Pennsylvania Avenue.

He had, in fact, been in the middle of a social glass of bourbon with Speaker of the House Sam Rayburn when the terrible phone call from Roosevelt's press secretary had come. Since then, in the whirlwind of crowded hours, the question of getting along with the Russians had been pushed to center stage in his mind while he was scrambling to fill the gaps in his readiness. FDR had died on Thursday, the 12th. That very evening Truman had sent a cable to Moscow, strongly endorsing U.S. Ambassador Averell Harriman's request that Foreign Minister Vyacheslav Molotov personally attend the organizing conference of the United Nations Organization at San Francisco on April 25, with a stopover in Washington. (Stalin and Molotov, eager to size up the new American chief of state, quickly agreed.) Then Truman had spoken with James F. Byrnes, Roosevelt's economic mobilization chief, and Charles Bohlen of the

State Department, both of whom had been at Yalta. And he had sent a message to Churchill, urging the Prime Minister to hold off on a denunciation of the Russians' alleged breach-of-promise for the time being.

He had held a Cabinet meeting that evening, too, asking all members to stay at their posts. Afterwards, Stimson had taken him aside for a moment and murmured something about a huge project under way—the making of an explosive of "almost unbelievable destructive power." That left Truman puzzled until Vannevar Bush, head of the Office of Scientific Research and Development, came in the next day to brief him on the nearly completed atomic bomb. Leahy was there, and snorted that it was all foolishness. "The bomb will never go off," he predicted, speaking as "an expert in explosives." But it was obviously something to keep in mind when thinking about the Russians.

At the funeral on Saturday Truman had exchanged a few words with the drawn and wraithlike Harry Hopkins. By Monday, after his first speech as President to the Congress, he was reading over back cables and talking to Assistant Secretary of State Joseph Grew. Whatever he said to the veteran diplomat encouraged Grew, who wrote happily to a friend that Truman would not "stand for any pussyfooting in our foreign relations." Leahy had also noted, with obvious pleasure, that Stalin's "insulting" language in the recent correspondence had inflamed Truman's "solid, old-fashioned Americanism."

Late that week Harriman had shown up, having flown back from the Soviet Union to brief his boss. The solemn-faced son of a railroad magnate ("How can a man with a hundred million look so sad?" Maxim Litvinov had allegedly asked another American), Harriman had been moving toward a hard-line position, convinced that the men in the Kremlin believed they could "force acceptance of their decisions without question upon us and all countries." He had conveyed his misgivings to the President, and had done likewise to Forrestal and several other officials in separate conversations. He was worried that the United States might be facing "an ideological crusade just as vigorous and dangerous as Fascism or Nazism."

Finally, by Sunday, April 22, Molotov himself had arrived. There had been a brief session of courteous, formal greetings involving Truman and other officials, and then Molotov was off to guest quarters at the nearby Blair-Lee House, where he startled the servants with the habits acquired in a lifetime of survivorship. He slept irregularly, prowled the garden in predawn hours, never sat with his back to a door or window, and had clothes that were back from the cleaner searched before donning them.

So there things stood at the special Monday meeting, and Truman was listening and weighing. Perhaps simply to get a reaction he threw out a line of argument for lawyer Stimson to deal with: Our agreements, he said, had so far "been a one-way street and that could not continue." Stimson responded as best he could in a difficult situation. The Russians, he declared, had kept their word on major military matters, even if, on minor ones, they occasionally needed lessons in manners. They took the Polish question very seriously as a matter of their own security—and while free elections sounded fine, in a country without a liberal tradition there was no real idea of what an uncoerced ballot meant.

The talk went on around the room—Marshall, Forrestal, General John Deane (who had headed the military mission to the Red Army), the other experts trying to outguess the future. The President listened, thanked them, and made up his mind. When Molotov showed up at 5:30, he was ready.

Molotov was probing, too, trying to find keys to the character of this newcomer to the stage, mentally composing his assessment for a report to Stalin. He spoke, Truman himself later noted, without hostility, after listening to the President's complaint that failure to implement the Yalta understandings would "seriously shake confidence" in British-American-Soviet "unity."

Not necessarily, was Molotov's response. The three governments had disagreed before, and always managed in the end to find "common language." But for two to combine against a third would not be acceptable to the Soviet government. Truman answered "sharply" that the United States only asked for execution of the Crimea decision on Poland. Molotov once again explained that the matter was difficult, but that Stalin was certain that an agreement could be reached. Truman thrust back: "An agreement *had* been reached on Poland and that it only required to be carried out by the Soviet government." Molotov said that "others"—meaning the London Poles—had some responsibility for the problem, and that surely Truman must understand that the Polish question was of special interest to the Soviets.

Truman's response was a crisp lecture. The United States wanted the Soviet Union's friendship, he said, but he wanted it "clearly understood" that this could only happen when there was "mutual observation" of pacts already made. Then Molotov bristled, either genuinely or as a tactic, and uttered what must have been, from one who worked for Stalin, a considerable exaggeration: "I have never been talked to like that in my life!"

"Carry out your agreements," snapped the Missourian, "and you won't get talked to like that."

A new spirit was abroad in Soviet-American relations.

I T WAS NOT A MATTER of an abrupt break, of a belligerent Harry
Truman suddenly replacing a peaceable Franklin Roosevelt. No
one would ever know for certain whether Roosevelt would have
retained his amiability toward Stalin in the face of post-V-E Day
events. Nor did Truman immediately abandon the path of negotiation. Though he told Joseph Davies proudly of his talk with Molotov
a week later, saying, "I let him have it," he followed up with a
question: "Did I do right?" He was open-minded enough to send
Hopkins on still another mission to Moscow in June—a tacit signal
that the Rooseveltian framework still endured. And Hopkins
actually won some points: a Soviet surrender of the veto on
discussions (but not actions) in the United Nations Security Council;
and even more, a hard offer of five ministries, out of some twenty in
the new Polish government, for nominees of the London Poles,
provided they were friendly to both the Western powers *and*
Russia.

But style sends its own signals. The shift from Roosevelt's sinuous
pragmatism to Truman's bluntness meant that messages had a
harder edge, arguments were more likely to end abruptly. Truman's
temperament, as he settled himself more firmly each day into the
Chief Executive's role, would insensibly have shifted the balance of
Soviet-American relations toward confrontation no matter what
formal positions he took.

It was a remarkable temperament. Born to a farming family on
May 8, 1884, he had attended the public schools of Independence,
Missouri. Weak eyes kept him from vigorous participation in sports,
but did not prevent his becoming an omnivorous reader, with a
special fondness for history and biography. In time, he would
surprise far better educated men and women with his grasp of past
events. Yet he did not get from his historical reading a sense of the
ambiguity or transience of the historical process, a sense of
skepticism or relativity. Truman believed that the values he learned
in American grade school were universal and timeless, and that
history simply provided him with insights into whether yesterday's
leaders had fulfilled or failed those values.

Life appeared to deal harshly with him. After unimpressive
clerical jobs he had returned to the farm to scratch out a living. Then
World War I brought him his finest moment up to then—the
captaincy of Battery D, 129th Field Artillery. He loved his combat
service in France, not out of misty infatuation with bugles and
banners, but because he enjoyed the no-nonsense order of an army
of citizen-soldiers getting a job done. He never doubted the justness
of the war's official cause—a fight against Prussian militarism.

After the armistice came a business failure, then local political
involvements and an appointment by Democratic patronage chiefs

to a county administrative post. In 1934 Tom Pendergast's Kansas City machine sent him to the Senate. He was reelected in 1940, and during the war headed a committee investigating performance on war contracts. Everyone was surprised when this supposed errand-boy of a "boss" turned out to be scrupulously honest and unremitting in his pursuit of profiteers and corner-cutters. By 1944 he had a modest name for himself, and then the lightning struck. Roosevelt was informed that his Vice President, Henry Wallace, was considered by many party regulars to be overly liberal, soft-headed, and hard to reason with. A replacement on the ticket was necessary. Passing over several choices—including Byrnes, by then a virtual "assistant President"—Roosevelt named the incredulous Truman, who had almost no political liabilities. Though he was well liked on the Hill, the consensus was that if he succeeded to the Presidency, he would be putty in the hands of the strongminded individuals in FDR's Cabinet.

No consensus could have been more mistaken, as the world would gradually learn. In the first, shocked meeting of that Cabinet on April 12, Truman told the hushed members that he would carry on, for the time being, with existing personnel and policies, but expected to be President in his own right. He would have to change staff habits to do that. A day or so later an official called Truman with a question about some appointment that had just crossed his desk, asking: "Did the President make that decision before he went down to Warm Springs?" "No," was Truman's firm reply. "The President made it today."

The willingness to meet possible conflict head-on was quickly demonstrated in another way, as Truman prepared to go to Potsdam for the next meeting of the Big Three. He had persuaded James Byrnes to take over the job of Secretary of State from the incumbent Edward R. Stettinius, Jr., a lightweight, wealthy appointee who had easily resigned himself to the fact that he would have little to do with decision-making, because in fact Roosevelt was his own Secretary of State. Byrnes, however, was of quite a different order. An Irish extrovert from South Carolina, he had entered the House of Representatives in 1911 and stayed fourteen years, practiced law, gone to the Senate for ten years, and then been named in 1941 to the Supreme Court. Roosevelt had asked him to give up that spot to take over the role of economic stabilizer, then to become head of the Office of War Mobilization. Byrnes could thus boast proudly that he had served in all three branches of the federal government, and was known to feel that his qualifications for the Presidency were considerably superior to Truman's.

All the same, Truman was willing to risk Byrnes's ambition in order to make use of his expertise. His place at the President's side would link the new Administration to the ghost of Hyde Park, but make it clear that the reins were firmly in the hands of the man from Independence. At least that's the way Truman saw it as they set off, with a large delegation, for the gathering in Potsdam (a suburb of Berlin—once home to major German film-makers—that had somehow escaped the worst of the devastation wrought on Hitler's capital).

Truman enjoyed the trip over on the cruiser *Augusta* in the early days of July. He kept everyone hopping to his by-now-familiar routine of early bedtime and a brisk 6 A.M. walk on the scrubbed decks. He enjoyed whiling away time with a few hands of cards—the loneliness of the White House had been one thing that bothered him, though he only admitted that in private letters. He read cables, listened to the serenades of the Navy band, and was delighted with gunnery practice, noting in his journal that he would "rather fire a battery than run a country" any day. By the time he was settled into his quarters in a former publisher's mansion in Potsdam, he was feeling feisty and ready to deal with Churchill and Stalin.

Oddly enough, he seemed to like the Russian the better of the two, at any rate on first impression. At their initial meeting he told Stalin he was "no diplomat" but usually listened to all the arguments and then answered yes or no. After Stalin's reply, and a luncheon of many toasts and official photographs, Truman recorded: "I can deal with Stalin. He is honest—but smart as hell." By contrast, he thought that Churchill had greeted him with "a lot of hooey" about his love for Roosevelt, but he believed that they would "get along if he doesn't try to give me too much soft soap."

As it turned out, Churchill was not to be a problem. Within two weeks of the conference's opening, the British electorate turned the venerable hero out to pasture, and replaced him with a comparatively colorless Laborite, Clement Attlee. So Potsdam would be different from Teheran and Yalta to the extent that Attlee and Truman differed from their flamboyant predecessors. In fact, though Truman did not yet know it, Potsdam would be a finale, the last meeting of the chiefs of the three great nations to be held against the dramatic backdrop of the war begun by their common enemy, the Third Reich. The President did note the fact that two of the three historical giants were off the stage now (though Churchill had plenty of public life left to live), and he wondered a bit uneasily what would happen if "Stalin should suddenly cash in" and a power struggle should convulse the Soviet Union.

But speculations about possibilities gave way to the basic facts of mid-1945 as discussions got under way. The first and uncontroverted decision was to confirm the Yalta understandings about the Pacific.

Russia would enter the fighting in Asia on August 15. She would, as promised, regain half of the island of Sakhalin (taken from Russia by Tokyo in 1905) and would jointly occupy Korea until a peace treaty was signed. She would also get her Manchurian concessions by treaty with Chiang Kai-shek, and a seat on the Allied Control Council for Japan; but it was clear and acceptable to Stalin that it would be uncontestably a backseat.

Not so with Germany, however. The reparations question was still full of thorns. The Russians wanted huge amounts of material and capital equipment both from their zone of occupation and those allotted to the United States, Britain, and France. But the Western powers knew that they would, for some time, have to feed the people in their shattered zones, which contained little farmland in contrast to what the Russians held. They insisted that whatever could be produced by postwar Germany should be taken to pay for food imports before any reparations were extracted; otherwise they would be feeding the German cow while the Russians milked it. But the Russians energetically fought this "first charge" principle, and finally an imprecisely worded compromise was struck. The Russians could take what they wanted from their own zone. They would also be entitled automatically to 10 percent of capital equipment "unnecessary" for peaceable use in the rest of Germany. And, in exchange for food and raw materials from Eastern Germany, they would be able to acquire up to 25 percent more of Western-zone machinery not convertible to nonmilitary production.

This arrangement was, of course, susceptible to haggling over definitions and figures, and was in fact a recognition that each side was tending to deal in its own way with its own half of the conquered Reich. But it was the best that could be achieved. In the same way, the Allies accepted the newly defined Polish boundary with Germany, being unable to do much about it. The same practical realization influenced the decision concerning peace pacts with Germany's allies—Italy, Finland, Hungary, Rumania, and Bulgaria. Great Britain and the United States had no enthusiasm for deals with the Soviet-dominated governments of the latter three, but in the end they were forced to a postponement and another verbal waffling. The newly created Council of Foreign Ministers—representing the Big Three, plus China and France—was to begin work on the preparation of treaties for the Axis satellites, which were eventually to be signed by "recognized democratic governments" in them.

There was some testing of remote possibilities by both sides. The Russians asked for a trusteeship of one of Italy's former colonies in Africa and for free access to the Mediterranean through the Turkish-controlled Dardanelles. Truman countered with the idea of an internationalizing of all waterways important to world commerce—which would have included not only the Suez and Panama canals, but such rivers as the Danube, whose banks were, that summer, lined with Soviet occupying forces. These proposals predictably came to nothing. On the basic issues of reparations, Germany's frontiers, and treaties with Axis satellites, there was simply a tendency to recognize that neither side could force the other's hand.

The most important development of all for future Soviet-American relations, however, did not reach the conference agenda. On July 16, Truman received the report of the "experiment" in the New Mexican desert, in which thirteen pounds of a new explosive vaporized the steel tower in which it was placed, dug a crater six feet deep and four hundred yards across, and lit the sky so brightly that it was visible two hundred miles away. Just for the moment, Truman was awed at this "most terrible bomb in the history of the world," which reminded him of the "fire of destruction" prophesied in the Bible for the valley of the Euphrates. But he did not hesitate to send the order for the preparations necessary to use it against a military objective in Japan. Nor was he unaware that the bomb gave him a diplomatic card to play, though the time was not yet ripe for it. He did take Stalin aside on July 24 and inform him that the Americans had tested a weapon of unusual destructive force, but the full import of the statement did not hit the Russian until he checked it with his own nuclear experts.

By the time the parleys ended, Truman had some cause for cheerful feelings. The spirit of wartime cooperation might be wounded, but it was still alive. The door had been left open for further dealings on European issues. There seemed to be no looming problems of cooperation with the Russians in Asia. Their entry into the war, according to promise, could not greatly change fundamental power balances, for the fighting could not last much longer, thanks to the atomic bomb, the ultimate ratification of America's power. If future top-level dealings were necessary, the President apparently felt, he could handle them. Stalin might be, in Truman's own words, "an S.O.B.," but he reminded him of Tom Pendergast, likewise a strong man with problems. Even twelve years later, when Truman felt that he had been an "innocent idealist" who had been hoodwinked by "the unconscionable Russian Dictator," he confessed: "And I liked the little son of a bitch."

He was not aware, as he boarded the Augusta for the homeward voyage, of how quickly things were actually moving. The bombing of Hiroshima opened the new era in warfare on August 6, while he was at sea. The next day, the Soviet Union declared war on Japan. One day later, the second atomic bomb hit Nagasaki. Two days afterward, Truman was back in Washington in time to receive the Japanese request for specific surrender terms. At last the greatest and most devastating war in modern history was over.

For every country affected, it was a time of rejoicing, but the cheers and the parades had special intensity in relatively unscathed America. The final victory appeared to be almost totally undiluted. The United States was at the zenith of her military and industrial power. The American people were almost unanimous in agreeing as never before or after that the cause had been just. There seemed every reason to believe that the unity and energy created by the war could be turned toward fashioning a peacetime era of untroubled prosperity. The world's problems, if any remained, would be taken care of by the forces and leaders liberated from Fascism, or by the new world peacekeeping organization. No shadows would fall on the American future that began with the shrieking whistles, ringing bells, and riotous street celebrations of V-J Day.

This euphoric mood was based partly on an incomplete realization of how the contrast between America's strength and the world's weakness would multiply Washington's responsibilities. Not everyone understood that a healthy giant in a world of cripples would have many burdens to bear. And of those who did, some overestimated the capacities of the giant. There were happy fantasies in 1945, which overlooked certain gritty realities, chief among them a vacuum in world affairs caused by the virtual destruction of Europe, for four centuries the globe's power center.

TRUMAN HAD GOTTEN A GLIMPSE of the state of Europe in a brief tour of Berlin during Potsdam. Bombed from the air for months, and fought over bitterly during the Russian siege, the German capital offered appalling sights. "The odor of death," recalled one American diplomat, "was everywhere," rising from the bodies and refuse that clogged streets and canals. General Lucius D. Clay, soon to be American Military Governor, picked his way around the rubble piles that had once been viaducts, buildings, and bridges, and said that he was in a "city of the dead." Looking at this inadvertent "monument" to Hitler, Truman thought of Carthage, Babylon, Nineveh, Genghis Khan, Alexander, and Darius the Great. He was even jolted into an uncharacteristic moment of pessimism: "I hope for some sort of peace," he noted privately, "but I fear that machines are ahead of morals by some centuries."

Yet Berlin was only one illustration of the overpowering devastation that the war had worked. In the most tragic statistic, loss of human life, estimates were that as many as 32 million people had been killed in the battles, bombings, extermination camps, famines, executions, and epidemics that the struggle produced. In military personnel alone the Soviet Union had lost 7.5 million men, and the Germans 3.5 million, while the European allies suffered 15 million deaths in their armed forces. A statistical sidelight showed how the war had fallen most heavily on one particular generation. One quarter of all Germans born in 1924, it was estimated, were dead or missing.

Those who remained alive in Europe had little to rejoice about as the hard winter closed in. Millions had been uprooted as conscripts, slave laborers, or prisoners of war; and millions of others had been expelled from their homes in population transfers to change the ethnic character of some regions (the Russians, for example, had forced Germans out of newly annexed parts of Poland). The simple initials DP, for "displaced person," concealed an enormous agony, as well as a huge task for relief agencies in feeding and relocating the wanderers.

Housing was almost impossible to find. Five million units had been wiped out all over Europe and many millions more severely damaged. Bridges were down, rail lines gone, roads pitted with bomb craters, so that food and fuel could only be distributed slowly and painfully. Industrial production was at a near-standstill. Germany's Ruhr, once capable of turning out 400,000 tons of coal daily, struggled to mine 25,000; in Belgium, France, Greece, Holland, Yugoslavia, and Poland, overall output levels were down to one-fifth of prewar totals. All of the nations involved in the fighting had debts measured in billions, no wherewithal for retiring them, and dizzying rates of inflation as faith in local currencies simply vanished. Prices in Italy were thirty-five times 1939 levels. In Hungary, the pengö was quoted at 2.5 *billion* to the dollar at one point; in Greece there was an almost equally catastrophic decline in the drachma. The hard currency of the day often consisted of cigarettes, chocolate, or other items from American encampments. To obtain it, and the precious food it could buy on black markets, once-affluent Europeans scrambled for menial jobs, or turned to swindling and theft and prostitution. It was a time of wolves. Officials of the United Nations Relief and Rehabilitation Administration (UNRRA), founded to deal with these problems in 1943, estimated that even long after V-E Day, up to 100 million Europeans were getting fewer than the 1,500 calories a day consumed by the average inhabitant of India. The triumphantly civilized Continent had become a place, in the words of a British observer, where "grey-faced ghosts in parodies of clothing . . . queued for bread and potatoes . . . rummaged for sticks and scraps. For them, this wasteland of rubble, rags, and hunger was a prison without privacy or dignity."

It would become an American article of faith, in time, that this debilitation left Western Europe naked to a possible Soviet invasion. Though theoretically true, this anxiety overlooked the desperate condition of the badly bled Russians themselves. The Soviet Union had lost 20 million dead altogether, 7 million horses, 20 million pigs, 4.7 million houses, 1,710 towns, 70,000 villages, some 3,000 miles of railroad track, nearly 16,000 locomotives, and 428,000 freight cars. Despite her large and victorious armies, she could hardly afford a war that would impose more privations on her people, already hard pressed to rebuild.

It was, nonetheless, a fact that Europe's shattered condition made a historic change in American policy inevitable. There was no way that the United States could, as in 1919, withdraw to its own side of the Atlantic, secure in the knowledge that French and British arms and diplomacy would keep the peace, even if in ways that did not always earn American moral approval. Moreover, it was certain that wretchedness and dislocation would breed a ready supply of disturbances to peace, not only in Europe, but in Africa and Asia, where the impotence of France and Britain guaranteed a speedup in the process of decolonization. So the surrender of the Axis "villains" was not simply the happy finale to the story of the war, but the curtain-raiser for more serious, perplexing, and demanding historical dramas, with the American people cast in a leading role.

Yet this sober thought was one that the American public mind was reluctant to entertain. Flushed with success, Americans seemed to believe that no problems were beyond quick solution, or would demand further long-range disruptions of their lives. The very contrast between conditions in the Old World and the New, in 1945, fed a sense of national superiority.

The new power of the United States was beyond both her experience and comprehension. At the war's end almost 12 million men and women were on active duty with the armed forces. Those in the Navy served in a flotilla that dwarfed all the armadas of history; even two years after V-J Day it numbered 15 battleships, 36 aircraft carriers, 72 cruisers, 630 destroyers, 206 submarines. The Army Air Forces, soon to become independent, were boasting of the role of the B-29s in subduing Japan, and eager to unveil the new generation of intercontinental bombers soon to come off the drawing boards, chief among them the B-36—twenty tons of airplane, powered by eight engines, able to carry a bombload five thousand miles and return. The bombload could include the ultimate weapon, the seal of power, the Faustian gift, the atomic bomb, which America alone possessed.

While these legions might soon be demobilized, the productive power that had armed them would endure. The output figures totted up at the war's end showed that in less than four years a United

States just emerging from the paralysis of the Depression had produced 299,000 combat planes, 3.6 million trucks, 100,000 tanks, 87,620 warships, and 5,200 merchant vessels, merely to list the large items. Prodigious quantities of other matériel were heaped up in dumps all over the world. Government auctions to unload $90 billion worth of surplus items suggested their infinite variety: 40,000 Signal Corps homing pigeons, $50 million worth of 60-inch searchlights, 10 million pounds of contraceptive jelly, and thousands of jars of Elizabeth Arden black face cream used by infantrymen on night missions. How could anyone regard such figures without a sense of mastery, or a conviction that they vindicated the "American system?"

The surge of pride in the golden moment manifested itself in many ways—first and foremost, in a mad rush to enjoy the good times that had been missing since 1929. The rush to dismantle the citizen armies was a major symptom of it. "Please," sang Americans in Italy, in a parody of *Lili Marlene:*

> *Please, Mr. Truman, why can't we go home?*
> *We have conquered Naples, and we have seen Rome*
> *We have licked the master race*
> *Now all we ask is shipping space . . .*

And indeed, as fast as shipping space could be found, whole divisions melted away into separation centers, the final stop before civilian life was resumed. The desire to cast off restraint broke out quickly among businessmen, politicians, and laborers. In November of 1945 Congress slashed taxes, especially excess profits taxes, by $6 billion. The following summer, over Truman's veto, it gutted the Office of Price Administration, whereupon prices promptly rose on various items anywhere from 10 to 1,000 percent. Unions stirred restlessly. The United Auto Workers was on strike against General Motors before the first peacetime Christmas, demanding a 30 percent wage hike to make up for the loss of overtime pay. The walkout lasted 116 days; but in the end, management granted many of the workers' demands, knowing that the cost would soon be recouped, for a car-hungry country would not wait long to snap up anything on wheels. Price hikes and wage demands played their usual game of leapfrog. By the spring of 1946 there had been strikes of electrical workers, meatpackers, steelworkers, coal miners, and railroad operatives. In all, during 1946, 4.6 million workers were involved in work stoppages costing 116 million man-days. The Republicans took traditional "out" party advantage of the general discontent, and won control of Congress in the November elections by repetition of the arresting slogan: "Had enough?"

Yet behind it all there was optimism. The 1940s were not the

1980s. The strikes were not considered squabbles for shares of a diminishing pie, nor was inflation seen as a chronic and irrepressible problem. Everyone assumed that the crunch, even in its most unpleasant aspects—the struggle to find housing, for example, since residential construction had virtually ceased for years—would be temporary. Everyone felt that the economy that had churned out the tools of victory would, in time, produce houses, cars, and consumer goods in abundance—as in fact it did.

But some people's visions soared even beyond that, and saw an American production apparatus that could fill the world's empty bellies and cover its roofless heads, that could undergird international leadership and paralyze totalitarianism by eliminating the poverty on which it supposedly fed. The ebullient message that age-old scourges were no match for an American will to end them came from many diverse quarters. It came from the publisher, Henry R. Luce, for example, no friend to the liberalism of Franklin D. Roosevelt, which he had often criticized in the editorial columns of *Life* magazine. In one of those same columns he contributed a phrase to the postwar vocabulary, "the American century."

It was the title of an essay in which Luce argued that "the world of the 20th century . . . must be to a significant degree an American century." America was already "the intellectual, scientific, and artistic capital of the world," and it "must undertake now to be the Good Samaritan of the entire world." It must "be the powerhouse from which the ideals [of Western civilization]" might spread throughout the globe, and "do their mysterious work of lifting the life of mankind from the level of the beasts to what the Psalmist called 'a little lower than the angels.' " Though the United States could not "impose democratic institutions on all mankind," it still had the duty and opportunity as the most "vital" of nations to exert "the full impact of our influence, for such purposes as we see fit, and by such means as we see fit." Though much of this was an echo of the missionary imperialism of the 1890s into which Luce had been born in China, it had a special ring in the hour of victory—which made even more remarkable the fact that the article first appeared in February of 1941, when the United States was still officially neutral, and Western civilization on the ropes.

At the other end of the political spectrum from Luce was Henry A. Wallace, a cantankerous agrarian radical and talented corn geneticist, and also Roosevelt's Vice President during his third term, who was dropped from the 1944 ticket because he was perceived as too far left for the public mood. In a 1942 speech Wallace had also spoken of the twentieth century, and said it must be "the century of the common man." The war's object, he claimed, was "to make sure that everybody in the world has the privilege of drinking a quart of

milk a day," and he had no doubt of America's capacity to help
reach that goal. Early in 1945, during hearings on his nomination to
the consolation prize of Secretary of Commerce, he promised to
work for an "economic Bill of Rights" that would produce roads,
houses, public works, and the then-high figure of 60 million jobs.

Luce and Wallace were articulating the same thought, namely that
America's material power could create a bright future for the whole
of humankind. Truman put its worldwide political implications in
condensed form, just after V-J Day, to some Missouri neighbors:
"We are going forward to meet our destiny—which I think Almighty
God intended us to have—and we are going to be the leaders."

The elements were therefore in place for what the English
historian, D. W. Brogan, would later call "the illusion of American
omnipotence." In that glow, Americans would be vulnerable to
special impatience with forces that seemed to delay the realization
of ambitious goals. As the peacemaking process dragged on, and
Soviet-American disagreements came to light, it was easy to
personify the persistent imperfections of the world in the shape of
Russian "obstructionism." Soviet bad conduct was magnified by the
particular check that it placed on optimism, as well as by three
decades of anti-Communist thought.

Ambivalence still shadowed the mood. Public opinion polls in
mid-1946 showed six out of ten respondents believing that the Soviet
Union had ambitions of ruling the world, but only one in four
thinking that this would lead to a war with the United States. The
discrepancy reflected an American sense of being somehow
threatened, but with that feeling there was coupled an unwillingness to undergo any new sacrifices to meet the presumed danger.
Over the ensuing two years, events would be interpreted so as to
give the anti-Soviet consensus some issues, slogans, leaders, and,
above all, acceptable programs of action. Eventually, all international events began to fit, so far as the majority of voters was concerned,
into the wider context of presumed Soviet expansionism; and
individual differences between such events were blurred and
muted.

Russian illusions were harder to document, and the debates
among Americans over whether the Russians were genuinely
fearful for their own security or merely power-hungry went on, as
usual, without the benefit of hearing any uncensored voices from
inside Soviet councils. There was a clue to Moscow's long-range
intentions in February of 1946, when Stalin announced a series of
five-year plans that would give "priority development" to heavy
industry, increasing steel and electric power production by over 100
percent, coal by over 60 percent, petroleum by over 75 percent, and
overall industrial output by 50 percent. The dictator declared the

program to be a guard against "chance happenings." It could have been a reflexive answer to American boasts and challenges. It could have been a warning to the West that Russia was on the move—the "declaration of World War III" that it seemed to be in the eyes of an American economic expert stationed in the Moscow embassy. Or it might have been an effort by Stalin to boost Russia, in a short time, to the status of a first-class military and technological power simply as a monument to himself, or as proof that his definition of Communism was in fact definitive.

In any of these cases, however, the plan would require enormous exactions and sufferings from the already ravaged Russian people. And even though he was well equipped with coercive devices, it was easier for Stalin to impose these demands if they were seen as one more patriotic effort to protect the homeland, this time from American imperialist machinations. Confrontation with the West had certain advantages for the Politburo. Confrontation with Russia fulfilled particular psychological needs for many Americans, and was a longstanding source of political strength in the United States. So confrontation became increasingly common as the postwar months continued to flick, one by one, off the calendar.

THE BAROMETER OF RUSSIAN-AMERICAN relations settled toward storm warnings as soon as the Council of Foreign Ministers (CFM) began to hold its sessions to carry out the Potsdam mandate for draft treaties with the lesser Axis powers. Unlike the wartime meetings, these were relatively open. Both sides, therefore, were conscious of the propaganda implications of their statements, and tended to speak over the heads of those in the meeting room to the wider audience beyond. Western newspaper readers began to receive a wearisome education in the conventional paranoid style of Soviet discourse, which consisted of lengthy excoriations of the motives of those "reactionaries," "Fascists," "ruling cliques," and others who disagreed with Moscow. The uniformly exacerbating tone of the debates concealed the fact that there was occasional progress. Only veteran leftists and negotiators with Moscow understood that the Russians could shift direction without skipping a beat in their denunciations. For the public at large, however, the contrast with the bland, upbeat communiqués issued after the Big Three conferences was ominous.

The first Council session, held in London in September of 1945, showed typical patterns and interesting stylistic contrasts between the American and British foreign ministers. Byrnes, the conservative South Carolina judge, hoped to win some agreements by the use of his well-honed political skills, and was externally the soul of geniality. Ernest Bevin, the Laborite radical dock-worker-turned-statesman, was much less accommodating in the face of Communist rhetoric. Once, at a closed session, he almost drove Molotov away in a huff by saying, in response to some harangue, that he " 'adn't 'eard" arguments so similar to Hitler's in a long time. Only a gruff apology forestalled the walkout. (The next year, however, in a Paris meeting and after a heavy-drinking dinner, Bevin actually exploded after a lecture on Britain's past sins, and muttering "I've 'ad enough of this," started for Molotov with fists knotted, before security men intervened.)

But even geniality and apologies could not keep the London discussions from running aground on the same disagreements that had surfaced at Potsdam a month earlier. Then, just as some movement was initiated on territorial and other questions in the treaties with Rumania, Bulgaria, and Hungary, the Russians abruptly reversed their field. At the meeting in London they had agreed that France and China should be represented on the Council, but they now took the position that France especially should have no part in discussing pacts with the three Balkan enemy states, since she had not fought against them. The suspected reason was that the Russians had originally expected the French to line up with the Soviets on many issues, and were disappointed in that hope once bargaining started. But whatever the cause, Byrnes reacted quickly by getting the chairman of the London CFM conference, who happened at that time to be the Chinese representative, to declare the talks ended. Byrnes was moderately and needlessly concerned over whether American opinion would sustain this firm message to the Russians that the rules could not be changed in mid-game. Unfortunately for his own future, he was less worried about promptly informing Truman of his daily activities, an omission that was duly noted in the White House.

A second foreign ministers' meeting was held in Moscow in December, and some movement was produced by a Byrnes-sponsored compromise. Under it the French would stay out of preliminary treaty negotiations but would be invited to a later, full-dress conference at which draft agreements would be put in final form and ratified. After this was accepted, Byrnes, on his return to the United States, made a public speech in which he tried, through somewhat heavy-handed humor, to enlighten the American people on his future tactics. Up until then, he said, the necessary qualities for dealing with Russia had been firmness and patience. Now there would be a switch to patience and firmness. With that, he began to prepare for the next session, which began in Paris in April.

Matters advanced somewhat at that point. While the foreign ministers themselves came and went, deputies hammered out the hard details in continuous sessions, so that by the beginning of summer the treaties with Rumania, Hungary, and Bulgaria were ready for submission to a general gathering of Allied representatives, as promised. At that parley Byrnes was in a genial frame of mind, according to the recollection of the *New York Times's* Cyrus Sulzberger. Byrnes received the journalist for an interview, offering him a drink of Truman's own special brand of seven-year-old bourbon, sold only by Kansas City's Hotel Muehlebach, and revealed something of his proposed methodology as well as his temperament. He hoped that the "small powers" would "raise hell" on certain disputed points to strengthen his position, and then he could "get to work behind the scenes, 'in the jury room.' " Byrnes needed some bargaining concessions from the Russians, because the American delegation included both Senators Tom Connally and Arthur Vandenberg and the official Republican expert on foreign policy, John Foster Dulles, each or all of whom might publicly push him to take a politically popular hard line.

The Italian treaty was not ready for discussion in Paris in the summer of 1946, because of a dispute between Italy and Yugoslavia over the ownership of the Adriatic port of Trieste and the territory immediately surrounding it. Both countries were still occupied and administered by British and United States military forces. Tito's claim to the whole region was vigorously backed by the Russians. Byrnes proposed a compromise, namely, the internationalizing of the city under UN control. Actually, this arrangement would, by reducing Anglo-American influence, improve the opportunities for Communist propagandists in Trieste to agitate for Tito's case and keep the issue alive, and the Russians knew it—for them, UN control was a perfectly good half-loaf, but they continued to insist on a settlement completely in Tito's favor. However, at a meeting of the foreign ministers in New York in November, Byrnes—according to his special adviser on Soviet matters, Charles Bohlen—adroitly broke the logjam with the kind of poker-playing maneuver that he enjoyed. He called on Molotov and said that he had decided it was best, after all, to withdraw the compromise proposal, since it was getting nowhere. He blamed the situation entirely on Yugoslav stubbornness, and pretended to believe that the only Soviet motive for taking Yugoslavia's side was friendship. It was too bad, he intimated, that Tito would not see reason, but for the time being the regrettably controversial status quo (of Anglo-American occupation) would have to stand. Faced with the loss of his half-loaf, Molotov stammered a request to "Mr. Byrnes" to take no hasty actions, and that afternoon, Bohlen recalled, showed up to "hand out concessions like cards from a deck." By the end of that session all four treaties were ready for formal signature in Paris in February of 1947. Bohlen thought of Byrnes as underrated, despite Byrnes's tendency to ignore the expertise available in the State Department. Byrnes had gained some ground.

But there was no way of denying two glaring failures of the peace process—the virtual abandonment of Eastern Europe and the stalemate on Germany. The first of these situations was basically unavoidable, given the facts of Soviet occupation of the area. In the countries east of Germany, coalitions of anti-Fascist forces had sprung up as the war waned, and installed interim governments. The Soviet "liberating" armies remained in charge of such matters as transportation, relocation of peoples, and internal security. The Soviet commanders used their powers to harass, detain, and muzzle all political elements but the Communists. Moreover, through reparations claims and one-sided economic treaties forced on their garrisoned "client" states, they could tighten the screws on any uncooperative leaders.

Unsurprisingly, therefore, coalition governments became Communist-dominated, at which point the Russians could step back, leave their friends in charge, and shrug off Western complaints over strangled liberties with the statement that these were "internal" matters. One by one, the satellites were created. In Bulgaria, a Communist majority was returned to the parliament at the end of 1946. In Hungary, Prime Minister Ferenc Nagy, head of a "Small Landowners" party, was ousted in favor of a Communist in the spring of 1947. In Poland, Peasant Party leader Stanislas Mikolajczyk complained to the British and American ambassadors late in 1946 that 13 members of his Executive Committee and 791 party members were in jail, and at least 95 had been executed. He was a refugee by the following autumn. In Yugoslavia, the only candidates for parliament were members of Tito's National Liberation Front, and the Marshal was, at that point, a loyal Communist. In Rumania, a coalition "National Democratic Front" was gradually turned Red as the heads of the Peasant and Liberal parties were arrested.

A capsule sketch of how the process worked was given to Sulzberger by an East German Social Democrat, who explained the routine faced by members of his party who opposed union with the Communists. First there was a persuasive dinner, with plenty of vodka. Then a "correct but firm" visit from the security police, the NKVD, with a warning, "Be careful. We are watching you." Next, if stubbornness persisted, was removal from office, and finally, "disappearance." The effect on those who hesitated was powerful.

There were islands of irregularity in the pattern. Stalin chose to let Finland alone so long as it kept itself isolated from the West. And in Czechoslovakia, despite the choice of a Communist premier in May of 1946, a strong opposition persisted for at least another two years. But Eastern Europe was sucked into Moscow's orbit in a relatively short time, leaving an unbleachable taint of suspicion on Soviet claims of peaceable intent.

The German problem remained impervious even to compromise throughout 1946. At best there were complex issues to resolve, even if a genuine will had been present to coordinate Russian and American policies. How, for example, did one "de-Nazify" Germany without gutting the middle-level bureaucracy necessary to the tasks of running a modern state? Were public-health administrators or rail traffic managers with long experience to be banned from rendering indispensable services because of forced association with the Party? And how did one decide what industries were purely "warmaking" in nature, and therefore subject to dismantling and shipment to Russia as reparations? Such riddles were even harder to deal with in an atmosphere of recrimination, and the Russians did not hesitate to denounce every American and British decision that seemed to favor German economic recovery as part of a plot to reunify and rearm Germany, and to incorporate her into a worldwide pattern of cartels. To allay Russian (and French) fears of a remilitarized Reich, Byrnes tentatively offered a long-term four-power treaty, in which the United States, France, Britain, and the Soviet Union would mutually react to any German attack. But the Russians, themselves experienced in ignoring unsatisfactory treaties, turned a cold shoulder to the proposal, continued to strip their own occupation zone, and delayed shipments of food into the Western zones. In May of 1946 General Clay, with top-level approval behind him, retaliated by halting deliveries of reparations matériel to the Russians. Clay was exasperated by Russian tactics, more than half convinced that they were aimed at producing economic distress that would thereby assist Communism, a fixed article of belief at the time.

The protests that followed simply confirmed the growing trend toward a de facto partition of Germany, and helped to put a terminal chill on what was left of wartime cordiality. As relationships congealed, a series of unrelated events, interpreted in the most negative ways possible, sped Washington and Moscow down the road to estrangement.

There was the matter of Azerbaijan. During the war the Russians had, by agreement, occupied the northern half of Iran, through whose ports crucial supplies reached them. They were scheduled to withdraw in stages as 1945 came to an end. But the Russians announced that they would delay their departure from the northern province of Azerbaijan, because separatist rebels there were conducting uprisings, which endangered the security of the area. Iran protested that this was a flimsy excuse to continue the Soviet

military presence, and perhaps to set the scene for an actual
takeover of part or all of the country. Teheran appealed to the
Security Council for an investigation of the actual situation by a
neutral commission, and was strongly backed, in January of 1946, by
the United States. The new and shaky United Nations Organization
was confronted with its first crisis, bearing an "ominous resem-
blance to the situation which confronted the League of Nations in
the cases of Manchuria and Finland," the *New York Times* noted.
If the Soviet Union, as she threatened, vetoed any action, the
ineffectiveness of the world organization in the absence of great-
power unanimity would be painfully exposed. If the UN (or UNO
as it was then usually called) tried to ignore the veto, it might
provoke a Soviet withdrawal from that body and its own collapse.
After a brief but tense period of breath-holding, Moscow made its
own deal with Teheran, and announced that it would complete its
evacuation by September. The moment of danger passed, but not
before the supposed analogy to the German aggressions of the 1930s
had been planted in public consciousness by headlines and
editorials.

Then, in March of 1946, Winston Churchill appeared on the scene
to crystallize growing suspicion of Russia in one of those phrases
that he spun off with incomparable ease. The setting was the town
of Fulton, Missouri, home to little Westminster College. Learning
that the former Prime Minister was vacationing in Florida, the
college president, Franc McCluer, conceived the ambitious idea of
inviting him to give a talk. Next, being a close friend of a fellow
Westminster alumnus, Brigadier General Harry Vaughn, who
happened to be an aide to fellow Missourian Harry Truman,
McCluer proceeded to Washington and came away with a genuine
prize—Truman's handwritten endorsement of the letter of invitation, and a promised introduction to Churchill.

Out of power and restless, the veteran leader seized upon the
chance to rally support among old friends by a renewed call for the
Anglo-American unity forged in the hour of battle. But what peril
could serve to bind the alliance now that Nazism had perished? The
answer came in the voice that had kindled resistance in the face of
despair in 1940:

> A shadow has fallen upon the scene so lately lighted up by the
> Allied victory. From Stettin, in the Baltic, to Trieste, in the Adriatic,
> an Iron Curtain has descended across the Continent. Behind that
> line lie all the capitals of the ancient states of Central and Eastern
> Europe. Warsaw, Berlin, Prague, Vienna, Budapest, Belgrade, and
> Sofia, all . . . lie in what I must call the Soviet sphere. . . . Police
> governments are prevailing. . . . In front of the Iron Curtain . . . and
> through the world, Communist fifth columns are established and

work in complete unity and absolute obedience to the directions they receive from the Communist center. . . .

Last time I saw it all coming and cried aloud to my fellow countrymen and to the world, but no one paid any attention. Up until the year 1933 or even 1935, Germany might have been saved . . . and we might all have been spared the miseries Hitler let loose upon mankind. . . . We must surely not let that happen again.

The Churchillian summons did not get an immediate enthusiastic reception, except from already committed and consistent Communist-haters. Most press reaction was wary of what was widely perceived as an appeal to help preserve the collapsing British empire, the alarm signal of an elegant and gallant Tory, but one past his time. Yet the term "Iron Curtain," so perfectly descriptive, passed at once and permanently into the common vocabulary, to be invoked again and again with increasing conviction as time went on.

Moreover, the presence of Truman on the platform seemed to imply an unofficial endorsement of the speech that understandably stung Moscow. Stalin sent the President a private note of reproach. Truman revealed this some time later, as well as his answer: an offer to Stalin to come and give a speech of his own, at the same place and in the same circumstances, with free passage on the U.S.S. Missouri. But such an impractical and theatrical gesture, while it might have satisfied Truman's sense of fairness to all parties, did not soothe Soviet sensibilities, already nettled by the fact that the American Congress had extended Britain a $3.75 billion loan on the State Department's recommendation, whereas a Russian application for similar reconstruction aid had gotten nowhere.

In June of 1946 fresh discord arose over the question of the future control of atomic weaponry. There had been a debate in the Cabinet on what to do with the superbomb almost from the moment of its use. Everyone knew that the American monopoly would be temporary. How might it best be used? Byrnes held to a conventional view. Keeping the "secret" for a time would give him, in Henry Stimson's words, "the bomb in his pocket . . . as a great weapon" in negotiations. And Byrnes did use precisely that figure of speech at the London CFM meeting in a joking context. "If you don't cut out all this stalling and let us get down to work," he said to Molotov, "I am going to pull an atomic bomb out of my hip pocket and let you have it." Molotov and his interpreter laughed, it was reported.

Stimson had a different plan, namely to offer information on the bomb to the Russians in exchange for specific concessions—in effect, to trade, but not to threaten with it. Forrestal and others dismissed this as an attempt to "buy understanding," and the Navy Secretary noted: "We tried that once with Hitler." A subsequent compromise was reached (Stimson, meanwhile, retiring from public service) in a decision to turn the bomb gradually over to international control. After many studies a proposal emerged that carried the name of Bernard Baruch, the elderly financial wizard, World War I industrial coordinator, informal adviser to Presidents, and good friend of his fellow South Carolinian, Byrnes. Truman had named him American delegate to the UN's committee on atomic energy.

The Baruch plan was sweeping, innovative, and ostensibly generous. An International Atomic Development Authority should be created under UN auspices, and commanded to survey facilities for making nuclear weapons in all nations. It would have a veto-proof right to inspect mines, factories, ports, power plants, transportation links—everything that could be involved in the process. Once this was done, America would furnish the agency with the information that would allow it to become the exclusive manufacturer of atomic bombs, a monopoly protected against cheating by unlimited powers of surveillance.

Predictably, the Russians rejected the scheme for internationalization. It was inconceivable in the Soviet scheme of things to open any part of their society to unlimited examination by outsiders. To ask them to do so was like asking a fish to walk. At the very least, as Moscow saw it, the inspection plan would weaken them militarily, providing data that intelligence officers the world over usually could only dream of getting. And, meanwhile, the United States would keep its hold on the bomb, dallying indefinitely until the atomic machinery of the UN—dominated by American clients—was ready.

Molotov offered a counterproposal consonant with reality as Russia saw it. The United States should destroy its entire stock of atomic bombs and yield up the secret. Then the two powers would sign a treaty binding each of them not to manufacture any more. Gradual steps toward international control might thereafter be taken by mutual agreement, through the traditional slow dance of diplomatic accommodation. In effect, the Russians, like the Americans, were asking for trust in their good intentions. The Americans rejected the idea without further exploration of the possibilities of reconciling the two approaches. Public opinion, in any case, was coming to share the view expressed by Senator Vandenberg to Molotov in Paris: "We have the atomic bomb and we are not going to give it up. We are not going to compromise or trade with you. We are not going to give up our immortal souls."

The Russian reaction, therefore, was not seen as one of possible fear and weakness, but as evidence of a probable intent to cheat. The aftermath of the plan was deepened suspicion. And even while it was being discussed, the United States flexed its nuclear muscles with tests at Bikini atoll, in which two more atom bombs were set off amid a group of expendable ships. The shattering explosion, the blaze of light, the mushroom cloud in Pacific skies once more, and the poisonous rain of debris spelled out an unmistakable, frightening message that humanity had a great deal to fear in the new age.

By midsummer of 1946, constant abrasions were wearing down Truman's capacity, such as it was, for dealing patiently with the problem of Russia. He was becoming irritated with the sole remaining voice of sympathy for Moscow, Henry Wallace. In July, Wallace addressed a long private letter to the President putting the case for a softening of tone. Wasn't it possible, the Secretary of Commerce asked, that the Russians had some grounds for suspicion, too? Might not the Bikini tests, the $13 billion military budget, and the plans for the B-36 seem to them to go "far beyond the requirements of defense?" And finally, couldn't American insistence on "establishing democracy in Eastern Europe, where democracy by and large has never existed," reasonably remind the Russians, thrice invaded since 1914, of the post-World War I attempt to create an "encirclement of unfriendly neighbors?"

Truman was not only unconvinced but later recorded that he wanted to fire Wallace then and there. He was deterred only by the conviction that Wallace still had important constituencies in the Democratic Party, and congressional elections were coming up. So Wallace remained to do cantankerous, isolated battle with what he called the "get-tough-with-Russia" boys (and the alleged Anglophiles and colonialists) in the State Department and the military. But in September he overstepped the bounds of prudence, a quality for which he was rarely noted. On the 12th, speaking to a campaign rally in New York's Madison Square Garden, he went public with his views. "The tougher we get," he declared, "the tougher the Russians will get." He went on from there to a frank espousal of a spheres-of-influence approach. "We have no more business," he insisted, "in the *political* affairs of Eastern Europe than Russia has in the *political* affairs of Latin America, Western Europe, and the United States."

The release of this speech in Paris, where the American delegation had been steadily battling for more freedom for the Eastern European nations, was a bombshell. It totally undercut the position of Byrnes, who frostily cabled to Truman: "If it is not possible for you . . . to keep Mr. Wallace . . . from speaking on foreign affairs, it would be a grave mistake . . . for me to continue in office." Truman was profoundly unhappy. He had actually seen and approved the speech in advance, still reluctant to let Wallace depart; but he realized that he could not simultaneously support the two sharply opposed men and their viewpoints, and he fumed in a letter to daughter Margaret that a President had to be "a liar, double-crosser . . . and a whatnot to be successful." In the end, when he could not bind Wallace to a promise of voluntary silence, he had to make the hard choice and demand Wallace's resignation a week after the fateful speech.

So the last counselor to urge a search for friendship with the Russians was gone. The triumph of Byrnes, however, was temporary. The President and he alone knew that he had already offered his resignation earlier, for reasons of health, and Truman now advised him that he would accept it, effective at the beginning of 1947 after the Italian and Eastern European treaties were signed. The two men had not gotten along well. Truman was irked at Byrnes's constant pattern of virtually ignoring the White House and keeping the spotlight on himself, and Byrnes was less than secretive about his own firm sense of superiority to the man who held a job that might easily have been his.

Byrnes's imminent departure, however, also had an impact on toughening the Administration's stance. Though he was as wary of Russian intentions and as frustrated by Russian intransigence as any hard-liner, Byrnes had still been committed to winning points through negotiation. With him out of the way, there was less resistance to a growing conviction in Truman's inner circle that negotiation was a waste of time, and possibly dangerous. That mindset was explored in July and August by Clark Clifford, a young and trusted Truman aide, whom the President had asked to prepare a comprehensive report on prospects for future Soviet-American relations. Clifford and a colleague, George Elsey, sounded out top officials in the War, Navy, and State Departments—the Russian experts in the last-named being particularly grateful for the consultation after what they saw as years of being bypassed. In his final report, Clifford testified to a "remarkable agreement" among them all that Soviet leaders clung to "the Marxian theory of ultimate destruction of capitalist states by Communist states." All international questions, in the long run, revolved around this basic threat. "So long as these men"—meaning the Kremlin hierarchy—"adhere to these beliefs," said the Clifford memorandum, "it is highly dangerous to conclude that hope of international peace lies only in 'accord,' 'mutual understanding,' or 'solidarity' with the Soviet Union." Concessions only raised their hopes and increased their demands. "The language of military power is the only language which disciples of power politics understand."

Clifford brought the report to Truman one September evening. The President read it until the small hours, then called his assistant the next morning and ordered him to put all copies under lock and key. "This is so hot," he explained, "if this should come out now it

could have an exceedingly unfortunate impact." But his concern
was with security and timing. He did not quarrel at all with the basic
premises of the document.

The era of negotiation was done with, the end of a road stretching
thirteen months from Potsdam had been reached. The great
anti-Hitler ally had been transformed into the number-one threat to
the world's peace. Those who had been Russophobes from the
beginning, like Leahy and Forrestal, were vindicated. The Russians
themselves had given ample cause for suspicion. Churchill had
contributed an articulation.

Something concrete was needed, some specific event to formalize
the reversal of policy, to arouse Americans to new efforts in the face
of the new danger. As 1947 dawned, happenings in the eastern
Mediterranean were to furnish that opportunity.

NEGOTIATION WAS NOT YET officially abandoned. Preparations
were under way for the next Council of Foreign Ministers
meeting, to be held in icy March weather in Moscow. The new
Secretary of State who would take part could not have carried more
home support with him. He was none other than General Marshall
himself, now retired as Chief of Staff and back from a fruitless
mission to arrange a truce in the civil war then racking China. He
had accepted Truman's request to serve in the post, and Congress,
cheering, had passed the special legislation enabling him to do so
without sacrificing his military rank and perquisites.

Unlike Byrnes, Marshall sought the help of his staff, especially of
the Soviet experts, Charles Bohlen and George F. Kennan. And, as a
newcomer, he relied heavily on his gifted under secretary, Dean
Gooderham Acheson. Acheson was the perfect deputy. Organized
and articulate, he could brief (and influence) his new chief, fill in
for him when testimony was to be given, and deal coolly with
problems, thanks to a massive confidence in his own talent and
judgment. An impeccably tailored Anglican and Anglophile Ivy
Leaguer, Acheson would come to play a larger part in American
diplomacy as time went on; but his basic attitude on Soviet issues
was fully formed as early as that spring of 1947, when he testified to
the Senate: "I think it is a mistake to believe that you can, at any
time, sit down with the Russians and solve questions." Nonetheless,
he continued his instructions to Marshall on what he would need to
know when sitting down with the Russians, until suddenly the State
Department was presented with an ugly situation that demanded
attention.

The government of Greece was undergoing hard times. A
coalition that took over after the Germans were ousted had
splintered into left- and right-wing elements. The rightists had put

down their opponents in bitter street fighting at the end of 1944, using weapons supplied by the British—and with no demur from Stalin, who apparently remembered the verbal agreement with Churchill that "gave" the Greeks to London. After a period of repression and "white terror," new warfare broke out in the northern provinces of the country, where guerrillas conducted an antigovernment "red terror." It was assumed in Washington that by then they were receiving aid from Greece's Communist neighbors— Yugoslavia, Albania, and Bulgaria.

On February 7, 1947, the American ambassador to Greece, Lincoln MacVeagh, sent a disturbing message. The government of Premier Constantin Tsaldaris was in trouble. It was beset by the usual postwar economic problems and by charges of corruption, and was rapidly weakening. It was only able to sustain the fight in the north thanks to financial help from the British. Even so, MacVeagh and two other American observers in Athens agreed, it might soon topple, and in the ensuing chaos the Communists would reap the harvest. "Soviets feel," ran the cabled text, "that Greece is a ripe plum to fall into their hands in a few weeks."

Two of those weeks had elapsed when, on February 21, another message came from Hugh Dalton, Britain's Chancellor of the Exchequer. His government, increasingly cash-pinched, could not continue its financial support of Tsaldaris. It was up to the Americans, if they cared, to take it over. Unaware of the "volcanic" effect his announcement would have, Dalton had made it seem that only the Americans could prevent the "ripe plum's" plummet into Stalin's lap.

That Stalin had expressed no previous interest seemed irrelevant. The new doctrine held that the Soviet Union was a powerful, purposeful beast, never so sinister as when it seemed asleep, indifferent, or friendly. "We're right up against it now," said Acheson.

An immediate meeting on the crisis was sought with the leaders of the Administration and Congress, for it was a given that any aid package would have to be passed by the newly elected legislators, who were in a budget-cutting mood and would have to be won over—along with lingering isolationists and the few members who might still believe in dealing with the Russians, or working through the UN.

The gathering took place on February 27. Marshall opened with a sober statement that this was merely "the first crisis of a series which might extend Soviet domination to Europe, the Middle East, and Asia." Acheson spoke, too, and added an educated gloss to the argument, which was turning the plum into a domino. "Like apples in a barrel infected by the corruption of one rotten one," he prophesied, "the corruption of Greece would infect Iran and all to the East . . . Africa . . . Italy, and France." The world had not been so polarized "since Rome and Carthage."

The congressmen were convinced, particularly Vandenberg, whose ample senatorial ego was, as the Administration knew and counted on, warmed by the role of senior Republican spokesman for internationalism—which he played with the zest of the recent convert from isolationism that he was, and with special happiness in an anti-Communist context. Though gratified to be a confidant, he warned that the matter could not, however, be settled only at the top levels. Congress could only go along if the President presented the issue to the American people at large, in terms as stark as those he had just heard.

So work began on a speech that would present the issue, as a State Department expert urged, "in such a fashion as to electrify the American people"—in other words, as George Elsey put it, an "all-out speech." Joined to the Greek question was another one, that of some assistance to Turkey, which was under heavy Soviet pressure to grant joint control of the Dardanelles. Discussing Greece and Turkey together would reinforce the theme of a Soviet threat to the eastern Mediterranean, and to its vital Middle Eastern supply lines.

On March 12, Truman stood before an emergency joint session of both houses, and presented the outline of what would come to be called the Truman Doctrine, and thereby be officially enshrined as a long-run policy. He began by referring to the "gravity of the situation which confronts the world today," and went on to anticipate the question of why action was not sought through the United Nations. The "urgent" problem of Greece required immediate action, and in any case the UN was not set up to give "help of the kind . . . required." What was needed was money to allow Greece "to become a self-supporting and self-respecting democracy," and Turkey "an independent and economically sound state." Both goals were "important to the freedom-loving peoples of the world."

Truman then set a historical framework. The effort to prevent coercion of nations by stronger neighbors was a "fundamental issue in the war with Germany and Japan." The UN had been founded to maintain that principle, but could not do so without American determination "to help free peoples . . . against aggressive movements that seek to impose upon them totalitarian regimes." Then the President came as near as he would do to naming Russia outright:

> The peoples of a number of countries of the world have recently had totalitarian regimes forced on them against their will. . . . The

government of the United States has made frequent protests against coercion and intimidation, in violation of the Yalta agreement, in Poland, Rumania, and Bulgaria.

Next he introduced the State Department's theory of Communist contagion. If Greece fell "under the control of an armed minority," there would be an immediate and serious effect on Turkey, and then "confusion and disorder might well spread throughout the entire Middle East." And the effect would be "far-reaching to the West as well," perhaps shaking the resolution of those in Europe who were "struggling against great difficulties to maintain their freedoms . . . while they repair the damages of war."

And so, after noting that the requested $400 million was less than one percent of the billions spent in winning World War II, he came to his conclusion:

> The free peoples of the world look to us for support in maintaining their freedoms.
>
> If we falter in our leadership, we may endanger the peace of the world—and we shall surely endanger the welfare of our own Nation.

So it was done, and the basic trumpet notes were sounded. American security depended on world peace. And world peace required American leadership in the struggle against totalitarian aggression, direct or indirect, everywhere. And everyone knew the name of the chief totalitarian state. They knew, too, that wherever Communism fed on "the evil soil of poverty and strife . . . when the hope of a people for a better life had died" that the Russian hand was at work. So in the end, world peace and American security required world prosperity and unimpeded trade.

It was an end and a commencement. Press reaction was varied. It ranged from the left-oriented criticism of New York's *PM* that the speech opened "a naked struggle for world power" to the isolationist *Chicago Tribune's* gruff warning that "the outcome will inevitably be war." From the high-minded judgment of the New York *Herald Tribune* that the President was asking for "the willingness to venture the belief in our own values, which can prove to the shattered peoples of the world that the American system offers a working alternative to the totalitarian order," to the pragmatic assessment of the *Los Angeles Times* that the requested sum was the "first premium on an insurance policy." From questions as to whether the money spent would really support democratic government in Greece, to flat affirmations like that of a Buffalo paper, that if Congress listened, "there [might] be no World War III."

Yet it was, oddly, Henry Luce's *Time* magazine, generally approving, that asked the most direct and penetrating question:

Human nature being what it is, the U.S. financial intervention might earn America the resentment, even the hate of beneficiaries. The program opened up a road with no visible end. Along that road were other nations in almost as desperate straits as Greece. Who would be the next to need U.S. help?

Chapter 3

QUEST FOR NATIONAL SECURITY
1947

THE ESTABLISHED RITUALS were still going on early in 1947. The Council of Foreign Ministers met in Moscow in March. Staff members, muffled to the ears against the savage cold, welcomed the temporary thaws of official receptions, tours, and ballet performances. Electronics experts in the visiting delegations searched the guest accommodations for "bugs." The French were said to have brought along, under diplomatic cover, czarist émigrés who could quietly circulate among the Muscovites and tune in to sounds of possible dissidence. Among the Americans, Secretary of State George Marshall's aides got to know him better, and to be impressed by his formidable memory, which retained, among myriad other things, telephone numbers that he had called in France while he was there in 1918 with the AEF.

But no decisions of consequence were reached.

Meanwhile, a new America was taking shape. The crusading spirit of the New Deal and war years was, at the very least, eclipsed by a popular concern with moving quickly into a less pinched future. As in other postwar periods, the nation was on the make and full of expectations, not overly concerned with remolding its social institutions. The "boys" had come home, surging down the gangplanks and into the arms of the sweethearts whom they were promptly to wed. There were 2,291,000 marriages in the United States in 1946 (as against 1,596,000 in 1940). In natural consequence, the number of live births in 1947 jumped to 3,817,000, a healthy increase from 1941's 2,703,000.

The dreaded economic results of the steep decline in government spending failed to materialize, as families rushed to convert into goods and services some of their increased personal income. Measured in current dollars, the average pretax income of what the Bureau of the Census called a "consumer unit" rose from $2,209 in

1941 to $4,126 in 1947. Even corrected for inflation, the figures
showed a jump of 20 percent in real income. The key number of all
that year was "housing starts" for privately owned dwellings—
845,600 of them, as against 138,700 in wartime 1944. That particular
figure would climb and climb; 13 million "dwelling units" would be
built between 1946 and 1958. Eleven million of them would be in
locations outside of America's central cities. Sustained on the baby
boom, the auto boom, and the happy anticipations of real-estate
developers and county assessors, modern suburbia was rapidly
coming into being.

The veterans dreamed in their new nests on freshly bulldozed
acres. They dreamed in the classrooms where they sat in faded
khaki, at government expense, finishing their educations and
pushing enrollments in institutions of higher education to over 2.6
million in 1948, close to double the 1940 total. They dreamed of the
new miracles that would be theirs to enjoy. Easy-to-care-for clothes
in synthetic fabrics, long-playing records, frozen meals ready in
minutes, television sets, cars that shifted their own gears. They
dreamed of not having to face hunger and fear ever again. Even
before the 1950s began, they were a generation programmed by
their times to put success ahead of radicalism.

They would, it turned out surprisingly in 1948, vote in large
numbers for Harry Truman when he reawakened Rooseveltian
echoes with promises of a "Fair Deal." But it was a mandate to
sustain rather than enlarge existing programs. As for remaking the
world, there was as yet no deep enthusiasm for the task. As late as
the summer of 1949, a random poll on aid to foreign countries if it
involved the risk of war showed 36 percent of respondents opposed
to any assistance under such circumstances. Only 7 percent
endorsed military aid to other nations, generally speaking. When the
question was sharpened to one of military help to Western Europe,
the support rose to 35 percent. A large number simply took no
position—like the 45 percent who, when asked what the United
States should do to prevent China from going Communist, had no
opinion.

There was fear of war, distaste for the Soviet Union, but also an
apparent wish to be let alone. There was a catch-phrase of 1947, the
"New Look," referring to women's fashions, which suddenly
featured lowered hemlines and full skirts. The American people
were wearing a New Look, too, but it was not yet very militant.

In Washington, however, and especially in the higher levels of the
Administration, that was not the case. New faces were appearing in
the offices where basic military and foreign policy decisions were
made. They belonged to a group of men who had been assistants
and deputies during the war (though they had come into govern-

ment service with distinguished backgrounds in law and business), but whose careers would ripen fully as the climate of international relations after 1945 grew steadily more frigid. Forrestal would be the prime example.

But there was also "Judge" Robert Patterson, who moved up to replace Stimson as Secretary of War—Union College, Harvard Law School (Class of 1915), wounded and decorated as a major of infantry in France in World War I, and then into the firm of Root, Clark, Buckner, and Howland. The Root was Elihu Root, Republican Secretary of State, mentor to Stimson, counselor to progressive American corporations making investments abroad as the American century, the twentieth, began. From that firm, Patterson went to the federal bench on President Hoover's nomination in 1930, and left it ten years later for the War Department at Stimson's side.

Patterson's chief associate when he took over as head of the department was Kenneth Royall, who was graduated from Harvard Law School two years behind Patterson and one ahead of Dean Acheson. He had pursued the law's windings for his clients in his native North Carolina after his World War I service, and had then reentered the military world as a special assistant to Stimson in 1942. Moving up to second in the chain of command under Patterson, he rose to the top job in 1947 when Patterson returned to civilian life in New York.

Royall and Patterson were both well acquainted with another wartime special assistant who had left their department in 1945, but whose opinions were still valued and would have effect when he later surfaced as president of the World Bank and then Military Governor and High Commissioner for Germany. John Jay McCloy, Amherst '16, had taken time to win a Distinguished Service Medal with the artillery in the First World War before going back to school—Harvard Law, naturally, Class of 1921—from which he had entered the world of corporate practice in the offices of Cadwalader, Wickersham, and Taft. McCloy was considered a formidable mind, especially in the field of military procurement in which he had specialized in the War Department.

One key job in that department was the post of Assistant Secretary for Air. It had been held during the late stages of the war by Robert A. Lovett, who had won the Navy Cross as a fresh-from-Yale pilot in 1918, and had thereafter entered Harvard Law School, from which he, too, would have graduated in 1921. But he had switched to the School of Business Administration and become a banker, specializing in the financing of transportation. Lovett had left the still-new Pentagon building after peace came, but only to move the short distance to the State Department where, in mid-1947, he became an adviser to Secretary Marshall on the intricate linkages that webbed together international finance and diplomacy. The man holding Lovett's old post early in 1947 was a Missouri businessman—though educated at Yale, Class of '23—Stuart Symington, who had previously headed the Surplus Property Administration.

Symington's Navy counterpart, the Under Secretary for Air, a former high official of the Treasury Department, was expert in devising ways for the Internal Revenue Service to collect wartime taxes. He had joined the Navy Department in June of 1945. He was slightly out of pattern, a New England Catholic Democrat with the robust Irish name of John L. Sullivan, but he did have the Harvard Law School label (Class of '24). He might even seem to have a touch of radicalism, having insisted stoutly on heavy levies on high incomes, but there was no question of his soundness on the key issue—his faith, as he expressed it once, that a "strong America" was "the best guarantee of peace in the years to come."

That credo, and its particular definitions of "strength" and "peace," were what truly linked together these men at the top of the 1947 defense hierarchy, putting them, at that moment, several steps ahead of the general public, which would require rapid education to catch up.

They were a special breed—not simply by virtue of their common background in Eastern colleges, Harvard Law School, and services to large-scale business enterprise. The main thing knitting them together was their immersion in the gigantic mobilization of 1941-45. They had been the expediters. They had talked the arcane language of industrial conversion from peace to war—at a profit. Start-up costs and tooling costs, lead times and down times, write-offs and penalties, bonuses and forfeitures, title transfers, inspections, deductions, advances, recaptures, units of output per shipyard and factory, and dollars in dazzling numbers. They spoke with production "czars" like Donald Nelson and William Knudsen, with the generals and admirals, the bankers and brokers, and with the legislative specialists who understood how congressional appropriations votes were translated into United States Treasury funds, payable on demand. And they brought all of the designs of these men together, and watched armies and armadas and victory come into being.

They were the heirs, these men, of the lawyers for the rail and steel and oil barons of the vigorous nineteenth century. They themselves had seen the American automotive, aviation, and electrical industries grow to swift maturity in the 1920s, to be only slightly slowed in the Depression. And they had coordinated these modern sources of power, in wartime, in a dream setting with a clear objective (victory), limitless public money and support, and a truce with politics, especially antitrust politics.

It was not surprising, then, that among the McCloys, Lovetts, Pattersons, Achesons, Royalls, and others like them a new world-view should take shape. It was one that synthesized their natural and instinctive anti-Communism with a prophetic vision of an ongoing struggle that would demand from the American people a new kind of internationalism and sophistication, and from their government a new efficiency. These architects of the future defense establishment defied the simplistic labels of friends and enemies, such as "patriot" or "imperialist." They spilled over conventional categories, just as they did in their politics, where, though nominally Republicans and Democrats, they would serve ad lib in administrations of either complexion. One clue to their thinking, in fact, was their willingness and need to deal with changing Congresses and administrations over long periods when majorities might change, but fundamental national interests did not. Those national interests, as they saw them, were shaped by events all around the world—the world over which, in their wartime jobs, they had ranged on airborne inspection trips as casually as aldermen touring their wards. They saw that world as small, interdependent, and capable, in 1947, of only two possible orientations—toward Moscow or Washington. It was, of course, unthinkable that it should be Moscow.

The goal of these mobilizers and managers and planners was no longer simply "defense," but the more elastic concept of "national security." National security involved more than soldiers on the ramparts. It required an international community that was stable, peaceful, and economically sound—as they defined all these terms. National security involved a constantly alerted populace; continuous, costly readiness for war; long-term commitments to allies; and political machinery immune to sudden election-time storms.

The fullest expression of these views was visible in what the leaders, with the President's help, created in 1947. The list included a rebuilt and at least partly unified military bureaucracy, a powerful new intelligence agency, and a remodeling and refocusing of the executive branch to coordinate national security planning. They also attempted to free security policy from the unsteady supervision of Congress, as provided by the Constitution, by stressing bipartisanship and secrecy as virtues. Their success in that effort was less than complete. But by the end of the year the key elements necessary for running the Cold War were set in place.

THE FIRST INSTRUMENTALITY to be forged was the Department of Defense. Talk of unifying the armed services had begun during the war itself, when it became overpoweringly clear that the scale and complexity of twentieth-century battle required continuous meshing of land, sea, and air actions, not only in the heat of combat, but in the long preliminary months of planning and supply. The need for merger was unarguable. The question was: on whose terms? Which of the joined services would be the centerpiece? Which stood to lose functions and responsibilities in a blending?

The Army did not contest unification. It saw itself as the core element in any important operation, its role unthreatened by any reshuffle. The quasi-independent Army Air Forces, secure in their monopoly of strategic bombing, welcomed the idea of equality with the other services in a combined setup. But it was the conviction of Navy leaders that unification would be, for them, a disaster. They were aware that one of its politically attractive arguments was that it would eliminate costly overlapping and duplication of weapons and facilities. If an efficient streamlining should be carried out, the Navy might lose its independent little infantry force, the Marine Corps, and, much worse, its air arm, the carriers that had replaced the vulnerable battleships as queens of the fleet. Without the flattops and the worldwide bases to sustain them, the Navy could sink to the status of an inglorious appendage.

The only defense, as Secretary Forrestal and the admirals saw it, was to fight for a new concept of maritime war, built around a Navy that had its own "global mission" and required its own specialized, seaborne airpower to carry it out. In presenting this idea to Congress and the public, Forrestal fought for time, holding off an impatient, economy-minded rush toward service reorganization.

All the armed forces leaders, in fact, did not find the long debate unwelcome, for it gave them a chance, through hearings and barrages of press releases, to define their missions and defend their claims for continued generous appropriations. It provided a seminar in which to enlighten opinion-makers who were prey to the notion that, with the Axis defeated, the country could return to a relatively modest level of military expenditure. Pentagon spokesmen, however much they might disagree among themselves, were united in efforts to replace this simple expectation with a new view of what preparedness meant. It meant, for one thing, responsibility for more than simply defending the continental United States. "The world," said John J. McCloy in 1945, "looks to the U.S. as the one stable country to insure [its] security." It also meant leaving behind the old notion of a clear demarcation between war and peace, with peace a time of relative relaxation, until some crisis developed. The new gospel was that the nation could not count on a sudden leap to mobilization, but must *always* be prepared to deal with the strongest possible *potential* adversary, to know its intentions and capabilities, and to counter them by diplomatic and economic means even when technically not at war.

Readiness for such a struggle required far more than mere arms. It demanded, in the words of a special report prepared for Forrestal, that "foreign policy, [the] military, and domestic economic resources should be closely tied together." Forrestal himself expanded on the concept, explaining to a Senate military affairs subcommittee that the United States must be able to defend lines of commerce all around the world, and that this required even more than the quickly mobile, floating air bases that carriers provided. "We have to take into account," he said, "our whole potential for war, our mines, industry, manpower, research, and all the activities that go into normal civilian life." The Navy Secretary was one of the first, if not the first, to leap beyond the simple word "defense" to describe the program in mind. "Our national security," he testified late in 1945, "can only be assured on a very broad and comprehensive front." At least one listening Senator was pleased, and assured him: "I like your words 'national security.' "

But security against whom? Stubborn isolationists could still point out that the only possible enemy of any strength, the Soviet Union, had no fleet to speak of at the time, and was still separated from the centers of American power by two oceans. Generals of the future Air Force were able to answer that by unveiling maps based on polar projections. With the North Pole at the center, and the earth flattened out like an orange around it, Siberian bomber fields appeared ominously close to the United States heartland. To counter that peril, there must be a wide-flung network of American bases sheltering radar installations, interceptors, and retaliatory bombing planes.

In the end, the country got something that was less than military unification and much more than mere military reorganization. In 1945, Forrestal commissioned a fellow financial expert from his Wall Street days, Ferdinand Eberstadt, to do a study of overall defense needs. Eberstadt's report was satisfactory from the Navy viewpoint in recommending against a single armed establishment. It called, rather, for "coordination" of the armed forces. But it went beyond that in proposing to create a whole new security planning structure. There should be a National Security Council of top-level policy-makers, composed of the Secretary of State, the Secretaries and commanding officers of the services, and the head of a new, unified intelligence-gathering body. There should also be a National Security Resources Board to direct economic mobilization, and there should be an effort to furnish more funds and direction to scientific research with possible military applications. (The services were unable to get control of atomic energy in 1946 when Congress created the independent, civilian Atomic Energy Commission with development authority in the field.)

Forrestal did not immediately throw himself behind the Eberstadt recommendations, but he and Patterson came under increasing pressure from an impatient President Truman, weary of interservice budgetary squabbling. (In one incautious moment Truman remarked that the Marine Corps had a propaganda machine equal to Stalin's.) Finally, early in 1947, there was agreement on the legislative package of compromises enacted by Congress as the National Defense Act. There was to be a single Department of Defense, but under its Secretary would be a Secretary of the Army, a Secretary of the Navy, and a Secretary of the free-at-last Air Force. These last three posts went, in that order, to Royall, Sullivan, and Symington, while Forrestal, not without some irony after his long resistance, became the first Secretary of Defense.

The commanding generals of the three services—and the Marines—would constitute the Joint Chiefs of Staff. The Central Intelligence Agency was created, as were the National Security Council and the National Security Resources Board envisaged by Eberstadt. The original aim of the reformed structure—to eliminate duplication of missions and procurement—was hardly achieved at all. And yet the 1947 law was a landmark, in that it created the skeleton, at least, of what was to become an overpowering national security apparatus. And the preliminary duels over its creation had prepared the ground for its public acceptance, and left little doubt about where, and from whom, future threats were to be anticipated by the United States.

ALMOST AT THE SAME MOMENT as the creation of the Department of Defense, two other events took place that were destined to furnish powerful reinforcement to the frame of mind that elevated national security, as it was defined in 1947, to an almost obsessive status. One was the appearance of a stunning popular rationale for a strong anti-Soviet diplomatic posture. The other was a program, originally presented as a safeguard against espionage, that rapidly made it not merely unpopular but actually dangerous to challenge that posture. When "security" was joined with the terms "containment" and "loyalty," they made up a dominating triad of ideas riveted into American policy-making for at least a decade.

Ironically, containment was the contribution of George Kennan, a certified intellectual—one of those beings who would later fall under suspicion as insufficiently zealous patriots. In an additional irony, Kennan would claim in the long run that he had been oversimplified and misunderstood, a fate common to many serious thinkers who fall into the popular embrace. From his post in Moscow, he had watched the events of 1945 and early 1946 in the melancholy conviction that FDR and Truman were vainly hoping to strike final bargains with Moscow over Eastern Europe and other matters, when in fact that was impossible. In a lengthy cable to Washington that came to be known as the "Long Telegram," he tried to explain the basic nature of Soviet international conduct.

"At bottom of Kremlin's neurotic view of world affairs," Kennan wired, "is traditional and instinctive Russian sense of insecurity." The Russians could only function "in patient but deadly struggle for total destruction of rival power, never in compacts and compromises with it." The desire to advance Communism was a factor in Moscow's aspirations, but the danger was fundamentally Muscovite, not Marxist. The often-jailed leaders of an often-invaded, often-isolated, half-Asiatic nation could not sleep soundly simply because of promises embodied in treaties. They found it "necessary that the international harmony of our society be disrupted . . . the international authority of our state be broken if Soviet power is to be secure." Yet they were not suicidal. "Impervious to logic of reason," Moscow was, all the same, "highly sensitive to logic of force. For this reason it can easily withdraw—and usually does—when strong resistance is encountered at any point."

The Long Telegram was received joyfully in Washington, still more frustrated than hostile in 1946. "Splendid analysis," was Byrnes's comment. "Magnificent . . . to those of us here struggling with the problem," said the head of the State Department's Office of European Affairs. Diplomatic missions and military authorities everywhere were familiarized with the contents, and James V. Forrestal had hundreds of copies made and, as an aide remembered, sent "all over town." Kennan was called home to head the department's Policy Planning Staff, and proceeded to write an article entitled "The Sources of Soviet Conduct" that was an elaboration of his earlier statements. It appeared in the spring of 1947 in *Foreign Affairs*, the prestigious journal respectfully read by American bankers, educators, journalists, and government officials. Kennan prudently signed the essay "Mr. X," but it was common knowledge who was behind the fig leaf.

Given more room, Kennan's natural articulateness blossomed. He described Soviet ambition as "a fluid stream, which moves constantly, wherever it is permitted to move, toward a given goal. Its main concern is to make sure that it has filled every nook and cranny available to it in the basin of world power." But it could be "contained by the adroit and vigilant application of counterforce at a series of constantly shifting geographical and political points, corresponding to the shifts and manoeuvres of Soviet policy." The eloquence of "Mr. X" actually provided a vivid picture of the world ideally suited to the views of men like Forrestal. It called not only for vigilance, but for the acceptance of an "implacable challenge" that would require Americans to accept "the responsibilities of moral and political leadership that history plainly intended them to bear." From the essay's pages sprang one word that defined all aspects of future security policy: "containment."

Kennan was, in a sense, the victim of his own gift for metaphor. He later insisted that he had not intended to advocate American armed intervention everywhere on the globe that Soviet power was visible; nor American support for every anti-Soviet government, however shaky or far from effective U.S. help; nor American economic penetration of "every nook and cranny" that might tempt the Russians. Yet all these things would, in time, take place, leading him, in academic retirement, to say that he felt "like one who has inadvertently loosened a large boulder from the top of a cliff and . . . helplessly witnesses its path of destruction in the valley below, shuddering and wincing at each successive glimpse of disaster."

Editorialists and speechmakers seized on the article (excerpted both in *Life* and in the *Reader's Digest*, in 1947), but tended to overlook Kennan's statement that war was not inevitable. They also failed to stress his argument that the United States might actually promote "a gradual mellowing of Soviet power," not only by standing firm, but by giving to the world's peoples "the impression of a country . . . which is coping successfully with the problems of its internal life . . . and which has a spiritual vitality capable of holding its own among . . . major ideological currents." Instead, to his later-professed dismay, they canonized the single idea that America was committed to an unending struggle with a sinister enemy.

Meanwhile, on March 22, 1947, only ten days after his speech on aid to Greece and Turkey, Harry S Truman signed Executive Order #9835, creating the Federal Employee Loyalty Program.

"Loyalty" and "treason" were not words that had much active currency in American life in peacetime. Only in war did they erupt in geysers of passion, and the images they conveyed then were clear enough: shaggy saboteurs, shifty spies, foreign accents, furtively passed messages, a strange combination of romance and tawdriness. In World War I hysterical patriotism had harassed German-Americans and left-wing war resisters, then blended into the Red Scare of 1919-20 and faded away. World War II had brought about the abrupt imprisonment of 110,000 West Coast Japanese-Americans on flimsy grounds, but thereafter the loyalty of most citizens was assumed. Few Americans of German or Italian descent had shown much sympathy for Nazism or Fascism, and Communists were, this time, vigorous supporters of the war.

What reawakened anxieties about hidden enemies in America's midst was the sudden possession of the atomic bomb. Although scientists freely predicted that any major industrial nation, the Soviet Union included, could produce the weapon in a few years of concentrated effort, many Americans vocally insisted that this was not so, and that only betrayal by a person or persons in the know could fatally crack the monopoly of the United States. These fears were strengthened in February 1946 when news broke that a Communist spy ring had been at work in Canada and had collected, among other things, significant bits of atomic research data. There had also been headlines made when a New York-based magazine of Far Eastern affairs, *Amerasia*, published material that came from classified documents passed to the editors by State Department employees. *Amerasia's* editors were alleged to have Communist contacts. And there were rumors about as-yet-unpublicized testimony to the FBI that charged various federal employees with Communist espionage in the 1930s. One of the allegations involved an Assistant Secretary of the Treasury, Harry Dexter White.

These developments were seized on by some Republicans in the 1946 congressional campaign as the basis for an assault, reminiscent of the Dies Committee days, on the New Deal's supposed tolerance for radicalism in inner circles. It was possibly with the idea of preempting and defusing this issue that Truman moved to create his own loyalty program early in the life of the Eightieth Congress.

Under the program, "review boards" were set up in every federal department or agency, charged with fulfilling a mandate to discover the "presence within the government of any disloyal or subversive persons," a presence that would present "a problem of such importance that it must be dealt with vigorously and effectively." The boards could hear any derogatory information about an individual accused of possible disloyalty—the term was never sharply defined—and could call on the FBI to make full field checks into his or her background, proclivities, and associations. (Ultimately the FBI ran checks on almost all the 2 million employees then on the federal payroll.) If, "on all the evidence," there were "reasonable grounds" to believe that "the person involved [was] disloyal to the Government of the United States," dismissal was authorized. The same investigative procedure was to apply to new applicants for federal jobs.

A person dismissed—or an applicant rejected—could appeal the agency's ruling to higher-level review boards, and ultimately to a coordinating Loyalty Review Board, but the rules governing appeal hearings offered little or no opportunity to identify accusers or confront hostile witnesses. What was significant about the program was that it was not designed to punish overt acts after they were committed. It was instead to make possible the ouster of a civil servant on the basis of a state of mind. The new premise of loyalty was that a spy might not be a figure of suspense fiction but an innocuous-looking bureaucrat. Moreover, since Communist spies had not done their work for foreign gold but in the service of an idea, it was possible that certain thoughts, attitudes, readings, and associations could prepare someone for spying, could become part of an intellectual journey that led down the road to treason.

These new ideas of what constituted treason, loyalty, and—an even spongier word—"subversion" were eventually to lead to a long, complicated, and tragic set of events. The full import of the federal loyalty program would take time to make itself felt. But in mid-1947, Truman's order fell into place as part of a fast-growing structure. Aid to nations resisting Communism had been authorized, the national security establishment had been founded, and a doctrine justifying a state of partial mobilization with no end in sight had been articulated. Now a process had been set in motion to make sure that Americans who worked for their government were careful not to entertain negative thoughts about what was happening— careful not to appear too friendly to the Soviet enemy.

It was against this background, and in this atmosphere, halfway through the year, that what came to be called the Marshall Plan came into being.

THE SECRETARY OF STATE spoke quietly, as was his fashion and as became the surroundings. A Harvard commencement was not a theater for stump oratory, and a Commencement Day meeting of the Harvard Alumni Association was not the kind of audience to respond to tub-thumping, even if Marshall had been capable of, or inclined toward, it. Yet the low-keyed remarks he was delivering to his influential listeners this June 6, 1947, added up to nothing less than a declaration of a historic new departure in foreign policy. He was suggesting that it was necessary for the United States, which then consumed 46 percent of the world's electric power, controlled 59 percent of its known oil reserves, and was its largest producer and consumer of coal and steel, to dip into its reserves of wealth and undertake the economic rehabilitation of a Europe that might one day become again a business rival. He was also stipulating that, as a prelude, the nations of Europe should bury generations of competition among themselves, and unite in drawing up a blueprint of exactly what would be needed for such a rescue operation.

These proposals actually had two sides to them, and historians still argue—perhaps fruitlessly—about which of their goals was paramount: to relieve misery or to thwart the Kremlin. Embedded in a vision of international economic cooperation, they were radical, innovative, and humanitarian, especially when they were obviously intended to include former enemies only two years after a devastating world war. Yet they also served the immediate needs of American capitalism, and they grew out of—and intensified—the divisions and anxieties of the ongoing battle with Communism, Moscow-style. Revolutionary in potential, the Marshall Plan was offered as an alternative to revolution.

The journey on the road to Harvard Yard had begun, for Marshall, early in the year. It was then that William Clayton, Under Secretary of State for Economic Affairs, returned from Europe with a gloomy report. Clayton was a onetime Mississippi cotton broker who had served on the War Industries Board in World War I and as a vice president of the Export-Import Bank from 1940 to 1942. He knew how to read economic indicators, how to tell with a banker's realism when an account was in trouble, and, setting aside Southern and diplomatic politeness, how to say so directly. "Europe," he recorded, "is steadily deteriorating." Production of basic goods was still far below 1939 levels. Savaged by two hard postwar winters, most Europeans were still hungry and cold and often unemployed and desperate. There was the possibility that the economies of some nations might go into total collapse. These words awakened ghosts of the Twenties and Thirties: strikes, hunger marches, riots, and armies of the dispossessed waiting for the right demagogue. Or the left demagogue. At any time the vista would have been frightening. In the state of international relations in 1947 it was, to the State Department, nearly apocalyptic.

Even setting aside the fear of political chaos, a sick Europe meant trouble for the American economy. Since V-J Day, economists (and, it was rumored, the Politburo) had been awaiting the "inevitable" postwar depression, the moment when consumers would have all the peacetime goods they could afford, and the artificially high prices of reconversion days would tumble, sending out shock waves of bankruptcies, foreclosures, and shutdowns.

But there was a hedge against this disaster in the export market. The United States accounted for one-third of all the world's exports in 1947. Many of them consisted of the products of the generous American soil, already being wooed to extra fertility by chemistry. One-half of that year's wheat crop went overseas, 15 percent of the fats and oils produced, and vast quantities of meat, rice, and cotton. But in addition, overseas customers took 10 percent of U.S. industrial goods, mostly in the form of transportation and construction machinery needed for rebuilding. It was a small figure, perhaps, like the 6 percent of those 42 million employed Americans whose jobs depended directly or indirectly on the export trade, but it was the margin of health. "Our foreign trade," said one businessman, "represents the difference between depression and prosperity." A State Department analyst was equally certain that any "serious failure" to keep up the export flow would ruin "millions" of American farmers, workers, and owners.

The trouble was that the export trade hung by a thread. Clawing for survival, Europe lacked either cash or products to pay for what it bought abroad. Already, the United States had helped with several billions in loans, either funneled through UNRRA, the International Monetary Fund, the International Bank for Reconstruction and Development, or directly to countries like Britain. But even so, the papers abounded in talk of the "dollar gap"—between the dollars that American exports cost and the pitifully small number of dollars that the Europeans could offer. It might appear to be Europe's problem, but America's economy could fall into that void and be badly damaged.

Reminded of this ugly political and economic prognosis by Clayton's report, Marshall lost no time in reacting. He needed no urging in any case. He had just returned from Moscow and another fruitless meeting of the Council of Foreign Ministers, with the suspicion that Stalin's stalling on German economic reunification might be part of a larger plan to delay overall European recovery and keep the Continent miserable for his own purposes. The delays were intolerable. "The patient is sinking while the doctors deliberate," said Marshall in a broadcast report on the conference.

He sat down to a series of discussions with his policy planners, and all of them rapidly reached the same conclusion. Europe's economy must be rebuilt, and the means must come from the United States. It would be a several-year commitment, costing as much as $5 billion each year—a staggering conclusion in the face of the fact that the annual federal total budget even in the "spendthrift" New Deal years had rarely exceeded that sum. Moreover, Congress was showing an indisposition to aid what one member later called Europe's "armies of mendicants and loafers." Nevertheless, a set of papers advocating such a course would have to be drafted, and Marshall set people to work with the terse advice: "Avoid trivia." While they were under way, a test dive into the waters of public opinion was made. The diver was Dean Acheson.

Acheson spoke, on the 8th of May, in Cleveland, Mississippi, to an organization called the Delta Council. It was a group of major farm owners and the men who financed, insured, and marketed their crops. These were regional leaders, Democrats but essentially conservatives, the very kind of people whose support and awareness would be most crucial. Unruffled as always, even in the heat, Acheson gave his shirtsleeved listeners a mixture of realism and uplift to go with their fried chicken as he unveiled the essential outline of the developing plan. He drew on draft studies to sketch out the "staggering" disparity between America's production and that of the rest of the world, and the insufficiency of previous U.S. credits to solve the problem. The "facts of international life" were harsh, and meant that "the United States [was] going to have to undertake further emergency financing of foreign purchases." Especially "in areas where it [would] be most effective in building world political and economic stability, in promoting . . . democratic institutions, in fostering liberal trading policies." The recipients, in turn, would need to set as a goal "the achievement of a coordinated European economy." It would all take time; Americans would have to answer the cry of need steadily, over years, and in big numbers.

Acheson spoke, for the most part in earthy terms, of concrete deeds and needs, of food, fuel, clothing, and the elements of people's dignity. But at the end he lifted the level when summing up the reasons for the rescue: "It is necessary for our national security. And it is our duty and privilege as human beings."

"I wanted everyone to know," he wrote later, "that I was putting a ball in the air and that we had all better be prepared to field it when it came down, because if it just landed *plunk!* on the ground, it would be a very bad thing." Acheson was not a man to leave a "plunk!" to chance. He hurried back to Washington for more meetings with his chief, and in anticipation that he would quickly hear from the congressional leadership when his words were reported. Sure enough, Senator Vandenberg promptly wanted to know what was going on—and was immediately assured that there would be no major foreign aid request during the current session, and that Capitol Hill would be constantly informed as well as listened to. In fact, charting the course of the program through anticipated political storms kept the department's top planners in a swirl of conferences. They decided, for one thing, that it would be best to distance it slightly from the President, who was at a low ebb of popularity that spring, and to emphasize its long-range aspects. Hence the Truman Doctrine was followed by the Marshall Plan. In addition, Kennan, at one of the meetings at which Marshall's Harvard speech was being drafted, stressed that there must be a call for active European involvement in the preliminary studies and estimates. Europe must not appear to be simply awaiting handouts.

And then there was the stickiest point. What about Eastern Europe and the Soviet Union? To block out the Soviet sphere could seem a hostile act, which might discourage some Western governments from participation—and further underwrite polarization. Yet to invite Communist participation would guarantee stiff congressional resistance. Besides, it was possible that if aid went to the satellites, Moscow would find means to siphon most of it away. Temporarily the question was fudged by leaving it untouched in the text, but Marshall would not let it rest there. What was he going to say, he later asked Bohlen and Kennan, if reporters asked him after the speech whether the Russians were included? The two experts pondered and then agreed on their recommendation. The answer should be yes. The Russians were certain to turn down the invitation. They would like neither the idea of the satellites looking toward the United States for help nor the idea of hard questions about the operation of their own economy.

So the Secretary, having decided to accept the invitation to Harvard as the proper occasion, went off to his June rendezvous with a new, civilian variety of fame. He received an honorary degree, along with General Omar Bradley, T.S. Eliot, and, ironically in the light of later developments, J. Robert Oppenheimer. Then, in his remarks to the alumni, he covered substantially the same ground as Acheson had done earlier. There was a significant sentence that read: "Our policy is directed, not against any country or doctrine, but against hunger, poverty, desperation, and chaos." It was Marshall's own emendation of Bohlen's version, which had said specifically "not against Communism." By making the change, Marshall shifted the focus, as Bohlen noted, to identifying opponents of the plan with friends of hunger and chaos. Otherwise, however, the Secretary offered no quotable jewels for the press, and was in fact not eager for too much early publicity that might arouse antagonism.

Not so Dean Acheson. Though he gave the appearance of disdaining mutual back scratching with members of the press, he was skilled at it. He was also especially eager that friends on the other side of the Atlantic should take particular note of the passage in Marshall's address that read: "It would be neither fitting nor efficacious for this Government to undertake to draw up unilaterally a program designed to place Europe on its feet. The initiative, I think, must come from Europe." And, therefore, two days before the speech, Acheson lunched with three British reporters (having already cued in some American journalist friends), and told them how important it was to get an early British reaction to what Marshall was going to say. He urged that they telephone the text to London immediately upon its release, and more: "[One] of you must ask your editor to see that Ernie Bevin gets a full copy . . . at once. It will not matter what hour of the night it is; wake Ernie up and put a copy in his hand."

That was precisely what was done, and Acheson knew his ally, Bevin, well. The pudgy Foreign Secretary was awakened by a messenger from a newspaper office, and bounded out of bed with alacrity to summon his senior advisers for a meeting. As a shrewd member of a beleaguered government, Bevin saw that Marshall had thrown out life jackets to the sinking British economy. As he later told the House of Commons: "I grabbed them with both hands."

What the grabbing involved was an initial contact with France's

Foreign Minister Georges Bidault, who in turn agreed on an almost immediate meeting in Paris to which Molotov should be invited. Though somewhat soured by the fact that Bidault and Bevin had talked privately first, the Soviet leader turned up, at the end of June, with a retinue of eighty-nine advisers, to listen to Bidault's projected future agenda. A series of special committees on different elements of economic health—transportation, farm machinery, energy, and so on—should be created at once to draw up a balance sheet of each European nation's needs, using information furnished by the countries themselves. These would become the bases of specific development programs and requests for aid.

Here was the Soviet Union's bugaboo once more: "prying" into what the Paris correspondent of *Tass*, the Soviet news agency, called "the internal economic problems of a State." Molotov picked up the theme, grumbling that the proposed committees of coordination would simply dictate future economic policies to the aid-receiving nations, most probably in accordance with Washington's dominating ideas. Yet he remained on the scene until the day when a sudden message was delivered to him at the conference table. Experienced Molotov-watchers knew that when he was agitated, the bump on his forehead became enlarged and reddened. Now, amid frantic whispering, it swelled and pulsated more than ever, and he rose to announce that he would no longer be a party to this scheme for American economic subjugation. Then he walked out. Clearly, orders from Stalin had arrived. And Bohlen and Kennan had scored impressively as prophets. There was no need to shut the Russians out; they had shut themselves out.

Sadly for the Eastern nations, they, too, were shut out—involuntarily. The French and British, ignoring Molotov's departure, invited all European nations to a general meeting in July to proceed with the "reconstruction programme." Poland and Czechoslovakia were known to be interested, but Poland never had a chance to accept even tentatively. Klement Gottwald, Communist premier of Prague's coalition government, did promise to send a delegation. But three days before the opening date of July 12, he was summoned to a "discussion" in the Kremlin. When he emerged, it was to withdraw Czechoslovakia from the proceedings.

Without the participation of the Communist bloc, then, all the other nations of Europe (Spain excluded) joined to form a Conference for European Economic Cooperation, in what was an impressive show of union. Former enemies (Austria and Italy) joined victims of Hitler (Denmark, Norway, Belgium, the Netherlands, Luxembourg, France, the United Kingdom, and Greece) and neutrals (Iceland, Ireland, Portugal, Sweden, Switzerland, and Turkey) in preparing the report on rehabilitation priorities, submitted in September. In time, when there was a West Germany, she, too, would be included in this seedbed of shared economic endeavor.

There was then a countermove by Stalin. After tightening the Soviet grip on Hungary and launching a "Molotov Plan" of mutual assistance among the satellites, he arranged a meeting of European Communist leaders in Moscow, out of which emerged the Cominform, a relatively short-lived organization to "coordinate" the efforts of all of them. French and Italian Communists were to abandon any efforts at working cooperatively with "bourgeois" regimes, thus burying the last vestiges of collaboration in the Resistance. And like their Eastern European counterparts, they were to recognize that the only acceptable method of "socialism" was that practiced by their liberator, benefactor, and protector, the Soviet Union. The new development simply intensified the political problems of the Western Communists. For the Soviet-dominated states, however, along with the rejection of the Marshall Plan, it was the final clang of the jailhouse door behind them.

If the developing Marshall Plan caused Western Europe to draw together and Eastern Europe to be herded together, it also had a unifying effect on politics in the United States. Defying a low standing in the public opinion polls and the minority status of the Democrats in Congress, the Truman Administration launched a superlative lobbying effort on behalf of the new idea. It was not hard to do, for the plan was an ideal amalgam of already popular attitudes. It was idealistic, and good business. It was practical charity, helping others to help themselves. It promised to bring prosperity, which automatically and unfailingly would enhance the survival prospects of democracy. It was anti-Communist, but not saber-rattling.

Its appeal cut sharply across old dividing lines. A Committee for the Marshall Plan to Aid European Recovery was formed (and fed by the State Department with information), numbering among its members attorneys like Allen Dulles of Sullivan and Cromwell (whose brother, John Foster, was already working at State), bankers like Thomas Lamont of the Morgan firm, and business executives like Philip Reed of General Electric, H. D. Collier of Standard Oil of California, and Paul G. Hoffman of Studebaker Motors (who later became the first administrator of the plan after its adoption). The committee advertised widely in major opinion-making journals (generally committed to the plan), circulated petitions, solicited letters, and underwrote pro-plan forums. In addition to this bipartisan body created for the occasion, there was an array of other groups—many of them old enemies—lined up in support: the AFL and the CIO, Americans for Democratic Action (at that time a young league of New Deal-oriented thinkers), the Veterans of Foreign Wars, the United States Chamber of Commerce, the American Farm Bureau Federation, and many more. The great middle-of-the-road liberal consensus of these early days of Soviet-American conflict was taking shape. Under the impetus of the Marshall Plan discussion and related events, what one historian and ADA founder would call "the vital center" of American politics for a generation was being formed.

There was a small chorus of opposition. Henry Wallace was critical, as he gathered around him a band of followers who would support him in a forthcoming bid for the Presidency. Representative Vito Marcantonio of New York, one of the few remaining radicals in Congress, charged that the plan had many strings—among them that the aid would be funneled through favored American banks and corporations, and would require recipient countries to cut off trade with others outside the plan's embrace, sometimes at a high cost to themselves. Ohio's Senator Robert A. Taft, still consistently isola- tionist, denounced the concept of a "global WPA." But the tide was running against men such as these, as was clearly evident when, during an autumnal congressional session, $640 million in "interim" aid was easily passed at the Administration's request—along with an unsolicted $100 million dollop to China.

Still, all was not completely clear sailing. The formal legislation submitted in December asked for a four-year commitment of $17 billion. Though Congress was almost sure to give ultimate approval, there would be inevitable snipping, trimming, and delay—perhaps even until the 1948 elections were over with. Yet time was of the essence if the help was to have an early impact. As the new year got under way, the creators of the Marshall Plan were worried about how much dilatoriness would be fatal to the patient. Then, late in February 1948, the Russians, through a mistimed and brutal maneuver in Prague, came to their aid.

Chapter 4

EUROPE DIVIDED
1948-1949

THE WINTER OF 1047-48 was a time of worry for the higher echelons of the newly reorganized and enlarged American security bureaucracy.

It was a time of worry for Marshall, who was obliged to sit through another intolerably unproductive session of the Council of Foreign Ministers in London, becoming certain that there was now no diplomatic exit from the deadlock over the future of Germany. He returned to Washington and a departmental staff bereft of the services of Acheson, who was back in private law practice, mending his personal finances. Marshall took up the courtship of Republican Senator Vandenberg, afterward recording that they could not have been closer "unless I sat in Vandenberg's lap or he sat in mine."

It was a time of worry for the United States ambassador to the Soviet Union, General Walter Bedell Smith, still another military man turned diplomat. He reported to Marshall that the Russians were working on their own atomic bomb and strategic air force. He predicted war inside of ten years.

It was a time of worry over the future of Italy and France. Both were due to hold spring elections. In Italy the Communists were expected to do very well, and win enough parliamentary seats for at least a share in any government. In France the Fourth Republic, beset not only `by Communists but by conservative followers of General de Gaulle, was shaky. One French official told correspondent Cyrus Sulzberger of rumors that the "Reds" would spawn a wave of strikes and assassinations before the balloting to set the stage for their takeover. Sulzberger asked why, if the French feared Communism that much, they did not give American diplomatic positions more support. The answer was simple fear. As Bidault had told Byrnes in 1946, in case of war the Russians could be at the English Channel in ten days.

It was a time of worry for those concerned with China's fate, as Chiang Kai-shek's position deteriorated, month by month.

It was a time of worry, also, for Harry Truman, facing a political revolt from the left. Henry Wallace was leading an organization called the Progressive Citizens of America. It called for a softer stance toward Russia, and for reenergizing programs of social reform, and was preparing to run Wallace for President. Wallace could not win, but his campaign could deny reelection to Truman—assuming that he could gain renomination from the demoralized, quarreling Democrats.

It was a time of worry, too, for the armed service leaders, convinced as always of their unreadiness to fight because of congressional parsimony. The Air Force complained especially of starvation, and called for funding at a strength of 70 Air Groups—the equivalent of Army divisions. The air generals got a wide public hearing for their case when a special Air Policy Commission created by the President and chaired by still another corporation attorney, Thomas K. Finletter, published its report under the title *Survival in the Air Age*. In its pages, everyone could read such testimony as that of Air Force Chief of Staff General Carl Spaatz:

> If Russia does strike the United States, as she will if her present frame of mind continues, only a powerful air force in being can strike back fast enough and hard enough to prevent the utter destruction of our nation.

This point of view was seconded by the aircraft industry, which had lost nearly $200 million in 1946 and 1947 through the shrinkage of the wartime market. But it was regarded warily by the other armed forces branches with claims for dollars. Secretary of the Navy Sullivan warned Capitol Hill that the Germans had nearly won the Battle of the Atlantic with only fifty operating submarines, and the Russians already had five times that number. Army spokesmen estimated that Russian armed manpower was at least double that of America.

Many American leaders were inclined to share the privately expressed concern of Admiral Leahy that there was a "very menacing situation," and to agree with his prescription for "a partial mobilization of forces of defense without any delay." The trouble was that such a step in peacetime went against the grain of American tradition. Even *Survival in the Air Age*, though faithfully endorsing the 70-Group Air Force concept, brooded that the needs of "relative security" would demand a permanent "force in being . . . greater than any self-governing state has ever kept," and would "put a disproportionate share of the power of the Government in the hands of the military."

But abruptly, in the third week of February 1948, it became much easier to accept those risks of constant armed readiness. This was due to events in what Neville Chamberlain had, in 1938, called "a faraway country of which we know nothing."

Throughout 1947, Czechoslovakia's President Eduard Benes and his Foreign Minister, Jan Masaryk, had been struggling to preserve the integrity of their tortured little country, betrayed at Munich in 1938, occupied by the Nazis, then "liberated" and garrisoned by the Russians. In a 1946 election the Communists had won 37 percent of the Czech vote and entered a coalition government in which they held the premiership. It belonged to Klement Gottwald, a party regular of no special distinction. In sharp contrast, Benes and Masaryk, particularly the latter, were well-known and respected in the West. Masaryk was the son of Czechoslovakia's founder, Thomas Masaryk, a longtime admirer of the United States. The very treaty that brought Czechoslovakia into being was signed, in 1919, in Pittsburgh, the home of hundreds of thousands of Bohemians and Slovaks who were happy to see Woodrow Wilson's principle of "self-determination" applied to their homeland.

On February 18, 1948, during a visit of the Soviet Deputy Foreign Minister to Prague, the twelve non-Communist members of the government resigned, Masaryk included. No one was certain why. Perhaps it was to give Benes the opportunity to call new elections in which the Communists would lose ground (though that was by no means a foregone conclusion). If so, it did not work. Day after day dragged by with public life paralyzed. The press buzzed with rumors of a Soviet invasion. And then, on February 25, came an announcement. The President had directed Gottwald to form a new government—without elections, and with only Communists included. Aging and ailing, Benes—who had also been President at the time of Munich—had somehow been forced to destroy Czech freedom for a tragic second time.

Jan Masaryk, a marked man, might have fled that day. He chose not to. Friends knew him as one whose patriotism was tempered by a sense of reality and ironic humor. (Once, asked if he objected to having a Communist deputy forced on him, he answered that he did not because it saved money on telephone calls to and from Moscow.) He may have hoped that he could still bridge the gap between factions or, at least, save some of his associates from forthcoming purges.

But two weeks after the new Gottwald government was named, a terse bulletin from Prague radio rocked the West. Jan Masaryk was dead. He had "fallen" from a bathroom window.

Was it actually a suicide leap? Was Masaryk pushed? No one would ever know. The one incontrovertible fact was the nakedness, the unmistakable horror of his death. It "dramatized, as few other things could have done, the significance of what had just occurred," said George Kennan. But exactly what was the "significance"? Clearly, the takeover was yet another Russian turn of the screw on the satellites. Perhaps it was also a sign of American failure to offer some timely early help to Czech anti-Communists. But Washington elected to read an even more ominous meaning into what had happened. This was the overture to the dreaded Soviet march westward—the move to conquer Europe before it could be revived. Again in Kennan's recollection, a "real war scare" swept the capital of the United States.

"Rumors and portents of war," wrote Forrestal in his diary for March 16, six days after Masaryk's death. The papers were full of such portents. General Clay cabled from Germany that fighting might break out with "dramatic suddenness." If so, the Secretary of the Army reported, disaster would follow: Without forward air bases in Alaska and Iceland, we would "lose all our troops in Japan and Europe." The CIA presented an estimate only a shade more reassuring. War was not probable within the next sixty days, but after that, nothing could be guaranteed.

Something urgent was necessary. The time lapse from Munich to World War II had been a year. The clock seemed to be running faster in 1948. Truman's advisers decided that he must, in a forthcoming speech at New York's annual St. Patrick's Day dinner, prepare the country for Armageddon. He should ask support for legislation to carry out the latest recommendations of the Joint Chiefs of Staff. They included renewal of the draft to fill existing manpower shortages, and, in addition, a program of universal military training on the European model—a year or two of automatic service for all young men when they reached eighteen. The Chiefs also wanted bigger appropriations and the return of atomic energy to military control. With the party conventions only three months away, the political implications of endorsing these recommendations were not forgotten. White House aide George Elsey, after one conference, noted: "Pres. must, for his prestige, come up with a strong foreign speech—to demonstrate his leadership—which country needs and wants."

The country would get what it wanted in full measure. The security counselors decided that the President should, in fact, not even seem to be waiting for a buildup of public opinion, but should go directly to Congress and then, the same evening, address the Friendly Sons of St. Patrick in New York. Marshall, consistent in his calmness, advised against a provocative speech. Elsey noted that the Secretary of State was "nervous—world keg of dynamite—HST shouldn't start it." But Marshall's call for a "simple, businesslike" speech drew a pragmatic response from Clark Clifford. "It has to be blunt, to justify the message. He asks for legislation—how does he explain it?"

Blunt it was. One year and five days after the Truman Doctrine was enunciated, the man from Independence once more confronted Congress and rang the alarm. This time he named the "aggressor" directly and often:

> The situation in the world today is not primarily the result of natural difficulties which follow a great war. It is chiefly due to the fact that one nation has not only refused to cooperate in the establishment of a just and honorable peace, but—even worse—has actively sought to prevent it. . . . Since the close of hostilities, the Soviet Union and its agents have destroyed the independence and democratic character of a whole series of nations in Eastern and Central Europe.

Though the emphasis of the speech was on military preparations and not on the Marshall Plan, the connection between them was self-evident. Truman—and Jan Masaryk—electrified Congress into a burst of activity, the first result of which was the passage of the plan's basic legislation. The House tally was 318 to 75. The Senate simply shouted it through by an overwhelming voice vote. Funding of $5.3 billion was authorized for the first fourteen months of the newly created Economic Cooperation Administration, with an extra $563 million to China and $275 million to the year-old Greek-Turkish aid program. Within twelve days a freighter steamed, with well-publicized fanfare, out of a Texas port, carrying wheat to Bordeaux. She was the first keel of an armada that would succeed, over the next four years, in dramatically reviving Europe's economy, just as predicted.

Suddenly, from the point of view of those who had been fearful that the United States was sleeping through imminent perils, there was good news. Congress did not authorize universal military training, but it did revive the draft. It also fattened the upcoming fiscal year's appropriation bill with $3 billion of additional military expenditure, $775 million of that earmarked for aircraft, so that as early as June 1948, *Business Week* cheerfully noted that plane manufacturing was "on its way out of the red ink for the first time since the end of the war." But all was not euphoria for the Pentagon. Truman still demanded an election-year military budget held to $15 billion, and groused about the "muttonheads," as he called the civilian Secretaries, who could not pare down the figures presented by their brass. He drove Forrestal into a nervousness that began to show itself by strange habits. (In meetings, the Secretary of Defense would, in total unawareness, scratch a spot on his scalp until blood flowed through the torn skin.)

At the same time, there was good political news for Truman. Henry Wallace foolishly chose to downplay the tragedy of the Czech coup. Seeking to damp down the mood of militancy, he pointed out that it was part of the general process of East-West fission in Europe that had been going on since 1945—and suggested that Masaryk might simply have yielded to a suicidal fit of depression. Whatever truth lay in these views, their apparent callousness achieved what Truman's inner circle had been seeking with regard to Wallace—to "isolate him in the public mind with the Communists."

There was better news from Europe, as well. Aided by a massive letter-writing campaign organized among Italian-Americans (and by unrecorded infusions of CIA and other money), the non-Communist parties of Italy won their April elections. In France, too, the expected Communist victory did not materialize, perhaps because French Stalinists were as much disorganized by Cominform policies as they were outbidden for support by political rivals.

Finally, there was one other piece of good news whose import was overlooked. For months, Stalin and Tito—lumped together in the American mind simply as two Communist dictators—had been quarreling. Tito resisted Stalin's plans for tying the Yugoslavian economy tightly to Moscow, for he saw potential profitable deals with the industrialized West, which could use the Danube basin's grain, meat, coal, and timber. The quarrel was couched in terms of Marxist theory, but was essentially over independence. In June of 1948, after bitter debate over certain proposals, Stalin threw Tito out of the Cominform, raging: "I shall shake my little finger and there will be no Tito."

The good news was in what Stalin did not do. He did not attempt a military solution—an invasion that would put Soviet armor in Adriatic seaports and on Italy's frontier. His alleged timetable of world conquest did not include a stop in Belgrade. He was either willing or compelled to think of other ways to bring Tito to heel, which in fact he was never to manage. He had lost Yugoslavia, though the West was not to win over the rebel state to its side.

But Washington was not ready, that June, to see a positive sign in the split within the Cominform. The atmosphere was still too sullen and electric. The state of apprehension of a storm about to burst was becoming habitual, almost acceptable. It was even endowed with a new name. Early in 1948, Walter Lippmann, celebrated as a journalist, columnist, and expert on public affairs, issued a book of essays, most of them critical of the drift of American policy toward confrontation with Russia. He called the collection The Cold War, his borrowing, he later explained, of the French term referring to something like the constant "war of nerves" that Hitler had waged against the democracies during the years 1938 and 1939.

The words were picked up and given a wider meaning. Cold War. A name for an epoch, a state of mind, a political climate. A definition of a state of enduring hostility between two powers, marked by short, sharp periods of instability during which there was danger of an explosion into full-scale armed encounter.

A T THE END OF 1947, the stalemate on Germany seemed beyond solution. The British and Americans were determined that Germany's economy must be unified and revived. The Russians vetoed every proposed step toward that end, still claiming that their reparations demands must first be fulfilled. "It is not possible to sit here with hands folded," the British zone commander complained in January 1948, and his government, among others, was fully prepared to agree. It was time to move beyond the merger of the French, British, and American zones, to go ahead without the Soviet Union and organize a separate West German government as the indispensable administrative framework for economic growth.

In February, representatives of the three Western occupying powers, plus delegates from Belgium, the Netherlands, and Luxembourg, met in London to agree to this in principle. It was a remarkable step for these countries, which had been under Nazi occupation only four years earlier, as well as for the British hosts who had endured Hitler's blitz from the air. It was a possibility, of course, that the move might be a bluff to force Stalin to accommodation by confronting him with what he evidently feared above all—a reborn, free, and potentially rearmed German state.

But the Westerners were not bluffing about their economic program. A vital measure that they sought was the issuance of a new, stable, and deflated German currency. Though the Russians, on the Allied Control Council, continued to reject all proposed monetary reforms, the Americans went ahead with the printing and storing of the new bills—and the Soviet side knew it. On February 1, when General Lucius Clay, commanding general of the American zone, urged currency action at a Council meeting, Russian Marshal Vasily Sokolovsky taunted him with pretending to seek agreement when in fact Clay already had the money in his pockets.

Several weeks later Sokolovsky, incensed at his failure to find out more about the five-power talks in London, stalked out of another session of the weakening Control Council. Immediately afterwards there was a suspicious flurry of new Russian "control" regulations, slowing and snarling road and rail traffic into Berlin. This "miniblockade" was a presumable hint of how hard it would be to do business in Germany without Russian cooperation.

But instead of accepting paralysis, the Western nations met once more in London in May. This time they sent the West Germans a

message to start working on a new constitution. The days of
purgatory were over, the purification from Nazism satisfactorily
achieved. For the French, especially, this was a giant step. Their
anxieties over German resurgence were understandably equal to
Moscow's, and Premier Bidault was always conscious of domestic
fire from his own parliament whenever he sat down to discuss
German matters. "Don't make it too hard for me," he pleaded with
the American ambassador in Paris.

The Americans did not intend to do so. They had already
provided reassurance for the French by encouraging the beginnings
of a Western military alliance. Exploratory talks on such a pact
among France, Britain, and the three small nations, whose names
were shortened for the convenience of headline writers and cable
editors to "Benelux," had already begun. On March 17—the very
day on which Truman was calling for American rearmament—the
five countries signed a mutual defense pact in Brussels. There was
implicit understanding that, in time, the United States would
support and even participate in the treaty, as soon as galloping
events could dissolve Senate resistance.

And this, too, the Russians knew. They were faced with a situation
that was getting out of hand. The Brussels Pact was not only an
anti-German but an anti-Soviet measure, inspired in part by the
reaction to events in Prague. The miniblockade was a partial
Russian response. Another was a Molotov proposal for bilateral
Moscow-Washington talks on Germany's future. But the Americans
saw in that move not a chance to discover Stalin's terms for a
German settlement, but only a divisive delaying tactic.

Then it was June 1948, and the pace of the game quickened. On
the 11th, the United States Senate passed a resolution, sponsored by
Vandenberg, approving in principle American participation in
"regional security" pacts. On the 17th, the announcement was made
that the new currency would begin to circulate in the Western zones
of Germany—that the West, in effect, would "go it alone" on the
question. And on the 24th, the Russians, while loudly protesting the
"illegal" currency move, shut down the rail lines and highways from
the Western zones into Berlin on the grounds of "technical
difficulties."

In another time, the maneuvers and countermaneuvers might
have seemed less threatening—simply moves on the board, the last
one a Russian attempt to force fresh high-level negotiations. But in
the tempestuous aura of the sixteen weeks since the Czech coup,
small events cast large shadows. The Berlin blockade was perceived
as a full-scale war crisis.

In emergency sessions of Truman's national security advisers, the
focus was on the potentiality of a showdown on Berlin, not on how

the traffic cutoff might fit into a larger Russian design to slow down the rush toward a West German state. Washington believed that the basic Russian intention was to throw the West out of the city. What was the safest and strongest response? Should they play for time by holding back the new money? Or even write off Berlin? The city was, at best (as the French especially pointed out), terribly vulnerable. And how Hitler's ghost might laugh at World War III commencing between the Americans and the "Bolsheviks," as he had predicted—in the very shadow of his Reich's ruined command post. Perhaps the line should be drawn, if at all, somewhere else.

But in cables from his headquarters, General Clay fought hard to give Berlin a larger significance. He was one of a new breed of soldiers, politically astute and a gifted manager. His father had been a United States Senator. He himself was graduated from West Point in 1918, first in his class in English and history, and with a specialty in engineering. During World War II he had been liaison chief between the Army and industry, serving as the link between the military and corporate high commands. Later, he was Byrnes's deputy war mobilizer. Byrnes recommended him for the post of Military Governor of Germany, one that perfectly suited his "get-on-with-it" temperament, since in that position, as Clay's civilian successor, John J. McCloy, recalled, "You could turn to your secretary and say, 'Take a law.'"

Clay begged his superiors to see the broader issue that would be posed by abandoning Berlin to Soviet supremacy. He evoked a theme that would reverberate again and again in the years ahead, the domino theory. If the United States gave in on Berlin, it would dishearten its supporters everywhere. "After Berlin will come Western Germany," he wired. "If we mean that we are to hold Europe against Communism, we must not budge. . . . If America does not know this, does not believe the issue is cast now, then it never will, and Communism will run rampant."

Clay won his first point. There would be no delay in distributing the currency, and moreover he was authorized to organize a supposedly temporary air relief expedition for the blockaded city. Amid all the grimness there was one moment of unwitting humor, when he first called General Curtis LeMay, the head of the Air Force units in Europe, to ask if he could deliver coal to Berlin.

The hardboiled commander of B-29 bombers removed the receiver from his ear, stared at it dubiously, then spoke.

"Uh, General, we must have a bad connection. It sounds as if you asked me if we have airplanes that can carry coal."

Clay got his flying colliers, but was thwarted in a second proposal to Washington. If the airlift proved inadequate, he wanted to send an armored engineer battalion out to deal with the "technical

difficulties." If it should be hindered in its "repairs," it was to open
fire.

No. The Joint Chiefs of Staff refused. They would not start a war
deep inside Germany over the printing of new *Reichsmarks*. Nor
would Harry Truman in 1948. At its most belligerent, American
public opinion stopped short of that. An airlift would be, for as long
as it worked, the perfect halfway measure. It avoided head-on
encounters, and it allowed both sides the fig leaf of legality, since
the air routes, unlike those on the surface, were guaranteed in
writing.

THE DRONING OF THE MOTORS overhead never stopped. Berliners
lucky enough to be still alive through the fourth winter after the
war would never forget the endlessness of it. Bright days and
cloudy, in fog and in pitchblack night, the noise was there, not
charged with alarm now, as in the terrible last days of the siege in
'45, but full of assurance.

It was loudest, of course, as one got near the airports. Templehof
in the American zone, with its concrete-over-pierced-steel runway
crumbling from hard use. Gatow in the British sector, an old
Luftwaffe training strip. And then Tegel, in the French zone, rushed
to completion in autumn of 1948 by civilian laborers—many in the
tattered suits that were their sole remaining clothing—struggling
with the cumbersome tools needed to create landing surfaces out of
earth, concrete, and the crushed-brick rubble that was everywhere
in sight, struggling not to faint on the limited diet allowed, even by
the special ration card for heavy workers.

The burdened planes lurched off or slammed down on the
runways in a permanent parade of overwork—at peak periods a
takeoff or landing every ninety seconds. Mostly they were aging
twin-engined C-47s, but there were C-54s, too, with four Pratt &
Whitney engines driving Hamilton propellers. The British were
using, in addition, some converted bombers. The pilots set them
down in Berlin, and men and trucks swarmed around the aircraft
and quickly emptied their bellies of sacks of coal, cartons of dried
milk and potatoes and eggs, medicine, blankets, and essential spare
parts for the machinery that kept a modern city going. Then they
took off immediately for the bases at Frankfurt and Hamburg, to
descend into another maelstrom of mechanics, who were squirting
oil, pouring gas, changing sparkplugs, gaskets, and fittings at a mad
tempo, while loading crews jostled their elbows. And then the
sturdy planes were airborne again, rarely grounded except for the
most essential overhauls. Heading back to Berlin and the welcome
voices of the stubbled men in the control towers who called out
weather information and approach directions, the pilots were

sometimes given warnings to avoid the wreckage of a flight that had gone wrong, ending in death for an aircrew that had been too weary, or too unlucky.

The Russians had tried to call the shots on Berlin, but the Americans, along with a few British crews and airplanes, were fighting back with a miracle, the supplying of the world's fifth largest city, 2.5 million people (plus six thousand occupation troops), by air alone. Sheer insanity on the face of it. From all over the world, veteran Air Force personnel had been jerked from peacetime billets and were now flying endlessly through three twenty-mile-wide air corridors, which, thanks to haste and oversight at the war's end, were the only means of access, guaranteed in writing, to blockaded Berlin. In the lumbering cargo-laden planes, the pilots would be clay pigeons for Russian fighter aircraft if Moscow chose to block the air lanes too.

Fortunately for the world, the Russians did not want war either. Yet as the world would also learn on ensuing occasions, any moment of tension had its hidden explosives: the transport gone astray, the trigger-happy fighter pilot, the nervous officer on a street patrol along the sector boundaries in Berlin, the misunderstood cable, the undelivered message, the tiny mischance on which destiny sometimes pivoted. In July, Lord Hastings Ismay, Britain's World War II Chief of Staff, summed it up well in a message to Eisenhower: "We are all standing on the edge of a precipice, and although all parties concerned are determined not to slip over the edge, there may be a puff of wind, or someone may get dizzy and trip up; or again, someone may be deliberately malicious."

But the Russians stuck to the letter of the agreement. They would not provoke a shooting incident in the air. They could wait. The airlift could not possibly fulfill Berlin's needs. They also held a truly high card: Two-thirds of West Berlin's power was generated in Russian-held East Berlin, and could be, and was, cut off. Shops and factories would close. Starved and shivering Berliners would demand a settlement, perhaps vote for Communist municipal officials on whom Soviet goodwill could shine. Then Washington, with London and Paris helplessly following, would have to negotiate its way out.

The Russians were totally wrong. Day after day, the planes kept coming, the runways were repaired, the crews were rotated, the planes refurbished and augmented. And the tonnage crept upward and upward, reaching the four thousand daily minimum, then exceeding it, and eventually, in the spring of 1949, reaching the old preblockade levels. There were bad weather periods, and hard weeks, and frightening moments, but the personnel of what the American press delighted in calling "Operation Vittles" continued to perform and enlarge upon the miracle.

And so did the West Berliners. Enduring tremendous hardships, they somehow lived on their daily rations of 17 ounces of bread, 2 ounces of Spam or powdered eggs, 3 ounces of flour or dried potatoes, 2 ounces of cereal, and 1 of fat. They picked their way afoot through the dark streets after public transportation stopped running at 6 P.M., and staggered out of bed, sometimes in the middle of the night, to do their cooking during the two hours in every twenty-four when power was supplied, on a staggered schedule, for home use. They listened to loudspeaker-launched bulletins that carried the story of the world's reaction to their ordeal. Still a little dazed, still living in a city of ruins and cripples and widows and orphans, they hung on. On December 5, 1948, 85 percent of their eligible voters went to the polls to give a staggering majority to Lord Mayor Ernest Reuter's anti-Communist Social Democrats.

And many of those who had time went to the airports to perch on whatever vantage points they could find and cheer the landings. Some scrounged pathetic gifts from their few possessions, pieces of family china, children's dolls, handknit scarves—and pressed them upon the crews. They were the same crews, in many cases, who four years earlier had been helping to batter the city to pieces. Now, they were not only pioneering in aerial logistics, but were also rewriting diplomatic history.

In an unexpected and ironic reversal, the citizens of the Western-held portion of Adolf Hitler's capital city had become America's wards and friends. In the words of the veteran diplomat Robert D. Murphy, Clay's political adviser, they were "for all practical purposes our allies." The airlines that made possible what Germans labeled the Luftbrücke—the air bridge—were roadways to an astonishing turnabout in America's definition of the "world enemy."

In August 1948, Stalin made it quite clear that he was after something bigger than Berlin. In a meeting with the French and British ambassadors he asked, over a cigarette, "Would you like to settle the matter tonight?" His offer was a lifting of the blockade in exchange for dropping the idea of a separate West German government.

It was an offer that could be refused, because the masterful technical exercise of the airlift was succeeding beyond all calculations. As early as the end of July, there had been 80 C-47s and 52 C-54s, each making two daily round trips, and month after month the number of planes and the delivered tonnage rose. When the final figures were recorded, a total of 124.5 million miles had been flown, at a cost of some $5 million per day.

By May of 1949 the battle was long over. By then, Harry Truman had won reelection. He saw his victory as an endorsement for his policy of avoiding either surrender or preventive war. By then, too, the Brussels Pact nations had formally invited the Americans and Canadians to join them, and on April 4, 1949, the United States abandoned a century and a half of isolation and entered the North Atlantic Treaty Organization, pledging that it would now regard an attack on the British, the French, the Dutch, or the Belgians as an attack on itself. America's frontier was now on the Rhine, and would move even further eastward in later years, when Greece and Turkey joined NATO.

On May 12, the new German constitution was ready for approval. Stalin, by then, had thrown in the towel. Early in the year, addressing an East European Communist delegation, he had correctly predicted: "The West will make Germany their own, and we shall turn Eastern Germany into our own state." With that much clear, there was no point in continuing the blockade, which was not only ineffective but a propaganda setback. Once again, as in opposing the Marshall Plan, the Russians had cast themselves as advocates of starvation for Europeans who resisted them. So Stalin, in a characteristically Byzantine way, chose to end the stalemate. In a newspaper interview with a Western correspondent, he talked of a number of outstanding issues, but made no mention at all of the German currency question that had provoked the blockade. That was a signal to sharp eyes in Washington that the door was ajar. Further conferences were called, and the barriers to Berlin were lifted on May 10 in exchange for token concessions by the West—a new meeting of the Council of Foreign Ministers and the abandonment of economic countermeasures against the Eastern zone of Germany.

The Berlin crisis was over. At the highest level, both sides had been clear about wanting to avoid war. But the world had nonetheless experienced the sensation of a long sojourn on the precipice. And out of that sensation, the major upheavals of 1949 were produced. The repercussions of the year of Berlin were enormous.

For one thing, the airlift was worth billions to the propagandists of air power and an expanded American military orbit. It was now clear that great bodies of troops, like great numbers of civilians, could be sustained by air transport, with tanks and guns taking the place of coal and groceries in the maws of the cargo planes. Entire new areas of the world were now possible theaters for the deployment of American force.

The year 1949 also completed a stunning diplomatic reversal. All pretense of four-power agreement on unifying Germany ended at last. The years of tortured Council of Foreign Ministers meetings were over. The Russians began to create their East German satellite, the German Democratic Republic, while the West formally recognized the Federal Republic of Germany, with its capital in Bonn, and began to integrate it into Europe's economy. The move paid off dramatically, as production figures began their long climb toward uncharted peaks. The "economic miracle" of West Germany went along with a psychological "miracle," too, in which former German occupiers, exploiters, and torturers became brethren—and were replaced in the popular imagination by a new Satanic adversary in the East. If this required a deep change of heart for Europe, it was equally profound in its impact on America, which, only a decade after living under strict neutrality laws, buried isolation at last.

In all, the Berlin blockade crystallized what had been happening since the war's end—the drift toward failure in joint peacemaking. Stalin's brutality had managed, at crucial junctures, to help American hard-line advocates. American anti-Communism had been heated to pre-1941 temperature. America's two main political parties had found a new unity in common anxiety about the fate of a world supposedly within the Soviet shadow, and together were writing a new foreign policy. But the new, tough, internationally minded United States position had further refining and tempering ahead of it. Throughout the last months of 1949 and the winter and spring of 1950, new events and developments, as dramatic and important as the great airlift and the emergence of East and West Germany, would plunge Americans deeper into the Cold War way of life.

SEPTEMBER 2, 1949, MAY IN THE LONG RUN prove to have been one of the most momentous dates of modern history. On that day, the Geiger counters in American monitoring planes over Alaska erupted in a fusillade of growls, as they responded to sudden, strong atmospheric radiation coming from the region of Siberia. What the monitors were checking on, but hoping desperately not to find for years to come, had in fact taken place. Soviet science—for the first but not the last time repudiating the myth of "backward" Russia—had created a nuclear explosion. The word was flashed to Washington. At last the Soviet Union had the bomb. At least one. And where one could be created, others would follow. The monopoly was over. A sobered Harry Truman publicly announced the truth almost at once.

At the topmost levels of government two new Cabinet members grappled with the implications of the bad news. One was Louis Johnson, Secretary of Defense. James Forrestal was gone, tragically, the victim of a mental collapse. Harried by the President, by recalcitrant generals and admirals, by liberal critics, by budget-cutters, by Zionists (because of his pro-Arab Mideastern policies), and above all by his own dark anxieties, Forrestal had become increasingly exhausted and erratic in his behavior. His proffered resignation at the start of 1949 had been gratefully and instantly accepted. Then, on May 22, he committed suicide.

Louis Johnson was the polar opposite of Forrestal. A gregarious businessman, a former American Legion commander, and a Truman fundraiser in 1948, he was suitably militant for his job. But he was also budget-minded, and not only willing but eager to stay within the presidential $15 billion arms-budget limit.

Over at State, the "new" face was an old one—Acheson. Marshall had asked for and finally gotten retirement, and Acheson had been called back in his stead, brisk and bristly as ever and deeply wedded to toughness with the Russians—a conviction that many people would later forget, for several reasons. One was Acheson's general association with the New Deal. Another, and better remembered, was his public profession of friendship for his friend Alger Hiss, which was based purely on personal loyalty, a strong Acheson characteristic.

Far from being indifferent to Communism, Acheson was, behind closed State Department doors, undertaking a shake-up to bring department policy more tightly in line with the national security outlook that meshed diplomatic, military, and economic activities in a concerted anti-Soviet drive. This meant overriding the conventional view of veteran diplomats that peace and war were clearly separable, that the goal of a "normal" foreign policy was to advance the national interest by agreements arrived at, even with rivals, through mutual bargaining. And, as it happened, Acheson was able to use the aftermath of the Russian bomb to complete the changes that he was seeking.

What America did not yet know in the autumn of 1949 was that the explosion of Russia's "device" touched off a debate in the most secret recesses of the Truman Administration, on whether or not to press on with research on a new nuclear weapon that would fuse atoms under intense heat, to produce explosions of even more apocalyptic destructive power than the "fission" bombs that had virtually destroyed Hiroshima and Nagasaki. The possibility of creating this "thermonuclear" or "hydrogen" or simply "H" bomb was first presented to the Atomic Energy Commission, which then passed it on to the President, who brought Acheson and others in on the discussions.

The specific way in which this happened, however, was part of a political story with fateful long-range results. The AEC, when first informed of the chance for making the "Super," as it was then referred to, turned for advice to the chairman of its General

Advisory Committee, the father of the atom bomb and the country's most respected physicist, J. Robert Oppenheimer. Oppenheimer counseled against going ahead, mainly on practical grounds. The new bomb would be expensive, uncertain, and would only temporarily restore the American edge. He added that it would pose major moral problems by loosing an even larger threat of annihilation than the A-bomb on an already shaken human race.

Three of the five AEC members, including Chairman David Lilienthal, agreed. Two did not, and they were strongly backed by other scientists, chiefly Edward Teller and Ernest O. Lawrence. Teller especially feared that the Russians might go ahead with their own superbomb if the United States did not. The minority members brought his view and theirs to Truman and to the Joint Congressional Committee on Atomic Energy, which was almost certain to favor the Super.

On November 10, Truman appointed Acheson, Lilienthal, and Johnson as a committee to advise him on the matter. In their report, Acheson and Johnson overrode Lilienthal with a positive recommendation—Acheson because he shared Teller's frame of mind and Johnson primarily on grounds of economy. He believed that with the H-bomb in the arsenal, conventional forces could be reduced—a policy to be defined by a later Secretary of Defense as "getting a bigger bang for a buck." On January 31, 1950, Truman announced that the United States would go ahead to "study the feasibility" of the weapon, meaning in fact to produce it. Whatever his own inclinations, which were probably approving, to do less would court serious trouble from the Congress.

Meantime, he had authorized Acheson to begin studies on the effect that the Soviet's "probable fission bomb capability and possible thermonuclear bomb capability" ought to have on future foreign policy. And not simply foreign policy, but on "our objectives in peace and war and the effect of objectives on our strategic plans." In this way, State was officially involved in a study of *overall* national goals—precisely what Acheson wanted instead of the conventional arrangement dividing diplomats from warriors. Moreover, the study was to be conducted under the auspices of the National Security Council, meaning that it could be undertaken without nosy and distracting questions from budgeteers, bureaucrats, and legislators. It played perfectly into a blueprint of Acheson's that went beyond approval of the Super—namely to lay the foundations for increased mobilization.

A first move was to neutralize conventional internal State Department objections as typified by those of Kennan. The chief advocate of containment actually felt increasingly isolated within the new, militant framework of official Washington. He had conceived his doctrine in a different context from that in which it was now applied, seeing it merely as a guideline to negotiation, which was difficult but not impossible, even with Russians. Knowing that this interpretation was unpopular, he asked to be relieved as chairman of the Policy Planning Staff early in 1950. But as a lame duck he duly registered his objections to the Super. It would, he believed, overstress purely military measures to counter the Soviets. He also thought (in anticipation of a later viewpoint) that small, mobile conventional forces were a much more useful and flexible defense investment. Finally, he worried that if the United States went ahead, it would incur world odium for leading in the race to Doomsday. At the least, he argued, it would be worthwhile, before plunging in, to try for a new agreement with the Soviet Union, which would keep both powers from entering a thermonuclear race.

Acheson countered that there was no such thing as agreement with Moscow, which was his unchanging opinion. "You can't argue with a river, it is going to flow," was the way he put it, and the only way to dam the "river" was to "create strength" and force the Kremlin to accept facts it was powerless to change. Of Kennan's moral objections, Acheson sniffed that a man with such scruples "ought to resign from the Foreign Service and go out and preach his Quaker gospel but not push it within the Department." His response to Oppenheimer's similar invocation of ethical dilemmas was: "Those are the kinds of problems with which men must live."

These Achesonian principles became dominant when Kennan was replaced at the head of the Policy Planning Staff by Paul Nitze, a Wall Street investment banker newly recruited to the State Department. Nitze's views were so close to Acheson's (and would remain unchanging through decades to come) that the Secretary declared him "a joy to work with because of his clear, incisive mind." Under Nitze's direction, the State Department's drafts of the forthcoming National Security Council paper became increasingly warlike, so much so that both Kennan and Bohlen objected that the end result would be exclusively a plea for military buildup, resulting in the virtual elimination of diplomacy.

Both old hands were soon away from the center of action, Kennan on a mission to South America and Bohlen as ambassador to France. The developing study on "objectives" passed now to a special task force called the State-Defense Policy Research Group, which gathered input from the AEC, the CIA, and other sources as it moved ahead. In the first week of March it invited an outside critic, the scholar-scientist James B. Conant, president of Harvard, to discuss one draft version. Conant spent the meeting in a duel with Nitze. He questioned the value of such broad terms as the "free world." He doubted that the zeal showed by Russia in defending her own soil was a sign that she would be equally vigorous in wars of conquest. And he believed that the goal of the ensuing twenty years should be "living with the Soviet Union on tolerable terms."

Conant was never invited back. Nor was any other comparable evaluator. The Policy Research Group, working behind closed doors with classified documents, preferred thereafter to recruit its experts from within, men like Robert Lovett, who argued: "We should fight with no holds barred . . . exactly as though we were under fire from an invading army."

One Defense official not consulted was Louis Johnson, who was represented through deputies. Johnson's recorded position was that to keep on hand "at all times armed forces large enough to win a major war . . . would be economically suicidal and inconsistent with our democratic form of government." Shown a draft version of the study on March 22, he objected angrily.

Nevertheless, he was outmaneuvered and outflanked. From March 28 to April 3 he was away, attending a parley of NATO Defense Ministers. In that period, the final paper, now officially labeled National Security Council Document Number 68, was approved by the three civilian service Secretaries and the Joint Chiefs of Staff. Johnson came home to find the entire hierarchy of his department behind the study. He had no choice but to sign or resign. He signed.

NSC-68, a document of dire expectations and Infernoesque predictions, bore Nitze's and Acheson's stamp from beginning to end. The Soviet Union, it said, was "animated by a new fanatic faith, antithetical to our own, and seeks to impose its absolute authority over the rest of the world." Going beyond Kennan's 1947 assumption that the Soviet leaders were insecure at root, NSC-68 painted them as positive in their malevolence, constantly seeking "to oppose and weaken any competing system of power that threatens Communist world hegemony." It was almost superfluous to point out how inimical the Soviet system was to "American ideals, which are predicated on the concepts of freedom and human dignity," ideals that must be defended "at whatever cost or sacrifice" by peaceful means if possible. However, "if peaceful means fail we must be ready to fight."

Readiness to fight was not easy to attain. By 1954 there would be an "approximate stalemate in nuclear weapons." Rapid Russian military growth would also soon offset the industrial and technical superiority of the West. Already, "the Communist military capability for conventional, or nonatomic, warfare" was "substantially superior to that of the West, and . . . continuing to improve at a more rapid rate."

The chances for a negotiated balance of power were "poor, given the immutability of Soviet objectives and its advantage in military power." The United States must, of course, keep trying because the danger of a "nuclear holocaust" demanded no less. But it must recognize that Stalin respected "the reality of force a great deal more than . . . the abstraction of peace." So the paper set up three fundamental premises that were not tested by debate within its pages: the Soviet design of world conquest, growing Soviet military superiority, and therefore the impossibility of negotiations with Soviet leadership. Then:

> Based on these premises an indefinite period of tension and danger
> is foreseen for the United States and for the West—a period that
> should be defined less as a short-term crisis than as a permanent
> and fundamental alteration in the shape of international relations.

The hope of things changing for the better was thus snatched away, though there was a token suggestion that the correct policy might bring on a "retraction of the Kremlin's control," and even "foster . . . seeds of destruction within the Soviet system."

What was the right policy? NSC-68 quickly set up and mowed down three straw men. One was a retreat to isolation, another preventive war, and the third a continuation of the status quo of "reduced defense budgets and limited military capabilities," which was how the draftsmen of the study described what a $13 billion outlay bought in 1950. The right choice was to "strike out on a bold and massive program of rebuilding the West's defensive potential to surpass that of the Soviet world, and of meeting each fresh challenge promptly and unequivocally," to change, in fact, the two-century-old framework of American thinking about war and taxes.

> This means virtual abandonment by the United States of trying to
> distinguish between national and global security. It also means the
> end of subordinating security needs to the traditional budgeting
> restrictions; of asking 'How much security can we afford?' In other
> words, security must henceforth become the dominant element in
> the national budget, and other elements must be accommodated to
> it.
>   The wealth potential of the country is such that as much as 20 per
> cent of the gross national product can be devoted to security without
> causing national bankruptcy. This new concept of the security needs
> of the nation calls for annual appropriations of the order of $50
> billion, or not much below the former wartime levels.

This staggering secret manifesto was laid on the desk of President Truman as the judgment of his topmost security counselors on April 7, 1950. He seems to have accepted its conclusions readily. The country at large, if let in on things, might have felt the same, though some would certainly have shared the reaction of Charles Murphy, Clark Clifford's successor as counsel to the President. Murphy reported that he took it home, and what he read, he said, "scared me so much that the next day I didn't go to the office at all."

Even in the national security state, however, presidential acceptance alone did not translate NSC-68 into active policy. Precise estimates had to be prepared and translated into legislative recommendations, and Congress would have to make the final disposition. That would require careful release of the document's volatile contents, and considerable salesmanship. Under Secretary of State James Webb put it compactly in a memorandum to the President. You will, he warned, face "the problem of how to get up enough public steam to support you in starting to build up our strength, and at the same time . . . not get up so much as to look provocative."

A trial heat within the executive department was not encouraging. An Ad Hoc Committee on Implementation met on May 2. Translated from the jargon of bureaucracy, this meant that Treasury officials were let in on the study for the first time. One of them, the Budget Bureau's William Schaub, found the study thoroughly "provocative." He asked the piercing, basic questions that had been mainly missing during NSC-68's birth. Wouldn't the buildup force the Russians into military action of their own? What were the specific commitments foreseen, and at what point did the United States fight to defend them? What would the total costs amount to? Was it sensible to reduce complex world problems to a clash between the "free world" and a "slave society?" Were there no valid reasons why people under corrupt and despotic governments turned to Communism? Why had the research group minimized "economic and social change as a factor in the 'underlying conflict' "?

Schaub's voice was being heard, naturally, in the inner sanctum only. Yet questions like his would be bound to surface, once specific programs were forged. To prepare the ground, Acheson took to the road, as he had done in the Marshall Plan days. But this time he was "preaching the premise of NSC-68" (without revealing its exact contents). As "a public officer seeking to explain and gain support for a major policy," he skipped "nicety and nuance," as he himself declared, in favor of "bluntness, almost brutality, in carrying home a point."

But even bludgeoning might not have won ready acceptance of the sacrifices asked by NSC-68, except that there suddenly arrived one of those moments when the entire focus shifts—when a new historic event smashes all previous calculations and catapults a people into a new phase of their history. Within a single year of the drafting of NSC-68, the budget for all security-related operations (which included military, military assistance, and intelligence expenses) leaped to $22 billion. And to $44 billion a year later. And, in fiscal 1953, to the figure mentioned in NSC-68—$50 billion—by which time Louis Johnson had long departed. Armed forces manpower, a year after April of 1950, jumped by a million. Armaments plants were humming again. The country, thereafter, would never turn back from the road of huge military spending, sustained by what a Truman economic adviser, Leon Keyserling, exuberantly saw as an economy rolling and roaring toward a trillion-dollar annual Gross National Product.

What miracle took place? For ten weeks or so after NSC-68 was set before Truman, it had faced a long, difficult, and problematical future as a foundation for policy. But then, as Dean Acheson explained it to a seminar at Princeton in 1953: "Korea came along and saved us." On the morning of June 25, 1950, tanks and troops of the Democratic Republic of North Korea, a Soviet puppet state, rolled across the border into the Republic of South Korea, an American protectorate. Within a few days Truman had committed United States military forces—under United Nations authorization—to repel the invasion. Within a few weeks, Americans were in a full-dress shooting war with Communist soldiers, and showing signs of serious deficiencies in military preparedness. It was not hard, in the long and bitter months of battle that followed, to win national support for the rearmament envisioned in NSC-68. The actual outbreak of hostilities began a new phase of the Cold War, and closed the book on the era of attempts at Soviet-American cooperation in the immediate aftermath of Hitler's defeat.

The shift to actual armed combat again, less than five years after V-J Day, had deep and long-lasting psychological repercussions. Chief among them was an intensified search for the "Communist enemies" at home who appeared to be linked with the Communism abroad that had forced us once more to take up arms.

Chapter 5

THE COLD WAR AT HOME
1947-1953

THE SPECTATORS WHO COULD CROWD into the hearing room of the House Un-American Activities Committee in the hot final week of August 1948 must have been struck by the odd contrast between the two men whom the members were successively questioning. Whittaker Chambers was rumpled, pudgy, and nervous in manner. His voice was sometimes strained with emotion as he appeared to dredge up his testimony, with pain, from a reservoir of black memories. Alger Hiss, slim and self-assured, appeared to betray no feeling other than irritation at the waste of his time. (When thanked by the chairman at the conclusion of a session, he answered coolly: "I don't reciprocate.") That two such men could ever have been associated seemed unlikely. That they could have been bound in a clandestine brotherhood appeared impossible, a violation of the self-evident fact that they sprang from different worlds.

Yet that, stunningly, was what Chambers was claiming—that twelve years earlier he (then an apparently drifting freelance writer) and Hiss (then a brilliant young lawyer working for the Treasury Department) had been Communists together, fellows in conspiracy and in a common distorted idealism. And as hours and days of testimony went by, it was Chambers who produced what sounded like a wealth of detailed, intimate, and supportive recollection, while Hiss, who steadfastly denied anything but a long-ago casual acquaintance with Chambers, using another name, slipped deeper into failures of recollection or denials contradicted by evidence. Chambers and the committee—especially a young member from California named Richard Nixon—became the pursuers, and Hiss the hunted.

The chase would end, for Alger Hiss, in the penitentiary, convicted of perjury and, by implication, of the far graver crime of espionage. Thirty-two years after those first hearings he would still be protesting his innocence and there would be no final agreement as to where the truth lay. But for both the enemies and the defenders of Hiss, the case worked powerfully upon their imaginations as the symbol of an era.

For Whittaker Chambers went on from the HUAC appearances to broaden his charges. He said that he had received secret documents from Hiss for transmission to a Soviet spymaster. What he was affirming was that the Communism that had recruited him as an anguished intellectual, guilt-stricken by the world's miseries, was not a mere ideology to be recanted on later reflection. It was a worldwide conspiracy in the interests of a totalitarian state. And that state, the Union of Soviet Socialist Republics, had used him and Hiss in its own interests, thus corrupting and betraying their high-minded intentions. So the two young men of the 1930s had become representatives of what the British journalist, Alistair Cooke, labeled "a generation on trial," particularly to those who believed in Hiss's guilt.

But if, on the other hand, Hiss was, as he insisted, the victim of a frame-up, then he stood for an era in which fundamental American freedoms had been trampled—a new Red Scare in which past association with Communist-supported causes became something so sinister that it justified harrying men and women from public life, gainful employment, community standing. For many, the Hiss case seemed to open an "age of suspicion" in which judicial honesty and intellectual freedom were cast away in the indecent pursuit of dissenters, with the performance masked under the title of protecting America's "internal security." That age, culminating around 1954, carried into history the name of the most prominent demagogue it created, Wisconsin Senator Joseph R. McCarthy.

Whatever significance people chose to attach to the years of investigations, trials, and purgations that made the headlines in the Truman and Eisenhower administrations, there was no doubt about one thing: They were the domestic side of the international confrontation between the United States and Russia, and what the two powers seemed to stand for. They were clashes behind the American lines in the Cold War.

What gave the Hiss case such a central role in popular consciousness was the extraordinary saga of anguish, guilt, and redemption that Chambers wove around it, particularly in his autobiography, *Witness*, which became a bestseller upon its publication in 1952. Born in 1901, Chambers had endured a difficult childhood in rural Long Island, helping to supplement the uncertain income of his commercial-artist father by peddling home-grown vegetables. Imaginative, talented, and a loner, he was haunted, like

Dostoevsky's Ivan Karamazov, by a desire for answers to his questions about the causes of human suffering. After high school he tried some manual labor, then a fling at college, then worked his way to hungry post-World War I Germany. There he encountered Marxist literature and a crisis of personal decision: What could he himself do in life about the world's wretchedness? "At that crossroad," he later wrote, "the evil thing, Communism," lay in wait with a simple response.

Chambers returned to America to serve the cause with his pen. Fluent and articulate in several languages, he wrote and edited for the *Daily Worker* and the *New Masses*. But in 1932, he said, there was a momentous change. The Party ordered him to go underground and become a spy. By day he earned a living for his young family as a translator of foreign works, including such tales as *Bambi*. By night he inhabited a dimly lit world of secret meetings with "contacts" known only by first names. In those shadows, he claimed, he dealt with Hiss.

Hiss's life, by contrast, seemed all sunshine (except for shadowed patches like the suicides of a mother and sister). A rich boyhood in Baltimore, academic success at Johns Hopkins, then Harvard Law School, where he became a protégé of Felix Frankfurter and, on graduation, law clerk to Supreme Court Justice Oliver Wendell Holmes. Then the jobs in New Deal Washington: counsel to the Agricultural Adjustment Administration, member of the Senate's Nye Committee (investigating the swollen profits and influence of munitions-makers), then to the Solicitor General's office and finally the State Department. Hiss seemed to be the quintessential brain-trust member, remaking society from his desk while enjoying a social life and Sunday birdwatching with his Quaker wife.

And, said Chambers, helping the Communist Party by providing a car and some rent-free living space for a pseudonymous organizer called "Carl," who was Chambers himself—just the kind of thing a guilty liberal would do for an unsung and impoverished apostle of the new faith, enduring hardship for others' sakes.

The association was not a long one. In 1938 Chambers reached another turning point in his soul's journey. He left the Party, and lived for a time in constant fear of being murdered as a man who knew too much. He carried a gun to his new job as an editor of *Time* magazine, was always watchful for possible "tails," and listened warily to every nighttime sound outside the Maryland farmhouse where he settled. For further protection, he hid some papers that were evidence of his espionage and that would incriminate and identify his pursuers if he should be killed.

In addition, he completed his expiation (he had now became a Quaker himself) by warning the government of potential enemies in its midst. In 1939 he talked to the FBI about his Communist past, and identified Hiss and some others as fellow believers, but he said nothing then about espionage. Nine years passed, during which Hiss went on to new career heights and finally left government work to become the secretary of the prestigious Carnegie Endowment for International Peace. Then, when HUAC began its investigation of alleged Communist penetration of the government, Chambers repeated his story, but again stopped short of accusing Hiss of treason. Only when Hiss sued him for libel did Chambers produce typewritten copies and microfilms (the latter concealed on his farm in a hollowed-out pumpkin) of government documents that he had long kept hidden. He had received them, he said, from Hiss.

The espionage charged by Chambers was too far in the past for prosecution, due to the statute of limitations. But Hiss was indicted for perjury in denying Chambers's accusations. A first trial was held midway through 1949, in the intensifying chill of the Cold War. A key piece of evidence was an old Woodstock typewriter said to have belonged to Hiss and his wife. The government offered expert testimony that some of the "pumpkin papers" had been copied on it. The defense contended that the incriminating Woodstock was no longer in Hiss's possession at the time of the alleged retyping. The jury could not reach a verdict, and a second trial was ordered. In January 1950, Hiss was found guilty and sentenced to five years' imprisonment, which began, after appeals were exhausted, in April 1951.

Far more damning than the mere verdict, however, were the reverberations and ramifications of Chambers's confession. For one thing, he implicated a number of other New Dealers (the highest of them an Assistant Secretary of the Treasury, Harry Dexter White) in Communist activities. His testimony thereby seemed to corroborate that of another informer, Elizabeth Bentley, who told HUAC members (among others) that she had been an underground Communist in Washington in 1938, gathering information for her lover, Jacob Golos, ostensibly a Soviet tourism official but actually a Red intelligence agent. Thanks to closet Marxists in government, including Hiss, she said, "we knew what was going on in the inner chambers of the United States Government up to and including the White House." Such affirmations were jubilantly welcomed by Republicans who had insisted for years that New Dealers and Reds were intimately linked.

But beyond these immediate partisan reactions came even longer-lasting echoes. Whatever its unmeasurable quotient of truth, Chambers's morbid memoir was wrung from an obviously tormented and thoughtful person. He thus lent respectability to other ex-Communist witnesses at trials and hearings throughout the 1950s, including many of considerably less sensitivity and possible credibility. Chambers's story also enhanced the view that the battles over Communism were part of the eternal struggle between light and darkness. He tended to transform political history into demonology, and where there were demons there seemed to be justification for inquisitors. Finally, by exposing certain bookish men and women, members of an elite, who had reasoned themselves into disloyalty, Chambers seemed to accord moral superiority to a simple Americanism that rejected all "alien" subtleties. Whether intentionally or not, he had helped to wipe out any lingering traces of wartime Soviet-American friendship. By exposing (or creating) the "Hiss case" he had reduced the odds in favor of critical examination of even the most bizarre anti-Communist charges. He had licensed Red-hunting at home in the same way that Kennan's "containment" article sanctioned a militant posture abroad.

JUDICIALLY SPEAKING, HOWEVER, the Hiss trials had followed the normal course of perjury prosecutions. Whether the accused had lied might be an issue, but there was no ambiguity about the definition of a lie. In another federal courthouse in 1949, however, a more debatable, disturbing, and theatrical inquest took place. Eleven men—scruffy but respectable-looking in their business suits—went before a jury for their actions as leaders of the Communist Party of the United States of America. They claimed, with passion, that they had merely propagandized on behalf of their candidates for office, as harmlessly—and constitutionally—as Republicans or Democrats. But the government charged that their "political" activities had disguised hidden, violent, and revolutionary purposes. Unlike Hiss, the defendants did not deny certain deeds. The question was one of meaning. It was the federal prosecutors' contention that in the post-1945 world, things were not what they seemed. The Soviet Union was not merely a powerful nation, but a center of global subversion. And the American Communists were not merely vote-seekers, but plotters, who deserved to go to prison.

The source of the trial was the Alien Registration Act of 1940, popularly known as the Smith Act (named for its author, Democratic Representative Howard Smith of Virginia), one section of which made it a crime to teach or advocate the violent overthrow of the government, or to "conspire" to do so. Few had thought then of applying the act to the feeble American Communist Party. It had never polled more than one hundred thousand votes. It had softened its revolutionary tone in favor of a more "American" approach late in the 1930s, and when the U.S.S.R. became America's wartime ally, its critique of capitalism took a distinct

second place to denunciations of the common Fascist enemy. For a
time its minuscule ranks were not even those of a party in the
ordinary sense, but of a mere "political association." But that was
only true until the month after V-E Day, when there were new
orders from Moscow. The Party must reconstitute itself, cast out its
"collaborationist" leader, Earl Browder, and end cooperation with
"class enemies." This, said the federal indictment, was the signal to
launch the "conspiracy." To support this contention, chief prosecutor John F.X. McGohey brought to the witness stand an array of
ex-Communists, at least two of whom had been members while
working for the FBI, and had successfully deluded their comrades
for years. Herbert Philbrick, Angela Calomiris, and Louis Budenz,
among others, testified that the Party's instructions to them were to
infiltrate unions, government agencies, and other institutions clan-
destinely (much as Philbrick and Calomiris had penetrated the
ranks of the Party), there to convert the vulnerable and await the
inevitable postwar depression, a spectre as real to Communists as to
the authors of the Marshall Plan. In the ensuing despair and chaos
they were to foment strikes, create paralysis, and seize power. The
model was 1917 Russia; the working plans were the writings of
Lenin and his associates. Proof of conspiratorial intent was to be
found in the forgeries and aliases employed by the members who
went underground. Even above-board utterances of the Party were
not innocent. Budenz explained that they were cast in "Aesopian
language," that innocuous barbarisms like "revisionism" or "oppor-
tunistic error," used to describe certain leaders' behavior, were
actually cues to how well or poorly they were implementing the
secret program.

The presumed conspirators, all members of the Party's national
executive board, met these charges in two ways. One was simply to
argue that the exhortations of Russian Bolsheviks in 1917 were in no
way intended to be taken as literal prescriptions for action in the
1940s, but were studied and propagated for their historical analyses
and general predictions. The other was to deny the legitimacy of the
entire proceeding, to adopt abrasive and dilatory tactics, and to be,
as one observant reporter, Bruce Bliven, noted, "constantly in
contempt of court except in the narrowest technical sense." For the
first two months of the trial, which began in January of 1949 in New
York, they and their six lawyers daily challenged the jury selection
system, claiming that it was stacked in favor of the affluent. Only
after an endless series of challenges and recesses did they secure
jurors and an alternate who were satisfactory to them—including
three blacks, eight women, and two manual workers. (Only one
juror, Russell Janney, a successful and sixtyish Broadway producer,
was later alleged to have a demonstrable bias.)

Then the defendants proceeded to illustrate their conviction that they were the suckers in a rigged game. They were an interesting assortment of personalities. They had worked variously at trades including those of furrier, lumberjack, metalworker, capmaker, and machinist. Two of them were black, of whom one—Benjamin Davis, Jr.—had been a New York City councilman. Another accused conspirator, Robert Thompson, was a decorated combat veteran. The only woman member of the board, Elizabeth Gurley Flynn, was not there—she would be tried later—and the Party's president and onetime U.S. presidential candidate, William Z. Foster, was likewise absent, too sick with a heart condition to stand trial. But Eugene Dennis, the general secretary, was there, along with John Gates, the editor of the *Daily Worker*.

Together they snickered at government witnesses, fed objections to their counsel, and interspersed their testimony with long harangues, couched in what an unfriendly news magazine called "ideological gobbledy-gook" that would look good in next morning's *Worker*. Among other things, they probably hoped to bait the presiding judge, Harold R. Medina, into angry outbursts that would justify a reversal on appeal. But though Judge Medina described their behavior, at various times, as "dilatory," "impertinent," "confusing," "repetitious," and "disorderly," he would not be goaded into judicial error. The contest between the bench and the defense, in fact, furnished the best drama of the agonizingly long trial.

For Medina was certainly, in his own eyes, a fine example of the success of "the American way." He was Brooklyn-born, to a Mexican father in the import business and a Dutch mother. He went to military school and then to Princeton. After his 1909 graduation came Columbia Law School, and years of hard work that led ultimately to a $100,000 annual income and a life-style that included a Long Island home, sailboats, and a midtown apartment. While he must certainly have found the defendants' diatribes exasperating, he responded to their jabs with patience and in a low voice, though at times he was obliged to declare recesses during which he could seethe privately in his chambers.

Pink-faced, moustached, and bespectacled, Medina looked like a kindly grandfather. Only in his charge to the jury did he appear to betray some prejudgment of the case. He told the jurors that they were not to decide whether Communist doctrine imperiled the republic (the premise of the Smith Act). That was already a matter of law. They were only to find if the defendants had in fact planned to say things "calculated" to produce the danger that congressional statute already insisted was clear and present. Since the Party leaders had hardly denied their interest in furthering Communism, this left little to decide. It was not really surprising when, in October, the jury's black forewoman read out a verdict of guilty on all counts. Medina sentenced ten of the guilty to five-year prison terms and $5,000 fines, but gave war veteran Thompson only three years. Then, with infinite satisfaction, he dealt out contempt-of-court jailings of thirty days to six months to the attorneys.

So the main show was over. Civil libertarians took exception to a general chorus of editorial approval, noting that the issue had never been one of Communist manners or sense of fairness (the defendants themselves having heartily approved of earlier Smith Act prosecution of "Trotskyite" members of the Socialist Workers Party). Rather, they said, the question was whether or not the United States had suppressed legitimate political activities on extremely thin grounds.

The Supreme Court, in 1951, said that the United States had not. In U.S. v. Dennis, it upheld the convictions, with only Justices Black and Douglas dissenting. Black's opinion hoped that, in calmer times, different views would be entertained. Douglas held that the Party was probably "the least thriving of any fifth column in history." As it turned out, Black's wish was fulfilled. In 1957, in another case (Yates v. the U.S.), a Court whose personnel had somewhat changed ruled that the prosecution must prove the advocacy of some particular action, not merely of the general desirability of upheaval. Under this more precise definition of the "crime," proof became far more difficult and the legal assault on the Party ended.

In the interim, however, Communist leaders had been zealously pursued. Seventeen "second-string" members of the Party's command structure were tried in 1952 in New York, and there was still a third Smith Act trial in the federal courthouse in Manhattan's Foley Square in 1956. Other Communists were brought to the bar of justice in Honolulu, Seattle, Los Angeles, San Francisco, Cleveland, and Baltimore. In all, there were 145 indictments brought between 1948 and 1956, and 108 convictions. Only ten were acquitted; the others who escaped sentencing did so on technical grounds. A total of $435,000 in fines was levied. Twenty-eight men and women actually went to jail. It was a modest enough purge by totalitarian standards, but the fact remained that not a single defendant had committed a violent deed, but only planned to present ideas that might result in violence. And if federal judges were so ready to go along with what was essentially thought control, it was no surprise that state anti-Communist ordinances should flourish and deprive a large number of people of jobs in teaching, government service, or "sensitive" industries. Or that the public at large came to identify Communism with treason automatically. Between 1949 and 1952 various Gallup polls showed that as many as 52 percent of a cross-section of respondents were willing to jail all Communists, 68 percent would outlaw the Party, and as many as 80 percent would at least strip its members of citizenship—although only 3 percent had ever actually met a Communist. The Smith Act trials might not have imprisoned many Communists, but they had obviously taught their lesson.

A third trial of the peak years of Soviet-American tension was not widely noted during its progress, but provoked the greatest judicial hysteria, the harshest sentence, and the most bitter aftermath of all. It was the prosecution and execution of two unprepossessing New York radicals, Julius and Ethel Rosenberg, charged with being, in headline parlance, "atom spies."

Their arrest was the end of a kind of "chain reaction." In 1949 a German-born British scientist, Klaus Fuchs, was seized in Great Britain, charged with espionage. He confessed and received a fourteen-year sentence. Since he had worked at Los Alamos on the American atom bomb project, Fuchs was interrogated by the FBI in his English prison. What he said was kept under security wraps, but it apparently included an admission of passing secrets, for transmission to the Soviet vice-consul in New York. His courier, the FBI claimed, was a chemist named Harry Gold. Gold, when arrested, was said to have named a machinist and draftsman at Los Alamos, David Greenglass, as an accomplice. And when the FBI picked up Greenglass, in June 1950, he told them—they said—that he had been induced to join the "ring" by his sister and her husband, the Rosenbergs. Greenglass's statement also led to the arrest of another New York left-winger, Morton Sobell.

Julius and Ethel were representative of the young idealists swept into Communism in the Depression years—and likewise fitted to perfection the stereotype of the "New York Jewish Red" nursed by right-wingers. Both were the children of impoverished immigrants, scraping their way toward a better life. Ethel Greenglass wanted to sing, act, compose, write poetry—but reality pushed her into the working world in 1931 at the age of fifteen. She showed a streak of toughness, leading a strike of 150 women against her boss, and getting fired at its conclusion. Julius, slightly younger, had attended religious schools as a child, but turned from the Talmud to social agitation and the Young Communist's League. At New York's yeasty City College he divided his time between an electrical engineering major and a political life of meetings, rallies, and appeals. He met Ethel at one of them, and the two were married soon after his graduation (near the foot of his class) in 1939. He found work as a civilian employee of the U.S. Army Signal Corps in Brooklyn. For a time both newlyweds openly sold subscriptions to the *Daily Worker* and collected funds for known "front" organizations. But when the

Army fired Julius as a Communist in 1945, he denied Party membership.

At first glance the Rosenbergs seemed to be simple-minded believers in the Party's platitudes. When finally tried for conspiracy to commit espionage, Julius testified: "I felt that the Soviet government had improved the lot of the underdog . . . made a lot of progress in eliminating illiteracy . . . contributed a major share in destroying the Hitler beast." These were, in fact, officially encouraged views during the war, and seemingly harmless.

But David Greenglass said otherwise on the witness stand. He and his wife Ruth swore that Julius had informed him, in 1944, that the project under way at Los Alamos was the creation of an atomic bomb, and that it was important for the sake of world peace that the Soviet Union share in the knowledge gained there. David, then in the army, was casting various models of high-explosive "lens molds"—devices to focus a small conventional explosion within the bomb that would trigger the atomic blast. Julius urged David to learn all he could about the application of his work, to pick up more information as unobtrusively as possible in conversations with scientists at the facility, and then to pass along the results, through Ruth, to a messenger, whom he would arrange to have sent out to New Mexico. (The man who appeared, after Greenglass agreed to go along, was Harry Gold.) Julius and Ethel boasted of having important friends in the Soviet Union who recognized the value of their efforts. Moreover, according to both Greenglasses, when the news of Gold's arrest nearly six years later made it clear that exposure was imminent, Julius urged them to flee the country and offered money, obviously from Soviet sources. Instead, the Greenglasses chose to stay and confess.

The Rosenbergs' defense was total denial of any complicity. The Greenglasses (and Gold) had been spies, perhaps, but when caught they chose to lighten their punishment by helping the FBI to frame a pair of fellow radicals who happened to be related to them. The U.S. government's purpose was to lend credibility to the claim that Communism equaled treason. Such was the argument of the accused pair and their counsel. Whether it was true or not, the trial could hardly have been held at a worse time for the accused. When they were arrested in mid-1950, the United States had just become involved in war with the Communist People's Republic of Korea, a Soviet satellite better known as North Korea. By the time the court convened the following March, there had been desperate seesaw fighting, intervention by Communist China, and a bloody stalemate midway up the Korean peninsula. Moreover, the shock of knowing that the Russians had an atomic bomb was still fresh. The public mood was fearful and unforgiving. Communist weapons were killing American soldiers. Someone had "lost" China; someone had given the secret of the bomb to the "backward" Russians; someone ought to suffer.

"Someone" turned out to be the Rosenbergs. On March 29, 1951, the jury returned a guilty verdict. Judge Irving R. Kaufman, in delivering the sentence, unburdened himself of a stinging anti-Communist diatribe. He lashed out at the couple before him for having "made a choice of devoting themselves to the Russian ideology of denial of God, denial of the sanctity of the individual," and of furthering the "basic Marxist goal of world revolution." By their "diabolical conspiracy to destroy a God-fearing nation" they had put nuclear weapons in the Kremlin's hands "years before our best scientists predicted," and they were therefore guilty of encouraging aggression in Korea and costing the lives of thousands of Americans. For such offenses, Kaufman grimly concluded, the appropriate penalty was death. Julius and Ethel were sent to New York State's Sing Sing prison to await electrocution.

The harangue owed something to Kaufman's natural feelings, and, some insinuated, to his desire to show anti-Semites that, while all the culprits in the case were Jewish, there were Jews like himself (and prosecuting attorneys Irving Saypol and Roy Cohn) who were unflinching Americans. Even so, the harshness of the sentence was a shock. Even if espionage had taken place and had made a difference in the pace of Russian research (an unprovable point), the other conspirators, Greenglass, Gold, and Sobell—a minor figure—got off with prison terms. The death sentence was not mandatory under the statutes violated. Russia was not an enemy nation at the time of the presumed crime. And finally, there was an especially strong motive for leniency because of the two small sons of the Rosenbergs, who would be orphaned.

But none of these arguments moved Kaufman. Nor did challenges to the trial record succeed in producing a reversal of the verdict despite numerous appeals taken as high as the Supreme Court, which twice found no cause for review. Nor did a petition to President Dwight Eisenhower in February of 1953, one month after he took office, persuade him to executive clemency. Meanwhile, during the two years following the sentence, the Rosenbergs—followers of causes—became one themselves. Their execution was protested by Communists, of course, but also by a variety of figures as diverse as Pope Pius XII and Albert Einstein. Worldwide demonstrations were held in their behalf. From their cells they wrote each other letters of touching devotion, laced with stilted and affectingly naïve passages of self-magnification. "Together," said Ethel, "we hunted down the answers to all the seemingly insoluble riddles which a complex and callous society presented. . . . It is because we didn't hesitate to blazon forth those answers that we sit within the walls of Sing Sing." And Julius: "Our case is being used as a camouflage to paralyze outspoken progressives and stifle criticism of the drive to atomic war."

Though a commutation of sentence was supposedly offered, at least for Ethel, in exchange for a confession, the two insisted on their innocence and, in consequence, their martyrdom. At 8 P.M. on a muggy June 19, 1953, the same day that a specially convoked meeting of the recessed Supreme Court hastily turned down a last bid for reconsideration, the Rosenbergs went to the electric chair.

The Hiss and Rosenberg cases in particular were the most spectacular judicial shows of the early Cold War period. They were the chief means by which government prosecutors—helped by ex-Communist informers—demonstrated what they perceived as the fatal linkages among liberalism, Communism, subversion, and espionage (much as prohibition lecturers had once traced the downward course from the first, innocent drink to a lonely, crazed death in the poorhouse).

But there were also other, later-forgotten cases, that supposedly taught the same lesson. One involved Judith Coplon, a brilliant 1943 Barnard graduate, described in her yearbook as "deeply philosophical about the fundamentals of life." She went to work for the Department of Justice and, in March of 1949, was arrested for passing secret counterintelligence memoranda to her lover, Valentin Gubichev, a Russian engineer working for the UN. She was convicted, but was later freed on a technicality.

And there was William Remington's ordeal, sometimes called the "little Hiss case." It also seemed to hint that academic excellence was the seedbed of "un-American" behavior. Remington, a star Dartmouth graduate of the 1930s, had gone to work in New Deal Washington and, like Hiss, progressed through several agencies, landing in 1948 in the Commerce Department with a bright future beckoning. Then Elizabeth Bentley implicated him as a member of her coterie of spies.

Remington was suspended, but cleared after exhaustive review by a federal loyalty board. Moreover, he sued Bentley for libel, and won. No matter; his troubles were not over. There were fresh Bentley charges that he denied. The government indicted him for perjury, and at the trial got his estranged wife to support parts of Bentley's story. (Saypol and Cohn were again the prosecuting team.) Remington was found guilty. A higher court overturned the conviction, but let the indictment stand, and the United States, remorseless as Ahab, bored in and finally got its man. A second trial brought conviction and a three-year sentence, and late in 1953 Remington entered Lewisburg Penitentiary where Hiss was a fellow prisoner. The next year an unknown inmate murdered Remington with a brick wrapped in a sock.

Such were some of the responses of the judicial system to the Cold War, counterparts to the executive loyalty program launched in 1947. The legislative answer to the anti-Communist summons was even more far-ranging and politically significant. But even outside the halls of government there was furious action. Official heresy-hunting was not enough. Communism as a virus infecting such institutions as schools and unions had to be—and was—purged.

THE HISTORY OF THE UNION MOVEMENT from 1947 to 1954 was an especially lush illustration of the self-policing that Cold War law and custom encouraged—a case study of what was also happening in educational institutions and government bureaucracies. Both the AFL and the CIO had emerged from the war with expanded membership and high confidence. But their hopes were shaken by the election of a Republican Eightieth Congress in 1946. It was Republican (and Southern conservative Democratic) gospel that the New Deal had been too "pro-labor," and the Taft-Hartley Act of June 1947 was supposed to redress the balance by banning such union activities as secondary boycotts and mass picketing. But the new law also reflected another long-cherished notion that unions, especially those of the CIO, were tainted with what the United States Chamber of Commerce called "Marxist economics."

To neutralize that toxin the act required every union official to sign an oath that he was not a member or affiliate of the Communist Party or of any organization that preached "the overthrow of the United States government by force or by any illegal or unconstitutional means." A union whose officers did not do so was rendered ineffective, since it could not be certified as a bargaining agent by the National Labor Relations Board. The penalty for a false oath was a $10,000 fine or ten years in jail.

There were objections to the affidavits on various grounds. Unions as wholly unradical as the United Mine Workers or International Typographical Union saw no more reason for labor officials to swear fidelity than for corporation directors or managers. Other unions did, in fact, have Communists and former Communists among their leaders (often seasoned and diligent veterans), and these men and women insisted that they could simultaneously be Communists and good trade unionists. They denied the prevalent view that by definition a "Red" unionist had a single goal: to make trouble at Moscow's instigation.

Such denials were in vain. The union "brass" quickly endorsed the orthodox view. The CIO's Philip Murray denounced Communists as "skulking cowards . . . lying out of the pits of their dirty bellies." The CIO's Walter Reuther declared: "We must get the Communists out of the political back alleys and walk them up Main Street in the full light of informed opinion." Such statements undoubtedly rested on personal conviction, but owed a good deal to political considerations as the 1948 election approached. The Democrats—whom the CIO's Political Action Committee heavily backed—were determined to seize the anti-Communist issue from their opponents and did. Truman's surprising victory seemed to validate that strategy and so, partly as a result, at the CIO's national convention of 1949 (addressed warmly by Dean Acheson and Chief of Staff General Omar Bradley), eleven unions branded as Communist-controlled were expelled from the body, and committees were formed to investigate the status of others. The AFL was not outdone—over half its unions, within the next five years, amending their constitutions to ban Communists or their "advocates" or "supporters" from office.

Reuther disavowed "repression" as a goal, but the ousted unions had reason to think otherwise. The United Electrical Workers, for example, found itself challenged by a new, rival CIO union, the International Union of Electrical Workers, as well as the AFL's International Brotherhood of Electrical Workers. It lost members to these competitors until, in 1955, it was down to some ninety thousand, or only one-tenth of their combined strength. In like fashion the United Fur and Leather Workers and the Mine, Mill, and Smelter Workers were pummeled. The Fur Workers were so heavily raided by the Amalgamated Meat Cutters that they broke up in 1954. The maritime unions, historically pugnacious, came under heavy attack. The International Longshoremen's and Warehousemen's Union was thrown out of the CIO, and its leader, Australian-born Harry Bridges, was stripped of CIO posts and subjected by the government to deportation proceedings, which he repeatedly fought off in the courts.

The United States, as in Bridges's case, rendered various kinds of help to union anti-Communist drives. There was further legislation, such as a Communist Control Act of 1954, which imposed even tougher restrictions than Taft-Hartley on "Communist-infiltrated" unions. One proof of such infiltration was the appearance of members' names on the Attorney General's list of "subversive" organizations. Originally the list had merely been advisory, simply suggesting to federal loyalty boards that an active role in, say, the American Council for a Democratic Greece might be something that warranted further scrutiny. But as time went on, it was assumed to be a checklist of "fronts" and an absolute test of disloyalty. (Eventually, the courts rejected this proposition as inconsistent with the First Amendment, but only in the late 1950s.)

Congressional committees, too, aided the unions' "housecleaning" by timely investigations in which reputed Communist officials would be publicly grilled about their membership, and would often refuse to testify under the Fifth Amendment privilege against self-incrimination (a prudent precaution in view of the Smith Act, or possible perjury prosecutions for denying accusations against them). Such "uncooperative" witnesses were then promptly fired from their jobs.

There were also additional special screening programs for workers in plants holding contracts under the defense or atomic energy programs, or in the critical shipping industry. An Industrial Personnel Security Program required "clearance" review for such employees. Some of the probing was done by examiners provided by the armed services, and some by private detective agencies hired by the employers, a potentially useful union-busting tactic for helping to isolate and get rid of "agitators." Under the Port Security Program established by an act of 1950, panels of Coast Guard officers investigated up to half a million merchant seamen and dockworkers and denied some 3,800 of them the right to work. The procedures employed offered few legal safeguards to those accused. And few of the victims had the resources to contest their dismissals in lawsuits.

The impact of the various clearance programs went beyond the mere dismissals themselves. Many workers, denied clearances, found themselves unemployable elsewhere. Others, after "exposure," were harassed by fellow employees. The atmosphere created was one of a constant credit check where, as one private screening company put it, a radical had a low rating—and where the penalty was not the denial of loans, but of livelihood. The unmistakable message was that it was healthy to agree with the official government line. "I would like to know," asked one Mine, Mill, and Smelter Workers official plaintively, "where in . . . the constitution of the CIO it says that we have to support the Marshall Plan?"

The key was the belief in the Soviet menace: the sense of outside events dictating internal changes. In January 1947, liberals for Truman founded Americans for Democratic Action, a group of articulate political elitists that clearly aimed to counter the influence of Henry Wallace's recently created Progressive Citizens of America. The ADA announced portentously: "The interests of the United States are the interests of free men everywhere." Domestic politics merged with the need to meet the international threat. From there it was easy to go on and accept the premise that the Smith Act was really a shield against foreign conspiracies, that American Communists, even when openly soliciting votes, were not the equivalent of ordinary political opponents. Much of the ADA's basic foreign policy argument, namely that resisting totalitarianism was the highest priority, was echoed and amplified by student associations, union-run programs of international education, and the publications of university research centers. It was not publicly known at the time that these organizations were surreptitiously getting some funds from the CIA. But even had that connection been known, the mood of the moment would quite possibly have accepted the justification later offered by a CIA official whose explanation was simple enough. "What you were made to feel," he said, looking back, "was that the country was in desperate peril and we had to do whatever it took to save it." Under that logic, most public figures allowed the need for anti-Communist orthodoxy to overcome any possible libertarian misgivings on grounds of overriding necessity. Self-censorship became the order of the day.

BY THE SUMMER OF 1948 the political potential of anti-Communism was rapidly becoming more evident than ever. Henry Wallace never freed himself of the albatross of Communist support, and the smallness of his vote contributed to Truman's surprising victory over Dewey. But the election result, though hailed as a liberal triumph, did not signal a truce in the war on "subversion." Liberals seemed eager, in fact, to prevent right-wingers from preempting the issue. Their ambivalence toward dissent was reflected by Truman himself. In his usual salty style he dismissed the clamor of Communist penetration of government as a red herring. Yet he began the loyalty checks on federal employees. His Department of Justice (and FBI) briskly pursued Hiss, Remington, Communist leaders, and "atom spies." And his Attorney General, J. Howard McGrath, declared: "There are today many Communists in America. They are every-where—in factories, offices, butcher shops, on street corners, in private business—and each carries in himself the germs of death for society." Sometimes it seemed that only Republican "Red-baiting" was anathema to the President.

Congressional Democrats, too, were in a prosecutorial mood. Thirty-eight anti-Communist bills were introduced into the Eighty-first Congress. The one that finally emerged bore the name of Nevada's deeply conservative, Catholic, Franco-admiring, and Democratic Senator Pat McCarran.

The McCarran Act (or Internal Security Act of 1950) declared in its preamble that Communism was a worldwide conspiracy to create a dictatorship in the United States through sabotage, terrorism, and infiltration. The law created a five-man Subversive Activities Control Board that could identify Communist, "Communist-front," and "Communist-infiltrated" organizations. Their members, like those of the Party itself, would then be required by the Attorney

General to register, in effect as conspirators acting for a foreign government. In addition, the measure gave immigration authorities virtually unchecked power to arrest and deport resident aliens suspected of Communist activities, or to bar the entry of any foreign visitors associated with "totalitarian" organizations abroad. Finally, there was a provision under which, in times of invasion, insurrection, or "national emergency," the President was empowered to throw Communists, without trial, into detention camps. Further provisions included denial of any federal job to a member of an SACB-branded "front" organization, and a requirement that such organizations stamp their "Communist" identification on anything they mailed out.

To his credit, Truman vetoed this legislative assault on the First and Fifth Amendments. He said, in fact, that the registration provisions were akin to asking thieves to "register" with the sheriff. Yet only seven Senators—all Democrats—voted against the McCarran Act, one of them being Glen Taylor of Idaho, Wallace's running mate. And only three more had the courage to reverse themselves, fruitlessly, to sustain the veto—one being Hubert Humphrey.

The legacy of the act was a great deal of litigation. In the end none of the twenty-three organizations ordered to register did so, and the courts eventually sustained them, though the process took years. In addition, international scientific and cultural gatherings in the U.S. were troubled by the visa difficulties imposed on suspect foreign intellectuals. (Among those barred was Pablo Picasso. Among those who made it after much difficulty were such distinguished novelists as Alberto Moravia and Graham Greene.)

The more lasting congressional contribution to the public safety from Communism came in the form of the klieg-lit hearings of the House Un-American Activities Committee into what it deemed Red poisoning of the American mind by Hollywood. In its first assault of 1947, HUAC was armed with the names of a number of screenwriters who had actually joined the Party in the 1930s and early 1940s. Ten of these refused to testify on First Amendment grounds—they called the probe an unconstitutional test of their political lives—and they went to jail for contempt of Congress. In one of the few humorous episodes of the period, the HUAC chairman at the time, Representative J. Parnell Thomas, was subsequently convicted of payroll padding, and shared time in the Danbury, Connecticut, federal prison with Ring Lardner, Jr., one of the Hollywood Ten. HUAC resumed the hearings, under new leadership, in 1951. This time a mostly contrite parade of witnesses either identified others as former fellow travelers and "front" members, or took the Fifth Amendment privilege of silence. These latter were promptly blacklisted by the industry, as were dozens, even hundreds, of actors, writers, and directors who were named as Red-tainted, and could not clear themselves. No specific evidence ever showed that those condemned for years to joblessness and despair had ever produced a frame of film at Communist instigation.

When the 1952 election returned the Republicans to the White House for the first time in twenty years, both President Eisenhower and his Attorney General, Herbert Brownell, were ready and willing to continue with the enforcement of loyalty. A new Executive Order Number 10450 broadened and extended the Truman program. A fresh category of dismissable employees was created, that of the "security risk." A security risk was someone whose past conduct was not in question, but who might, in the future, disclose classified information through carelessness or under the pressure of blackmail—in short, a person with psychological or alcoholic problems, or, in that less open era, a homosexual. During investigation a suspected security risk was suspended without pay, a practice that forced many to resign so that they might earn a living elsewhere.

In all, some 6,000 civil servants quit and about 1,500 were dismissed under Eisenhower. Vice President Nixon happily announced: "We're kicking the Communists and fellow travelers and security risks out of the Government . . . by the thousands." But, in fact, the totals were close to those of the Truman years. Among the various charges brought against the alleged security risks were: contributing to a defense fund for Harry Bridges, reading books by the Communist novelist Howard Fast, and listening to records by the outspokenly pro-Soviet artist, Paul Robeson.

But the most celebrated casualty of the new program was no obscure bureaucrat. It was J. Robert Oppenheimer. On December 23, 1953, his security clearance was "temporarily" suspended. By that time Oppenheimer had left full-time government service to become director of the renowned Institute of Advanced Studies at Princeton. He had long been a thorn in the side of security officers. Multilingual, widely read in both the humanities and sciences, he had publicly supported Communist causes while teaching at the Berkeley Radiation Laboratory of the University of California before the war. He was married to a former Communist and had encouraged and protected several students who were, in all probability, also Communists. The government had swallowed hard and overlooked this dossier when bringing Oppenheimer into the Manhattan Project that created the A-bomb, because his skills were indispensable. In the words of one project official, a convicted murderer with the right qualifications would have been cleared.

In the postwar era Oppenheimer had run into trouble. His initial opposition to the H-bomb was resented by conservative members of

the Atomic Energy Commission. Moreover, his intellectually dis-
dainful treatment of the AEC's 1952 chairman, Lewis Strauss, a
former admiral and conceited autocrat, had filled Strauss with
hostility. When Oppenheimer challenged the suspension of his
security clearance the AEC was obliged to conduct hearings, but
did so under rules that worked to Oppenheimer's disadvantage. His
attorney was not cleared, and therefore was denied access to key
parts of the testimony for possible exploration and rebuttal.

All of Oppenheimer's old associations were once again examined,
especially one damning wartime incident in which he allegedly had
been approached by a fellow traveler with a veiled proposition to
leak atomic data. Oppenheimer had dutifully reported the matter to
security officers, but had given several conflicting and untruthful
versions, to protect others involved. ("I was an idiot," he explained
at the hearings.) Primarily on this ground, and despite almost
universal support from other scientists, the final commission report
found that Oppenheimer's behavior exceeded the "limits of
prudence and self-restraint." He was no longer worthy to be trusted
with official secrets. And so, to a far, far greater extent than Hiss,
whose attainments were less significant, Oppenheimer became an
example of an intellectual-in-government whose past connections
made him a Cold War casualty.

Over the Oppenheimer hearings a shadow had loomed, spurring
the Commission to weigh the balance in favor of "security." The
shadow belonged to a late boarder of the anti-Communist band-
wagon. This was the junior Senator from Wisconsin, Joseph R.
McCarthy. He had been elected in 1946, partly as the result of
accusing his campaign opponent of being "used by the Communist-
controlled PAC [Political Action Committee]" of the CIO. Yet
McCarthy did not discover the full potential of what news analyst
Richard Rovere called his "oil gusher," the Communist threat, for
almost three years. Then, early in 1950, in a routine speech to a West
Virginia audience, he attracted newspaper attention by claiming
that the Truman Department of State was still employing 205 known
Communists. He had in his hand, he said—gesturing—a list of their
names.

The celebrated "list" was illustrative of a basic McCarthy tactic,
the simple lie. Pressed later to elaborate his claim, he declared that
the alleged 205 were merely security risks. Then he juggled the
figures—down to 57, up to 81. In the end, it turned out, he had
simply cited a 1946 figure of persons under investigation. The
fifty-odd still working at State four years later had all been
cleared.

McCarthy's other major device was the claim that made headlines
by its dazzling outrageousness. He was willing to tackle big targets.

Dean Acheson himself, despite his vigorous anti-Soviet stance, became the victim of a McCarthy assault as "the great Red Dean." Even the respected General Marshall was denounced for such sins as urging a second front in 1944, pressing at Yalta for Soviet participation in the Pacific war, and attempting to negotiate peace between Chiang Kai-shek and the Chinese Communists. The attacks on the State Department coalesced in an overall charge that all the melancholy events in foreign relations after 1945—the "loss" of Eastern Europe and China, the Soviet nuclear bomb, and the Korean War—were not accidental, but engineered. They were part of a "conspiracy on a scale so immense as to dwarf any previous such venture in the history of man."

McCarthy's standard riposte to critics was to point out that Communists also attacked him, and therefore his enemies must automatically be Communism's friends. Time magazine, for example, made some negative judgments on McCarthy. He replied that while the Luce publication might "throw pebbles at Communism generally," it would also "parallel the Daily Worker's smear attack upon individuals who start to dig out dangerous secret Communists," thereby rendering "almost unlimited service to the Communist cause."

For a time this style rendered the Senator formidable. A bearish, dark-jowled man, his deliberately rough-and-tumble approach appealed to a recurrent strain in American thought—a dark thread of distrust of the nonmuscular: of intellectuals, Easterners, "striped-pants" diplomats, tea drinkers, Ivy League snobs, homosexuals. McCarthy was perceived by numerous voters as a forthright he-man, unafraid to tackle skunks. They sustained him against his foes. When, after a 1951 investigation, the Senate Foreign Relations Committee dismissed his charges against Acheson, McCarthy took out after its chairman, Maryland's Millard Tydings—and Tydings lost his next election. It became conventional wisdom that to defy McCarthy was a high political risk. In 1952, General Eisenhower, campaigning in Wisconsin as the Republican presidential candidate, was even persuaded by nervous advisers to greet the Senator, although Eisenhower was infuriated by the McCarthy attack on his old friend and mentor, Marshall. And more—Eisenhower deleted a favorable paragraph about Marshall from a speech delivered on that leg of the campaign tour.

Reelected in 1952, and given the chair of a Senate Committee on Government Operations (almost no Senator dared vote against liberal funding of the committee), McCarthy continued to reap headlines and terrify the bureaucracy, especially in the State Department. To the dismay of many Republicans, McCarthy continued his battle as if there had been no change in the political complexion of Washington. Under McCarthy pressure the department's chief security officer, an ex-FBI man named Scott McLeod, demoted or fired several Far Eastern experts whose error had been to report accurately the impending Communist victory in China, and urge accommodation with the new regime.

McCarthy finally overreached himself, however. He apparently did not realize the extent to which some Republicans—who had privately disapproved of him but found him useful before 1952— were changing their minds. And since, strangely, he seemed to bear no personal malice toward his targets, he could not understand the gathering backlash of hostility to him. In 1953, looking for fresh woods and new pastures, he opened an attack on the Army for allegedly sheltering Communists in its Signal Corps electronic research installations. This time he met with White House-approved resistance. A series of televised hearings followed in which the impact of the new medium was given early demonstration. Millions now saw McCarthy's hectoring and bullying directly for the first time—such as his tongue-lashing of a decorated general (who had promoted a "pink" Army dentist) with the words: "You are a disgrace to the uniform." On one memorable afternoon the Army's counsel, Joseph Welch, a cherubic-looking but scrappy Bostonian gentleman in his sixties, went after the Senator, who had just smeared one of Welch's young colleagues. "At long last, sir," cried Welch, "have you no sense of decency left? Have you no sense of decency?" The chamber burst into spontaneous applause, while McCarthy looked on, uncomprehending.

His public support weakened, McCarthy suddenly became vulnerable. The Senate itself now investigated his previous conduct. Still full of what Welch had earlier called his "recklessness," McCarthy fought back with his usual bellowings. He referred to one senatorial adversary, Missouri's Thomas Hennings, as "a living miracle, without brains or guts." On December 2, 1954, the Senate responded to assault on its own majesty by passing a vote of censure against McCarthy, 67 to 22. Every Democratic Senator—and exactly half the Republicans—voted aye. McCarthy was ineffective thereafter, and drank himself to an early death in 1957.

In an odd coincidence, the censure vote came in the same week that Alger Hiss was released from Lewisburg and William Remington was killed there. A period was ending, or at least there was a change in the air. McCarthy's reign was the climax of the age of suspicion, the era in which almost any deviation from a strong anti-Communist line was suspect. He had, possibly, helped to end it by his very exaggerations and the reaction they finally provoked, though with the perversity of history, many people would call the entire episode of heresy-hunting by the name "McCarthyism."

There were other reasons, too, why the fever abated somewhat in 1954. It had reached some natural limits. Antibodies in the political system had had time to develop. And more. The fuel that fed McCarthy, especially when he saw betrayal in Asia, had been the bitter war in Korea, which had harshly confronted Americans with defeats and limited expectations. That war had reached its formal end in mid-1953. But its aftereffects would linger on. It had, in many ways, besides the spurring on of McCarthy, deeply changed the pattern of twentieth-century United States history.

Chapter 6

THE KOREAN TEST
1950-1953

HE WAS FIFTY YEARS OLD, and he had soldiered in some hard places, but General William Dean had never seen anything as bad as what was around him in the exploding, bullet-swept town of Taejon, Korea, this 20th of July, 1950.

Only four weeks earlier he and his 24th U.S. Infantry Division had been part of General Douglas MacArthur's 83,000 garrison troops in Japan. His men were in good measure teen-agers, ripened just too late for involvement in World War II, and like all occupation forces, they had been bored, diverting themselves with local girlfriends, plenty of beer, joyriding. Then on June 25, hell had broken loose in Korea. Armored columns from the Democratic People's Republic of Korea, a Soviet satellite, had smashed southward in a surprise attack on the Republic of Korea, an American- and UN-sponsored nation that took up the half of the Korean peninsula south of the 38th parallel. "North Korea" and "South Korea," as they were more compactly described in headlines, were in fact parts of a single country, divided "temporarily" between Russian and American armies in 1945 and then, like Germany, locked into the split by the Cold War. Now North Korea had struck to force unification on Communist terms.

Within hours, Harry Truman had told MacArthur to assist the South Koreans. Then the UN Security Council authorized member nations to contribute troops to repulse the "illegal" attack. It was not supposed to be a war, but a "police action." One of Dean's GI's spluttered to a war correspondent: "Some cops! Some robbers!"

Dean's job was to stall the "robbers," and buy time to organize a defense. With the help of the Air Force's strafing P-51s and new, jet-powered F-80s, it was supposed to be easy. It wasn't.

The North Koreans had Russian T-34 tanks, well manned, and able to outgun American defenders. They were good at dispersing and taking cover. And when Dean's units, fed piecemeal into action, set up roadblocks, something bad happened. At night North Korean infantrymen filtered around the American flanks, climbing ridges, eating what they found in villages, drafting civilians to carry shells and gasoline cans, one by one, over narrow trails. Except for the tanks, the North Koreans didn't seem to need roads as the Americans did, nor supply dumps, aid stations, motor pools, message centers, or a huge supporting network of noncombat personnel.

Dean had learned how easy it was for his troops to be overpowered because they weren't prepared to scramble up steep slopes and through rice paddies stinking of human manure in 80-degree heat. Nor were they ready to move with their many vehicles over roads jammed with refugees, some of whom were disguised guerrillas, or to fight as isolated groups, separated by mountains that blocked communications. In their unreadiness, companies and battalions were collapsing, and some individual soldiers were already known to be flinging down weapons and "bugging out."

Dean was doing what he could to bolster morale in person this July 20th. He had come up from his division HQ into beleaguered Taejon, carrying a 3.5-inch bazooka to show his men, by example, that its rocket could stop T-34s, and to make sure that his orders were getting through in the chaos of retreat, as U.S. and South Korean troops fell back.

But generals were not supposed to be so far forward, and Dean soon paid for his rashness. His position was overrun. Racing toward safety through an inferno of burning buildings, sprawled corpses, and shrieking refugees, Dean's driver became lost. For three weeks the general was missing in action, wandering the countryside, losing 70 pounds, until he was betrayed by peasants to North Korean captors.

Dean was lost in a new kind of political and military landscape, as well as in Korea's rough terrain. He was caught in a war by proxy, a war without formal declaration or clear objectives, a civil struggle in which allies and enemies looked identical. He, like his country, was embroiled in a conflict that could neither be won nor lost. It was a special agony new in the national experience.

Following closely on the downfall of Chiang Kai-shek's Nationalist China, the explosion in Korea had come as a special jolt to Americans. Yet Chinese and Korean developments were actually episodes in a wider, continuing upheaval in Asia, triggered by World War II. That story, with roots of its own, was largely ignored or oversimplified by an Atlantic-centered United States press steeped in Cold War assumptions.

After Pearl Harbor, it had taken the Japanese only six months in

1942 to wipe out the Dutch, French, and many of the British outposts of empire in Southeast Asia. It was abundantly clear after Tokyo's surrender in 1945 that the peoples of Malaysia, Indonesia, and Indochina would never willingly accept the restoration of colonial rule. But what would fill its place? The politics of liberation swirled around two poles. At one of them stood strong Asian figures who combined traditional authority with modern techniques of subjugation. They included former native leaders who had been supported by the Europeans, and the Asian bankers, businessmen, and generals who had partly shared in the profits and culture of imperialism. These men used the slogans of nationalism, and also of Christianity and democracy, no matter how autocratically they might behave in practice.

Against them were other nationalists and "rebels." Many of them professed to be Communists, meaning that they shared in yet another Western philosophy—and some had actually learned their Marxism in the Soviet Union. They tended to seek support among the dispossessed, primarily the hard-pressed peasantry.

Both sides produced chieftains of profound intensity and high-handedness who were advocates of modernism, or of changes to be superimposed on ancient and rooted faiths and habits, with results that would be definably Asian. Yet as these modernizers turned for support to Washington or Moscow from 1946 onward, that indigenous quality was often overlooked. The two superpowers bid strongly for Asian followers, recognizing the enormous value of the continent's resources and population. But in their propaganda they forced their own patterns of explanation on matters, describing conflicts between "socialism and reaction" or "Communism and democracy"—labels that did not quite fit the contents of the bottles. For American public opinion in particular, this led to some perilous misunderstandings and policies.

Americans might have been expected to grasp some of the intricacies of political infighting in the Philippines, since the islands had been a United States possession from approximately 1901 until formally freed on July 4, 1946. There were 7,100 islands, in fact, stippled over 115,600 square miles of blue southwest Pacific, supporting a population of some 16 million, including Chinese, Japanese, Spanish, German, and British settlers and their descendants. "Native" Filipinos spoke a variety of languages, and worshiped as Catholics, Protestants, and Muslims, with some 680,000 still listed as "pagans." Yet American public attention focused less on the problems of steering a ship of state with such a mixed crew than on the post-1948 struggle with the Hukbalahaps. That was the name given to a group of guerrilla fighters who had harried Japanese outposts during the war. Afterward, they had militantly taken up the cause of tenant farmers growing sugar and tobacco on Luzon, the main island. Using captured weapons, they descended on villages, summarily executed "exploiters," and extorted supplies. President Elpidio Quirino, a conservative whose term began in 1948, denounced the "Huks" as Communists and pooh-poohed their "so-called social and agrarian reforms" as camouflage. He launched a large-scale police and army campaign against them, and boasted, after some three years of the killing and resettlement of villagers, that he had brought terrorism under control.

American newspaper readers followed a similar story in dispatches filed from the Malay Federation, a patchwork of tiny sultanates and one major city, Singapore, all under British control and strung out along Malaya's serpentine equatorial peninsula. London insisted that the federation, set up in 1946, was "autonomous" and fairly distributed power among nearly 6 million Malayan, Eurasian, Chinese, and Indian merchants, tin miners, rubber workers, and rice growers—some of them Muslim, some Christian, some Hindu, and some Buddhist. There was apparently strong dissent from this view deep in the interior jungles, where rebellion flared. As in the Philippines, there were raids on the villages, and a government response that branded the attackers as Communists. The British brought in troops from remnants of their empire Nepalese Gurkhas, Dyak headhunters from Borneo, police squads from Hong Kong—and claimed by 1950 to have killed some 1,500 terrorists, arrested hundreds more, and saved the situation.

Americans read about the antiguerrilla campaigns without learning much about the underlying social tensions that filled men's hearts with violence. They knew even less about Malaya's neighbor, oil-rich Indonesia, freed from the Dutch in 1949 and also containing a many-tongued populace, separated by history, beliefs, and geography. Yet Americans would hear, in time, of civil war there and thousands of slayings by Communists and anti-Communists.

And Americans who could not have named the provinces of prewar French Indochina knew that there was a revolt in progress there, too, after 1946. It was led by a bearded wraith named Ho Chi Minh. Of Ho's Communism there was no doubt; he had been one of the founders of France's Communist Party. There was no doubt, either, about his total dedication to the liberation of Vietnam, the name he preferred for his country. He had worked his way to France on a freighter before World War I to agitate for Vietnamese independence, tried to press the issue on the 1919 peace conference, then dodged and starved his way in and out of China, Malaya, and Siam (and their jails), organizing, teaching, speechmaking, and leaving cadres behind him. In 1946 the French reshuffled their administration, and gave Ho an "autonomous" republic comprising only part of the peninsula. It was not enough. A guerrilla war began, following familiar tracks. The French called in more troops, including the Foreign Legion. By 1947, the Westernized cities were controlled by one hundred thousand soldiers, while the countryside, especially at night, fell increasingly under the rule of Ho's Viet Minh, who were either patriotic liberators or Red terrorists according to one's point of view.

Americans contemplated these Southeast Asian struggles and were confused. The persistence of war after 1945 mystified them. Generally, they had expected the end of colonialism to produce familiar, recognizable, European-style republics with strong cultural and economic ties to their former masters. It was upsetting to find these new nations savaged by terrorists who were, it seemed, Communist-led. Obviously there was an explanation for the disappointment. The popular mind of the late 1940s believed uncritically that a Communist anywhere, from Paris to Peking, was a letter-perfect follower of a script written in Moscow. The wars of Asians against Asians, therefore, must be part of a drive for monolithic world Communist rule, which had to be resisted.

So the anti-Communist measures designed for Europe in 1947 and 1948 were applied to the Pacific area. No Asian NATO—as yet—but weapons and supplies to the hunters of insurgents in the Philippines, Malaya, and Indochina. There was an effort, too, as in the Marshall Plan, to deny Communism its "nutrient soil" of poverty. A reelected and contented Harry Truman, snapping out his inaugural address on January 20, 1949, ticked off the points in his new foreign policy. "Point Four" called for help to "undeveloped" nations, then the preferred term, in the form of modern industrial and agrarian technology and skills. This would presumably cure sickness, improve transportation, boost crop yields, spur manufacturing, and produce dynamic, revolution-proof, well-fed economies linked by trade to the United States. In time, Congress responded with appropriations and agencies to forward the work.

Yet there was a tentativeness about large-scale spending on Asia. For one thing, much aid seemed to be misapplied by the governments to whom it went—to stick to elite fingers. Some American liberals even argued that the Communists were, in fact, genuine reformers who should not be crushed. Many conservatives, for their part, hesitated to face the heavy long-term outlays required to help faraway, unfamiliar peoples. Finally, top planners in the State and Defense Departments did not want to scatter over the globe the resources needed to confront Russia in Europe. There was no strongly organized opposition to this view before 1950.

Thus aid to "free" Asia came in smaller dollops than that which was conferred on Europe, and with less clear-cut results. The "insurgencies" dragged on, or were settled by sweeping, authoritarian assumptions of emergency power by the supposedly democratic and constitutional regimes favored by Washington. And Americans, on the whole, continued to be uncertain of what was happening, but to assume that it all made sense in some grand design of Cold War conflict.

Nowhere was this illusion so self-defeating and bitter as in the case of China.

I N THE AMERICAN CONSCIOUSNESS, China occupied a particular shadowland of well-meaning fantasy. "Old" China was a land of jade, silk, tea, dragon paintings, gongs, and inscrutable sages. Modern China, under Chiang Kai-shek, was a solid republic, an enormous potential customer, and a possible Pacific power. Roosevelt's vision of a postwar world kept peaceable by four "policemen" included China on the force.

Moreover, America was China's friend. American missionaries had worked valiantly to convert and educate the Chinese people. American diplomats had supported China's territorial integrity against attempts by other nations to dismember her. America had tried to halt Japan's "grab" of Manchuria in 1931, as well as her undeclared war, begun in 1937, that slowly put Nipponese troops in control of China's ports and major cities.

There were elements of truth in this picture, but some deep flaws, too. America had not hesitated to share in the trade advantages wrung from Peking in the nineteenth century. Americans in China lived, for the most part, in imperialism's enclaves of plenty set amidst Chinese poverty. Chinese residents in the United States had suffered from harsh discrimination. To an unsuspected degree, our presumed ally had anti-American thoughts.

But above all, the China of World War II was not a unified country. She was in the midst of a turbulent civil war that went back as much as twenty years, and was in a state of temporary suspension because of the Japanese invasion. Chiang Kai-shek was not master in his own house. He had, of necessity, left uncurbed the powers of some of the strong provincial chiefs, or warlords. And he was also pitted against the Communists, who had been part of the struggle to create a modern Chinese nation since the 1920s, and who had once been Chiang's allies.

Chiang's life story was at the center of the history of China in the twentieth century that began when he was twelve years old, the son of a successful wine merchant. Army life attracted him. He entered an Imperial Chinese military academy, and then was sent to Japan for further training, the government of China being obliged to use any available foreign experts to educate its youth in modern ways.

There, Chiang met radical young fellow Chinese under the spell of Dr. Sun Yat-sen, the father of the Chinese Revolution. Sun and his followers overthrew the empire's rulers in 1911 and proclaimed a republic. Thereafter, Sun was in and out of power, but by 1923 he headed a shaky government, its capital in Canton, with little support in the provinces. Chiang was his star soldier, and Sun, willing to accept Soviet help, sent him to Russia to learn still more. Sun had organized what he called the Kuomintang, or People's Party, a coalition of merchants, workers, and intellectuals dedicated to building a new China. The young Chinese Communist Party was in it, too, thus joining the fight against what it called the feudal, reactionary warlords.

Among the more important Chinese Communists was Mao Tse-tung, five years Chiang's junior, son of a well-off peasant. Mao had been trained as a teacher, fallen in with Sun's adherents, and then plunged into a lifelong absorption of Marxist works. He was a forceful organizer, and was good at creating unions and study groups among miners, railroad workers, government employees, and peasants.

Chiang became head of the Kuomintang's armies, which were aided by Russian advisers. All seemed harmonious until Sun died in 1925 and a power struggle broke out in the Kuomintang. In 1927 Chiang did a dramatic turnaround. He broke with the Reds in a bloody coup, took help from major financiers and businessmen, and, with the resources they afforded, managed to battle his way northward into Hankow, Peking, Shanghai, and Nanking. He married Mei-ling Soong, daughter of a prestigious, Westernized banking clan (one of her sisters was Sun Yat-sen's wife), and in 1930 he was converted from Confucianism to Christianity. Was Chiang an opportunist and turncoat? Or was he a far-seeing statesman choosing an alliance with the classes who possessed the most power to help China? Perhaps a little of both, just as he remained, to the end, an amalgam of Confucian aristocrat and Christian activist.

Whichever was the case, the central theme of Chinese political life now became the civil war between the Communists and the new, more conservative Kuomintang, which had ousted them. Mao and associates like Chou En-lai and Chu Teh organized a Peasants and Workers Army, and became strong enough to set up a Chinese Soviet-style state in central China. But in 1934, for various strategic reasons, they undertook an extraordinary change of base, conducting a "Long March," in which thousands of their supporters, guarded by troops, moved six thousand miles through twelve provinces, in what was described as "the biggest armed propaganda tour in history." The migrants carried printing presses, collected taxes from landlords and other "class enemies" en route, recruited new soldiers and organizers, and fought fifteen battles with Kuomintang forces. By late 1935 the Communists were resettled in Shensi province in northwestern China, in effect making it a separate state with its capital at Yenan.

The year 1937, therefore, found Chiang fighting against the Reds, as well as those warlords who were not yet subdued. Then the Japanese invasion gave him another front to worry about. Tokyo claimed, in fact, that its occupation was only intended to protect its nationals from the chaos in China. The new war created a wave of Nationalist Chinese sentiment that helped the Kuomintang, but there was still a certain vagueness about Chiang's priorities. Was he committing his full strength against Japan's armies, or hoarding it to fight the Communists, despite the fact that they were also strongly anti-Japanese?

Even if the first assumption had been true, Chiang's underequipped divisions were no match for the Japanese war machine. Within two years, China's seacoasts and rich eastern provinces had been overrun. Though Chiang was recognized by world governments, including those in Washington and Moscow, as China's official ruler and unifier, he was forced to hole up in a temporary, refugee-swollen capital at Chungking, deep in the mountainous west. Meantime, the Communists in Yenan more or less suspended the fighting against Chiang, and welcomed a few friendly foreign correspondents, some of whom they convinced that they were more interested in agrarian and social reforms than in ideological purity or conformance with Soviet policy.

That was where matters stood on December 7, 1941, when suddenly Chiang's luck seemed to improve, and he found himself with rich America as his partner in battle.

The marriage was less happy than depicted in official propaganda, which made much, for example, of Chiang's appearance with Roosevelt and Churchill at the 1943 Cairo Conference. In truth, China was effectively cut off from all but an airborne trickle of supplies over the Himalayas from India, and had a near-zero priority in overall strategic planning. Chiang was given an American chief of staff, a pungent and dedicated career soldier, General Joseph Stilwell, who was fluent in Chinese and certain that he could create a potent fighting force out of a properly equipped and led Chinese army. But for his purposes Stilwell needed far more control over Chinese officers than Chiang was willing to yield, and far more matériel than Roosevelt had to spare, and he did little to conceal his frustration and his disdain for both heads of state. (In his private diary he called Chiang "the Peanut.") He was ousted in 1944 and replaced by General Albert C. Wedemeyer, who was more diplo-

matic and supportive of Chiang. Yet the China theater remained a
military orphan.

What was worse for Chiang was that his own government was
slipping. The war was hard on all the elements of the Kuomintang.
Intellectuals and salaried government employees suffered from
disastrous inflation. Business and industrial figures were isolated in
the Japanese-occupied regions, vainly awaiting rescue. The rural
peasantry, never strongly wooed by the Generalissimo, as Chiang
had become known, was especially hard hit by conscription and
taxes from which their landlords appeared to be easily exempted.
Above all, Chiang's associates and kinsmen were doing suspiciously
well. Foreign aid, in cash and goods, seemed to find its way into the
black market or directly into high-ranking pockets (as Stilwell had
raged). Even Clarence Gauss, the American ambassador to Chungking in 1944, in a moment of discouragement wondered unofficially
if "we should pull the plug and let the whole Chinese government
go down the drain."

By contrast the Communists, as American observers reported,
seemed to be tougher, more attuned to the ghastly sacrifices and
sufferings of the Chinese people, and more likely to do well when
the fighting with Chiang inevitably resumed after the Japanese were
defeated.

Still, for all the grumbling, Chiang's was the legal government.
Even Stalin recognized that. He signed a mutual defense treaty with
Chiang and promised to restore Manchuria to him six months after
the war was over. (Turned into the puppet state of Manchukuo by
Japan in 1932, the province had been quickly seized by Soviet troops
in August 1945.) But Stalin's interpretation of the deal was in a
familiar Moscow pattern. Chinese Communist units were allowed to
enter and take over Japanese equipment. And, though Chiang
counted on Manchuria's industrial resources in his recovery plans,
the Russians picked the area clean as they withdrew. Hence the
Nationalists, as Chiang's forces were being called in late 1945, took
over a shell that they barely controlled.

On the other hand, meanwhile, the United States moved the
Generalissimo's troops back into eastern China and ordered the
Japanese to wait and surrender only to them and no other—
meaning, Communist—authorities. Chiang also got considerable
American matériel left behind by homeward-bound U.S. units. But
beyond this, the dwindling American encampments were ordered to
stay strictly neutral if warfare was renewed between the Nationalists and Communists.

It *was* renewed, almost immediately, and the rekindling of the
civil war put American policymakers in a dilemma. To secure a
strong and stable China, the United States might try to give the

Kuomintang unlimited backing. But some veteran Far Eastern experts in the State Department, especially John Paton Davies, John Carter Vincent, and John Stewart Service, saw problems in that course of action. They predicted that Chiang would continue his downward slide, and that aid to him might be lost. Prudence might warrant keeping lines open to the Communists. For this candid advice, the three were to have their careers ruined during the McCarthy era.

The fact was that it was impossible to "pull the plug" on Chiang or tilt toward the Communists even in the earliest stages of postwar Soviet-American tension. The case of America's last wartime ambassador to Chiang showed why. His name was Patrick Hurley. He was an oilman and loyal Democrat, a patronage appointee. At one time, after meeting top Chinese Communists, he had opined that they were something like the Oklahoma Populists of his youth. But he changed his mind later, and in October 1945 he angrily resigned his post, charging that the striped-pants professional diplomats in his embassy were selling Chiang down the river in favor of Mao Tse-tung, whose name Hurley pronounced as "Moose Dung." Hurley's attitude was shared widely enough to make it highly inexpedient, politically, to do Mao any favors.

If there were clear disadvantages in supporting either side, a third option was to seek a compromise. In December 1945, Truman chose to play this card, and led with an ace. He asked no less a person than General Marshall, who then had everyone's confidence, to go to China as a mediator. Marshall had been looking forward to retirement, but with characteristic uncomplaining promptness, he accepted.

He flew immediately to China, there to begin an exhausting and frustrating year of airborne trips and lengthy conferences. From time to time agreement seemed possible on concrete matters, such as integration of the rival armies, or the degree of material help furnished by the United States. Marshall even arranged two temporary truces. But in the end the oil and water would not mix. Even Marshall was unable to isolate and clarify issues for resolution when dealing with the embattled Chinese. (Of Mao he declared: "That is a real iron curtain when you get there.") At the end of 1946 he abandoned hope and returned home, stating in a final report that those moderates who would yield principle in the interests of a unified China were hopelessly outgunned by the "dominant group of reactionaries" on Chiang's side and "dyed-in-the-wool Communists" on the other.

That conclusion left the State Department with the agonizing choice, by default, of simply waiting out events. Chiang's hold on China continued to slip as millions became, if not pro-Communist, at least neutral. In 1947 General Wedemeyer was sent over on a fact-finding mission. Sympathetic to Chiang though he was, he recorded that "nepotism [was] rife"; that the Nationalist secret police "operate[d] widely, very much as they . . . did in Germany"; and that the Nationalists, restored to power in the eastern cities, acted like "conquerors instead of liberators." Wedemeyer did not believe in a passive policy. He proposed options, among which were major financial help and up to ten thousand American troops for Chiang, or even a great-power trusteeship for Manchuria to keep it from the Communists who were taking it over, town by town. Yet the Administration suppressed the Wedemeyer report, in good part because its forthright criticisms of the Nationalists were sure to anger a small group of ardent Chiang supporters in Congress who, with their backers in some business and religious circles, were becoming known as the China Lobby. And therefore, Wedemeyer's recommendations for helping Chiang were never discussed against the background of an honest appraisal of his chances.

Nothing was done, and matters continued to become more desperate for Chiang. Marshall Plan aid sent to him at the insistence of the China Lobby vanished without visible effect. Armies went unpaid or never received available equipment, and melted away along with the Nationalist will to fight—or were surrendered by their corrupted generals.

The final mop-up stage came in 1949. The Communists captured Peking, followed, in the next four months, by Nanking, Shanghai, and Canton. In October Mao proclaimed the People's Republic of China as the sole government in the land. In December Chiang's remaining officials fled to Taiwan (long known to Americans by its European-bestowed name Formosa). There the Generalissimo awaited them, vowing that he would someday regain control of the mainland. That same month, Mao journeyed to Moscow and came back with a treaty of recognition, mutual defense, and economic aid. The civil war had ended in Red triumph, and the Truman Administration summed up its position in a white paper that declared: "Nothing that this country did or could have done . . . within reasonable limits . . . could have changed that result."

At the same time, nothing could have been more devastating than the failure to prepare the public for that result. Chiang's fall ended a historical tragedy, a long trip through the bloody labyrinth of China's past. But Americans capable of seeing the struggle as one of "the Peanut" against "Moose Dung" could not fathom that complexity. Dazed, they could only respond to what they saw as a sudden, seismic upheaval. China, one of the Big Four, one of the victors of 1945, had been overwhelmed. China, America's old friend, was now apparently a Communist satellite, increasing the strength of Moscow's side by more than half a billion people. It was impossible to believe that nothing could have been done. Somewhere there had to be guilty parties who had made China an enemy. How much of an enemy would be clear within a year of Mao's victory, when Chinese and American soldiers began to kill each other in Korea, a nation about which most Americans knew practically nothing.

FOR THOSE AMERICANS who were following the news closely in 1950, South Korea was synonymous with its president, Syngman Rhee. The key to Rhee's character was to be found in a small, revealing habit. When he was excited or in deep concentration, he would blow on his fingers. He had begun to do that as a young man in the 1890s, to ease the pain after they had been broken in jail. His torturers were policemen of the kingdom of Korea, and he was a student rebel already obsessed by the vision of an independent Korean republic, dominated by none of its powerful neighbors— China, Japan, or Russia.

When Rhee was born, of a good family, in 1875, it was China whose political and cultural shadow fell across his country. His boyhood education was on the Chinese classical model, in fact, aimed at readying him for a career in Peking's bureaucracy. But he also studied English in a mission school in Seoul. That, plus his republicanism and subsequent arrest, proved decisive in his life. Behind bars, he was converted from Confucianism to Christianity and passed his time studying economics, religion, and more English. In 1904 there was a general amnesty. Rhee, released, booked passage for America.

He stayed eight years, earning degrees in economics from George Washington and Harvard, and in theology from Princeton. He came back to work for the YMCA as Doctor Rhee, but in a Korea now formally annexed, under the name of Chosen, to Japan.

Though Rhee was to found the Korean Methodist Church, his kind of Christianity did not preach passive resistance. He and a group of followers proclaimed a Korean Republic in 1919, hoping that the peacemakers in Paris would accept Woodrow Wilson's talk of self-determination for all peoples and would recognize his government. He was doomed to disappointment, and had to flee from Japanese police.

Settled in Hawaii, he earned a living as a translator, but gave most of his life to lobbying for his goal among American legislators, editors, and church figures. He wanted a "Korean Commission" that he had set up in Washington to be recognized as a government-in-exile. This expectation, too, was fruitless. But at last, in 1945, when he was an old man, Japan toppled and his hour came. It was barren of joy, for it offered him only a half-loaf. Divided at the 38th parallel by its liberators, Korea would have to wait to have its fate determined by a future peace conference.

Still, Syngman Rhee was optimistic. Back in his native land, bouncing about like someone half his age, playing tennis, composing Chinese poetry for relaxation, tirelessly organizing, he awaited an election that he felt sure of winning in a united Korea. He was the best-known figure in Korean political life, a fact probably more important than his program, which was a mixed bag of state socialism and autocracy. He envisioned tight national control of the economy, tempered by universal suffrage. But it was clearly his intention to use his formidable influence to make sure that the voters "democratically" endorsed his every wish. Above all, he wanted no interference from Communists, whom he distrusted and despised. "Your government must learn, as we have," he told an American reporter in 1950, "that there is no compromise with the Reds."

Unfortunately, the Red motherland was in command of half of Korea, and what was more, the half containing most of the mines, dams, hydroelectric plants, and factories developed by the Japanese. A United Nations Commission on Korea tried hard to prepare for the nationwide vote desired by Rhee, but the Russians barred it from their zone, within which they contrived, as in Eastern Europe, to make organization virtually impossible for anti-Communists. In 1948 the UN gave up and authorized elections in South Korea alone, easily won by Rhee, who still nevertheless considered himself a man without a country. The Russians, in turn, held elections in North Korea, which, not surprisingly, chose Kim Il Sung, a Moscow-trained bureaucrat, as party leader and chief of state. Soon, he had a "People's Army," with excellent Soviet-furnished equipment, after which the Russians withdrew. The United States pulled its troops out of South Korea in mid-1949, and mulled over the thorny choices it faced regarding its future relations with its new, small, and vulnerable client.

Heavy arms support to Rhee, or an American presence in Korea, or a mutual defense pact all had drawbacks. They would be costly at a time when high defense expenditures were under attack. It would be foolhardy to risk United States troops and weapons on a small peninsula that could be quickly overrun. And there was another factor. Given a really potent army, Rhee himself might thrust into North Korea. Exactly like his Communist opposites in Pyongyang, the North Korean capital, Rhee denied the legitimacy of the partition and claimed the right to rule all of Korea's thirty-odd millions. If he began a war, it could spread dangerously. If he became unpopular at home while enjoying strong American backing, it would be a propaganda defeat.

Yet he could not simply be ditched. So Washington's compromise was economic aid to stabilize his inflation-ridden realm, and military assistance shorn of weapons with strong offensive capabilities, such as tanks. As to what might happen in case of a Soviet attack directly or by proxy, Secretary of State Acheson tried to spell out a proposed response in a speech, early in 1950, to Washington's National Press Club. If there was aggression outside the basic U.S. Pacific defensive perimeter, which included Japan, the Aleutians, the Ryukyus, and the Philippines, the "initial reliance" for resistance would have to be placed on "the people attacked," and afterwards "upon the commitments of the entire civilized world under the Charter of the United Nations."

Later on, Republicans would bitterly charge that the statement was a virtual invitation to invade Korea (or Taiwan) without fear of American retaliation. The accusation could never be verified without access to secret archives in Pyongyang and Moscow, confirming actual Communist reaction to the speech.

Whatever his reasons, Kim Il Sung prepared, late in the spring of 1950, for a stab at unification by force. On the fateful last Sunday in June, he sent his tanks across the 38th parallel in the first open attempt to change the postwar status quo by direct invasion. The dreaded war was on.

The initial rush of the People's Army swept the ROK (Republic of Korea) forces and the first American units that reached Korea under General Dean back through and beyond Seoul and Taejon. The North Korean spearheads raced on, relatively unhampered by U.S. air and naval interdiction, and unheeding of the Security Council resolution that gave UN authority to the American intervention. That resolution escaped a Soviet veto, thanks to a major Soviet policy miscalculation. Since early 1950, Moscow's delegation had boycotted the Council's meetings, because Nationalist China's permanent seat there had not been vacated in favor of a nominee from Peking. (Russia quickly amended her stand after the crucial ballot that declared Pyongyang to be an outlaw.)

A wave of popular support buoyed up the White House through July. The Munich analogy worked a magic spell. Once more an aggressor was on the loose, but this time he would encounter steel. Yet, for a while, each day's news proved that it was easier to preach resistance than to make it effective. The retreat went on through August, until finally U.S. and ROK elements were penned up in a small perimeter around Pusan, the major port of entry for supplies and reinforcements coming through Japan. There, the perimeter held, while fresh troops and war machines poured ashore daily, until the entire area around Pusan's harbor was, in a correspondent's recollection, a "vast arsenal and supply depot." There were new, unwearied American regiments, and a sprinkling of Britons, Turks, Filipinos, Netherlanders, and other non-Americans composing a polyglot army of combat and service units from fifteen nations. However, 90 percent of the total UN force was made up of U.S. and ROK troops.

Even as early as mid-July, General MacArthur knew that his total control of the air and sea would allow him a counterpunch in short order. The one he planned was a classic textbook maneuver, a dash around the enemy's flank that would confront them with the instant choice of retreat or encirclement and destruction. Leaving General Walton Walker at Pusan, MacArthur would take a seaborne Marine division up to Inchon, a Yellow Sea port just outside Seoul, land and capture it, and force the North Koreans to race back homeward before the Americans could dash all the way across the peninsula and cut them off.

Inchon was actually a difficult target, thanks to strong harbor defenses, wicked tides, and tricky currents and channels. When MacArthur first proposed the operation, his stunned naval and Marine commanders came as near mutiny as military propriety allowed. But MacArthur convinced them at a Tokyo staff meeting by a display that caused one to say later that if the general had gone on the stage, the world would never have heard of John Barrymore. "I can almost hear the ticking of the second hand of destiny," MacArthur's presentation concluded. "We must act now or we will die . . . Inchon will succeed."

And, with incredible good luck, Inchon did—a model amphibious battle, fought on September 15, that seized its objective in a matter of hours at a cost of some 550 dead and 2,500 wounded. Within another seventy-two hours the Americans were back in Seoul, and the North Koreans who had hemmed in Pusan were in pell-mell retreat, pursued by General Walker's army. Two weeks after Inchon, all of South Korea was again free. Ninety days after beginning her invasion, North Korea was open to attack by superior forces.

Though many would later think otherwise, it was not exclusively or originally General MacArthur's idea to push on into North Korea and punish the international wrongdoers. Halfway through September the National Security Council directed him, when he asked for orders, to "make plans for the occupation of North Korea" if—a significant "if"—there was "no indication or threat of Soviet or Chinese intervention." The question of who would gather and interpret such "indications"—MacArthur in the field or the intelligence apparatus surveying the world from Washington—was left open. Equally vague was the question of UN support for moving up to the border where Korea, China, and (just barely) the Soviet Union touched. As MacArthur moved ahead, the General Assembly, under American prodding, passed a resolution calling for a "unified, independent, and democratic" Korea once again, but failed to say whether it meant to reach the goal by force or negotiation. It was just enough of a green light to take any restraints off MacArthur, except for orders not to use air power over Chinese or Soviet soil.

There was no ambiguity, however, about China's reaction. Foreign Minister Chou En-lai said in a monitored broadcast on October 1 that Peking would not "supinely tolerate" an American invasion of North Korea, and added within another few days: "We cannot stand idly by." If MacArthur was chargeable with an initial fault, it was in downgrading these warnings, along with later ones relayed through India. Instead, he pushed on, and then displayed exorbitant self-confidence by dividing his forces into two wings, the X Corps and the Eighth Army, and sending them up North Korea's two coasts, where they became ever more widely separated by rugged mountains.

The dangerous decision to split his expedition in the face of the enemy seemed justified at first. Pyongyang fell, and then the ports of Wonsan and Hungnam. But meanwhile, unknown to MacArthur, up to two hundred thousand Chinese infantrymen were filtering into Korea and taking up positions in the central ridges. There were alarm bells. By November 1, ROK troops had encountered the Chinese, and even civilian military analysts for the press knew that many "volunteers" sent by Peking were somewhere in front of MacArthur. On November 6, however, the general ordered the bombing of the bridges across the Yalu River, which was the dividing line between North Korea and China. The Joint Chiefs of Staff immediately countermanded MacArthur.

Angry but still not frightened, and convinced he had only a beaten foe to deal with, MacArthur pushed on. "Asiatics . . . respect aggressive leadership," he explained to the press, and expressed hope that he might be able to get some troops started on the way home by Christmas, which seemed likely enough when ROK troops reached the Yalu at Thanksgiving.

Then, on the dark, bitter cold night of November 26, the well-hidden Chinese army boiled out of its jumpoff positions. With bugles and whistle blasts providing commands, Red China's soldiers swiftly overran the forward positions of the startled and badly frightened and confused ROKs and Americans. The Chinese were in the war "with both feet," as Harry Truman put it. In a matter of days they had surrounded one of the wings of MacArthur's force and bent the other back into a horseshoe. The X Corps had to fight its way out of the noose. Blizzards tore at retreating columns carrying their frostbitten wounded and frozen dead to the transports at Hungnam, for evacuation by sea.

MacArthur, suddenly discredited, poured out communiqués that spoke of a "fluid situation" or of "retrograde disengagement." The second American retreat in six months tumbled back down the peninsula. By New Year's Eve of 1951 the Chinese and revived North Koreans, some 485,000 strong and back at the 38th parallel, broke through and took Seoul again. But then the Americans stiffened. They had a new commander, Lieutenant General Matthew B. Ridgway, who had taken over after General Walker was killed in a jeep accident. MacArthur left the field command pretty much to Ridgway, who began to fight a new kind of war, with low expectations and high costs—a war of small unit actions, bitter struggles over strategic slivers of real estate with names like Heartbreak Hill and Bloody Ridge. Supported by artillery and armor, Ridgway's straining infantrymen stabilized a new line and battled back northward by inches. The inches added up to the recapture of Seoul and a battle line of March 1, 1951, more or less along the 38th parallel, the starting point of it all.

There, after eight months of violent surges from Pusan to the Yalu, the war settled into a stalemate. The Joint Chiefs of Staff had no appetite for a "victory" in the form of a new northward incursion that could further widen the war. They wanted American strength saved for possible encounters elsewhere. Yet they could not simply write off South Korea and so send out signals of irresolute weakness. Hence the war became a trap for the United States, and especially for Matthew Ridgway's men, who could no longer anticipate the big push that would send them all home to victory parades, but who lived instead for day-to-day survival and felt largely forgotten.

The nation itself was neither fully informed of how the war had changed, nor of what was being asked of it. But the issue was framed dramatically in April 1951, because foremost among those who passionately rejected the concept of the "limited war" that had taken over in Korea was General Douglas MacArthur.

THE OUTBREAK OF THE FIGHTING in Korea had given MacArthur his final chance to perform upon the luridly illuminated stage of war, an activity that he loved even while proclaiming its horrors. He was a looming figure, a man of the nineteenth century, something like Charles de Gaulle, but without the French general's luck of finally becoming his country's chief of state.

MacArthur's father was a general, too, and young Douglas, born in 1880, was raised on army posts. Pushed by an ambitious, adoring mother, he shone in study, and read avidly, thrilling especially to tales of courtly combat among noble warriors who embodied and guarded, in their sovereigns' names, such noble virtues as sacrifice and honor.

After graduating from West Point in 1903 with top honors, he began a turbulent career. He commanded a division in France in 1918, and simultaneously won medals for valor under fire and vexed superiors by disregarding the rules that were supposed to keep high-ranking officers out of the front lines. Later he saw duty in the Philippines, was a forceful superintendent of West Point, and finally came to Washington as the country's ranking soldier, the Chief of Staff, in 1930. But this meant that he had to struggle with lean Depression budgets, which fed in him a lifelong sense of injury. He believed that Roosevelt was deliberately starving the services for funds. The general also enjoyed striking attitudes. In 1932, wearing all of his decorations, he supervised the routing of the so-called Bonus Army of hungry veterans from their ramshackle camp in downtown Washington as if it were a Napoleonic charge. His assistant on that occasion, Major Dwight Eisenhower, was once asked if he knew MacArthur. "Know him, Madam?" he replied, "I studied dramatics under him."

MacArthur retired in 1937, but accepted, in the presumed twilight of his active life, the post of chief military advisor to the government of the Philippine Islands, which was preparing for promised independence in 1946. Then Pearl Harbor made him legendary. His little force was overwhelmed and driven into the Bataan peninsula, but he became a symbol of heroic resistance. Roosevelt ordered him to flee to Australia and assume command of United States forces in the southwest Pacific. He was not grateful, having argued privately for months that the President, in malice, was denying him reinforcements. But he left, announcing over the Philippine airwaves: "I shall return." He kept the pledge, and the result was power undreamed of. He became commander of the occupation forces in Japan, and the virtual ruler of that defeated power. For five years he presided—by all accounts successfully and with great popularity among his "subjects"—over the relative democratization of Japan, spurring important constitutional reforms in land tenure, social welfare, educational and human rights. He was a contemporary Shogun, the "Dai Ichi," or Number One, the actual master in the Japanese emperor's house. He had become himself something of an Asian autocrat—like Rhee or Chiang, a man in his seventies, full of himself and his mission, and used to having his way.

And like those two, he blended Communism and the Antichrist in his mind. An example of his feelings, in the bombastic style that became one of his hallmarks, was his message to a religious journal in 1931. "History teaches us," he wrote, "that religion and patriotism have always gone hand in hand, while atheism has invariably been accompanied by radicalism, communism, bolshevism, and other enemies of free government."

This was the man elevated to his last combat command by Kim Il Sung's aggression, and, given his background, it was inevitable that there would be severe problems in asking him to preside over a stalemated battlefront. He was unprepared to yield the right of judging worldwide strategic priorities to a Washington that he had always distrusted and had not visited in fourteen years, and from the very start of the fighting he had been in conflict with Truman, Acheson, and the Joint Chiefs. The first round of their battle came as early as July, 1950, over the question of a role for Taiwan in the new war.

MacArthur did not fear a Communist threat to Asia immediately after V-J Day. Even though he spoke of "the Muscovite bulging his muscles and lusting for power," he thought, correctly, that Russia was not ready for a renewal of large-scale warfare. But he had not speculated on the possibility of a Communist China, and was appalled when the mainland was overrun. Of Chiang, his view was that "if he has horns and a tail, so long as he is anti-Communist, we should help him." After Chiang's flight to Taiwan, MacArthur thought it crucial to strengthen him there.

In the first week of the Korean hostilities, both Chiang and MacArthur were heartened—MacArthur by a Truman order to the 7th Fleet to protect Taiwan, and Chiang because he thought that a general Asian war was about to erupt that would, as in 1941, redeem his fortunes. Chiang promptly offered three of his dubious divisions for Korean service, which might then and there have provoked Peking's intervention. MacArthur was ordered to turn them down, but was authorized to visit the island and check its defenses. He turned the inspection trip into a virtual declaration of alliance, saying in a communiqué that the Generalissimo's determination "parallel[ed] the common interest and purpose of Americans that all peoples in the Pacific shall be free." Chiang, too, spoke to the press in terms of initiating "Sino-American military cooperation."

This turn of events was far from pleasing to Acheson, who did not intend to reverse course and become entangled again in Chiang's faltering future. Averell Harriman was sent to Tokyo to warn MacArthur: "You must not permit Chiang to be the cause of starting a war with the Chinese Communists . . . which might drag us into a world war." MacArthur, with justice, may have been puzzled as to why the Administration, which had just risked a world war two years earlier over Berlin, was suddenly so circumspect.

So round one ended. Round two began when MacArthur was asked to send a message to the August encampment of the Veterans of Foreign Wars. Majestically he held forth. Taiwan was an "unsinkable carrier-tender" that must be preserved against "the lustful thrusts of those who stand for slavery as against liberty, for atheism against God." The public release of this message a few days before the VFW gathering stunned Truman, who, in cold fury, made it clear to a meeting of State and Defense brass that the general's words flouted official policy and must be withdrawn. MacArthur did so, claiming to be "utterly astonished" at the reaction.

The conflict went into remission after Inchon, which sent MacArthur's stock soaring. There was a strange mid-October episode in 1950, when Truman asked for a conference with the general and offered to meet him at Wake Island, far closer to Japan than to Washington. It was not usual for a Chief Executive with as high a sense of White House dignity as Truman to go two-thirds of the way around the world to talk to a subordinate, and Truman afterwards expressed irritation at what he saw as MacArthur's attempts to upstage him in front of reporters. But he had created the situation himself, and knew precisely what he was about. Congressional elections were around the corner; MacArthur was then riding high, and Truman saw advantages in publicly coddling the general. Nothing of importance was settled, but each man carried away different impressions. Truman later claimed that MacArthur had foolishly assured him that the Chinese would not intervene. MacArthur insisted that he had been given a promise of unlimited support, and was later betrayed by the restrictions imposed on him.

The setback of December 1950 opened round three. MacArthur's sense of the global nature of the struggle now fused with wounded pride. He wanted to return to the Yalu as he had returned to Manila. From headquarters in Tokyo he cabled sweeping suggestions for action to the Joint Chiefs of Staff, including a blockade of China, the landing of Nationalist troops with U.S. support on the mainland, and the bombing of Manchuria. The proposals made some sense in terms of Cold War propaganda about inflexible and indivisible world Communism. But the JCS fought shy of imprisonment in propaganda. Apocalyptic warnings to frighten the public were one thing, but reality was another. Reality dictated that a war with Peking would be a drain that left Europe, still recovering and rearming, in peril. The word to Tokyo was firm: no major adventures. The war could not be widened.

Very well, was MacArthur's reply, in effect. If he could not take these strong steps, he might be thrown off the peninsula altogether. The Chiefs did not know whether the old warrior was actually in panic, or twisting their arms, for the Administration could not face the political repercussions of actually "losing" Korea as well as

China. In either case, they responded that MacArthur should have Ridgway hold the line. If new disasters developed, bolder counter-measures might be authorized.

At that point, MacArthur determined to force the issue and brought matters to a boil.

First, he flung aside a White House gag order to clear all press interviews with the Pentagon. To one reporter he predicted that the war would become a "savage slaughter" unless the right decisions—those he wanted—were made "on the highest international level." To another he complained of being halted short of "accomplishment of our mission in the unification of Korea," which had never, in point of fact, been defined as a military objective. On the 20th and 23rd of March 1951, he scaled the heights of insubordination.

On the first of those days, he wrote a letter to Republican Representative Joseph W. Martin of Massachusetts, the House minority leader and former Speaker. Martin had recently delivered a New York speech in which he claimed that the President was blocking the use of nearly a million Chinese Nationalist troops in Korea, though they might be the means to turn the tide. "If we are not in Korea to win, Martin intoned, "then this . . . Administration should be indicted for the murder of thousands of American boys." Martin had sent a copy to MacArthur for comment, and now the Supreme Commander answered, not confidentially, that he was in accord. "If we lose the war in Asia," he warned, "the fall of Europe is inevitable; win it and Europe most probably would avoid war and yet preserve freedom." Then he added six words that were a virtual campaign slogan: "There is no substitute for victory."

On the same day as MacArthur was writing these words, however, the Administration was sending notes to U.S. allies proposing a very distinct substitute for victory in the form of a truce proposal to the Chinese and North Koreans. To get both sides out of the trap there might be a freeze of military positions, followed later by withdrawal of all "foreign" troops, Peking's included, as part of a general settlement. An information copy went to MacArthur with the notation to plan no important military action until the feedback from other capitals was recorded and studied.

MacArthur proceeded at once to wreck the plan.

Publicly, he issued his own offer to the commander-in-chief of the Chinese armies. Red China, his proclamation ran, had shown her total inability to achieve the "conquest of Korea" and had exposed weaknesses that guaranteed her "military collapse" in the event of strong countermeasures. Therefore, he was ready to confer any-where in the field with his opposite number on the best way to realize UN objectives in Korea "without further bloodshed." Where his own government was offering a truce, MacArthur was demanding a capitulation, and making talks an impossibility.

It was obvious that MacArthur had gone beyond the limit. A late-night meeting of senior statesmen, held in Acheson's house, agreed that MacArthur was trying to pursue an independent foreign policy, and must be sacked. But several days of study and conference would be needed to thrash out details and forestall problems. In the midst of the huddles, the final detonation went off. On April 5, Joe Martin happily read MacArthur's "no substitute for victory" missive on the floor of the House. Action could not be delayed much longer.

Acheson warned Truman that the ouster would trigger "the biggest fight of your Administration." But by then Truman had been through enough fights to be toughened. On April 10 he signed the terse order by General Marshall—who after the start of the Korean War had become Secretary of Defense—directing MacArthur to turn over all of his commands to General Ridgway and to "order" himself to any place he chose. Because of a communication foul-up, the brusque and blunt notification did not reach MacArthur until after a White House press conference had broken the story. The dismissal seemed needlessly ungracious, but MacArthur's response on actually receiving the official envelope was a quiet sentence to his wife: "Jeannie, we're going home at last."

Going home would not be a quiet pilgrimage, however, but rather the final phase of the battle with Truman. Leading Republicans urged the general to hurry back before the President's publicists could "smear" him with "their side of the story." He did so, and cast himself into the vortex of a shrill debate over Cold War priorities.

The firestorm surpassed even the worst fears of Acheson. White House mailroom clerks staggered under bags of letters condemning the dismissal. They stopped counting at 78,000. MacArthur, the incarnation of total victory against Japan only five and a half years earlier, was saying what Americans, still thinking themselves omnipotent, wanted to hear. Congressmen raged. Senator Nixon of California said: "The happiest group in the country will be the Communists and their stooges. . . . the President has given them what they always wanted—MacArthur's scalp." Senator McCarthy called it "treason in the White House," while Indiana's Senator Jenner (who had already denounced General Marshall's mission to China as treasonable) put into words the most extreme accusations. "I charge," he said, "that this country today is in the hands of a secret inner coterie which is directed by agents of the Soviet Union. Our only choice is to impeach President Truman."

MacArthur landed amid mobs at San Francisco's airport on April 17, and was followed by thousands on the drive to his hotel. He encountered more cheering mobs when he touched down in Washington. On the day following his arrival there, he reached his theatrical pinnacle in an address to a floodlit, televised joint session of Congress. Promising "neither rancor nor bitterness," he nevertheless made his case once more for an enlarged war against what he saw as appeasement. Interrupted over and over by applause, he came to his final words. He had joined the army before the century began, he said quietly, thus fulfilling all his boyhood hopes and dreams. "The hopes and dreams have long since vanished. But I still remember the refrain of one of the most popular barrack ballads of that day, which proclaimed, most proudly, that 'Old soldiers never die. They just fade away.' And like the old soldier of the ballad, I now close my military career and just fade away—an old soldier who tried to do his duty as God gave him the light to see that duty. Good-bye."

The chamber reverberated with cheers. Tears flowed unashamedly from hundreds of Congressional eyes. Representative Dewey Short said to the press: "We heard God speak here today, God in the flesh, the voice of God." At the other end of Pennsylvania Avenue, Short's fellow Missourian, Harry Truman, had other ideas, spoken years later into a biographer's tape recorder: "It was a hundred percent bullshit."

In truth, MacArthur did not intend to fade away. He paraded through Washington cheered by half a million spectators, and next day went on to a huge ticker-tape procession in New York while Truman, throwing out the ritual first toss of the baseball season in the capital, was drowned in boos.

And yet, all was not lost for the man from Independence. His own political future was finished. But he may have hoped, though he did not say so, that once the people had paid homage to MacArthur and the past, they would begin to listen to reason about the present and let the tempest subside.

Which was, in fact, what happened. The Senate Armed Services Committee held hearings on the dismissal, the Republicans cheerily anticipating the benefits to come, in 1952, from exposure of the "plot" against MacArthur. They had their turn first when MacArthur, guided through his lead-off testimony by friendly questions, presented his view that the professional soldiers had all agreed with him, but had been forced to yield to the sinister politicians.

Unfortunately for him, it was next the turn of the Joint Chiefs themselves to testify, and it became clear that they did not agree with MacArthur. The hearings gave them a forum to publicize their case. Chairman of the JCS Omar Bradley gave utterance to his feelings in words that would become famous. A war on the Asian mainland, he insisted, would be "the wrong war in the wrong place at the wrong time and with the wrong enemy." Air Force Chief of Staff Hoyt Vandenberg, always happy to show the need for more airplanes, said that a full-scale war in China's skies would take all available U.S. airpower and leave us "naked" elsewhere. The Chief of Naval Operations, Forrest Sherman, liked the idea of a blockade of Red China, but also concurred that it was preferable to keep conflict limited. And all of them thought the dismissal warranted. They might pity MacArthur's humiliation, but they knew the rules and who was boss under the United States Constitution. As Eisenhower, interviewed on the firing in Europe, had said, when one put on the uniform he "accepted certain inhibitions."

Without overtly acknowledging it, the public swung quietly toward the JCS view. Slowly it lost interest in MacArthur. Attendance at the hearings dwindled, and by June 4 they were moved to a smaller room. The China Lobby had not been able to keep control of the headlines with "proofs" of an anti-MacArthur cabal. They did have one success; they absolutely froze policy toward China. Acheson, on the griddle as a witness, said that there would be no recognition of Peking: "We are not contemplating it, haven't contemplated it; we have been against it." Into the deep-freeze went American relations with some 600 million Chinese, for twenty years.

And there was no surge of popular opinion in favor of MacArthur's hoped-for measures—of America's landing Chiang on the mainland, or raining bombs on Manchuria or Siberia. As the excitement faded to indifference, the polls showed that people were not really ready for Armageddon. The hearings ended in a kind of stalemate, with the committee simply voting to "transmit" the records to the Senate without comment, over the minority protest of eight of its Republican members. In the end, the hearings exposed some confusion and conflict in American policy, but nothing to cause its repudiation. The response to the probe revealed that, as in the case of the Berlin blockade, no one was in a hurry to go over the edge of the abyss.

And when that was clear, the stage was at last set for the truce.

THE SIGNAL CAME FROM JACOB MALIK, Soviet delegate to the Security Council, who suggested, in a June 1951 speech, that a ceasefire and mutual withdrawal from the 38th parallel would benefit all sides. As was expected, the North Koreans and Chinese soon after accepted an invitation from General Mark Clark (MacArthur's successor in Tokyo) to parley. Early in July, high-ranking officers from three of the four parties actually engaged in combat—China and North Korea on one side and the U.S. (representing the UN) on the other—convened under a flag of truce. South Korea angrily refused to send a representative. But the others sat down around a green table in a tent in the hamlet of Kaesong, between the opposing lines. What happened then was simple and heartbreaking. The UN offered in essence a demilitarized zone between the two Koreas, to be patrolled by a truce commission, and an exchange of prisoners. These basic terms were accepted by the North Koreans. But to reach final concurrence took two years and many lives: another 22,000 Americans dead in combat (added to the 11,000 already killed in action), plus the major share of the war's other casualties, which included 47,000 ROK battlefield deaths, an estimated 1.4 million Chinese and North Korean soldiers slain, and some 2 million Korean civilians wiped out by bombings, hunger, or disease.

Negotiations in the Cold War, like battle itself, were bizarre. Talking and fighting proceeded simultaneously. American military negotiators, led by Admiral Turner Joy, had to learn what American diplomats had learned earlier—how to sieve out hard proposals from Communist rhetoric that denounced the "atrocities" of the "murderer Rhee," or the "puppet Chiang"; how to deal with long lapses in communication, such as a two-month break-off when an American plane accidentally strafed Kaesong (after which the talks moved to Panmunjom); how to be patient when proposals from the other side, already rejected, were simply repeated in new forms.

There was, nonetheless, barely perceptible movement. By the end of November 1951, ceasefire positions were agreed on. "Time," said Admiral Joy wearily, "is the price you pay for progress." But the time was earned by the hundreds who fell weekly along the battle line, now honeycombed with bunkers, machine gun nests, artillery emplacements, dugouts, and tunnels like a replica of World War I's devouring Western Front. Early in 1952, however, an apparently immovable obstacle was struck by the negotiators over the exchange of prisoners. It appeared that as many as 83,000 of the 132,000 North Koreans in UN hands did not want to go home, a devastating indictment of Kim Il Sung's regime. Large numbers of Chinese, too, were ready to resist repatriation. Unable to accept such a propaganda black eye, the Communists insisted on both sides' returning all prisoners, by force if need be. But the UN spokesmen held firmly that they would order no one back into political slavery. By midsummer the parleys were at a standstill. It took the oncoming American presidential election to make the last breakthrough possible.

The Republicans, after a sharp convention battle, named General Eisenhower as their candidate. His enormous popularity virtually guaranteed his election over Adlai Stevenson, the Democratic Party's choice to succeed Truman. Yet there was an additional significance to the choice of the universally liked "Ike." As the victor of Europe, and then the first commander-in-chief of NATO, Eisenhower symbolized the American commitment to internationalism and especially to the defense of Europe. His nomination itself was therefore a defeat for the MacArthur position, and for lingering isolationism within the GOP.

It was true that the platform appeased the deposed Supreme Commander's partisans by denouncing Truman's " 'Asia last' policy" and saying there was "no intention to sacrifice the East to gain time for the West." But Eisenhower, like all candidates, knew that platforms were primarily rhetoric, and on October 24 he gave his already high prospects a lift when, speaking in Detroit, he announced that the first act of his Administration would be "to concentrate on the job of ending the Korean War—until that job is honorably done." The use of the word "end" rather than "win" was a tip-off to inevitable compromise, but Eisenhower promptly overshadowed any discontent with his next words: "That job requires a personal trip to Korea. I shall make that trip." By promising to bring his own five-star judgment to bear on the situation, Eisenhower made it seem that military professionalism would have the final say.

True to his word, he was in Korea within four weeks after his easy electoral victory, lurching over frozen roads by jeep and chatting before the cameras with troops and officers of units from fifteen nations. Studying the bristling enemy fortifications through binoculars only confirmed what was obvious to him: No new UN drive would succeed without either vast bloodshed or the unallowable risk of bombing China. New ways would have to be found to move the talks along and produce the "tie game" that Eisenhower's prestige alone made acceptable.

Pressure was put on the Communists, still dug in on the prisoner question. It took the form of warning that new Red offensives might meet undefined "retaliation," and a hint of what that might mean in the form of tactical nuclear weapons moved to Okinawa in April 1953. The information about the atomic artillery was "leaked" to China through India. Other forces were also at work to soften the postures of Pyongyang and Peking. Among them were the death of Stalin in March, and growing discontent among Soviet satellites in Europe. These cast doubt on how much support Russia would continue to furnish.

And, therefore, the logjam loosened. April saw a preliminary exchange of sick and wounded prisoners. After that, a general prisoner deal was worked out. Those who did not wish to be repatriated would be turned over to neutrals for temporary detention while "explainers" from each side would attempt to persuade them to change their minds. After a set time they would, if not convinced, be released to find new homelands. But just as the peacemakers reached the doorway to peace, there was a final struggle to push Syngman Rhee through it. The old man had bitterly resisted the entire negotiating process, unwilling to yield his dream of presiding over a single Korea. On June 18, he suddenly threw open the doors of camps in which some 27,000 North Korean prisoners, disaffected with their rulers, had been kept under ROK guard. The captives melted into the populace at large.

With that act of defiance behind him, Rhee was willing to be pacified by an American promise of virtually permanent postwar military and economic aid, sorely needed, since 43 percent of the country's industrial capacity and 33 percent of its housing were devastated, and the land swarmed with millions of crippled and homeless people.

The North Koreans and the Chinese, too, though outraged by Rhee's act, were ready to swallow the pill, which was a bitter one for them, since an additional 22,000 North Koreans and some 14,000 Chinese finally chose not to go home, as against only about 7,500 ROKs and 21 Americans.

At last, on July 27, 1953, in a temporary wooden hut at Panmunjom, the top field commanders spent twelve minutes signing some eighteen documents of agreement, then turned and left wordlessly. Later there were signatures from higher authorities. Rhee never signed at all, but he made no more trouble. And General Clark, himself a believer of the no-substitute-for-victory school, put his name down with a golden pen provided by the Parker Company, but said: "I cannot find it in me to exult in the hour."

But on the truce line the unsung fighting men exulted, emptying remaining clips of ammunition harmlessly into the sky. Theirs was the joy known only to frontline soldiers, the sudden awareness for the first time in years that they could count on going home alive. Eisenhower, who understood that mood, showed one reason for his popularity in a nonbombastic address to the nation that night. "The war is over," he said quietly, "and I hope my son is going to come home soon."

With that, the three years of bloody education by test of arms were over. The United States had learned something about itself, about the recalcitrant nature of the new world it shared, about the limits of its strength. Not enough to prevent future errors and agonies, but enough to open a new phase of the continuing confrontation with the Soviet sphere.

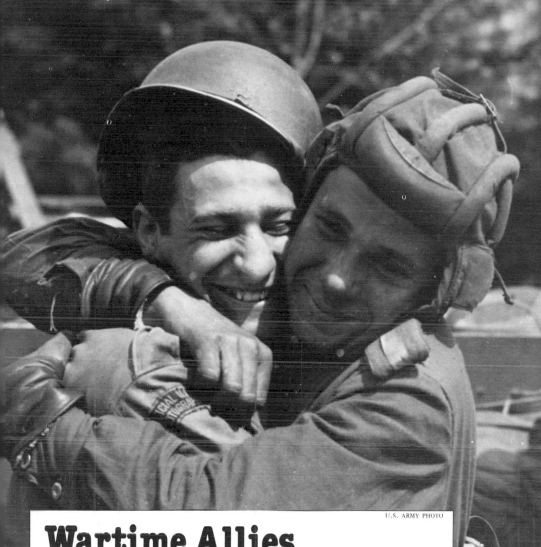

Wartime Allies

American and Soviet troops come together at the Elbe River, April 1945.
Inset: Stalin, Truman, and their staffs at Potsdam, 1945.

The Marshall Plan sent coal to Western Europe in 1948. The U.S.S.R. refused to allow its satellites to participate in the program.

An American plane lands in West Berlin during the airlift that broke the Soviet blockade of that city in 1948.

The Iron Curtain Falls

Right: George Marshall and Dean Acheson, architects of America's postwar policies. Below: Churchill introduced the phrase "Iron Curtain" in a speech in Fulton, Missouri, in 1946.

In Yenan in 1946, George Marshall (center) met with Mao Tse-tung (far left) and Chou En-lai (left) to try to mediate in their war against Chiang Kai-shek. Marshall's mission failed, and the United States turned its back on the mainland for twenty-three years.

Two Chinas, Two Koreas

As Chiang's forces disintegrated, this American cartoon depicted some of his U.S. supporters propping up his regime.

On September 15, 1950, four LSTs put 15,000 U.N. and American troops ashore behind enemy lines at Inchon, Korea, in a drive to recapture the peninsula from North Korean forces.

By December of 1950, allied forces were in retreat, pushed back from the Yalu River by Chinese troops who joined the war in support of the North Koreans.

Joseph McCarthy cites numbers of Communist Party members and fellow travelers at the McCarthy-Army hearings in 1954. Army counsel Joseph Welch (left) called McCarthy a reckless character assassin.

Richard Nixon's dogged pursuit of the Alger Hiss case launched his career, and he remained militantly anti-Communist until his surprise overtures to China and the U.S.S.R. in 1972.

Nine of the Hollywood Ten await fingerprinting for refusing to answer questions at a 1947 House Un-American Activities Committee hearing.

Cold War at Home

Right: Ethel and Julius Rosenberg were executed in 1954 for crimes that might have drawn prison sentences in calmer times. Below: Both Albert Einstein and Robert Oppenheimer came under attack by Red baiters.

ALFRED EISENSTADT/*Life*

Ships sunk by Egypt in October 1956 block all traffic on the recently nationalized Suez Canal.

Back-to-back Crises 1956

British and French troops parachute into Egypt to try to protect their stake in the canal. With Russia backing Egypt, war seemed imminent.

In October of 1956, a statue of Stalin was torn from its pedestal (above), and photos of the hated leader were burned in the streets of Budapest (left) during a week-long revolt by Hungarian freedom fighters.

Soviet tanks promptly moved into Budapest to put down the uprising. Some 25,000 Hungarians died.

WIDE WORLD

Above: Khrushchev and Nixon engage in their famed kitchen debate at an American trade exhibition in Moscow in 1959. Below: Kennedy and his advisers confer outside the Oval Office during the tense week of meetings about the Cuban missile crisis in October 1962.

STANLEY TRETICK

JIMMI SCOTT

A cartoonist's view of the crisis.

A quarter of a million people turned out to hear John Kennedy proclaim "Ich bin ein Berliner" in June of 1963, when the front line of the Cold War was the wall running through that city.

The Super Powers Face Off

An East German guard escapes across the barbed-wire barricade that separated East and West Berlin in August 1961. When the Berlin Wall was completed, such escapes became impossible.

Brezhnev visits Nixon in Washington in 1973 during a calm period in Soviet-American relations that coincided, paradoxically, with bitter fighting in Vietnam.

Nixon dines with Chou En-lai during his startling 1972 trip to Peking—a personal about-face that was a diplomatic masterstroke.

During a 1966 search-and-destroy mission south of Ben Luc, Vietnam, American infantrymen move warily through a mangrove swamp.

Warmer Peace, Hotter War

One of the last groups of evacuees from Vietnam crowd up a ladder to a waiting American helicopter perched on top of a building in Saigon on April 29, 1975.

Rebel Afghans, resisting the 1979 Soviet invasion of their country, seize control of a downed Soviet helicopter.

Angry crowds demonstrate outside the American Embassy in Teheran in November 1979 where the American hostages were being held captive. The Iranians were outraged by America's support for their hated, deposed Shah.

/MAGNUM

An unarmed Czech confronts a
Soviet tank crew in Prague, 1968.

Passionate Resistance

Lech Walesa, leader of Poland's
independent union Solidarity,
receives a hero's welcome in
Cracow in 1980. Even after being
outlawed by Poland's military
regime, Walesa and his supporters disrupted an official May Day
parade in 1984.

ATLAN/SYGMA

At a Regional Military Training Center in Honduras, a U.S. military adviser instructs a Honduran soldier in the use of an American weapon.

Below: American students in Indiana protest U.S. policy in El Salvador.

Chapter 7

ILLUSION OF MASSIVE RETALIATION:
1953-1956

THEY WERE AN ODDLY MATCHED PAIR, the President and his Secretary of State, as unusual a coupling as the conservative George Washington and the closet revolutionary Thomas Jefferson. Dwight Eisenhower, at sixty-two, still seemed somehow boyish despite his international renown. A reporter noted that he liked "poker and bridge, bourbon, dialect jokes, vegetable gardening." Even when he stood listening to "Hail to the Chief," the nickname "Ike" seemed to fit him.

No one, however, could have imagined calling John Foster Dulles "Jack." Even to intimates he was "Foster." Wrapped austerely in the mantle of two generations of distinguished diplomatic and Presbyterian ancestry, he was well described by a Washington correspondent as "a card-carrying Christian." Rectitude was his trademark, and his lectures on the perils of "atheistic, materialistic Communism" sometimes taxed the public attention. Eisenhower's, too. Presidential speechwriter Emmett Hughes noted how, in conference, the President would nod his head briskly to move Dulles along to a conclusion, tapping a pencil on his knee or gazing at the ceiling while the sermon wound on. (Later, however, after a split with Hughes, Ike would deny the tale.)

Yet the two functioned well together, for they did not differ at root. Both wanted to maintain American global power and leadership in the face of Soviet "expansionism." Both saw the material abundance of the United States as evidence of the success of her moral and political system. Both wanted to use the American economy as the model for what they called "the free world." Dulles never challenged Ike's leadership, and Eisenhower shed genuine tears when, in 1959, Dulles died of cancer.

Where they differed was in manner and emphasis. Eisenhower, the soldier, was at heart an accommodator. He was happiest when proposing international cooperation on such projects as the peaceful use of atomic energy, or disarmament. He disliked indictments of the Russians. Once, he snapped to advisers that the United States must "cut out all this fooling around and make a serious bid for peace." By contrast Dulles, the civilian, was forever in rhetorical combat. He hated negotiations that gave even the appearance of conceding the Soviets "a moral and social equality." He talked of "massive retaliation" or of going to the brink of war. A capsule version of the two variant styles was evident in the final negotiations for the Korean armistice. Eisenhower was perfectly willing to let the enemy know quietly that he would consider escalating the war, but he hoped that they would accept a deal and allow him to avoid that choice. Dulles, on the other hand, wanted no settlement until America had convincingly demonstrated firmness by "giving the Chinese one hell of a licking."

The dual nature of the pair was suitable to the new era of Soviet-American relationships that opened, in 1953, with fresh leadership in both nations, since Josef Stalin died less than two months after Eisenhower took office. True, the confrontation remained a central fact of life. The Cold War was now an established pattern, and the search for subversives at home a routine operation. The starting point of all analysis of events abroad was how they would weight the scales in favor of Moscow or Washington. The terrifying weapons race accelerated. A generation was reaching adulthood without ever having known anything but a climate of international tension.

Yet there were also forces making for peace. Each side felt constraints on its power. The rearmament of the United States and of Western Europe braked Soviet ambitions. So did the breaking away of Tito, the early rumbles of conflict with Peking, and the struggle for succession within the Kremlin. But even so, the United States did not enjoy a totally free hand. To risk nuclear war over a peripheral clash in Eastern Europe or anywhere on the globe was too appalling a possibility to consider seriously. Neither side could push too hard toward chaos.

With that realization, a new range of policy choices appeared for the United States. Options opened, as in the 1917-33 era, with regard to Communist Russia. Should she be ringed with armed force, isolated, warned to stay within bounds? Or accepted into partnership of trade and cultural exchange, on the theory that everyone would thereby benefit economically, and an easement of tension might even soften Moscow's harsh regime from within? Was an American position of toughness too provocative? Was a softer line likely to lead the Russians into dangerous miscalculations? Debate swung from position to position. Sometimes the result was a tentative thaw. Sometimes it was a flirtation with the dreaded "brink." Sometimes, it seemed, one after the other, in quick succession.

FROM EARLY INDICATIONS, it seemed the accession of Dulles to the stewardship of the State Department would force the Cold War's temperature down to record depths of frigidity. And that was odd, because few men, in actuality, seemed better prepared to understand the world. Dulles came from a diplomatic clan. His maternal grandfather, John W. Foster, had been Secretary of State to President Benjamin Harrison in the relatively tranquil days from 1885 to 1889. His uncle, Robert Lansing, had held the same job under Woodrow Wilson. Young John Foster Dulles himself, only ten years out of Princeton, went to Versailles in 1919 with the American delegation, and thought of himself as a Wilsonian internationalist, committed to a world kept peaceful by agencies like the League of Nations and the World Court. Between wars he worked for Sullivan and Cromwell, a major Wall Street law firm whose clients' interests encircled the globe. In 1945 he attended the organizing conference of the UN, and was later a delegate to its General Assembly. What Eisenhower once said to him in jest was literally true: "You've been training yourself to be Secretary of State ever since you were nine years old."

But Dulles's expertise was matched by a religion-based moralism whose foundations were laid during boyhood in a Presbyterian parsonage in Watertown, New York. During the 1930s he often attended conferences on how to achieve peace, sponsored by such organizations as the World Council of Churches and the Federal Council of Churches. There he came to believe that what humanity needed was basically to apply the moral force of the Gospel to its problems, and by the late 1940s he had come to see complex issues in terms of the duel between Christ's persecuted followers and their foes. Once, a friend remembered, some unflattering references were made to Chiang and Rhee during a conversation. Dulles, blinking rapidly as was his habit when excited, leaned forward in his chair and said: "No matter what you say about them, those two gentlemen are modern-day equivalents of the founders of the church. They are Christian gentlemen who have suffered for their faith."

Dulles's apocalyptic rhetoric fitted in with a political fact of life that he faced on taking office. All Secretaries of State need to play an active role in selling Administration policies to Congress and the public. When Dulles, who willingly embraced this chore, went up to Capitol Hill to testify, he found a peculiar grouping. Most Democrats and all so-called "Eisenhower Republicans" supported the treaties and arrangements already negotiated with allies abroad, even those who, in Dulles's own words, unfortunately did not share "our view that Communist control of any government anywhere is in itself a danger and a threat." The Secretary himself recognized the indispensable nature of this cooperation. But a hard core of conservative Republicans—isolationists, McCarthyites, and China Lobby supporters—denounced pacts with any nation that did not ardently believe that Moscow was the root of all evil. To appease this group Dulles spiked his testimony with such inflammatory phrases as "the black plague of Soviet Communism." More significantly, and to the dismay of professionals in the State Department, he appointed as the department's "security" director Scott McLeod, a McCarthy ally. McLeod's security procedures purged the department of many experts who seemed insufficiently zealous in their anti-Communism. Moreover, even veteran critics of the Soviet Union like Kennan and Bohlen, who were holdovers from the days of Roosevelt and Truman, were given the cold shoulder by the Secretary. This was calculated to deepen the impression that American foreign policy was being put on a course of direct confrontation with the Soviet Union—and that this was somehow a change from the policies of the preceding eight years. "Isn't it nice," Vice President Nixon was quoted as saying, "to have a Secretary of State who stands up to the Russians."

Dulles's pronouncements to the public at large were equally bellicose, even though in fact the Secretary recognized the actual constraints of diplomatic behavior when dealing with other heads of state. Just after Eisenhower's inauguration he spoke to a radio and television audience, warning that the United States would challenge Soviet domination of the vast area from Korea to East Berlin, and telling those nations who were captives of Moscow: "You can count on us." A year afterward, in Paris to prod the French into accepting German rearmament, he told a press conference that foot-dragging by France might provoke the United States to an "agonizing reappraisal" of its foreign policies. The message seemed to be that nations that did not fall in step with U.S. initiatives would be abandoned. Then, in a speech to the Council on Foreign Relations, Dulles spoke of a "new look" in American world strategy, one in which the United States might confront aggression by a "deterrent of massive retaliatory power," presumably the newly developed H-bomb. And in January of 1956, Dulles, in an article in *Life* magazine, told James Shepley: "You have to take chances for peace, just as you must take chances in war. . . . If you are scared to go to the brink you are lost." Speech by speech, and slogan by slogan, Dulles was emerging as the spokesman of impending apocalypse.

What he actually did was somewhat less drastic and spectacular. He worked on a grand design for a worldwide bulwark of anti-Soviet alliances within which to hem Communism. And to achieve this he took spectacular advantage of the air age, becoming the most widely traveled Secretary of State in the nation's history up to that point. The flights, which added up in varying estimates to at least half a million miles, gave him opportunities to focus on his plans and to escape the trap that awaited Secretaries who stayed too close to their desks—that of becoming enmeshed in their department's internal quarrels and bureaucratic entanglements. His closeness to Eisenhower spared him the risk of being undercut, in his absence, by other presidential confidants. So he would gratefully head, at the end of a working day, for the air base where a Lockheed Constellation bearing the United States seal awaited him. He would change into informal clothes, amuse himself with a glance at the navigation charts (he was a skilled amateur sailor), then settle down to conferences with legal advisers, area and public-relations specialists, and other associates. While the four-engined magic carpet headed toward far-off destinations, he would eat dinner (still conferring), down a couple of highballs, and curl up in his berth with a yellow legal pad on which to jot down ideas before sleep came. So frequently was he airborne that the three-year-old son of one of the security officers who constantly flew with him once looked at a picture of an airliner and confided to his mother: "That's where Mr. Dulles lives." These five-mile-high and three-hundred-mile-an-hour days and nights gave Dulles a sense of command and control, and were, of course, flattering to the visited heads of state who could feel that they were talking directly to top U.S. authorities.

After having made many of these trips, Dulles succeeded in putting together, by late 1954, a Southeast Asia Treaty Organization, consisting of Britain, France, Australia, New Zealand, Pakistan, and the Philippine Republic. The purpose of SEATO was to dam the Red tide that threatened, in Dulles's view, to engulf Malaya, Indochina, and Taiwan. Dulles also negotiated a treaty of defense with Chiang Kai-shek's government, committing the United States to defense of the Nationalist-held island, but leaving it somewhat vague as to whether or not Communist Chinese attacks on other small islands off the mainland, such as Quemoy and Matsu, would be regarded as preliminary to assaults on Taiwan itself, and therefore would trigger American military action.

Dulles flew to the Middle East, too, to press for the formation of a coalition of anti-Communist regimes there. He encouraged the signing of the Baghdad Pact of 1955, which united Great Britain, Turkey, Iraq, Iran, and Pakistan in a defensive linkage against Russia. Though the United States did not join the pact, due to complications arising from America's support of Israel, Dulles was satisfied that the alliance plugged the gap between NATO's eastern flank and SEATO's western one. Finally, in his tireless journeyings, Dulles added links to an existing chain of American air bases, maintained by treaty, in such places as Libya, Morocco, and Saudi Arabia. Added to those already operated in NATO and SEATO nations, they encircled the Soviet Union with launching sites from which airborne "retaliation" might come.

On the surface these actions appeared to be triumphs for the seven-year-old policy of "containment." Yet they harbored future dangers. NATO involved stable, experienced Western nations, slowly emerging from post-1945 impoverishment, and consistently friendly toward the United States even as they tried to break free of dependence on her. But SEATO tied together two colonial powers, two white nations in the Pacific, and three newly independent Asian states in a relationship of questionable mutual interests. And America's client states in the Middle East were often swept by fiercely contradictory waves of religious and political passion, and were ruled, in most cases, by princes or generals who could be and were assassinated and replaced overnight. Dulles had, therefore, committed American prestige and power to the defense of nations bound to suffer shocks of internal upheaval. Walter Lippmann, the severest conservative critic of the Cold War, called Dulles "a gambler . . . more lavish than any other Secretary of State has ever dreamed of being with promissory notes." Democratic Senator Henry Jackson, of Washington, though a sturdy anti-Communist, said that the Secretary was "the original misguided missile, traveling fast, making lots of noise, and never hitting the target." Whether or not these criticisms were justified, it was a fact that the "promissory notes" would be hard to fulfill. And meanwhile, out of the public eye, the Secretary was giving his blessings to some other operations that were potentially risky.

WITH THE KOREAN TRUCE in effect as of July 27, 1953, the United States found itself freed from its shooting war with two Communist governments. But another kind of secret conflict—a halfway house between open combat and diplomacy—was in full progress. It was made possible by the growth of the CIA. The young but ambitious agency was about to show its "operational" muscle in Iran and then in Guatemala.

After the Azerbaijan episode in 1946, American public opinion had allowed Iran to recede back into a fantasyland of minarets and veiled princesses. This innocence was matched by the belief of some politicians in Riza Shah Pahlevi's slowly modernizing kingdom that the United States was their permanent friend, and would give them unlimited backing in any future stormy weather.

The stormy weather broke when Iranian nationalism ran head-on into the Western powers' thirst for Iran's oil. The Iranian oilfields were worked by a British government-owned corporation, the Anglo-Iranian Oil Company, which remitted to its "partner," the Shah's government, a share of the profits. In 1950 the Iranian parliament, or Majlis, demanded a larger slice, plus the assignment of more Iranians to high-level administrative and technical positions in the AIOC. When the response was unsatisfactory, the Majlis confiscated the AIOC's properties in April of 1951.

It was a fresh blow against crumbling imperialism, and it revived an old dilemma for Washington. Acheson had no wish to back the old, British-dominated order unquestioningly. But he worried about a surge of nationalist excitement that might destabilize Iran's political parties and cause riots or deadlocks. In that case the Tudeh, Iran's Communist Party, might use the emergency to seize power. Social change in the developing world could not readily be disentangled from Cold War politics.

The entanglement in Iran's case was particularly troublesome because of the personality of her Prime Minister. Mohammed Mossadegh was seventy years old, suspicious, eccentric, given to public fits of weeping, interviews in pajamas, convenient fainting spells, and a histrionic ability to switch quickly from the role of frail petitioner of powerful America to master manipulator who could deliver Iran into the Soviet camp. Mossadegh hoped to use the battle with London to solidify his hold on the turbulent Majlis factions, including the Tudeh, Islamic fundamentalists, friends and foes of the Shah, progressives, and traditionalists. Having done so, he would get U.S. support by suggesting that the only alternative to him was Communism.

Mossadegh's behavior added a rare note of comedy to the Cold War drama. Once, visiting Washington, he was met by Acheson at Union Station. The old man descended from the train leaning on the arm of his son, and probing feebly for the ground with a stick. When he saw his American host, however, he straightened, flipped the cane to an aid, and ran down the platform in greeting. At another moment in the negotiations, Averell Harriman was sent to deal with him—and was ushered into the bedroom where Mossadegh sat propped up by pillows, buttoned to the throat, palms crossed meekly on his breast. He then proceeded to demand U.S. aid on an "or else" basis. Once Mossadegh, talking to Acheson, sighed: "I am speaking for a very poor country. . . . Just sand, a few camels, a few sheep." Yes, answered Acheson, "and with your oil, rather like Texas."

But at root the situation was serious and getting worse. By 1952 a Western boycott of Iranian oil, in support of AIOC, had shut down the fields. Iran's economy was in disarray, and unemployed crowds were ready to be led in dangerous directions. The United States sought mediation, worried about a possible British invasion, but at the same time, to be fair, tried to bring Mossadegh around to a reasonable settlement by denying him aid money. How convenient it would be, thought many in the Truman Administration, if Mossadegh disappeared. But there was, alas, little chance. He resigned once, whereupon street mobs demonstrated in his favor, and he returned to win from the Shah a decree dissolving the Majlis and giving him emergency powers. By that point, late in 1952, the CIA was privately proposing to the State Department a plan of its own. Given some money to be properly spread around, Mossadegh might, in fact, be quietly put away.

Acheson either did not wish, or did not have enough time left in office, to choose this solution. But the matter of Iran was on Dulles's desk when he took office, and he had no hesitation in adopting a hard line, particularly as the new director of the CIA was his own brother. Allen Dulles, a pipe-smoking man who did not share John Foster's tendency to sermonize, emphatically shared his convictions and was tough as nails when it came to acting on them. Allen Dulles got the go-ahead for a plan that he had worked out with his CIA predecessor, former general and former ambassador to Moscow, Walter Bedell ("Beetle") Smith. The two of them cued in the British, and then secretly dispatched one of the CIA's rising stars, Kermit Roosevelt, to Teheran, for duty with the American embassy. Only Ambassador Loy Henderson and a few trusted aides knew that Roosevelt's true mission was to get access to the Shah and to a group of pro-American Iranians, and funnel through them a million dollars in bribes to get rid of Mossadegh.

The plan was for the Shah to leave Teheran suddenly for safety's sake, and from a remote location order the dismissal of Mossadegh and his replacement by Fazlollah Zahedi. It was hoped that the army could keep order. But when zero hour arrived the operation sputtered and lurched toward disaster. On August 16, 1953, Mossadegh refused to quit. Anti-British, anti-American, and Tudeh-controlled mobs roared, at his bidding, through Teheran's streets. But as the hours ticked by, Roosevelt's funds began to take effect. By August 19, new gangs of Iranians boiled out of the shops, raged through the marketplaces, waved pro-Shah and pro-Zahedi banners, and efficiently beat up Mossadegh adherents. The pressure finally forced the stubborn old man into hiding. Roosevelt vanished into invisibility in the embassy (and later slipped out of the country). The Shah, who had at first prudently fled as far as Italy, returned to his now-safe capital. Zahedi's government was offered a package of economic and military assistance by the Eisenhower Administration, and soon thereafter accepted a deal on compensation to the

AIOC for their expropriated properties. Mossadegh went to jail until 1956, when he was released. But only to be placed under virtual house arrest until his death in 1967.

The affair was over, and jubilation seemed in order. Iran had been spared from either a British or Soviet takeover, and at a relatively modest cost, thanks to a textbook-perfect CIA maneuver. In 1953 no one was apt to worry about unanticipated long-range consequences. The United States was now fully committed to the support of the Shah, who could thereby be branded by hostile propagandists as a puppet, kept on the throne by American guns and dollars. Future anti-Shah dissidents would automatically cast the United States in a Satanic role. The ultimate, surprising harvest would not be reaped for another twenty-six years, but the seeds were in the ground.

The CIA was not clairvoyant, however, and boldly pushed on to a second show of strength. This time the target was the president of a small republic in America's front yard. His name was Jacobo Arbenz, elected in 1951 to lead Guatemala. Though he had miscellaneous backing, he had proceeded to commit two sins, in the eyes of Dulles and his brother, equivalent to those of Mossadegh. First, he had seized American property, some four hundred thousand acres of plantation land owned by the United Fruit Company, whose banana empire had been, for decades, the most potent force in Central American politics. In addition, he had legalized Guatemala's Communist Party.

In simpler times a regiment of Marines would have been landed to set things straight, but such crudeness was outdated in the 1950s. This time the CIA offered a plan of combined psychological warfare and armed insurgency against Arbenz. (Among the officials of the agency involved in working it up was E. Howard Hunt, then a Political Action Officer.) Few people outside of the CIA knew what was coming, and when, in fact, a hint reached the desk of the Assistant Secretary of State for Latin American Affairs, he protested bitterly—and vainly.

The CIA's instrument was a Guatemalan army officer, Colonel Carlos Castillo-Armas, trained, as were many like him from all over the world, in the United States Army's command and staff schools. Twenty million dollars were earmarked to send Castillo to Guatemala's neighbor state of Honduras, and to equip him with an "air force" consisting of a few World War II fighters and medium bombers (flown by CIA pilots), a handful of trucks, and some followers who were to invade their homeland in order to liberate it from Arbenz's yoke.

Early in May 1954, clandestine CIA transmitters began to announce this forthcoming event over Guatemalan airwaves. More broadcasts came from a source called "The Voice of Liberation," scattering alarming rumors. There was an aerial landing here, a key defection there. So-and-so had joined the rebels. Such-and-such a town had fallen. So effective was this campaign of befuddlement that the Arbenz administration became, in fact, incapable of organized response.

The "invasion" began on June 18. Nine days later Arbenz resigned and fled. Colonel Castillo-Armas arrived almost immediately thereafter in the capital, Guatemala City—on the private plane of United States Ambassador John Peurifoy. Neither the Organization of American States nor the UN could mount an effective protest, so fast had it all happened. And the CIA became convinced of its ability to handle the Communist threat anywhere in Latin America, a burst of confidence later to have unpleasant results in Cuba.

Three days after Arbenz went under, John Foster Dulles explained matters to his countrymen by radio and television. "For several years," he said, "international Communism has been probing here and there for nesting places in the Americas. It finally chose Guatemala as a spot which it could turn into an official base from which to breed subversion which would extend to the other American republics." But the story had a happy ending. "Led by Colonel Castillo-Armas," Dulles reported (without mention of the American role), "patriots arose in Guatemala to challenge the Communist leadership—and to change it. Thus, the situation is being cured by the Guatemalans themselves."

It was a view not universally shared. In London, the head of Britain's Labor Party, former Prime Minister Clement Attlee, said that the episode "left a rather unpleasant taste in one's mouth." The former Foreign Minister of Guatemala (under Arbenz) put it more drily. The operation was, he declared, "the internationalization of McCarthyism."

FROM 1953 TO 1955, WHILE BOTH superpowers tested their new weapons (the Russians had an H-bomb of their own by late 1953) and continued their propaganda duels and shadowy battles between intelligence services, small signs began to appear indicating that prospects of peace might not be completely extinct. A new, and possibly less suspicious, leadership took over in the Soviet Union, speaking soft words and compelling an American response in similar terms. During that period the continuing war of the French in Indochina was ended—or so it appeared—at the conference table, thus eliminating a possible tinderbox. And finally, in 1955, a summit meeting would be arranged, in which U.S. and Soviet heads of state would meet face to face for the first time in ten years.

It was 6:30 A.M. on a rainy March 4, 1953, when Eisenhower was awakened with startling news. The Soviet radio had announced that Josef Stalin was gravely ill. He was, in fact, dying of a massive stroke. "Well," snapped the new President to his advisers, "what do you think we can do about this?" The answer would depend on what happened after Stalin's actual death, which took place two days later, and after the period of elaborate compulsory mourning. Who would speak for the U.S.S.R. now, and what would he say to the United States?

As it happened, the first high Communist official to emerge in a helmsman's role was Georgi Malenkov, and what he did, in a speech to the Supreme Soviet, was to offer Washington both an olive branch and a dilemma. "At the present time," he said, "there is no disputed or unresolved question that cannot be settled peacefully by mutual agreement. . . . This applies to our relations with all states, including the United States of America."

The dilemma was simply that America was unprepared for peace talk. Policy had been built for a decade on the foundation of Russia's unrelenting hostility. What happened when the bear cooed like a dove? Was there a true mending of ways? Or was this a device designed to buy time for some new and diabolical machination—in Dulles's words, "the classic Communist manouver known as 'zigzag?' " Men like Dulles were always ready to believe the worst and to reject such overtures.

But by 1953 that was not so easy. Still another Cold War front had opened, the psychological contest for the allegiance of the world's other independent nations, which, whatever their politics, feared incineration in a Soviet-American clash. It was increasingly important for both the U.S. and the U.S.S.R., therefore, to avoid being cast in the role of the intransigent "warmonger." There had to be an American response to Malenkov's feeler that would effectively counteract the propaganda impact of his conciliatory words.

The form it took became classic, to wit, a high-level American statement urging the Soviets to prove their honesty by some "good behavior," some yielding on points at issue. A speech was prepared for Eisenhower to deliver, in April, to the American Society of Newspaper Editors, entitled "The Chance for Peace." It was Emmett Hughes's recollection that Ike was enthusiastic at the prospect of making it a genuine opening. "The slate is clean," Hughes later quoted him as telling his speechwriters. "I am not going to make an indictment of them. The past speaks for itself."

Nevertheless, the talk itself was double-faceted. In some ways it was a moving argument for pacifism. "Every gun that is fired," said the ex-general with evident sincerity, "every warship launched . . . signifies, in the final sense, a theft from those who hunger and are not fed, those who are cold and are not clothed." Yet he went on to say that peace was possible only if the Russians would sign a peace treaty with Austria, support an armistice in Korea, concede the "full independence" of Eastern Europe, accept a "free and united Germany," release their remaining World War II prisoners, and enter disarmament agreements calling for international monitoring—in short, if they would abandon most of their positions since 1945.

Yet the very fact of the exchange of speeches was significant. The Kremlin hierarchy obviously was contemplating a breathing spell to get itself organized. Not until mid-1954 would Malenkov be replaced by Nikolai Bulganin and Nikita Khrushchev, and not until 1956 would the latter—the bald, pudgy, emotional Secretary General of the Executive Committee of the Communist Party of the U.S.S.R.—become the sole authorized voice of the Kremlin. In the interim there was clearly an internal debate in which some voices could press the point that an easing of tensions and the arms race was needed to give relief to the hard-pressed Soviet and satellite peoples.

The American high command, too, was hearing dissenting voices from France and Britain, who were insisting on a share of participation in policymaking. If nothing else, they were interested in continuing their economic recovery through trade with Communist-bloc nations without cries of outrage and threats of retaliation from conservatives in the United States Congress. They sought and got a "Western summit" in Bermuda in December of 1953, where Churchill—Prime Minister once more—and France's Georges Bidault strongly urged this point on Eisenhower.

Immediately on the conclusion of the meeting, the United States struck another psychological-warfare blow. Eisenhower was scheduled to deliver a speech to the United Nations, and in it he set forth what was called the "atoms-for-peace" idea. This was a proposal that the U.S. and the U.S.S.R. should each contribute, from their nuclear stockpiles, some fissionable material to an internationally controlled agency that would develop atomic power and other peaceful applications of nuclear fission and fusion for the benefit of undeveloped areas. Since the American supply at that time comfortably exceeded the Russian, the idea caused little worry to Pentagon planners, while it powerfully reinforced the image of the country's determination, in the President's words, "to devote its entire heart and mind to find the way by which the miraculous inventiveness of man shall not be dedicated to his death but consecrated to his life."

The beginning of 1954 brought a stepped-up peace offensive from Europe, and another moment of hard decision for the Administration. The French in Indochina were in the last ditch. By February, Viet Minh forces had surrounded a major garrison at Dienbienphu and were slowly starving and shelling it into submission. If it fell, it would take most of France's remaining strength in the area with it, and probably the French will to continue the whole war as well. Either some new, sizable American aid must be forthcoming, Bidault informed the Americans, or a "political solution," namely a compromise with the Communists, would be unavoidable.

In fact, the pressure was already on for what Dulles saw as a deal with Satan. As a result of the slightly thawed atmosphere, a Big Four foreign ministers' conference was held in Berlin in February. It got nowhere on European questions, but out of it came a proposal, over strong U.S. objections, for a conference of "interested parties" to meet at Geneva on April 26 for the purpose of dealing with the Indochinese and other Asian questions. Red China would be included. Dulles could not head off the move, but he could not let the discussions proceed without some American participation, either. So an "unofficial" U.S. delegation was on hand, which studiously ignored the presence of Peking's Foreign Minister, Chou En-lai, in just the same way that the French pretended not to notice the presence of representatives of the Viet Minh.

Before the parleys opened, however, Dulles fought a hard two-month battle to preserve a tough bargaining position by rescuing Dienbienphu. The instrument of salvation was suggested by Admiral Arthur Radford, chairman of the Joint Chiefs of Staff, and was called Operation Vulture. Sixty Philippine-based B-29s would join 150 carrier-based attack bombers in a massive strike against the encircling Vietnamese. The admiral was convinced that a taste of modern airpower's awesome destructiveness would demoralize and scatter the unsophisticated besiegers.

The trouble was that public and congressional opinion, enjoying America's recent liberation from the stalemate in Korea, were cool to new involvements. A campaign of persuasion was launched. The President, at an April 7 news conference, did his part by expressing how "incalculable" the loss of Indochina would be to the "free world." "You have," he explained, "what you would call the 'falling domino' principle. You have a row of dominoes set up, you knock over the first one, and what will happen to the last one is the certainty that it will go over very quickly." The dominoes would include the Malay peninsula, Burma, Thailand, and Indonesia with their tin, rice, rubber, tungsten, and oil, and their millions of people to join the 450 million Chinese already swallowed up by the Communists.

Vice President Nixon was even more convinced that the situation was grave and warranted high risks. "If in order to avoid further

Communist expansion in Asia," he said publicly, "we must take the risk now by putting American boys in. . . . I personally would support such a decision." But most daring of all, if the memoirs of Georges Bidault can be trusted, was John Foster Dulles. At a meeting of the council of NATO foreign ministers he asked the Frenchman: "What if we were to give you two atomic bombs?" (Bidault's response was, in effect, nothing doing!)

In any case, Congress, without which Eisenhower would not move, was wary. Conservatives felt that the United States had been shortchanged by its allies in Korea, so that even someone like Senator William Knowland, sometimes called "the Senator from Formosa," would not go along without assurances that England would carry a full share of any new anti-Communist war. On the other side, liberals were unenthused about rolling back the tide of Vietnamese nationalism for France's sake. Massachusetts Senator John F. Kennedy expressed the view that the French would be better off simply to grant Laos, Cambodia, and Vietnam their full independence.

So time ran out on Dulles. As the delegations gathered in Geneva, he tried to win from the Churchill government a promise of at least token participation in an American attack—perhaps a few bombers from bases in Hong Kong and Malaya. But even the aging lion of imperialism was unwilling or unable to put further strain on Britain's resources. On April 24, London pulled out of talks concerning a joint move. The conference opened. The peacemakers talked and drank and dined pleasantly while men died daily by the hundreds around Dienbienphu. Finally, however, the French folded their hand. The fortress surrendered on May 7. The following month the government in Paris fell. The new premier was Pierre Mendès-France, who was committed to getting out of Indochina peacefully.

Thereafter there was little that the United States could do. Dulles called home Walter Bedell Smith, the chief American delegate, and left underlings to observe, as the accords—which they did not sign—were finally reached. These provided for an independent Laos and Cambodia, and for Vietnam a Korean-type arrangement—not the most promising precedent. There would be a temporary division along the 17th parallel, with a "provisional" North Vietnam (which Ho Chi Minh would head) on one side and an equally short-term South Vietnam, under Emperor Bao Dai, on the other. There would be a cease-fire at once and, in June of 1956, free nationwide elections to decide the form of government for a unified Vietnam.

Though the United States pledged not to interfere with these arrangements, Dulles had wired Smith even before their completion: "Since undoubtedly true that elections might eventually mean unification Vietnam under Ho Chi Minh, this makes it all more important they should be only held as long after cease-fire agreement as possible and in conditions free from intimidation to give democratic elements best chance."

What that meant would later become clear. A secret National Security Council paper laid out a future plan for South Vietnam. Bao Dai was a French puppet, but his premier, Ngo Dinh Diem, was well regarded by many Americans whom he had met during a sojourn in the United States. The NSC's recommendation was that military and economic aid should be furnished to Bao Dai and Diem, while reforms were pressed upon them that would make them an attractive alternative to Ho. There seemed to be heartening signs that such a policy would work, for soon after the cease-fire South Vietnam severed her last ties with the "colonialist" French, and in 1955 her voters deposed Bao Dai in favor of a republic with Diem as president. But the ultimate result of the new American approach was that the United States had assumed the French role of supporting Western-oriented, anti-Communist elements in a still strife-torn Indochina. Unwittingly, a time bomb had been planted and it began to tick.

Nevertheless, the war had been ended, leaving Dulles no choice except to step up the pace of the talks that finally led to the creation of SEATO. Peace had won an apparent victory in 1954, and from the point of view of conciliators, 1955 would appear to be even better.

Eisenhower and Dulles had been resisting the urgings of the French and British for a four-power summit meeting with Russia, especially because they were sensitive to the constant refrain of right-wing Republicans that the last two such meetings, at Yalta and Potsdam, had resulted in "sellouts." They continued to say that nothing could be gained without a Soviet demonstration of good deeds.

But early in the new year the Russians seemed to do precisely that. They offered a peace treaty to Austria under which Soviet troops would be withdrawn if the Austrians agreed not to enter NATO or any other armed Western alliance, as West Germany was on the verge of doing. Moreover, in May, a Soviet delegate who had been dispatched to join disarmament talks in London offered a seemingly generous proposal to the French, British, Canadian, and American representatives—basically an acceptance of their suggested limits on nuclear and conventional weapons, with even a possibility of inspection by an international agency thrown in. To be sure, Moscow simultaneously created the Warsaw Pact, linking seven East European countries together in a counterforce to NATO. But their earlier pacific moves undercut American claims that they were not seriously trying to ease matters, and Eisenhower and Dulles knew it. On the day that the Austrian treaty was proposed, the Secretary walked into the President's office, grinned ruefully, and said: "Well, I think we've had it."

They had. The conference was set for mid-July, in Geneva. State Department planners prepared for it with position papers on American goals, which included a unified and rearmed Germany allied to the NATO powers, Soviet relaxation of its grip on the Eastern European nations, and an arms control program that would leave American superiority substantially untouched. They also guessed at the probable Russian objectives, such as more trade with the West, recognition of Red China, and that "moral and social equality" so dreaded by Dulles. To prevent that last contingency, the President was asked to avoid too many jovial meetings before news cameras with Bulganin and Khrushchev. When with them, he should preserve "an austere countenance."

But one of Eisenhower's strengths was his natural, spontaneous warmth, and he greeted the Soviet delegation with the same smiles that he showed to new British Prime Minister Anthony Eden, and France's Edgar Faure. He was especially cordial, at a formal dinner, to his old wartime comrade, Marshal Zhukov—now Soviet Minister of Defense—to whom he presented gifts for his daughter, a portable radio, and a pen-and-ink desk set. He also arranged a private lunch with Zhukov, agreed to by his staff provided that the talk was confined to old soldiers' gossip. In the benign atmosphere of toasts and laughter, it was easy to detect a new "spirit of Geneva," a ray in the clouds, but the realities were actually unyielding. Bulganin and Khrushchev, for example, privately told the British and French that there was no way they could agree to a reunified and rearmed Germany only ten years after the war that had devastated Russia. But when this was passed on to Eisenhower, he denied that it was a problem. The real issue for the West, he said, was how to deal with Communist zealots.

At a final plenary session, Eisenhower unveiled a proposal worked up by a special task force under his assistant for Cold War strategy, Nelson Rockefeller. Turning directly to the Russians, he announced that the United States would be willing to exchange with them a complete blueprint of military establishments in the two countries, to be verified by mutual aerial photographic missions. That would reduce each side's anxiety over the possibility of surprise attack by hitherto unsuspected weapons. The "open skies" plan was a striking notion, but the President was aware that while most American bases were open to the public and could be located by any newspaper reader, the same was not true of Soviet installations. In effect, U.S. intelligence would be the chief gainer in the exchange, and, as was expected, the gambit was refused. At a postsession reception, Khrushchev smiled at Eisenhower, and shook his head in an unmistakable no. In the end, the main result of the summit gathering had been to boost Eisenhower's popularity at home and abroad, and to leave matters of substance untouched.

Still, there *had* been top-level dialogue. The two sides, even if they were talking as much to the world's propaganda-consuming audience as to each other, *were* talking. Murmurs of accommodation might be misleading, but they were easier on the world's nerves than threats of annihilation.

But then, in the summer and autumn of 1956, wrenching news burst into headlines from the pavements of Budapest and the sands of the Sinai. The Cold War was still on, and getting more frightening—neither ending nor exploding, but merely changing.

I F THE NEW SOVIET LEADERSHIP made John Foster Dulles's nights uneasy with fear that its peace offensive might weaken the will of the European allies, he had even more cause for worry in 1955, when Khrushchev and Bulganin undertook goodwill tours to Burma, India, Afghanistan, and various Mideastern countries. Dulles had to accept the neutralism of a few Asian nations like India, even though he regarded it as "immoral and shortsighted." But at that time he still hoped somehow to sculpture an anti-Soviet alliance in the Arab world, and it was this project that Moscow's traveling salesmen threatened to upset.

But there were difficulties in Dulles's plan. For one thing, such states as Saudi Arabia, Egypt, Syria, Jordan, Lebanon, and Iraq were not eager to join hands with France and Britain, their former colonizers. For another, the United States had a special relationship with Israel, to which it had been a particular patron since 1948. The unrelenting hostility of the Arab nations toward what they referred to as the "Zionist" republic in their midst made it hard for Washington to entertain simultaneous good relations with Tel Aviv and the Arab capitals.

The French, and to an even greater extent the British, likewise faced complexities. They still furnished arms and advice to the Arabs, and felt reduced in rank and undercut when America wooed their formerly "backward" client states as equals to themselves. But they also disliked it when the U.S. offended the Arabs by any leaning toward Israel. Angry Arabs might take their wounded feelings to the Russians, who had, in 1955, the freest hand of all, since they were burdened neither with a colonialist record in that particular region nor with partiality to Israel. True, the autocratic and Islamic rulers of the Arab states had no ideological sympathy whatever for Communism. But friends could be won in the undeveloped world with the loans, technical assistance, and arms the Russians had to offer.

Hence the bizarre ballet of Mideastern diplomacy—the United States urging France and Britain to deal gently with Arab nationalism, the French and British urging Washington to cool its sympathies for the Jews, and the Russians watching and waiting. Nowhere was it illustrated better than in the course of events in Egypt after 1952.

In that year a revolt of progressive and nationalistic army officers ousted fat, sybaritic King Farouk from the throne of the longtime British protectorate. Two years later, with some encouragement from Washington, the British pulled out of their military bases in the country. By February of 1955, Gamal Abdul Nasser, one of the revolutionaries, had become Egypt's strong man. He inherited not only its severe economic problems but the ongoing border battles with Israel, and in that particular month he learned how costly they could be, when an Israeli raid on Gaza wiped out an Egyptian garrison and inflicted heavy casualties.

Nasser needed an infusion of arms, and he first approached the United States. But Washington was loath to escalate the Arab-Israeli arms race, and had even agreed with France and Britain as far back as 1950 to try to cap it. Rebuffed, Nasser went off to a week-long April conference of twenty-nine "unaligned" African and Asian nations, members of what was then labeled the Third World. When he returned, he asked the Soviet ambassador to Cairo how Moscow would respond to a request for military hardware. The answer was satisfactory. In August, to the consternation of both British and Americans, a military assistance pact between Nasser and the Soviet Union was concluded. Egypt had vanished from the fold! But then came a fresh chance to bring back the errant sheep.

Nasser wanted to build a huge dam at Aswan, on the Nile. It would control the devastating annual flooding of the mighty river, the lifestream of the great Egypt of antiquity. The harnessed waters would bring richly irrigated crops to the hungry, would generate kilowatts to light homes, commence industries, and lift modern Egypt to new plateaus of prosperity. But it would take vast sums of money to get started. And so Nasser's ambassador turned for help to the primal fountain of money at that time, the United States, and asked for help.

Dulles was willing. It was the kind of deal often put together in the offices of Sullivan and Cromwell. Fifty-six million would come at once from the United States and $14 million from Great Britain, and there would be loans from the World Bank (of which the United States was the chief prop), adding up, over fifteen years, to an additional $330 million. Meanwhile, Nasser would agree to a new mission from the United States to make a try at patching things up between himself and his Israeli neighbors. By the start of 1956 everything seemed in order and in motion.

But in six months it all fell apart. To begin with, Eisenhower's special emissary, Robert B. Anderson, spent a frustrating month of flights between Tel Aviv and Cairo (via Rome and Athens), but ran into an absolute blank wall in efforts to arrange talks between Nasser and Israeli Prime Minister David Ben Gurion. With the failure of the peace effort, some Administration officials assumed that the entire package, the dam included, was lost. Moreover, Eisenhower's reelection campaign was opening, and, as world leaders were coming to know, American foreign policy took erratic flights during each presidential contest. Secretary of the Treasury George Humphrey urged on his fellow Cabinet members a course of fiscal prudence that would be popular with some voters who were grumbling about "excessive" foreign aid. And, finally, Nasser compounded his problems with the American establishment by recognizing Red China, thereby provoking new Dulles preachments on the sins of neutralism. The combination of all these factors caused the United States to reexamine the question, and on July 19, 1956, the Egyptian ambassador was bluntly told that it was all off. There would be no money for Nasser's dam.

It took one week for Nasser to come up with his counterstroke. On July 26 he nationalized the Suez Canal.

The news broke like thunder on Britain and France. They owned the waterway through the Suez Canal Company, a joint-stock corporation in which each nation held 44 percent of the shares. Egypt had a small portion, too, but only five of thirty-two directors were Egyptian, and of the canal's $99 million in earnings in 1955, only $5 million went to Nasser. But the money from users' fees was not the only consideration. For the British in particular the canal appeared vital. One-third of all the ships that "transited" it in 1955 were British; two-thirds of all Britain's oil imports passed through it. It was no wonder that Anthony Eden declared: "The Egyptian has his thumb on our windpipe." Eden's hatred of Nasser was intense; to an aide he had raged, with a total loss of his studied British calm, "I want him destroyed, can't you understand that?"

The Americans, who had provoked the crisis, found themselves in the middle, reluctant either to offend Nasser further or make the British unhappier. Dulles suggested various alternatives, such as the possible internationalization of the canal, that were rejected by one side or the other. He also warned the British and the French—who were equally indignant at what they called Nasser's "robbery"— against the use of force. They listened. And privately ignored the warning.

Quietly and effectively they had turned to the one other power that had a lively interest in unseating Nasser. Letting bygones be bygones, Israel was working with Eden and French Prime Minister Guy Mollet, former Arab supporters, on a plan. The Israelis would mobilize, but apparently against Syria. Then, aided by Mystère jets supplied to them by the French, they would instead make a swift surprise jab across the Sinai peninsula toward the canal. Whereupon the French and British, to preserve international trade, would send in their troops to occupy the canal and save it from destruction by the armed forces of either Egypt or Israel.

So during September and October, while the two former owners of the canal were seemingly looking for a nonviolent solution, their ships, soldiers, and airmen were stealthily taking up attack positions.

Meantime, many hundreds of miles away from the Suez region, another powder trail was being laid that would lead to an explosion at the exact moment when the Suez affair reached its climax.

Ever since the post-Stalin Politburo had taken over, Soviet Russia's involuntary allies, the nations of Eastern Europe, had been testing the tightness of Moscow's controls. In 1953 East Germany had witnessed some resistance, quickly squelched. In the summer of 1956 the Poles had demanded the reinstatement of their leader, Wladyslaw Gomulka, imprisoned in 1951 as a foe of Stalin, and Khrushchev, though angry, had let it happen in October. Then the contagion spread to Hungary, chafing under especially severe privations and a harsh police regime, imposed by a Kremlin-blessed state chief. Loud demands now began to be made for the return of Imre Nagy, a relatively mild Communist boss, who had been ousted in 1955 for "Titoism."

On October 22, shouting crowds poured into the streets of Budapest demanding Nagy's return. The next day, evidently with Kremlin approval, Nagy was actually named Premier. But rioting went on, the police fired on demonstrators, casualty figures mounted. No one seemed to know for certain whether Hungary was in the grip of chaos or on the way to some Titoist version of Communism, or was actually trying to end Communist rule altogether and break all ties with Moscow.

Washington assumed the latter. It was an article of faith that everyone in the captive nations yearned for the total rejection of Marx, Lenin, and all their heirs. Moreover, it was good politics in American cities with large Slavic populations to hint that the United States would help. In his 1952 campaign Eisenhower had promised to use "every political, every economic, every psychological tactic" necessary to help each satellite "maintain an outward strain against its Moscow bond." But such promises were risky. They tended to make the Russians believe that American propaganda was exacerbating every discontent in Eastern Europe and turning it into an anti-Soviet weapon. And, in point of fact, Radio Free Europe, the American broadcasting system that beamed "truth" behind the "Iron Curtain," was exhorting the Hungarian "freedom fighters," as it had dubbed them, to keep fighting. Denouncing the return of Nagy as a sly maneuver, it urged: "Do not hang your weapons on the wall until [the ministries of] Interior and Defense are in your control."

On October 29, a Monday, it looked as if the happiest of endings might be in sight. A Soviet broadcast announced that the Russian troops in Hungary, long an affront to the local populace, would be withdrawn. And the process actually began immediately.

On the same day, early in the morning, Israeli paratroopers tumbled out of their planes to seize positions thirty miles east of the Suez Canal.

The Hungarian and Suez crises each peaked within the next few days, crowding the imminent U.S. election out of the headlines. The news of the Israeli assault was not a total surprise to Eisenhower. Secret U.S. aerial reconnaissance had revealed troop buildups, but as Tel Aviv had hoped, it was assumed that the blow would fall on Syria. When it hit the Sinai, instead—and when, on Wednesday, October 31, British planes bombed Cairo—the Administration was livid. Walking to the White House staff mess, Sherman Adams, Ike's chief of staff, muttered through clenched teeth to an associate: "What your friends won't do behind your back!"

Eisenhower's temper erupted. When first informed of Israel's sneak punch, he stormed to Dulles: "All right, Foster, you tell 'em that, goddamn it, we're going to apply sanctions, we're going to the United Nations, we're going to do everything that there is so we can stop this thing." There was little doubt that he felt the same way about the British and French as the final hours of October heightened the tension.

Then, on the morning of November 1, the ugliest depths of Soviet behavior were nakedly exposed to the world. While the U.S.S.R.'s armed units had been evacuating Hungary, Moscow radio had issued an astonishingly conciliatory statement, praising the Hungarian workers and trumpeting the virtue of a "great commonwealth of Socialist nations," built on the principle of "full equality . . . and noninterference in the domestic affairs of one another." The ink was still wet on newspaper copies of the proclamation when the tanks and weapons carriers marked with the Red Star rolled back into Budapest—firing! Whether the broadcast had been a ruse or whether Nagy had blundered fatally by announcing Hungary's withdrawal from the Warsaw Pact remained unclear. But there was nothing vague about what happened next. Nagy fled to the shelter of the Yugoslav embassy, later to be lured out by a trick, kidnapped to the Soviet Union, and executed. In a few days of street fighting thirty thousand Hungarians were killed. Armored power was too much for Molotov cocktails and sniper fire from clandestine rifles. The battle ended with a Moscow puppet government in total control, the jails jammed, and many thousands of refugees in flight to Austria and safety. Some of them complained there that Radio Free Europe's bold words had led them to expect American help that never came.

Wherever justice and truth lay in the quarrels, the brute facts were that as of November 1 the United States was confronted with two disruptive acts of aggression, one by its closest allies and one by its most implacable enemy. Rarely had Dulles enjoyed the chance to be so righteous at the expense of both friend and foe. The United States put resolutions calling for immediate cease-fires and with-drawals in both Hungary and Egypt before the Security Council. When they met with expected vetoes, they were resubmitted to the General Assembly.

There was almost a note of black comedy in the proceedings. The Russians, with the blood of the Hungarians on their hands, spoke in outraged tones about the "Western aggressors." The French and British, in turn, wanted to cosponsor the condemnation of the Hungarian atrocity. They were promptly told by Washington to call off their own invasion before joining the ranks of the indignant. Eden professed astonishment at American objections to a simple "police action," even though angry Londoners were demonstrating in protest outside his windows. And then, as if God wished to confuse the players further, on the night of November 3, Dulles was taken out of the swirl of events. Stricken with the first attack of what proved to be cancer, he was rushed to the hospital for emergency surgery.

On the night of Monday, November 5, French and British paratroopers hurtled down on the northern end of the canal, and troopships carrying reinforcements neared Port Said. Bulganin went on the air with messages to Israel, France, and England. He condemned their "colonial war," and said that the Soviet Union might send "volunteers" to the area or even use her long-range rockets, if need be, to halt the subjugation of Egypt. (A few hours earlier he had set some kind of record for effrontery by proposing a joint Soviet-American expedition to restore peace in the Mideast, an offer immediately rejected by Eisenhower as a bid to divert attention from Hungary.)

Almost instantly, the emergency was at a crisis point. The disaster of a Soviet armed incursion into the eastern Mediterranean and North Africa was imminent. And more—there could only be one response to a threatened Russian attack on two NATO allies, even the most errant. Was war a matter of hours away? "We must stop this before we are all burned to a crisp," said one State Department officer at one of many urgent meetings that filled Tuesday, November 6.

All during that election day, Eisenhower sat conferring with his military and naval commanders discussing combat options, or with his diplomatic staffs seeking ways to use the two peaceful weapons against the Suez invaders that good fortune had put into his hands. They were, simply put, oil and money.

The British had overplayed their hand. Their bombing of the canal had sunk an Egyptian ship in such a way as to block through-passage. Meantime, the Syrians and Saudis either destroyed or shut down the pipelines through their territories that fed the waiting tankers of the "imperialists." Not only England and France but Europe and NATO were facing a destructive oil cutoff.

In 1956, the United States could help. America controlled large reserves of petroleum produced domestically or in Latin America. Dwight Eisenhower was now spelling out a clear rule. No cease-fire, no help.

In addition, the daily cost of the miniwar was shattering to the shaky British economy. London's thin gold and dollar reserves were melting away. On world markets, the pound was dropping. The French, already bled by Indochina, were in worse condition. The United States could help there, too, by making dollars available. And Eisenhower explained again, through the desperate hours: no cease-fire, no help.

Late on Tuesday afternoon, the capitulation came. The French, British, and Israelis would accept a cease-fire.

That night the returns sent Eisenhower back to the White House with 57 percent of the votes cast behind him.

It was not quite all over. The invaders had to be gotten out of Egypt to remove any vestige of a Soviet excuse for further troublemaking. But the leverage of cash and oil remained potent. The British government fumed that Eisenhower had been less moralistic, less insistent on a common law for the strong and the weak when Guatemala had taken United Fruit's acres—but by the 28th of November they agreed to withdraw. The end of that month saw the British and the French depart, while the Israeli forces remained in Egypt through the following March.

Unfortunately, there was nothing in the United States' hands that could be used to get the Russians out of Hungary.

So the worst period since the Berlin blockade was over, after a nightmarish few hours during which Americans had come close to the brink, and just fourteen months after the smiles that testified to "the spirit of Geneva."

There was much hard work to do for a recuperating Dulles. The French and British would need to have their feelings soothed. They felt triply punished. The United States had chided them when they backed Arabs who menaced Israel. Then it had spanked them when they joined Israel in a war on Arabs. Finally, it had equated them with the Russians. It was hard to swallow, and harder still to choke down a basic fact. They had flopped ignominiously in their attempts to restore the status quo without American help. Even Khrushchev, at a Moscow reception, laughed at their "hopeless attempt to restore lost colonial bastions," adding the words much quoted later, "We will bury you." For France it was the second such humiliation in two years, and for Britain a clear sign that the sun had finally set on the age of Kipling.

For Americans, the impact was enormous. The vacuum left by Britain and France had to be filled by the United States if the assumptions of Cold War thought were true, and already France was being replaced as defender of Indochina. Now, unless the whole "containment" frame of mind was changed, the British would be replaced as the major Western presence in the Middle East, and the U.S. would take up the burden of excluding the Russians. The military, economic, political, and psychological responsibilities of the American people had become global, just as the creators of the national security system had anticipated and desired.

But there were some clear limits to U.S. power, too, sadly demonstrated in Hungary. All of the brave talk of liberation was unavailing. Nothing had changed the situation that Roosevelt had had to accept in 1945. Where Russian armies stood, the Russian will could not be challenged without full-scale war. And "massive retaliation" became a less and less endurable prospect as the stockpiles of appalling nuclear weapons grew.

So the Cold War went on in new arenas, shaping policies to its needs. As in Berlin in 1948, the ultimate holocaust had been avoided. The 1956 crises, too, passed into history, leaving the nations to face fresh choices between peace, surrender, and destruction.

Chapter 8
ERA OF CRISES
1957-1960

THE SOUND WAS UNLIKE ANYTHING that American radio listeners had ever heard. Through a background rasp of static, an intermittent "beep" forced itself—a high-pitched noise like the chirp of a newborn chick. And yet that tiny signal, first heard on October 5, 1957, separated two eras in human history as decisively as the lookout's cry of "Land, ho!" from the masthead of the *Santa Maria* 465 Octobers earlier. Nineteen fifty-seven's mechanical hail also opened a New World. It came from a tiny transmitter in a hollow 185-pound steel ball that was circling the globe every ninety minutes—an artificial satellite of earth, blasted into orbit by a rocket of enormous power, made in the Union of Soviet Socialist Republics. The Russians humorously called their minimoon Sputnik, or "fellow traveler."

The United States did not laugh.

For Sputnik, though a tremendous beginning for humankind, marked the end of an era for Americans. It slammed the door on their long-standing faith in unchallenged U.S. technological supremacy.

The mind of every American schoolchild teemed with storybook images of Yankee geniuses and their contributions to progress: Eli Whitney contriving the cotton gin; Samuel Colt whittling out the wooden model of the six-shooter that won the West; Morse and his telegraph; Singer's sewing machine; George Eastman's "Kodak"; Edison's light bulb, talking machine, and pictures that moved; Henry Ford building his "quadricycle" in a backyard garage in spare hours. Popular pride ignored European pioneers in both theoretical and applied physics and chemistry, on whose work all these "discoveries" rested. The Russian achievement, however, forced a confrontation with reality—a second jolt like the detonation of the Soviet nuclear bomb in 1949. But in that case the Russians had

177

merely caught up with the United States. In the matter of artificial satellites, even though America had ongoing programs of rocket and space research, the Reds had gotten unmistakably ahead.

Though knowledgeable U.S. scientists were not wholly surprised, public leaders reacted at first with shock, then bewilderment, and then attempted to belittle the Russians. Presidential press secretary James Hagerty declared that America's own embryonic space effort was not "in a race with the Soviet's." The appraisal of Sherman Adams, Eisenhower's chief assistant, was crisp: "an outer-space basketball game." And according to American Admiral Rawson Bennett, chief of the Office of Naval Research, Sputnik was a "hunk of iron almost anybody could launch."

The Russians made such remarks sound hollow within a month. On November 4, they sent up a second Sputnik. This one weighed 1,120 pounds and obviously had room for a payload of research instruments that was mouth-watering to scientists studying upper atmospheric radiation, density, temperature, and composition. What was more, a tiny dog named Laika was on board, wired with devices to measure the effects of extragravitational flight on animal functions. The Russians were obviously preparing to put men in space, or even to undertake that perennial tease to the human imagination, a journey to the moon.

Another thirty days passed, and a new gulf of humiliation was plumbed. An American program to "fly" a satellite (code-name: Vanguard) had been in the works. It was put on a furiously accelerated schedule. On December 6, in a glare of publicity, a three-stage Navy rocket, with Vanguard on top, was ignited. It wobbled a few feet off the pad and exploded. The grapefruit-sized American rival to Sputnik fell to the ground and beeped its last amid geysers of smoke.

At that point, an almost inevitable American overreaction set in. First there was fear. Could Soviet satellites be orbital platforms from which to rain devastating explosives on a defenseless world? Or in even more earthbound terms, if the Russians had rockets with thrust enough to hurl half a ton into orbit, were they equally able to send rockets with nuclear warheads halfway around the world to U.S. targets? Were they leading in the sprint to develop a new weapon with initials that would soon be chillingly familiar? ICBM. Intercontinental ballistic missile.

And underlying that initial, immediate panic was a sudden anxiety about the very foundations of American society. An explosion of criticism of the U.S. school system ripped through the press when it was learned that Russian educators stressed hard training in scientific fundamentals instead of driver education, typing, and home economics. If Russian youngsters graduated at eighteen with ten years of math, four of chemistry, five of physics, and six of biology under their belts—whereas only half of American high school graduates had training in physics, and only two-thirds had a slight acquaintance with chemistry—did this mean that Americans were, as a people, too easygoing with their children? Too relaxed about the future, too soft, too consumer-oriented—yes, even perhaps a bit decadent?

The answer was, in fact, "not necessarily." Media overkill exaggerated America's "defeat." The Russians had the rocket power for ICBMs but not, as yet, the finely honed guidance systems. And although the U.S.S.R. would soon become first to put men in space, the Americans would presently begin to win solid laurels of their own in exploring and mapping the heavens with rocket-propelled vehicles. Finally, the Russian "spectaculars" simply proved that forced industrialization and scientific development, under totalitarian rule, could bring about remarkable accomplishments but did not prove the superiority of the totalitarian way of life. Unlike the Americans, the Russians were unable to provide military hardware and journeys by "cosmonauts" while simultaneously furnishing their people with the fundamental amenities of life. A French newspaper correctly noted that the first Sputnik was "a brilliant star" carrying the light of Soviet power into the skies, but only "thanks to millions of pots and shoes lacking."

Yet, all the same, that autumn of 1957 marked a major turning point in the history of the Cold War. For the first time, Americans scrutinized their entire culture in terms of how well it prepared them for the ongoing conflict. The battle against the Russians, it seemed, would have to be fought in classrooms and supermarkets as well as in embassies and on battlefields. The Soviet-American power struggle had become the prism through which even nonpolitical aspects of life might be viewed, interpreted, and changed.

Proof was shown in some of the sequels to the Sputnik launch. Congress voted heavy appropriations for "defense-related" study and research, greatly expanding academic offerings in fields as diverse as astrophysics and Slavic languages, and in the process reworking the priorities, funding, and control mechanisms of American universities. The "space race" continued, and was not seen as a mighty adventure of humankind but rather as a series of theatrical "spectaculars" staged by the two national rivals in the vast auditorium of the solar system. On the American side some spin-offs of the space program, such as new lightweight materials and microcircuitry, flowed into the general economy in the form of minicomputers, portable television sets, lightweight cameras, and recorders, all of them accelerating ongoing social change.

But there was one surprising element in the American reaction.

There was no upsurge of nervous belligerence. Whereas the first Soviet nuclear test blast had been followed, in the United States, by NSC-68 and the rise of Senator McCarthy, the follow-up to Sputnik was, after a brief interval, a slackening of tension. In the case of the United States this was due to an array of new forces at work. America's culture, as the 1950s neared their end, was not necessarily weakening, but neither was it geared for stern sacrifice or tuned receptively to battle cries. Paradoxically, a prosperity partly due to the Cold War was loosening the Cold War's grip.

AMERICANS IN 1958 had not forsaken the underlying assumption of the day, namely that the world was threatened by Communist ambition and guile. But they were something like the second generation of settlers of New England; Puritan zeal for holy war was diluted with everyday, earthly concerns. The greatest preoccupation of Eisenhower's America had become the absorption of swift, gigantic changes in patterns of life and work.

The changes began with an explosive rise in the birthrate, labeled "the baby boom." The fundamental statistic was a jump in live births per thousand of population from 18.8 in 1950 to 25 in 1960, and that abstract census-taker's number became startlingly visible in a landscape that seemed increasingly crowded with toddlers. The escalating infant populace made fortunes for obstetricians and pediatricians (and their publishers, most notably Pocket Books, which sold millions of copies of Dr. Benjamin Spock's relaxed *Pocket Book of Baby and Child Care*); for those who made and sold baby foods, diapers, highchairs, playpens, carriages, strollers, "kiddie clothes," toys, and games; and for those who supplied educational equipment to thousands of school boards struggling to deal with the most far-reaching statistic of all—an annual jump of over a million grade-school-age children throughout each year of the decade. The budgetary strain on state and local resources was insupportable, and was only relieved, over time, by various kinds of federal help.

The baby boom gave rise to, and was articulated with, a stampede to suburbia. The virtue of country living was a deeply established national conviction, and as a wave of prosperity floated thousands of couples into middle-class status, they easily adopted the gospel that their children had to be spared the frustrations and limitations of growing up in apartments and city streets. To meet the demand for escape from urban centers, "developments" boomed on what had once been farmlands, now bulldozed down to raw earth and then covered with several dozen or several hundred modest look-alike homes priced within young families' budgets, thanks to the economies of mass purchasing. The developer, buying stoves, refrigerators, and washer-dryers in carload lots, could offer a "fully equipped" home on as little as a quarter of an acre and sell it for $15,000 to $25,000. The buyer could get as much as 90 percent of the total sum in a low-cost loan, which a bank would happily grant because repayment was guaranteed by the Federal Housing Administration or the Veterans Administration. The government wanted to subsidize home building and home ownership, and added an extra inducement by exempting interest payments on mortgage loans from taxation. And so the number of Americans owning their own homes rose from 23.6 million in 1950 to 32.8 million in 1960, an impressive validation of the national dream of independence for everyone. For these new owners it often did not matter that the walls were thin, the backyard small, and the design identical with the neighbors'.

Suburbia both nursed and fed on the auto boom. Commuters of the 1920s had ridden the railroads or interurban electric trolleys, but their sons and daughters thirty years later took to the driver's seat, traveling as much as 75 miles daily with carefree minds, since a dollar bought as much as four gallons of gasoline, enough for that distance. Government poured money into road building, the capstone of the effort being the almost completely federally funded Interstate Highway System of superexpressways, begun in the mid-1950s. Suburbia also spawned the two-car family, for while the breadwinner had one vehicle at work, the other was indispensable to the homemaker, who needed it to get to the shopping malls. These, which were long rows of stores surrounding enormous parking lots, were built to take advantage of cheap land. Schools in suburbia tended to spread out over large tracts for the same reason. They, too, could only be reached by bus or car. Since the auto was the "environment" in which all family members spent many hours a week, it was axiomatic that manufacturers would compete in making each year's new models more luxurious than ever. By 1960, 74 million passenger cars were on the roads.

The car was the master machine of national existence, but the American family also lived with an arsenal of lesser gadgets whose manufacture and sale kept the economy running at high speed. The "ideal" suburban mother depicted in advertisements required electric vacuum cleaners, polishers, waxers, dishwashers, freezers, juicers, toasters, and rotisseries to keep her domain neat and her brood fed. The suburban father of popular image tended the lawn and garden, built shelves and rumpus rooms and backyard barbecues, and "redid" entire kitchens and bathrooms, using a variety of power tools. It might have occasionally occurred to perceptive couples that they worked hard for the "freedom" of homeownership. A young mother, urged by the culture to be fecund, found herself bound to a relentless routine of meal-making, laundering, shopping, and above all chauffering (for suburbia's children were not within walking distance of dance classes, piano lessons, or scout meetings), while she handled the infinite variety of crises generated by sibling rivalry and prepubescent anxieties. A "development" father often started his commuting day at 6:30 A.M. and finished it thirteen hours, many office problems, and two traffic jams later, only to be faced then with accumulated chores. Many marriages were invisibly fraying under the strain.

Yet there was some leisure time, too; the grind was offset by liberalized employment patterns that made forty-hour weeks and long vacations almost standard. There was time to invite friends over for drinks on the newly acquired outdoor furniture—$145 million worth bought in 1960. Time to light the charcoal and consume—also in 1960 alone—about a billion pounds of hot dogs and 532 million pounds of potato chips. Time to gypsy off into the beckoning woods (national forest campground users increased from 1.5 million in 1950 to 6.6 million in 1960), with a tent-trailer behind the station wagon and a boat with an outboard motor (3 million more of them in use in 1960 than in 1950) strapped to the roof.

Above all, time to watch television, whose growth was phenomenal. Five million families owned sets in 1950. Each year thereafter, 5 million were added, until, by 1962, 90 percent of all households had at least one tube. Television's enormous influence on American life—on child-rearing, violence, the national sense of reality, the political process—would not be felt and debated until much later. But even in the Fifties, the lighted screen in the living room was becoming a major family presence, and was one more indispensable item to buy on the installment plan.

The whole nation appeared, at times, to be committed to a festival of consumption held in an atmosphere of inoffensive sterility. Social analysts worried because many college students reported to pollsters that they were eager, on graduation, to land jobs with large organizations and earn their way as quickly as possible to security and married happiness in split-level suburban homes, complete with two-car garages. Those who actually found such corporate jobs, in fact, were quickly programmed into attitudes designed above all to emphasize team behavior, according to William H. Whyte, Jr., in his popular book, The Organization Man. Whyte reported that the junior executive sure to rise was one who seemed to be without kinks or abrasive qualities or strong opinions or distinctive accents, customs, or skin color—someone, in short, who fit the title of another Fifties bestseller, The Man in the Gray Flannel Suit by Sloan Wilson. Or one who took his opinions exclusively from others and was therefore a member of what sociologist David Riesman named The Lonely Crowd.

A SOCIETY APPARENTLY SO STEEPED in material comfort was hardly one eager to undertake an ardent, self-sacrificing struggle with the world's Communist zealots. But "apparently" is a key word. In actuality, life in the United States was nowhere near as seamlessly idyllic as it was painted by American information officers abroad— or by the Republican Party in its 1956 convention when it turned Eisenhower's renomination into a virtual coronation. There were hidden booby traps that would be detonated within a few years, and merely to tick off a checklist of them was to furnish a preview of the issues of the Sixties and Seventies.

For one thing, there were soft spots in Eisenhower prosperity. It rested in part on a narrow base of high military expenditures that produced relatively few consumer goods and jobs. It was true enough that Pentagon billions for "research and development," when spread through the automotive, aircraft, and electronics industries, stimulated the economy generally. But the stimulus pushed up prices, wages, and production costs in what later become a dangerous inflationary cycle. To escape those rising-cost pressures, major industries either retarded modernization or else pursued it through automation, thereby reducing manpower demands and also raising the spectre of a permanent unemployed class composed of those who, for one reason or another, could not acquire technical skills. Yet efforts to reduce armaments budgets ran into the combined influence of what a political orator called an "immense military establishment and a large arms industry." This orator further declared that the nation must "guard against the acquisition of unwarranted influence . . . by the military-industrial complex." The voice was not that of a soapbox socialist; it belonged to President Dwight D. Eisenhower, saying farewell to the nation as he left office in 1961. In the same address he called attention to another item on the nation's future agenda, namely conservation. We must, he warned, "avoid the impulse to live only for today, plundering, for our own ease and convenience, the precious resources of tomorrow."

Eisenhower prosperity was unevenly spread. Left out of its embrace were migratory workers, marginal farmers, the chronically unemployable, and the people who clung to their hometowns in regions whose economic heyday had passed—places like rural New England or the valley of Appalachia. Social security and welfare programs kept such souls barely solvent, and "invisible" as a problem. They did not ride in the good-times caravan. Even those Americans who did were periodically jolted by periods of recession (as in 1957-58).

Strong tremors of economic distress were felt in the nation's major cities. Thanks to the exodus to suburbia, many of them were left in a squeeze between shrinking tax revenues on the one hand, and on the other, rising maintenance costs for their aging transportation, sanitation, school, police, and fire protection systems. Moreover, the remaining urban population contained a high proportion of low-income workers and public dependents—the old, the sick, the jobless, the nonwhite—unable to escape. The cities' solution was often an appeal to Washington for help, but when the help came it enlarged both the federal budget and bureaucracy, already swollen by the nation's worldwide responsibilities.

And those same responsibilities were beginning to weaken the mighty dollar. The United States spent heavily abroad to maintain its network of bases and aid programs. In the early 1950s that money had come back home to pay for American exports. But by the decade's end, a recovering Europe and Japan were becoming self-sufficient, and buying fewer American articles. The balance of trade began to tip against America. At the end of a year her government and businessmen would owe money abroad, and would have to pay a premium for gold and foreign currency or credits.

Such were the submerged economic dilemmas waiting to snag the national well-being. There were also cultural and social pressures and anxieties that would afterward be overlooked by sentimentalists who waxed nostalgic about the 1950s. For one thing, there was the overpowering fact of the hydrogen bomb casting its shadow across life. In the back of everyone's mind was awareness of the inconceivable destruction that would follow what strategists euphemistically called a "nuclear exchange." A sign of that was in the failure of sporadic efforts in the United States to promote public or private air raid shelters. One hopefully launched backyard model called the Mark I Kidde Kokoon included a portable radio, airblower, chemical toilet, generator, and gasoline stove among its amenities. But customers proved rare, for it was widely realized that the family that survived in such a womb, on canned food and water, would sooner or later have to emerge into a corpse-strewn, poisoned wasteland. Sanity could only be preserved by ignoring, rather than trying to prepare for, such a catastrophe.

One social issue could not be suppressed—that of race. In 1948, a modest civil rights plank was inserted into the Democratic Party platform. Next, the armed forces were desegregated. Then, in 1954, the Supreme Court unanimously struck down racial separation in public schools. In 1955, a charismatic young minister named Martin Luther King, Jr., led a boycott by his fellow blacks of the bus system in Montgomery, Alabama, finally forcing abandonment of the Jim Crow seating pattern that reserved the front of the buses for whites. In 1957 Congress passed the first federal civil rights legislation in decades—and a reluctant Dwight Eisenhower had to send federal

troops into Little Rock, Arkansas, to bring about peaceful compliance with a court order to admit black students to the city's
Central High School. Throughout the Fifties Negroes were finally
raising their long-silent voices.

There were other kinds of cultural protest as well. White
middle-class teen-agers, however little they seemed overtly to
question the "organization" mentality, flung themselves joyfully into
the orgiastic gyrations of "rock and roll," and particularly relished
the performances of a rural Tennessee ex-truck driver named Elvis
Presley. Dressed in skin-tight, flamboyant clothing, Presley moaned
and gasped as he sang, bumping his guitar with his hips in explicit
sexual pantomime, and his attraction was obviously that he
embodied the very opposite of the passionless self-control that was
the organization model.

There was also a chorus of nay-saying from a small group of poets
and writers who called themselves "beat." They celebrated a
life-style of voluntary poverty, marijuana and alcohol jags, jazz
sessions, excursions into Oriental philosophy, and road-roaming in
search of elusive and mystical bliss through suppression of the ego.
Their poet laureate was Allen Ginsberg, and their Tolstoy was Jack
Kerouac, whose picaresque novel On the Road, published in 1955,
won a wide following among collegians. It was an intriguing fact
that while the "beats" were a tiny group largely ignored or rejected
by "established" Americans, those same solid nonbeat citizens
consumed, in 1960 alone, 19 million gallons of gin, 9 million gallons
of vodka, and 18 million pounds of aspirin—plus uncounted
capsules of frequently prescribed tranquilizers such as Miltown.
They had their own quest for forgetful bliss.

THOUGH THE BLACKS and the beats challenged the Eisenhower-era
blandness, they had no interest in sharpening hostilities toward
the Soviet Union. Blacks (and their white liberal allies) were
inclined to believe that the battle for equality at home needed more
attention than, say, the liberation of Eastern Europe. And those who
took their cultural cues from Ginsberg or Kerouac, were not inclined
to leap to the defense of an American way of life that they found
stultifying.

So by 1958 the attitudes of both the satisfied and the rebellious
Americans dictated a slackening in the Cold War's momentum.
Sometimes Eisenhower and Dulles appeared to be working hard to
fan cooling embers into fresh flames. In January of 1957 they had
sought from Congress a resolution authorizing the President to use
American power, if necessary, to repel any threat to the Middle East
from "international Communism." This so-called Eisenhower Doctrine was supposed to fill the power vacuum left by the British and

French defeat over Suez. But Congress whittled down the White House request to an approval of force only if "consonant" with the charter of the United Nations and with existing treaties. And not until the spring of 1958 did the State Department find an appropriate emergency for demonstrating the Doctrine at work.

It occurred in tiny Lebanon, one of three Arab states in the region that looked westward for support. The other two were Iraq and Jordan. Nasser's Egypt, however, was receiving arms and assistance from the Russians, and Nasser won over as an ally Lebanon's strong neighbor, Syria. (Syria and Egypt even briefly experimented with fusion as the United Arab Republic.) Syria, too, began to acquire Soviet weapons and training.

Lebanon's president, Camille Chamoun, attempted in May of 1958 to amend his country's constitution so as to authorize a second term for himself when his first expired in the autumn. His act provoked rioting in Beirut, whereupon Chamoun sounded the tocsin in Washington and at UN headquarters. The demonstrations, he said, were the start of a Communist uprising, to be supported by a Syrian invasion.

Eisenhower promptly ordered the United States Sixth Fleet into the eastern Mediterranean, but while he thus put the weapon to his shoulder, he did not yet pull the trigger. Until the night of July 13, 1958. Then, suddenly, there was a coup in Baghdad, capital of Iraq. Young nationalist officers, known admirers of Nasser, assassinated King Faisal and his chief minister, Nuri es-Said. They installed in his place General Abdul Karim el-Kassem, who they believed was certain to repudiate the Dulles-inspired anti-Soviet Baghdad Pact.

Chamoun was now in extreme alarm, as was Jordan's King Hussein. Were they next on the "hit list" of pro-American regimes to be overthrown? Were Syrian tanks and Egyptian planes at that very moment warming up their engines for a devastating strike? Quickly, Lebanon and Jordan appealed to Eisenhower. And, just as quickly, radioed orders snapped through the air, warships took station, and, finally, landing craft churned through the warm blue swells toward the beaches of Beirut, disgorging some nine thousand U.S. Marines in combat gear.

The entire scene was watched and applauded by happy crowds of sunbathers and ice cream vendors enjoying a pleasant July afternoon. There was neither a revolution nor a Syrian invasion anywhere within eyeshot.

Eisenhower put as good a face as possible on the comedy by explaining, on television, that the "uprisings" in Iraq and Lebanon had been "actively fomented by Soviet and Cairo broadcasts," and that the cause of freedom had required the dispatch of the Marines, as well as of a contingent of British paratroopers to Jordan. The Marines, slowly reinforced, spent a tranquil three months in the area. Then, at the request of the UN, they—and the British in Jordan—left. Chamoun, equally quietly, ended his term in office. The affair was finished.

September of 1958 brought another small flap. Nationalist troops were still encamped on the tiny islands of Quemoy and Matsu, only a few miles off the Chinese mainland near Amoy and Foochow. Chiang Kai-shek resolutely insisted that, given the proper support, they could be used as the spearhead of an invasion that, he was convinced, would topple the Mao government. Possibly to forestall any such intentions, the Chinese Communists began to shell the two small outposts. (They could not simply send out landing parties to seize them because the United States Seventh Fleet was still protecting them under orders dating from 1950.) As the high explosives pounded Quemoy and Matsu, Dulles ordered the fleet on alert status and probed among the European allies for support for some strong action. There was none. After a time, the shelling ceased. No one had changed positions. This crisis, too, was over.

It was getting harder to find plausible Communist threats like those of the 1940s. During the summer of 1958, Vice President Nixon, on a goodwill tour to Venezuela, had encountered spectacular ill will. In Caracas he had been stoned, heckled, spat on, and nearly seized and murdered by anti-"Yanqui" mobs possibly, if not probably, under Communist instigation. But it was difficult to turn that sorry episode into an immediate, tangible menace to American security. And, on the final day of 1958, a young Cuban guerrilla leader named Fidel Castro entered Havana with his followers and sent packing the last adherents of the government of Fulgencio Batista, friendly to American interests. But few saw at that moment that Castro might become a Soviet client and, therefore, a breach in the American wall around the western hemisphere.

The year 1959 was marked by a personnel transition. John Foster Dulles passed from the scene. In February he entered a Washington hospital with a recurrence of the cancer that had felled him during the Suez ordeal. He had recovered from surgery then, and had worked dutifully despite his growing pain and weakness to quell what he perceived as a national and international retreat from the demands of the battle to preserve Christian civilization. But after many more months of travel and conference, he was spent. God retired him from the fray. On May 24, he died.

Not entirely by coincidence, the remainder of 1959 saw a sudden shift toward accommodation, if not downright cordiality, in Soviet-American relations. The culmination was a spectacle that would have been deemed incredible as little as six years earlier—the

Communist boss of the Soviet Union, Bolshevik Russia's strong man, and Stalin's heir, Nikita Khrushchev, breaking bread at the White House.

THE CHUNKY, BALDING KHRUSHCHEV was a man of surprises, despite what appeared to be a conventional record as a Soviet *apparatchik* or sinuous bureaucrat. He was a true product of the Revolution. Born in 1894 to a family of peasant stock, he worked in coal mines as a child, then joined the Bolsheviks as a "political officer" during the civil war with the Whites. Afterward he went to "workers' schools," impressed his superiors as a comer, and inched up the ladder—supervisor of work on the Moscow subway, first secretary of the Moscow Communist Party (akin to being mayor), member and secretary of the Central Committee of the Communist Party of the entire U.S.S.R. He was faithful, careful, and not above ruthlessness in carrying out orders. He escaped the purge trials of 1936. He helped crush nationalist stirrings among Ukrainians and Poles in 1940. He survived the paranoid rages of Stalin in the old man's final years, when, in Khrushchev's own chilling phrase, "all of us around Stalin were temporary people." When Stalin died, Khrushchev's own excellent Party connections helped him move toward the center of power. He helped get rid of Lavrenti Beria, Stalin's long-time chief of secret police. Then he slipped and shoved his way past Malenkov and Bulganin into key posts, stood off challenges from oldtimers like Molotov and Zhukov, and by 1958 was chairman of the Council of Ministers, in effect premier, the ultimate reward of wisely controlled and focused ambition.

Yet in 1956 Khrushchev had already taken an astonishing step. In a speech to that year's congress of the Communist Party he had exposed to world view Stalin's grisly regime of mass arrests and executions, and had torn down the edifice of sycophancy and adulation that the dictator had taken years to build. The reasons for destroying the "cult of personality" could have been ideological, aimed at breaking the identification of "socialism" with a single figure. Or it could have been political, designed to discredit older rivals who had been close to Stalin. But whatever his motives, Khrushchev's de-Stalinization campaign, which helped confirm years of foreign anti-Soviet propaganda, clearly bespoke him as someone not quite in the playing-it-safe mold.

That was, perhaps, the key to understanding him. He was the first Soviet ruler willing to venture out into the world, debate Soviet positions, and test the stereotypes of *Pravda* against his own observations. In spite of what he had done to Hungary, he was willing to talk of "many roads to socialism" and of "peaceful competition" with capitalism. His freedom from xenophobia seemed to rise from a genuine conviction that Russian progress validated the Russian system. There was nothing artificial in his vocal pride (shared by his countrymen) in Russia's leap from an industrially backward nation, twice devastated by war within thirty years, to the world's second greatest armed power and first trailblazer in space. He was convinced that somehow, eventually, butter could be provided along with the shiny new guns. Russia, like Khrushchev, had come a long way, far enough to feel almost secure.

Nikita Sergeyevich Khrushchev had his dark side as well. He remained hard to fathom, if only because no one knew for sure when he was expressing his own convictions and when he was under pressure from rivals in the Kremlin. He could be outgoing, verbose, full of earthy jokes—a thick-faced, rotund little comedian. And he could explode in a temper, threaten, bluster—and then, at the right moment, compromise. No one, after all, survived years of totalitarian intrigue without flexibility and shrewdness, and Khrushchev, in the end, would pull off the most amazing feat of all for a Soviet leader. He would be forced out in 1964, yet live to write his memoirs.

During 1958 Khrushchev had sent both conciliatory and threatening signals to the West, first intimating a desire to accelerate disarmament talks, and then threatening to force a new Berlin crisis by turning over full control of the city to East Germany (the German Democratic Republic), which was not bound, like Russia, to agreements providing access corridors. By the spring of 1959, however, the sunny side was uppermost and the Soviet chief made a proposal to a group of visiting American governors (whose presence in Moscow was in itself a sign of warming trends). Much was to be gained by such face-to-face exchanges, Khrushchev suggested; it would be useful if he and the American President could, in turn, visit each other's homeland to discuss pending issues.

When the message was relayed to Eisenhower, he was cool, at first, believing that more spadework must be done at the foreign ministers' meetings, and more progress in "sincerity" shown by the Russians. But the post-Dulles State Department was pleased at the possibility of getting the universally popular Ike to make appearances and remarks inside Russia. It would help, said a high departmental official, to clear up the "monotonous Soviet diet of official distortion and misrepresentation regarding the United States." Two sides could play the game of wooing the enemy's people, and Eisenhower was a high card. Accordingly, the President was prevailed on to invite Khrushchev for a visit in September, which would be returned the following year.

In effect, a public relations game was in progress, and the opening phase actually took place in July. The momentum of events had begun once again to interest some American (and European) businessmen in prospects of trade with the Soviet Union's vast, untapped markets. The Russians, in turn, were tempted by such an idea, and set up a trade exhibit in New York that was opened with a flourish by deputy premier Frol Kozlov. Diplomatic niceties therefore dictated that when a comparable United States "fair" opened in Moscow, Vice President Nixon should be on hand. With Khrushchev, Nixon toured the exhibits and paused before the centerpiece, a complete six-room model ranch house, laden with gadgetry, living proof of America's power to create consumer goods. Its mere existence was a psychological victory for the United States. Nixon, aware that the event was being filmed for later American television release, smilingly but pointedly declared that the house was "typical" and within the reach of any American worker.

Through his interpreter, Khrushchev flashed back: "You think the Russians will be dumbfounded by this exhibit, but . . . all newly built Russian homes will have this equipment." He added that Americans needed dollars to acquire a house, and those without dollars had "the right to . . . sleep on the pavement. . . ."

Nixon, his mind on the approaching 1960 election, continued to play to the cameras and go beyond the required formalities. The beauty of the house, he continued, was that it was one of many models made by different builders. "We don't want to have a decision made at the top by one government official saying that we will have one type of house." Khrushchev shunted the issue aside. "On political differences we will never agree," he said. But Nixon rattled on, provoking Khrushchev into a show of belligerence for Russian watchers. "Your generals say they are so powerful they can destroy us," he asserted. "We can also show you something so you will know the Russian spirit. We are strong. We can beat you."

Then Nixon returned to the mood of good fellowship, raising a glass to Khrushchev in a Russian toast: "May you live to be one hundred." Amiably, the premier replied that when he was ninety-nine, they might reopen the discussion. Whereupon, Nixon could not resist a final dig. "You mean," he asked, "that at ninety-nine you will still be in power, with no free elections?" End of the great "kitchen debate." Later, Nixon led Khrushchev over to the Pepsi-Cola booth and induced him to consume several bottles for the cameras.

The episode had revealed both the genial and the boastful facets of Khrushchev's personality. When the Russian landed at Andrews Air Force Base on a cool day two months later, in September 1959, he remained in character. First, there was a thirteen-mile ride into town, at Eisenhower's side, past unenthusiastic crowds. Next came the presentation of gifts to the President: vodka, caviar, an elk's head, a shotgun, and one slightly barbed offering—a model of a Soviet rocket called Lunik, which had only recently been fired and had hit the moon, another "first."

A White House dinner followed. Khrushchev wore a simple black suit, while his wife (one of an entourage of sixty people) dressed in modest green, touched off by a capitalistic diamond brooch. At the table Allen Dulles joked with Khrushchev. "You may have seen some of my intelligence reports from time to time," said the CIA chief. Khrushchev nodded. "I believe we get the same reports—and probably from the same people."

"Maybe," ventured Dulles, "we should pool our efforts."

"Yes. We should buy our intelligence together. . . . We'd have to pay the people only once."

On the following day Khrushchev was taken on an eye-opening helicopter ride over Washington's suburbs, highways, shopping plazas, and drive-ins. Then he motored to the National Agricultural Research Station at Beltsville, Maryland (waving amiably in his shirtsleeves to passersby), where he gazed on what seemed to excite him most in America, fat cattle and rich crops.

That same afternoon he gave a relaxed talk at the National Press Club, but then was exposed to an American free press conference, and did not like it. A question came from the floor, asking, in effect, where he was and what he was doing during the Stalin purges that he had later denounced. Khrushchev grew steely quiet. "I shall not reply to this question," he enunciated slowly through the interpreter, "which I look on as being provocative." Inevitably, Hungary came up. But instead of parroting his own propaganda, Russia's leader dropped into a folksy tone. "Hungary has stuck in some people's throats [like] a dead rat." (Pause.) "We could think of some dead cats we could throw at you."

On Capitol Hill he talked with various members of Congress. Minnesota's Senator Eugene McCarthy sized him up and was impressed. "He's a little like a candidate in the late stages of the campaign," was McCarthy's judgment. "He has heard all the questions many times and his answers are sharp as hell."

The agreed-on plan of the visit was that Khrushchev should leave Washington for twelve days of touring the United States, and should then return for talks with Eisenhower at Camp David, the presidential retreat in the Catoctin Mountains in south-central Maryland. The talks were to cover Berlin, arms control, and the future of Laos, one of the Indochinese states created by the Geneva accords, which was showing signs of instability. The journey of the former political commissar became a kaleidoscopic set of scenes, daily replayed on the newscasts. Khrushchev in New York, ignoring Hungarian and Ukrainian pickets, goggling at Manhattan from the Empire State

Building. Khrushchev laying a wreath on the grave of Franklin D. Roosevelt at Hyde Park. Khrushchev fending off reporters with a cheery: "Gentlemen, I am an old sparrow; you cannot muddle me by your cries."

On to Los Angeles, where he ran into one of his few problems on the pilgrimage—local politicians who sought to score points at home by "standing up to him." Mayor Norris Poulson, in an after-dinner speech, warned Khrushchev that Americans would "fight to the death" if attacked, and Khrushchev, annoyed at the needlessly hostile tones in view of his own friendly statements to the press, snapped that in the United States "I trust even mayors read." His temper flared in California only when a proposed visit to Disney-land was canceled, supposedly because security arrangements would be too hard. For some reason he was especially outraged at missing the fantasy kingdom. "Is there an epidemic of cholera there or something?" he roared. "Do you have rocket-launching pads there? . . . Or have gangsters taken hold of the place?" He was mollified by a visit to Hollywood where he saw the shooting of a scantily clad dance number from the film *Can-Can* and opined prudishly that people's faces were more beautiful than their backsides.

And then a procession back eastward, with a stop in San Francisco to shake hands with union leader Harry Bridges, a look at the Detroit auto factory and a Pittsburgh steel mill, and a day at the large, mechanized Iowa farm of Roswell Garst, where so many newsmen crowded Khrushchev's steps that Garst, an impatient host, flung handfuls of silage at them, to the visitor's vast amusement. Farms brought out Khrushchev's most jovial side. He teased his official escort, the patrician Henry Cabot Lodge, about Lodge's unfamiliarity with barnyard smells. Shown some imported Russian pigs, he posed a question: "These Soviet and American pigs can coexist—why can't our nations?"

Finally, a pleasant weekend at Camp David, with a side trip to Eisenhower's Gettysburg farm. There was no joint communiqué issued after the last meetings, although it was announced that Khrushchev had agreed not to set any timetable for resolving the Berlin question. Modest though this outcome seemed to be, the American papers nonetheless editorially hailed the "spirit of Camp David," and looked forward to more productive peacemaking sessions the following May, when there would be a European summit meeting from which Eisenhower would go on to Moscow.

FRENCH, BRITISH, AND UNITED STATES diplomats worked hard in preparing for the May 16 opening of the 1960 summit conference in Paris. There was a heavy agenda, including the future course of NATO, the rearming of West Germany, and the presence of U.S. nuclear weapons in Britain. The host would be the craggy General de Gaulle, called on in 1958 to take over his faltering country as president under a new constitution. De Gaulle was insistent on restoring France's grandeur and independence by removing her from NATO and having her achieve her own nuclear capacity. He was pleased when, in February, 1960, the first French atomic device was exploded in the Sahara; he was more pleased when Khrushchev paid him a special visit in March; and he clearly looked forward to presiding at the gathering of chieftains.

On May 1, Parisian workmen were busy getting the city in readiness for the invasion of dignitaries. In Moscow, Soviet citizens watched the May Day parade. And in Peshawar, Pakistan, a thirtyish ex-lieutenant in the United States Air Force, Francis Gary Powers, climbed into the cockpit of a delicate and beautiful creation of twentieth-century technology called the U-2, and prepared to use it to violate the airspace and spy upon the military secrets of the U.S.S.R.

The U-2 was a gliderlike airplane with thin wings, a high tail, an arrow-slim fuselage, and the capacity to climb twelve to fourteen miles into the sky and fly as long as ten or twelve hours. It carried only the pilot, instruments, fuel, and a battery of astonishing cameras that photographed the earth below through seven portholes. They could reproduce a strip of geography 125 miles wide and up to 3,000 miles long on film, with such accuracy of focus that when the shots were blown up, it was said, the headlines of a newspaper in the hands of a man on the ground were readable.

The U-2 was priceless to American intelligence. It could "overfly" Russia beyond the then-known range of Soviet radar and antiaircraft weapons, and sweep into its cosmic vision railroads, highways, factories, missile bases, troop concentrations, airfields, power grids, every sinew of Soviet strength or hint of Soviet movement. If the value of such flights was huge, so were the risks. Though clandestine intelligence-gathering was as ancient as the Bible, aerial spying in peacetime was a violation of accepted international standards, and at the very least a major diplomatic insult. Therefore, U-2 missions were authorized—one at a time—directly by the President, and with misgivings. "Well, boys," said Ike at one meeting of top brass, "some day one of these machines is going to be caught and then we're going to have a storm."

Yet he had chanced the storm once again with an O.K. for Powers's mission. The young Tennessee-born flier was to follow a zigzag route that would take him over much of central and northern Russia and would end at Bodo, in Norway. In Powers's pockets was an assortment of items, including his draft and Social Security cards, and some currency and gold jewelry for bartering if he should be shot down in strange territory.

But what if he were to come to ground in Russia? The CIA's plans for this contingency were ambiguous. The plane was supplied with self-destruction devices to protect its secrets. And Gary Powers carried, on a chain around his neck, a silver dollar hollowed out to hold a tiny needle whose tip was treated with curare, an instantly fatal poison. One quick scratch would do the job. But Powers was not under orders to use the needle. He was a hired civilian (at $30,000 a year) and the agency left the decision up to him, assuming that patriotic instincts would triumph. Allen Dulles, for one, was sure that no U-2 pilot would ever be taken alive.

Powers roared into the air at 6:20 A.M. In his silent, lonely, instrument-crammed cocoon he watched the wrinkled mountains of Central Asia unroll under his wings like a white-tufted carpet of brown. At precise checkpoints noted on his maps he flipped on the cameras. All was well until, somewhere over the central Russian industrial city of Sverdlovsk, the U-2 suddenly lurched as if it had hit a wall, then dropped into a high-speed dive while an orange blaze filled the windshield. A Soviet missile had scored a hit or a near-miss, killing the engine. Powers, pressed into his seat by enormous gravity forces, nonetheless managed to tear away his harness and oxygen hoses, blow the canopy, and jump free at thirty thousand feet. But in his haste he did not arm the switches that would blow up the stricken plane, though, drifting down into the heart of the Soviet Union, he did have time to think about whether he wanted to reach for his silver dollar and die a hero.

He did not.

Five days later, Nikita Khrushchev went on the air from Moscow. In mock distress he reported "aggressive acts" by the United States in the form of aerial violations of Soviet frontiers, but gave no details. By then the CIA knew that neither plane nor pilot had reached Norway. So it released the official cover story through the National Aeronautics and Space Administration. NASA announced that it did, in fact, base nonmilitary, high-altitude aircraft for weather reconnaissance in allied nations such as Turkey, and that one was recently missing. Probably a malfunctioning oxygen system had caused the pilot to black out and thereby fly inadvertently into Russian territory. Where, NASA indignantly wanted to know, was that innocent pilot?

That was what Khrushchev had craftily been waiting for. On May 6 he revealed the cards he was holding. The U-2's fragments, unburned, were being taken to Gorky Park, in Moscow, for public display, and the pilot had given the full details of his mission to interrogators. He would soon stand trial for espionage. America's government had lied outright.

American papers were shocked. "Uncle Bungle has done it again," said one of them. Others assumed that a runaway CIA had ordered the mission. "Do our intelligence authorities," asked the St. Louis *Post-Dispatch*, "enjoy so much freewheeling authority that they can touch off an incident . . . by low-level decisions unchecked by responsible policy-making power?" Perhaps to protect the CIA, the President admitted, on the ninth of May, that the flight had been sanctioned by him. A State Department news release tried a propaganda counterattack. The reason for the spy flights, it said, was Soviet rejection of Eisenhower's "open skies" plan of four years earlier, which would have made it unnecessary for the United States to take such preventive actions against another Pearl Harbor-type sneak attack. Khrushchev's rejoinder was to caricature the statement: "It is not the burglar who is guilty, but the owner of the house . . . because he locked it, thereby compelling the burglar to break in."

Khrushchev headed for Paris in a steaming rage. Some of his indignation might have been self-protective. Hard-liners in the Kremlin were possibly claiming that his softened attitude toward America had encouraged Eisenhower to think that the Soviet Union would calmly accept violation of her frontiers as if she were a third-rate power. Khrushchev had to show compensatory toughness, and he did. He wanted Eisenhower's personal apology, punishment of the guilty parties who had planned the flights, and guarantees that there would be no more of them.

Eisenhower arrived in Paris in time to learn of these demands from de Gaulle and British Prime Minister Harold Macmillan. His reaction was: "I hope that no one is under the illusion that I'm going to crawl on my knees to Khrushchev." Yet he was willing to suspend further U-2 activity over Russia indefinitely. He could hardly take any other public stand without opening the door for a Soviet claim of the "right" to fly over Omaha or Denver. Moreover, the United States could afford to give up the U-2 missions because they would soon be obsolete. In a short while the stepped-up American space program would yield satellites that would do the surveillance job as well.

But ending the spying was not enough for Khrushchev's needs. At the opening session of the conference he stood up and virtually shouted that there was no point in holding a summit meeting so long as the United States was guilty of "treachery" and "bandit" behavior. Then he fired a second shot. The Soviet people, he declared, had ingenuously been preparing to accept Eisenhower's visit as a sign of friendship, but it was now clear that the gesture would be false and hollow. The visit was off, and the entire summit gathering, in fact, had best be put off for at least another eight months. Everyone in the room was slightly embarrassed. They knew that in exactly eight months Eisenhower's term would be over. Khrushchev had turned a diplomatic protest into a personal insult.

So the parley broke up after brief but temperate remarks from Eisenhower. He would not accept Khrushchev's tone, but simply repeated that missions like that of Powers would not be undertaken again. With that, he walked off to cool things down. But Khrushchev continued to fume. At a later press conference he explained why he thought the guilty instigators of the spy flights should be punished. As a young boy, he said, he had known of farm families whose cats stole cream from the family jug. One could only teach such animals manners by seizing their tails and banging their heads against the wall.

On that note ended the brief springtime of the spirit of Camp David.

EISENHOWER RETURNED HOME to a desk full of problems that indicated major shifts in the focus of the Cold War. New areas were requiring attention. Africa, for one. A summer crisis suddenly boiled over in the newly liberated Republic of Congo, formerly the Belgian Congo. The young nation's thirty-four-year-old premier, Patrice Lumumba, was suspected by the CIA of being, in Eisenhower's words, a "Soviet tool." Lumumba was at once confronted with a secessionist movement in the province of Katanga, rich in gold, silver, cobalt, and uranium. The rebel leader was Moise Tshombe, denounced by Lumumba as a puppet of Belgian mining interests. Fighting between Lumumba's and Tshombe's soldiers and mercenaries spilled over into violence against remaining European businessmen and missionaries in Katanga. Belgium—America's NATO ally—dropped in paratroops to take control and preserve "order." There were cries of outrage from Russia. Lumumba appealed to the UN, which sent in an all-African peacekeeping force to replace the Belgians.

In September, Lumumba was ousted from power by President Joseph Kasavubu and Colonel Joseph Mobutu; he was arrested and later murdered. There were persistent rumors that the ubiquitous CIA had arranged the affair. Whether that was true or not, there was much talk from Washington about Soviet penetration of Africa. The American people, who could scarcely find the unfamiliarly named new African countries on the map, now had to learn from the headlines that these nations were arenas of danger.

As the Congo cooled off, there was more bad news from southeast Asia. Laos, presumably under heavy Communist infiltration, continued to be an irritant.

The situation in Cuba was souring, too. Fidel Castro began to move toward an alliance with "socialist" countries, including the Soviet motherland. Latin America, once thought securely in the American fold, needed a new appraisal and fresh policies.

Castro actually made an appearance in New York for the September session of the United Nations. He stayed, with his party, in a modest suite in a Harlem hotel. Its staff members later reported that the Cubans left the place a mess and, among other things, plucked chickens in the rooms. Castro was part of an all-star UN cast that month that included Macmillan, Tito, and even Khrushchev, who came with his country's delegation for a second and last look at America. This time he had no red-carpet welcome, only eight thousand New York police, professionally impassive, guarding him from demonstrators.

Inside the UN building Khrushchev found only frustration. His attempt to get a resolution condemning intervention in the Congo failed, and his candidate for president of the General Assembly was trounced. During debate he showed some of his old form by angrily pounding on his desk with his shoe. He and Eisenhower addressed the organization on successive days, but exchanged no courtesies with each other.

Both men, in their speeches, stressed their friendship for, and desire to help, the nations bursting out of colonialism. The era of the Cold War, when its zones of tension were confined to the boundaries between Eastern and Western Europe—the final battle lines of World War II—was daily becoming more remote in memory. Names like Trieste, "Bizonia," or Masaryk meant nothing to people under twenty-one.

More than anything, the approaching United States presidential election signified that not only a decade but an entire phase of history was passing. The campaign was the first not dominated by the reputations and recollections of the Depression or the great battles of 1941-45.

The candidates were young, both born in the twentieth century. John F. Kennedy, the Democratic nominee, was only forty-three, potentially the most youthful Chief Executive since Theodore Roosevelt. The public spotlight on his 1917 birthdate (and his Roman Catholicism) obscured the fact that the Republican standard-bearer, Vice President Nixon, was only four years older. Both of them had been teen-agers when Franklin D. Roosevelt was elected. Both were junior naval officers in the war. They took American global reach for granted, and had hardly known an America not militarized.

Despite enormous personal differences in class and style, and disagreements on domestic liberalism, there were strong similarities that linked the two. Both had been shaped in the era of the bomb, the tube, the jet airplane, the "new politics" that took away individual voters' faces and accents and lumped them into "blocs" on pollsters' charts. Both were at home with the national security establishment and the multinational corporation. Neither had the small-town mentality of Truman, the corn-fed simplicity of Eisenhower, the preacher rhetoric of Dulles. Each, whatever attitudes he might strike for ceremonial purposes, was a nonideological pragmatist, fully ready to use the huge power of the executive office; to rely heavily on staff work and technical advice; to ignore or manipulate Congress and its parochial, divisive interests; to innovate. Truly modern men, the two of them. (There were almost eerie parallels in their careers, too. Both entered the House of Representatives in the 1946 election and went on to the Senate. Nixon achieved the vice presidency, and Kennedy barely missed nomination to that slot on the 1956 Democratic ticket. Eventually, each man would become President and serve a term dominated by Cold War issues. And each one's Presidency would end tragically.)

Only Kennedy tried, during the actual campaign, to stress change. He charged that Eisenhower had allowed the nation to stagnate and lose its sense of mission, its worldwide reputation for social justice and idealistic leadership. He promised to "get America moving again." Nixon, tied to the defense of the Administration of which he was part, had to play a more conservative role. But when it came to concrete questions of foreign policy, there was no genuine debate, no clearly enunciated and separate stands on Laos, the Congo, Berlin, or a nuclear test ban. The old bipartisan consensus held; the conventions of Cold War discourse were observed. Kennedy insisted—as the nonincumbent candidates would go on insisting at each election thereafter—that the Administration had allowed the United States to fall behind in the arms race, that there was a "missile gap" in Russia's favor. And Nixon, as spokesmen for the party in power would always do, denied the charge. The possibility of a real clash of views arose during one of four televised debates between the two. What would be the response of each candidate, asked a questioner, to a Communist Chinese attack on Quemoy and Matsu? For a moment it seemed as if the two might replay the "Asia-first" versus "Europe-first" argument of Korean War days, and, this time, give voters a choice. Nixon took a hard line. Failure to defend the islets would be "the road to war. . . . We must not give up an inch of territory." Kennedy said at first that he would "not risk American lives and a nuclear war . . . at the wrong place at the wrong time through an unwise commitment."

But in the end, after clarifying speeches, Kennedy and Nixon agreed that U.S. military forces should not rescue Quemoy and

Matsu unless the assault on them was a "prelude to an attack on Formosa." That was the official position of the State Department, now under Christian Herter. Its vagueness left room to maneuver, to keep the Red Chinese guessing, and to preserve the grudging support of pro-Chiang Congressmen. So, in the end, the ranks were closed behind the President as they had been since 1947.

Nonetheless, when the election went to Kennedy by a whisker, there was a sense that a generational change had occurred. The old warrior passed off the stage and the untested young hero stepped forward to establish what he called new frontiers. How would he deal with the Cold War that now extended as far as space itself? How would he relate to Khrushchev, the tough and wily old Red professional? Would his leadership enhance or reduce the risks of disaster?

The world would have approximately a thousand days, some of them the most anxious in its history, to find out.

Chapter 9
CLOSEST TO THE EDGE
1960-1963

JOHN FITZGERALD KENNEDY OPENED his Presidency in smashing style. The January 20 of his inauguration was a day of crackling cold and bright sunshine, of light bouncing off the snow that lay around the Capitol, and words rising in plumes of frosted, mortal breath. The hard glare almost interfered with a fine gesture. Kennedy had honored the poet, Robert Frost, a four-time Pulitzer Prize winner, by asking him to read a few lines on the occasion—a sign that the arts would have a prominent place on what was being labeled "the New Frontier." But Frost's eighty-six-year-old eyes could not decipher his own handwriting on the sun-whitened sheets until the President and others helpfully shaded them with their hands. So a small symbolic drama was played.

The Inaugural Address, too, delivered topcoatless despite the weather, was a glittering performance. It rang with biblical, literary, and historical allusions, skillfully interwoven by various advisers, including Arthur M. Schlesinger, Jr., who had won the Pulitzer Prize at age twenty-eight for his biography of activist President Andrew Jackson. He had interrupted his work on the life of activist President Franklin D. Roosevelt to serve Kennedy, who was himself the owner of a Pulitzer Prize in history for his *Profiles in Courage*.

After the formal ceremonies came the parties, with everyone looking splendid, and none more so than the President himself and his stunning wife, Jacqueline, thirty-one. They danced and laughed and gossiped the night away, and were at work the next morning, as if to sleep were an antiquated custom. For the Kennedy entourage behaved, in those first days, like a family of eager newcomers flinging open windows in a long-shuttered Washington. They flaunted their youth, talent, and energy. There was the National Security Adviser, McGeorge Bundy, only forty-one, straight from the deanship of Harvard College, a post he had been awarded after a brief, brilliant career as an instructor in government. (His most successful course was called "The U.S. in World Affairs," and his successor in it was a young émigré named Henry Kissinger.) Bundy's deputy was Walt Whitman Rostow, another academic, whose book, *The Stages of Economic Growth: A Non-Communist Manifesto*, was a best-selling description of how underdeveloped countries could, or should, achieve a "takeoff" into industrialism. The Secretary of Defense, Robert McNamara, forty-five, was a statistician acclaimed as a genius, who had previously gone from teaching at the Harvard Business School to the presidency of the Ford Motor Company, which he and his assistants, collectively known as the "whiz kids," had thoroughly modernized and made into a marketplace winner. And closest of the presidential counselors was the Attorney General, Robert F. Kennedy, "Brother Bobby," not yet thirty-six, whose relentless drive and toughness already terrified the slow-moving.

Around these major figures revolved a constellation of new appointees, all of them spirited and unlike the conservative, established, and generally senior civil servants who had set the tone for Eisenhower's official family. The new team seemed intent on keeping the promise to "get the country moving again," to cut paperwork, jostle the party chiefs on Capitol Hill, and infuse the ruling process with—a favorite Kennedy word—"vigor." Precise blueprints were as yet lacking, but on every front there would be change, as the President had said in the very opening paragraph of the Inaugural Address. The word should go forth that "the torch has been passed to a new generation of Americans." The occasion was one of "renewal."

But did that include the Cold War?

Yes and no. The Inaugural Address itself gave conflicting cues. It sang two refrains. One was a battle hymn, the other a lullaby of accommodation. "We shall pay any price, bear any burden, meet any hardship, support any friend, oppose any foe to assure the survival and success of liberty," said Kennedy. "Only when our arms are sufficient beyond doubt," he added, "can we be certain beyond doubt that they will never be employed." And John Foster Dulles himself could not have improved upon: "In the long history of the world, only a few generations have been granted the role of defending freedom in its hour of maximum danger. I do not shrink from this responsibility—I welcome it."

Yet Kennedy also urged "those nations who would make themselves our adversary" to join America in a new "quest for peace, before the dark powers of destruction . . . engulf all humanity." "Let both sides," he urged, "explore what problems unite us instead of belaboring those problems which divide us." Let both formulate arms control proposals, and unite to "undo the heavy burden" of poverty throughout the earth.

The address was as burnished as a metal mirror, but it did not give clear reflections. When the rhetoric was removed, and Kennedy's actual stances up to January 20, 1961, were examined, it was clear that he firmly shared the leading assumptions of the Cold War—that the United States was the champion of freedom in the world, and the Soviet Union the prime sponsor of tyranny, that a struggle between them was foredestined, and that American armed supremacy was essential. These postulates were shared by his inner circle, most notably by the new Secretary of State, Dean Rusk, who did not fit the "whiz kid" mold. A low-profile former foundation executive, Rusk had won the job only after Robert Lovett, one of the fathers of the national security apparatus, had refused it on grounds of age and health.

To judge by the proposals initiated early in his Administration, Kennedy was considering the introduction of some new elements into the equations of power, some adaptations to changing realities—such as more flexible military forces, allowing options other than "massive retaliation"; a set of new approaches to Africa, Asia, and Latin America, to deal with the social problems that supposedly made them vulnerable to Communism; and an acceptance of the genuineness of Soviet scientific progress. His innovative side was generating ideas that were not precisely articles of truce in the Cold War, but, rather, new rules for its conduct.

He was not wholly free to innovate. His zigzag course would be shaped by the conflicting pressures of good intentions and immediate necessities. Every President involved in the Soviet-American conflict often had to choose, on short notice, among unplanned-for alternatives.

AFTER THE CIA'S EFFECTIVE OPERATIONS in Guatemala and Iran, it was not unreasonable to assume, in 1960, that it could perform as unerringly in solving the United States' latest hemispheric problem, namely how to rid itself of Fidel Castro. The Agency's director, Allen Dulles, had no doubt that a project aimed at Castro's destruction would get support from Eisenhower's White House, or in fact anyone's White House.

For Castro was perceived as a true threat. He was also an enigma, and would always remain one. Voluble, individualistic, an opinionated tornado, he was a lawyer by training, drawn (like many middle-class Cuban intellectuals) into opposition to the dictatorial regime of Colonel Fulgencio Batista. He had good reason. Batista, like many of his predecessors, lined his pockets with bribes and exactions, did little for Cuba's illiterate and impoverished peasantry, and winked at the role of American crime syndicates in operating Havana's tourist-catching racetracks, casinos, and brothels. He lived at peace with the fact that his island realm was in most respects a Yankee protectorate. American corporations owned the better part of its mines, forests, ranches, and plantations. American consumers ate most of its annual sugar crop.

When Castro attempted his first, unsuccessful anti-Batista coup, in 1953, he was only twenty-seven years old. Jailed and later released into exile, he returned secretly in 1956 with a small band of followers, holed up in the central mountains, and conducted a three-year guerrilla war that ended in his 1959 victory. The fatigue-clad Castro, his brother Raoul, his friend Ernesto Che Guevara, and their fellow barbudos (bearded ones) seemed to be romantic, even heroic, figures to a few journalists who penetrated their headquarters. They enjoyed a good press in the United States. The American government itself was willing to gamble that a democratically reformed Cuba might actually be a strong asset, and it expended neither effort nor tears on Batista's behalf.

But Fidel as a ruler proved something different from Fidel as a liberator. He unloaded verbal scourgings and heavy taxes on the big businessmen, landowners, and bankers of Cuba, and the professionals and tradesmen, from lawyers and engineers to hairdressers and tailors, who served them. Meanwhile, he courted the rural masses through lowered rents and populistic harangues, promising that they would inherit Cuba's future. When many of his original followers quarreled with him, they were muzzled, jailed, or forced to flee. Increasingly, their replacements came from Cuba's small Communist Party.

Inevitably, Castro fell afoul of the United States by seizing American-owned properties. Washington retaliated by freezing Cuban assets, banning critical exports to the "misbehaving" neighbor, and closing American markets to Cuba's sugar. Finally, just days before Kennedy took office, diplomatic relations were severed. Hard-hit by these measures, and the growing exodus of Cuba's limited number of managers and technicians, Castro looked for and found a friend—the Soviet Union. Moscow announced that it would be happy to buy Cuban sugar and to lend Castro money and experts to build his economy anew. And so, Fidel's revolution turned a progressively deeper shade of red.

Was he a dishonest demagogue, a closet Marxist from the start as he later claimed? Or a colorful, energetic folk leader who, whatever his sins against democracy, was struggling to bring such unaccustomed amenities as schools, good housing, and medical care to Cuba's dispossessed? Was he a willing Soviet pawn? Or had America's economic warfare pushed him in that direction? Debate on such questions (in effect, on whether the United States had "lost" Cuba) filled columns in American journals of opinion, but for Washington's security planners the controversy was wastefully abstract. The brutal fact to deal with was that before 1959 Cuba had been within the American sphere of interest—there was a U.S. naval base at Guantanamo Bay to confirm it—and now it was literally an enemy island in the very waters that lapped at the U.S. Gulf and south Atlantic coasts. An unthinkable Soviet foothold, ten minutes from Miami by jet plane.

And that was why Allen Dulles felt he would have no problem in securing Eisenhower's approval in 1960 to devise an anti-Castro operation. Heading his committee of planners was Richard Bissell, whose record in the Agency was superior, and who was the father of the U-2 program—within the CIA the planes were known as Bissell's Air Force. Bissell's initial idea was simply to infiltrate Cuba with a small cadre of trained spies and saboteurs, recruited from Miami's large and willing community of exiles. They would conduct against the Fidelistas the same kinds of hit-and-run raids that had undone Batista.

Bissell's projects had a way of mushrooming ambitiously. Encouraged by reports that Castro's regime was rife with dissent, Bissell conceived a paramilitary operation. Instead of a handful of scattered agents, a landing force big enough to carve out and hold a beachhead would be set ashore. Within that enclave, an anti-Castro government would be established. It would become a lawful authority that could broadcast orders to disaffected Cubans all over the island. It might even receive recognition from the United States and the Organization of American States. Castroism would be mortally wounded by this spearpoint of freedom in its very vitals.

The new concept involved challenges that Bissell and Dulles found stimulating, and well within their generous and unaudited budgetary allowances. An entire infantry battalion, over one thousand men, as well as frogmen and paratroopers, would have to be recruited and trained. A private navy, eventually numbering five supply ships and seven landing craft carried in a mother vessel, would need to be created—likewise a private air force. And a "Cuban Revolutionary Council," the government-to-be, would have to be organized from among the quarrelsome group of exile leaders. All of it was to be done in darkest secrecy. And all of it added up to a clandestine invasion of Cuba by the United States behind a smokescreen of exiles, a fact that did not trouble the Agency.

Nor did it disturb Eisenhower, who apparently did approve the concept, though a little warily. Nor Kennedy, who voiced no misgivings when he was first briefed on it as President-elect. True, the plan was ethically flawed. Invading a small neighboring country, even by surrogates, was a dirty trick. But the Communists, too, played dirty. It was how the real world worked; the Devil had to be beaten at his own game. The CIA lived by that justification, and it found special favor among the Kennedy men, who fancied themselves as unusually cool, realistic, and "hard-nosed." They were impatient of rhetoric and poses, even—or especially—liberal poses. They saw themselves as idealists who knew the score, who knew that to fulfill high-minded visions it was necessary first to get, and then to use, *power*, without hesitation or hand-wringing.

So Kennedy interposed no barrier, and through his first days in office the machinery ground on, having already produced a complete air base and a training camp in willing (though nervous) Guatemala and Nicaragua. Kennedy paid Cuba little heed in February. His trouble spot that month was Laos, where the Communist-led Pathet Lao continued to do well. There was, therefore, a vacuum of inattention in which the landing scheme moved into its final phase, and in that silence all parties to the operation acted out a perfect scenario of how to march, with all goodwill and intelligence, straight into a disaster.

To begin with, the premise that the landings would trigger uprisings was never examined by State Department or civilian experts on Cuba, or even by relevant specialists within the CIA itself, thanks to tight internal security in which the Agency took pride. Bissell never heard, therefore, from those who could have told him that Castro had already eliminated his strongest enemies, and enjoyed considerable popularity.

Next, the enlarged scale of the operation made it perilous. General David Shoup, Commandant of the Marine Corps, and a veteran of Pacific invasions, knew how many vital and vulnerable parts had to mesh precisely to make an amphibious assault work. Although, like his fellow members of the Joint Chiefs of Staff, he gave his OK, he suffered "a lot of sleepless hours," fretting over a lack of air power. Only two prelanding air strikes were scheduled. If they did not wipe out Castro's own small air force, the "Exiles' Brigade" faced annihilation.

Planning those very air strikes underscored two other critical dilemmas. How could surprise be maintained once the first bombs were dropped on Cuban airfields? And more, how could American complicity be hidden so as to avoid the inevitable negative repercussions throughout the world? These last formed the biggest overhanging cloud. When Kennedy confided the plan to the powerful chairman of the Senate Foreign Relations Committee, J. William Fulbright, the Arkansas scholar's reaction was explosively negative. "To give this activity even covert support," he wrote to the President, "is of a piece with the hypocrisy and cynicism for which the United States is constantly denouncing the Soviet Union. . . . The Castro regime is a thorn in the flesh; but it is not a dagger in the heart."

And yet in the end Fulbright went along rather than fight the President. The Joint Chiefs also went along, because Dulles and Bissell insisted that the operation was workable, that time was on Castro's side since he would soon be getting Russian equipment, and that it would be impossible at a much later date to break up and disperse the Brigade; the moment was now. When Adlai Stevenson, ambassador to the UN, was informed of what was afoot— incompletely and at the last minute—he, too, went along as a good soldier.

Even the free American press went along. For some time, perceptive journalists in Miami had been hearing details about the impending action from the Cuban refugees there. They were a gregarious and strongly patriotic group, too proud and excited to be tight-lipped. The *New Republic* got hold of some aspects of the story and was about to go to press with it when word reached the White House, and presidential assistant Schlesinger successfully persuaded the magazine's publisher to kill the piece. Meanwhile, the *New York Times*'s Tad Szulc, briefly vacationing in Florida, got a virtually complete picture, and rushed to New York to write a report. Senior editors at the *Times* agonized over what they saw as a conflict between their obligations as journalists and as Americans, and finally fudged matters with a compromise. They ran Szulc's revelations under a single-column head, "Anti-Castro Units Trained to Fight at Florida Bases," and deleted all references to the CIA and to the imminence of the invasion, by then less than a week off.

Even so, Kennedy fumed when he saw the article. "Castro doesn't need agents over here," he snapped to his press secretary. "All he has to do is read our papers." But he had to deal with the issue at an April 12 press conference, and he did so with a ringing half-truth: "I want to say that there will not be, under any conditions, any intervention in Cuba by the United States armed forces." As he spoke, the Brigade was boarding its ships.

Still, Kennedy was literally correct—there would be no use of United States armed forces. The carrier *Essex* and escorting vessels were ordered into observation positions off the invasion site—*Bahia de Cochinos*, the Bay of Pigs—but under strict hands-off rules. There was to be no excuse offered for the Russians to take action because of a U.S. attack on a Soviet ally. No American could visibly participate. At all costs the operation must "look Cuban."

But those costs proved fatal. With the security so porous, Kennedy might justifiably have canceled the mission. Instead, he hedged the bet. He ruled out one of the two preliminary air strikes, thus guaranteeing that Castro would have some undestroyed planes of his own left. Moreover, the exiles were to land in darkness, and their supply ships could only unload by night, which would double the time required. All of this would reduce what Kennedy called the "noise" of the attack, but also its effectiveness. At that point some of the CIA planners were angry enough to call off the invasion, on the grounds that the new rules made failure certain. Finally they, too, went along. In their minds may have been the same thought harbored by the Joint Chiefs: If things went awry, Kennedy would, at the very least, authorize U.S. air support rather than accept total defeat.

So, on the fatal tide of inevitability that can sweep a nation into war, the government drifted toward the sorry outcome. At dawn on Saturday, April 15, the one preparatory air mission—against three Castro airfields—was flown from Nicaragua. To cover its origin in a neutral country, the CIA put exile pilots in six World War II B-26 twin-engine bombers with Cuban Air Force markings. The official story was that these planes were from inside Cuba, with defectors at the controls. (Once the invaders had seized an airstrip, they could bomb to their limit from Cuban soil.) To strengthen the deception, an extra "Cuban Air Force" B-26, bullet-punctured in advance, was flown into Miami, its "defecting" pilot announcing that he had barely escaped pursuit and was seeking asylum. But no one was convinced, except, perhaps, Ambassador Stevenson, who solemnly and innocently repeated the story in the United Nations session hastily convoked on the call of the outraged government in Havana. Only two of Castro's planes—both transports—were destroyed, and he now was forewarned, left in ignorance only of the exact spot where the blow would fall.

Near midnight on Sunday, the actual landings took place at the Bay of Pigs. With the sunrise, Castro's fighter-bombers appeared over the beach. Though they were only reequipped U.S. jet trainers and British World War II-vintage naval planes, they quickly blew up two of the sitting-duck supply vessels. The other ships fled, their civilian captains fuming because they had been falsely assured of air protection. The unarmed B-26s of the exile force were helpless as they tried to fly support missions. Two, piloted by American civilians, were shot down. By Tuesday morning Castro's troops, responding energetically under his personal leadership, were hammering the stranded men of the Brigade with artillery, automatic weapons fire, and strafing attacks. Agonized American navy fliers, circling overhead in planes whose U.S. insignia had been painted out, were watching in frustration and rage as men on "our side" were destroyed. Some CIA training officers on the headquarters ship wept as radioed messages from their friends in the Brigade arrived, pleading for help that would never come.

And in constant top-level meetings, Kennedy was holding firm against pressure to step in. The United States, he was convinced, simply could not officially commit itself to the success of the landing. To do so would justify the charge that Cuba was America's Hungary. The final pleas were made in a late-night White House conference that ran into the predawn hours of Wednesday. There had been a reception for members of Congress, and the President was still in white tie and tails as the death-rattles of the attack were reported to him. After his final no, he walked out onto the South Lawn to be alone with his emotions. A few hours later the Brigade gave up the fight. One hundred and fourteen of its members died in action, and 1,189 were captured.

It was time to pick up the pieces. The President gave orders: no buck-passing, no finger-pointing. The Administration was responsible, and no one in it—no matter how he might actually have felt—was to disavow a role. Robert Kennedy, it was reported, was seen poking Assistant Secretary of State Chester Bowles in the chest and saying: "Let me tell you something as of right now. You were for it." Allen Dulles and Richard Bissell were kept in their jobs until the heat dissipated and only fired months later. Personal explanations were made to leaders of both parties, including Eisenhower and Nixon. And Kennedy met the Cuban exile leaders, some of whom had had sons in the Brigade, and told them face to face, "I lost a brother and a brother-in-law in the war. I know something of how you feel."

The cool style was maintained. "We got a big kick in the leg and we deserved it," was the President's final wrap-up. But the long-term effects could not be dismissed with a stoical shrug. The legend of Kennedy invincibility was sunk along with the CIA supply ships. Almost exactly a year after the U-2 affair, America had suffered a new setback, been caught in fresh lies, and this was under the "new" management. Castro, more firmly entrenched than ever, jubilantly celebrated his victory over the Yankee imperialists. Khrushchev joined the cheers, and promised the Cubans more assistance, with a pledge whose ominous significance would not become clear until some sixteen months afterward.

Above all, future positions were frozen. Kennedy became rooted in absolute hostility to Castro. As late as December 1962, when he managed to ransom the imprisoned Brigade members for $53 million worth of drugs and foodstuffs, he greeted them on their return with the promise that their flag would one day fly over a free Havana. Such a position, while emotionally satisfying, limited room for diplomatic maneuver in the Caribbean and made it difficult to learn any but military lessons from the expedition's failure.

More than ever, too, Kennedy was under pressure to display firmness, for in the rulebook of the Cold War it was especially necessary at exactly such a moment not to tempt the enemy by a show of weakness. That April, Kennedy believed that as a young President still untested by the Russians, he had to make it clear that he could not be bullied. And he had to face this challenge to show toughness in the immediate aftermath of the Cuban fiasco, for he was scheduled to visit Europe in June and to meet, in Vienna, with Khrushchev, who was once more, and brusquely, demanding a new arrangement on Berlin.

BY EARLY JUNE, KENNEDY HAD already had two opportunities for muscle-flexing. Laos had offered one of them. In March, in fact, it had seemed to be far more swollen with ominous portent than Cuba. The battle there was labyrinthine, feudal, and Asian, an ancient conflict renewed in Cold War garb. There was a recognized neutralist government under Prince Souvanna Phouma in 1954. It was assailed by the pro-Communist Pathet Lao, led by Souvanna Phouma's brother, Prince Souvanouvong. It was also under attack from a right-wing faction that gave its loyalty to still another member of the royal Laotian family, Prince Boun Oum. Under Eisenhower, the United States had shifted support away from Souvanna Phouma to Boun Oum and his chief general, Phoumi Nosavan. By the time Kennedy took office, Souvanna had fled, and the Pathet Lao, strengthened by many of his former followers, was beating Boun Oum's conservative forces badly. Boun Oum and Phoumi Nosavan then claimed the Pathet Lao was getting Soviet and North Vietnamese help, and called for Western assistance.

Kennedy and his staff secretly discussed various ways of answering that cry, including the possible use of up to 140,000 U.S. troops, in addition to military advisers already on the scene, and tactical nuclear weapons. At a March 25 press conference Kennedy reiterated the domino theory, saying that if Laos fell it would "shake the faith of every small nation we were pledged to protect." He ordered the Seventh Fleet to the Gulf of Siam, moved five hundred Marines to Thailand, put U.S. forces on Okinawa on combat alert, and sought commitments of help from SEATO nations. Whether as a result of these moves or not, Khrushchev announced on April 1 that he would willingly see the conflict submitted to a renewed session of the 1954 Geneva Conference. That defused the situation, and soon after, a battlefield cease-fire took effect.

On April 20, Kennedy also asked Congress for $2.4 billion to be added to the Eisenhower defense budget that he had inherited. He wanted more airwings, warships, and combat-ready divisions. This was partially in fulfillment of his campaign promise to "rebuild"

American military strength, though he had discovered, on taking office, that the so-called "missile gap" was in fact not a sign of national weakness. Missiles—that is, rockets that flew at thousands of miles per hour—were the most dramatic of military "delivery vehicles," as the curiously bloodless language of experts labeled weapons. Of those, the United States had some 80 in Polaris submarines and 100 of long and medium range in land-based launching sites. The Soviet Union, according to the best intelligence estimates, had perhaps 50 intercontinental missiles and 400 of medium range. But what truly mattered were the payloads—the nuclear warheads. In addition to those in her missiles, the United States had 3,000 of them of varying sizes: 1,700 usable in bombers that could span half the globe and 1,300 capable of being carried by land-based or carrier-borne fighter-bombers. In terms of destructive power, the balance was awesomely favorable to America.

Nonetheless, Kennedy made his arms buildup request, and followed it up with another on May 25. This time he asked for money to beef up the nation's conventional forces, to prepare special units for quick transportation to hot spots anywhere on earth, and to prepare select forces for "counterinsurgency" programs. All of these would improve the "flexibility" of the U.S. position. It was in this speech that Kennedy also left one of his most durable legacies. A few weeks earlier, the Soviet Union had lofted "cosmonaut" Yuri Gagarin into earth orbit, the first man to fly in space. The United States had countered, on May 5, with the three hundred mile sub-orbital rocket ride of Commander Alan Shepard. In the afterlight of that moment, Kennedy called for achievement of the goal of landing a man on the moon "before this decade is out." The first funding for the voyage to the heavens came out of the drive for second-to-none arms.

Dealing over Berlin would prove harder for Kennedy than summoning defense dollars from Congress, or even showing the flag in faraway Laos, because Berlin was at the very center of things, especially for Khrushchev. The Soviet ruler wanted the sixteen-year-old "temporary" arrangements of 1945 replaced with a long-term German settlement. He was demanding a new four-power conference, and holding to his threat that if he did not get one by the end of 1961, he would sign a separate peace with East Germany, thus automatically canceling existing arrangements for Western access to Berlin.

His motivation was not clear. American planners liked to think, with wistful envy, of Soviet dictators who could devise moves without keeping an eye on public-opinion polls or Senate committee chairmen. But in reality Khrushchev had rivals in Kremlin inner councils who were carefully watching his missteps. He had lost face over the U-2; the split with China was widening; his attempts to produce more consumer goods were failing and perhaps weakening the Soviet Union in the weapons competition with the United States. But if he could bring the Western powers to the table to talk once more about neutralizing and reuniting Germany, it would be a stroke to recoup much of his shaken prestige. It would also be especially helpful to Walter Ulbricht of East Germany, perhaps the unhappiest leader of any Soviet satellite. The reason for Ulbricht's concern was simply that his German Democratic Republic's economic failures were especially glaring in contrast to a booming West Germany, and were publicized by a steady flow of refugees, who found escape particularly easy through Berlin.

For Berlin, in 1961, was a Western island in the Red sea. It was where Russia and America actually had a contiguous frontier. The two superpowers stood face-to-face there in ordinary city streets. The "free" and "slave" worlds, the "socialist" and "imperialist" camps, were separated by only a few guard posts. People took subway rides between the two systems, daily. They phoned friends, delivered packages, swapped visits. Hence East Berliners—and all East Germans who came to Berlin—could easily see a humming West Berlin, full of consumer goods and promising jobs for the skilled, a magnet for the young and ambitious, and within easy reach. Too easy, from the Communist viewpoint. There were, of course, rules, necessary passes, checkpoints. But those who were willing to leave behind families and possessions had little trouble. One could invent a reason, forge a pass, and never return—or simply catch a guard with his back turned and dash across the street to freedom, opportunity, unrationed meat, milk, eggs, and clothes, and a future with a car and a radio in it. Thousands of East Germans a month were slipping away from Ulbricht's realm—the total for the first six months of 1961 was 150,000. It was small wonder that Khrushchev called Berlin an aggravating "bone in my throat." From his standpoint, almost any new setup, even a reunited Berlin under some kind of international guarantee as a free city, would be an improvement.

But Kennedy saw possible Russian intentions differently. In March he had appointed Dean Acheson to study the issue. In Acheson's eyes, Khrushchev's purpose was to get Western troops out of the city and thereby abandon the West Berliners to harassment and eventual seizure. Such an outcome would destroy the West's credibility, so hard won in the airlift of 1948. Once again, the issue was the "free world's" will. There was nothing to negotiate. The United States, France, and Britain had a right to stay in Berlin.

With this advice in mind, Kennedy took wing to see Khrushchev in Vienna. There was a brief stopover in Paris to get acquainted with de Gaulle. Then on to the historic Hapsburg capital and the first encounter with Khrushchev, amid the usual amenities. There were lunches on successive days at the U.S. and Soviet embassies, punctuated by an Austrian government state dinner at the Schoenbrunn Palace, and a ballet performance. The stocky Russian in a gray suit, wearing his Lenin peace medal, joked easily with the young American about various matters, as the two posed for photographs among their sober cadres of accompanying experts. At dinner, when Kennedy touched a match to one of the Upmann cigars he enjoyed and dropped the burnt stick behind Khrushchev's chair, the Soviet premier asked: "Are you trying to set me on fire?" "No," laughed Kennedy. "Ah," said Khrushchev through his interpreter, "a capitalist, not an incendiary."

But the good humor did not mask an absolute stalemate. As Kennedy said in a later television report to Americans, it was a "very sober" two days. He and Khrushchev had "wholly different concepts of where the world is and where it is going," even though there was "no discourtesy, no loss of temper." At the final meeting, Khrushchev repeated that he was going to sign a peace treaty with East Germany by the year's end if the Berlin matter was not renegotiated.

"If that is true," said Kennedy, "it is going to be a cold winter."

So they parted, with Kennedy left to ponder hard alternatives. What response should there be to a Soviet or East German effort to force matters by a new attempt to isolate West Berlin? Token ground resistance? A new airlift? Or nuclear war? What was the proper price tag on Berlin? On July 25, in a special message to Congress, Kennedy asked for still another $3.25 billion for military purposes— to augment the permanent armed forces by 350,000, to call up 150,000 reservists, and, most ominously, to identify and mark places suitable for public air raid shelters. Nothing could more clearly underline that the President was thinking the unthinkable.

Nineteen days later came the Soviet and East German answer. At 2 A.M. on Sunday, August 13, the noise of hundreds of gasoline engines battered the moist air as trucks and generators rolled through East Berlin to the twenty-five-mile-long sector demarcation line. Floodlights suddenly blazed as workmen and soldiers wrestled concrete slabs and rolls of barbed wire into position. By daytime a harsh, bare, bristling wall was under construction. By Tuesday it was completed, a literal embodiment of the divided world. The "iron curtain" was a figure of speech, but the Wall—invariably capitalized—was all too real, especially to the hapless East Berliners.

"What next?" West Berliners wondered as they came to stare at it. Was this merely a first step? Would the next one be a thrust by armored vehicles across the boundary? In the command posts of NATO that had recently been reinforced, and in Washington, too, nerves were taut.

On deeper consideration it was plain to America's leaders that the Wall itself changed nothing. It was a fence to keep Ulbricht's people penned in, nothing more. The best thing to do about it (save for a formal protest filed by the Western sector commander, formally rejected as "absurd" by his Soviet counterpart) was to leave it alone, but make some nonthreatening gesture that said: "Thus far but no further."

Quickly, two such "signals" to the Russians were arranged. First, Vice President Lyndon Johnson was dispatched at once to Bonn, and then to Berlin, to assure Chancellor Konrad Adenauer and Mayor Willy Brandt of the American resolve never to abandon them. Next, a 1,500-man combat team of the U.S. 18th Infantry Division was ordered to leave its base at Mannheim, on the border between West and East Germany, and to drive the 110 miles to West Berlin. At 6:30 A.M. on Sunday, August 20, the first group of thirty-five vehicles set out, the men in them spit-polished to a fare-thee-well under their Texan colonel's orders not only to be the best soldiers in the U.S. Army, but to "look the damn best." At a deliberate twenty miles per hour they approached the first East German checkpoints, fingers nervously on their weapons, wondering if they would be challenged. They were, instead, formally and stiffly waved through. By midday they rolled into West Berlin to be welcomed by the Vice President, while ten thousand cheering civilians threw flowers at them and at a band that blared out "The Caissons Go Rolling Along."

There was a collective exhalation of relief. "We felt," said Robert F. Kennedy later, "that war was very possible then." But war had been avoided, partly because under the odd rules of the Cold War, conciliation was possible after the fists had been displayed to show toughness. On August 21 the United States, at the urging of British Prime Minister Harold Macmillan, agreed to four-power talks. Then it was Khrushchev's turn for rituals. First the fist: On September 1, he announced that the Soviet Union would resume its airborne nuclear bomb testing program. Then the handshake: He would enter the new talks, and withdraw his December 31 deadline. And so, again, the doomsday clock was arrested. The basic issue remained unsettled, and the talks actually lasted for ten years, resulting in a new occupation agreement in 1971, during one of the calm periods of Soviet-American relations. The Wall also remained.

But the political aftermath yielded one more memorable moment of the Kennedy Presidency. On June 26, 1963, during a visit to Europe, Kennedy spoke to a tumultuously enthusiastic crowd of

West Berlin citizens. Long ago, he told them, a man's proudest boast had been citizenship in Rome. "Today," he said, "in the world of freedom, the proudest boast is *'Ich bin ein Berliner'* [I am a Berliner]. All free men, wherever they may live, are citizens of Berlin. . . . I take pride in the words *'Ich bin ein Berliner.'* "

IF KENNEDY TRULY HOPED for a peacemaker's role in history, the twelve months following the Berlin crisis seemed to offer him breathing space in which to execute the design. With no major emergency pending, he was able to win congressional enactment of two imaginative concepts that seemed to fulfill the constructive aspirations of his Inaugural Address. One was the Peace Corps, the "army" of primarily young Americans who would give two years of their lives to working side by side with people in the developing countries, sharing their hardships while teaching them basic skills. Finding in such work an answer to Kennedy's challenge to "ask . . . what you can do for your country," five thousand volunteers were enrolled by early 1963.

In March of 1961 Kennedy had also proposed the Alliance for Progress, a program primarily funded by the United States to raise living standards in western hemisphere nations by stimulating economic growth. Kennedy called it "a vast, cooperative effort, unparalleled in magnitude and nobility of purpose, to satisfy the basic needs of the American people for homes, work and land, health and schools." The details were worked out at a conference in Punta del Este, Uruguay, in August. The United States was to make a ten-year commitment of $20 billion (including $300 million annually from private capital). Eighty billion dollars in investments were pledged by the Latin American nations. The goal was to reach an annual excess of economic growth over population growth of 2.5 percent, and thus gain on poverty. Political and economic reforms were promised by the participating governments. Thus the liberating vision behind the old Marshall Plan and Point Four programs was to be revived and renewed.

Giving substance to the dream was a hard task. Two years after the Alliance's kickoff, Kennedy told a news conference that there was "a long, long way to go, and in fact in some ways the road seems longer than it was when the journey started." By that time there had been at least three military takeovers of civilian governments in hemisphere nations—with many of the participating generals trained in U.S. armed forces schools. It was not supposed to work that way. The theory behind a military component of "foreign aid" was that the local army needed help in defending the emerging democratic order against Communist guerrillas, who would try especially hard to overthrow reformist governments that were proving that Marxism was not the only road out of exploitation. Thus arms support was an appendage to the program, not the essence of it.

Yet the difficulties of Kennedy's Latin American program were partly due to rampant militarism. Moreover, similar problems with balancing the martial and peaceful parts of foreign aid were visible throughout the globe. In the ideal tableau of the New Frontier's new kind of Cold War, Peace Corps volunteers would be in the fields of Third World nations teaching peasants to dig wells and read, to organize marketing co-ops and village councils. Money and specialists would be coming from the Agency for International Development (AID), the U.S. foreign assistance coordinating body, for rural electrification and local handicrafts factories. And the nation's army, trained for "counterinsurgency," would be protecting everyone from terrorist disruption. Only as a last resort would it need help from America's guerrilla-fighting Special Forces, the Green Berets.

The trouble with the engaging scenario was that military aid seemed to consume more and more of the dollars allotted to "helping" other peoples. It was the form of support most readily asked for by client governments and granted by Congress. In Asia this imbalance was becoming most noticeable in South Vietnam, where the effort to stabilize the country under Ngo Dinh Diem produced only frustration. Attacks by anti-Diem rebels, known as Viet Cong, were increasing. A series of special emissary-observers were dispatched in 1961. Vice President Johnson visited Saigon, where he ebulliently called Diem "the Winston Churchill of Asia." Then General Maxwell Taylor, Kennedy's special military adviser (later made Army Chief of Staff), went out with Walt Whitman Rostow. They submitted virtually identical reports. What was needed was expansion of the size and role of the five-hundred-man contingent of American military advisers so as to buy Diem time for peacefully winning elusive Asian hearts and minds.

Despite such headaches the spring and summer of 1962 offered time to assess and reflect on the future of Kennedy's foreign and domestic policies. But on October 15, a period of relative diplomatic calm was shattered abruptly. That Monday morning, CIA photo-interpretation teams made an electrifying discovery in rolls of film taken by a U-2 flight over Cuba on the preceding day. By nightfall their news had been reported to "Mac" Bundy, who prudently decided to let John Kennedy remain ignorant of them until he had enjoyed a good night's sleep, knowing that there would be no more such nights for some time to come. On Tuesday, at 7:30 A.M., Bundy entered the President's bedroom and found him, in his bathrobe, sipping coffee and scanning the morning papers.

"Mr President," said the National Security Adviser, "the Russians have offensive missiles in Cuba."

Cuba was Kennedy's "bone in the throat." After the Bay of Pigs, he created a special committee of Defense, State, and CIA officials, with Robert Kennedy as his personal watchdog on it, to work on toppling the bearded nemesis. This "Special Group, Augmented" (SGA) ordered new radio propaganda, sabotage operations, more pressure on the OAS for the economic strangulation of Cuba, and—with or without the Kennedy brothers' knowledge, it was never clear—attempts to assassinate Castro.

Khrushchev was presumably unaware of these steps, but was convinced that the Americans might, at any time, find some pretext to invade Cuba. He had openly announced his intention to bolster Castro's defenses with fighters, radar, and antiaircraft guns and rockets. But in May of 1962 he decided to go further—secretly. He ordered preparations for the additional installation of four Cuban bases, from which Soviet medium-range ballistic missiles (MRBMs), with ranges of 200 to 500 miles, and intermediate-range ballistic missiles (IRBMs), with 1,100-mile to 2,000-mile ranges, could be launched.

Those missiles, if equipped with nuclear warheads, would drastically change the complexion of affairs in the Caribbean. It was true, as Robert McNamara was later to point out, that the basic power balance between the U.S. and U.S.S.R. was unaffected. Russian intercontinental missiles were already aimed at American cities; it made little difference whether New York was obliterated by a warhead hurled from Cuba or Siberia. But the Russians had only a few ICBMs, of doubtful accuracy, at that time. Those in Cuba would put many new American cities and military bases—and all of Central America—under siege. No U.S. Administration could accept such a change.

Khrushchev's motive in taking what was, therefore, a grossly reckless step was never clear. Possibly it was to satisfy critics both in the Soviet hierarchy and in other Communist countries, most of all China, who reproached him for allowing the U.S.S.R. to become strategically inferior. Perhaps it was to create pressure on the United States for a trade, say, a yielding on Berlin in exchange for removing the weapons. Or just possibly Khrushchev really meant the missiles simply to guarantee American good behavior toward Cuba, and underestimated the reaction.

Whatever his reason, during the summer Havana's docks became crowded with Soviet freighters and troopships unloading the men, the supplies, and the extraordinary collection of machinery and buildings needed to maintain and protect modern weapons systems, including the controversial IRBMs and MRBMs, and also a number of IL-28 light bombers with a six-hundred-mile striking radius that would allow them to hit most of Florida.

Such large-scale activity could not escape CIA observation, and it was deeply worrisome to the Agency's new head, John McCone, a sixtyish California Republican who had made his business fortune in steel and shipbuilding, before joining the march of managers to the defense establishment in the late 1940s. He had been a deputy to General Marshall, an under secretary of the Air Force, and chairman of the AEC before taking the CIA job. Now he wanted a fuller picture of what the Russians were up to, and asked White House approval for both low-level and U-2 surveillance flights. He was turned down on the grounds that an unpleasant incident might be provoked. The Kennedy team was willing to believe that the activity only involved the placement of purely defensive weapons— jet fighters, torpedo boats, and even surface-to-air missiles (SAMs)—just as Khrushchev had publicly and privately assured the President. But early in September the situation changed. Word of the Soviet buildup leaked to some important Republicans, possibly with McCone's help. Faced with an embarrassing issue in forthcoming midterm congressional elections, Kennedy delivered a speech on September 4, saying that the United States was not ignorant of events in Cuba, but would do nothing unless evidence were discovered of a "significant offensive capability." Then, secretly, he gave the OK for some U-2 flights over Cuba.

Three flights were thwarted by cloud cover. But on October 14 Major Rudolf Anderson, Jr., who was later to play a sad role in the crisis, took off on a fourth. The thirty-five-year-old South Carolinian, a onetime accountant and the father of two small boys, switched on his astonishing cameras over the island. Bright sunlight helped them to capture the images that were unmistakable to the experts: at least two sites containing the necessary trailers, launching scaffolds, fuel tanks, and cables for large-sized missiles.

Galvanized by this news, Kennedy assembled an advisory team of people he trusted. Some of its members were there by virtue of their office, like Taylor, Rusk, McNamara, Bundy, and the Vice President. But there were others who were especially close to him, such as speechwriters Theodore Sorensen and Kenneth O'Donnell, Treasury Secretary Douglas Dillon (his Cabinet Republican), and above all his brother. And there were some whom he asked to serve because of their special expertise in Soviet affairs or their long experience: such men as Charles Bohlen and Dean Acheson. They were a temporary executive committee of the National Security Council, ExCom for short.

He set two ground rules. One was that at first, at least, the gravity of the situation must be concealed. He would go about his ordinary

business, which included campaigning for Democrats. Those with
official public chores, like Rusk, must sandwich those obligations in
somehow, which they did at heavy cost in sleep. Kennedy's second
rule was that time was of the essence. Defense experts told him that
the missiles could be operational in as little as two weeks. Once that
happened, he felt, American bargaining power would be limited.
The loaded gun would already be leveled at the southeastern
United States.

Within the limit set by clock and calendar, ExCom was free to
propose any method of accomplishing their task of coming up with
an appropriate response. The President would have final say as to
the proper mix of toughness and restraint, but all sensed a shared
responsibility for whatever might go catastrophically wrong.

After the first shock passed, Excom settled down to its fateful
debates. Taylor and Rusk led in calling for an instantaneous hard
smash, an air strike without warning, to knock out the missiles.

The President left for lunch with a visiting Libyan dignitary, and
then to confer an award on astronaut Walter Schirra. Adlai
Stevenson was at the lunch. Kennedy took him aside and showed
him the pictures. He warned that there might be a bombing raid and
that the ambassador should be prepared for the aftershock in the
UN. An upset Stevenson urged the President then and there not to
think only of military options, but to consider negotiations. He
believed that Cuban President Osvald Dorticòs, speaking at the UN
earlier in the month, had opened the way to a possible deal. If the
United States, Dorticòs had said, would give Cuba "effective
guarantees" against invasion, Cuba would no longer need any arms
support from her Soviet friends.

So the lines were drawn on the first day between two extreme
alternatives—immediate air strike and no military response at all.
Although the terms "hawk" and "dove" first appeared in later
descriptions of these meetings, not all positions were firm or
clear-cut. Men felt free to play devil's advocate. Others took
common ground for differing reasons. McNamara opposed the air
raid, for example, because he doubted the Air Force's promise of a
clean, "surgical" strike to "take out" the missile bases. He feared
that many Cubans and certainly some Russians would be killed.
That could force Khrushchev into a retaliatory move, perhaps on
Berlin.

By Thursday's dawn, the ExCom members were sleeping sporadi-
cally on cots in their offices, dodging reporters' questions about their
mysterious absences, living on sandwiches, growing red-eyed and
short-tempered. Robert Kennedy, at this point, emerged as the chief
opponent of the hawks who were demanding the air strike on the
coming Sunday, insisting that the U.S.S.R. could not retaliate since it

was too weak in ICBMs and too overextended in Cuba. He claimed that such an attack would be "a Pearl Harbor in reverse and would blacken the name of the United States in the pages of history." His brother was not going to be the Tojo of the 1960s. Douglas Dillon said afterward that the Attorney General's persuasiveness reversed his own decision. But Dean Acheson was outraged, called the analogy "false" and "pejorative," and later characterized such moral arguments as "silly" and "unworthy."

McNamara and others now came up with a halfway measure, a Caribbean "quarantine," with U.S. naval forces halting all Cuba-bound vessels for search, and banning those with offensive weapons. Hard-liners argued that it would only delay matters, give the Russians more time to arm the missiles, and place the government under pressure, as Robert Lovett put it, "from the bleeding hearts . . . and the peace-at-any-price units." But the blockade advocates had a powerful consideration on their side. If their measure did not work, it could be followed by a bombing, whereas to start with a rain of explosives on Cuban soil might slam doors irretrievably shut.

On Thursday at 5:30 P.M. Kennedy had a prearranged visit with Andrei Gromyko, who had come down from New York where he was attending the UN session in progress. Kennedy did not mention the missiles; he appreciated the freedom of maneuver that he would lose once the news was public. And Gromyko did not refer to them for reasons of his own, including possible ignorance of them. But when the Soviet Foreign Minister reassured Kennedy that the Soviet presence in Cuba was "by no means offensive," Kennedy, stung by what he saw as Khrushchev's attempt to deceive him, was sorely tempted to show the incriminating pictures. Instead, he carefully reread, aloud, his September statement warning that "offensive capabilities" in Cuba would not be tolerated.

On Friday the President took off for some campaigning in Cleveland, Chicago, and Springfield, Illinois, where he laid a wreath on Lincoln's tomb. Then, by presidential command, his doctor "ordered" him to return to Washington and give some rest to a "cold." Behind that thinning smokescreen against the press, the President could meet with ExCom on Saturday morning for a final decision.

It was a dark hour for Adlai Stevenson. Against the hawks' demands for the air strike (with one service chief recommending nuclear weapons), and the moderate call for the blockade, he argued that something be offered to the Russians as a quid pro quo. Perhaps an offer to neutralize Cuba, even if it meant giving up America's Guantanamo Bay base. Or, Stevenson suggested, since the United States had MRBMs of its own in Italy and Turkey—the latter on the Soviet border—a swap could be arranged, with both parties taking out their missiles. In that way Khrushchev, doubtless under pressure from Kremlin hawks, could afford to back down without humiliation.

Stevenson's idea was not novel. The Turkish missiles were obsolete "Jupiters," and Kennedy himself had already said that the fifteen of them and the thirty in Italy should be "taken off the board." What had held up the order was NATO politics. The Turks might resent the move as a gesture of abandonment. Nonetheless, on that morning of October 20, Stevenson became the lightning rod in the weary gathering. Why, almost everyone virtually shouted, should Khrushchev be "paid" to end his adventure? What an invitation to future blackmail! And what ultimate proof of the softness of the prematurely aging Stevenson, already burdened with a reputation as an indecisive "egghead." Now another label— "appeaser"—would also be affixed to him. He bore it unflinchingly. That night he told Kenneth O'Donnell that "perhaps we need a coward in the room when we are talking about nuclear war." Privately, the President actually expressed admiration for Stevenson's "guts" in taking the unpopular stand. But his final choice was for the blockade, to be announced on Monday night, leaving forty-eight hours to prepare for the war that might break out.

On Sunday morning the gray ships of the fleet steamed out to battle stations. The Strategic Air Command's planes went into their alert pattern, some of them—carrying nuclear bombs—always airborne to avoid surprise attack on the ground. Four transports evacuated civilians, suffering from fear and the sticky heat, from Guantanamo Bay. Ninety Atlas and forty-six Titan intercontinental missiles were fueled and armed. An armored division rolled, convoy by convoy, into Florida. Dispatches were sent to alert heads of foreign governments. (Acheson was asked to go and speak to Charles de Gaulle personally, and did.) Navy procedures for halting Soviet vessels were reviewed: first a hail from an interpreter-officer, if no response a shot across the bow, and if still no response, a crippling shot to the rudder. Low-level Cuban reconnaissance flights were ordered. Finally, a politically aware Kennedy had seventeen campaign-trail-riding congressional leaders, of both parties, tracked down and flown to Washington.

Monday afternoon the President briefed these legislators on the contents of the speech he had announced for that evening. He listened politely to some dissenting opinions (all of them in favor of stronger action), and, though bone-tired, had enough steam left to josh Senator Hubert Humphrey, his 1960 rival for the nomination: "Hubert, if I'd known the job was going to be this tough I would never have beat you in West Virginia."

At 7 P.M. Kennedy gravely faced the network cameras and microphones. In a thirteen-minute talk he explained that the "offensive" missile sites had been found, that he had asked for emergency meetings of the OAS and the UN, and that as an "initial" step he was proclaiming the quarantine. He avoided bluster, but issued a dire warning. Any missiles fired from Cuba toward any place in the hemisphere would lead to "a full retaliatory response upon the Soviet Union." As the television floodlights snapped off, he confronted the possibility that the Soviets would attempt a first strike at once. Every hour now was anxious.

Tuesday, October 23. All the ExCom members, and millions throughout the world, awoke and probably shared Dean Rusk's feelings. Rusk went into George Ball's office and found him asleep on a sofa. He nudged him awake. "We have won a considerable victory," he said. "You and I are still alive." . . . Throughout the day, pro- and anti-American demonstrations kept police and reporters busy in world capitals. . . . UN Secretary General U Thant asked the Soviet Union to halt its shipments and the United States to lift the blockade until talks could be arranged. . . . In Moscow, Khrushchev attended a performance of *Boris Godunov* and invited a visiting capitalist, William Knox of Westinghouse International, to his office for a chat. . . . And of the twenty-three Soviet ships known to be bound for Cuba, the nine closest were swiftly closing in on the blockade line set up five hundred miles from the island.

Wednesday, October 24. ExCom was in session. Radio messages poured in from the blockading task force. Suddenly there was a paralyzing report: A Soviet submarine was discovered, positioned between two of the approaching freighters. Kennedy went gray, his fist clenched spasmodically. What was the sub's purpose? The carrier *Essex* raced toward the submarine, under orders, if the sub was submerged, to have a plane drop a depth charge "near" it to bring it to the surface for communication. . . . A secretary distributed cards containing instructions for those officials who would be evacuated to a secret shelter outside Washington before it was vaporized. . . . At 10:25 John McCone rushed in. "Mr. President, we have a preliminary report which seems to indicate some Russian ships are stopping." Rusk turned to Bundy. "We're eyeball to eyeball," he said, "and I think the other fellow just blinked." Kennedy ordered an immediate message, uncoded and audible to any Russians listening, to the *Essex*: Do *not* go after the submarine. . . . A long few minutes passed, and then there was more news. All the Russian ships outside the blockade line were stopping. Everyone would live for a while yet. . . . Later, Khrushchev went on the air to announce that he was honoring U Thant's request. But the American blockade was still "unacceptable," and his ships would try again in the morning. . . . The clock continued to tick.

Thursday, October 25. In the UN, Adlai Stevenson confronted Russian spokesman Valentin Zorin. "Do you, Ambassador Zorin," he asked, "deny that the U.S.S.R. has placed . . . missiles . . . in Cuba? Yes or no? Don't wait for the translation. Yes or no."

Zorin: "I am not in an American courtroom, sir."

Stevenson: "You are in the courtroom of world opinion right now, and you can answer yes or no."

Zorin: "You will have your answer in due course."

Stevenson: "I am prepared to wait for my answer until hell freezes over."

Then, with clear enjoyment of his new, tough role, Stevenson produced gigantic, damning blowups of the U-2 photos. When news of the exchange reached Kennedy, he smiled. "I never knew Adlai had it in him." . . . On the blockade line the Navy let through some neutral ships and even a Russian tanker. But, finally, the *Marucla* approached to furnish a test case of the recognition and effectiveness of the quarantine. It was chartered by Russians, owned by Panamanians, flew the Lebanese flag, and had a mostly Greek crew. It was loaded with Soviet truck parts, electronic gear, asbestos, sulfur, and lathes. The destroyer *Joseph P. Kennedy, Jr.* (named for the President's brother killed in World War II) radioed the *Marucla* to prepare for search. The captain cheerfully assented, showed his papers, offered coffee to the American visitors, and was allowed to proceed. The United States had demonstrated its will. The Russians backed away. Sixteen more Soviet ships turned back before reaching the line. The first act was complete.

Rejoicing on Friday the 26th, however, was limited and premature. No new missiles would be entering Cuba. But work continued on those already there, and there was no sign of further Russian softening. The United States continued preparations for the invasion of Cuba. Hard-line pressure mounted. Arthur M. Schlesinger, Jr., received a telegram—one of hundreds pouring into the White House—from fellow academic Zbigniew Brzezinski. It read: "Any further delay in bombing missile sites fails to exploit Soviet uncertainty."

Then two messages arrived from Moscow via unconventional channels. The American Broadcasting Company's State Department correspondent, John Scali, quite naturally had a number of Soviet contacts in Washington. One of them was Alexander Fomin, an embassy official, thought by some Americans to be a KGB agent. That Friday afternoon, Fomin called Scali with a lunch invitation. Across the table he hinted that if the United States pledged not to invade Cuba, the missiles might be removed and the UN allowed to verify the fact. Would Scali be willing to convey that possibility to the American government to get its reaction? Scali did precisely that. He was rushed from Roger Hilsman, then director of intelligence for the State Department, to Rusk, and by Rusk to the President. Kennedy was ready to bargain. He told Scali that Scali could tell Fomin, citing only "a very high source," that such an arrangement could work. Scali passed the word that very night at the Sheraton Coffee Shop. The Russian was so relieved or agitated that he dropped a five-dollar bill on the table to pay a thirty-cent check and rushed out.

Meanwhile, a cable had come in from Moscow that proved the "back channel" approach to Scali to be no fluke. It was a personal message from Khrushchev to the President. Robert Kennedy recalled it as "long and emotional," full of passion to avoid the "death, destruction, and anarchy that nuclear war would bring to his people and all mankind." Khrushchev repeated that the missiles in Cuba were not offensively intended. He hoped the President would lift the blockade, for sooner or later the Russians would be forced to defend by arms their ships' right to travel freely on the high seas. But the military solution was not a good one. At best, the accumulation of armaments, he said, "damages the economy," and if used, they would "destroy people on both sides." If the President would guarantee not to invade Cuba and to end the blockade, he himself would send no more missiles and take away or destroy those already there. "We must not succumb to intoxication and heady passions," said the Chairman:

> We and you ought not now to pull on the ends of the rope in which you have tied the knot of war, because the more the two of us pull, the tighter that knot will be tied, and a moment may come when . . . even he who tied it will not have strength enough to untie it, and then it will be necessary to cut that knot. Let us . . . relax the forces pulling on the ends of the rope.

It was pure Khrushchevian imagery. Coupled with the identical offer through Fomin, it was a way out that Kennedy would accept, and so everyone went to bed convinced the worst was over. They awoke, instead, to what proved to be the most dangerous day.

Saturday, October 27. The country, knowing only that the blockade was "working," prepared for a day of raking autumn leaves and watching football, weekend leisure rituals that offered some reassurance that life could go on. . . . A new message arrived from the Soviet Union for Kennedy, completely different in tone from that of the day before. It had upped the ante. "We will remove our missiles from Cuba," it said brusquely. "You will remove yours from Turkey." The no-invasion-of-Cuba pledge would still be expected. Dazedly, ExCom gathered and speculated. Was Khrushchev still there? Or had he been replaced or bullied into a new position by his hawks? . . . Suddenly, news came that seemed to imply that very development. Major Anderson, on a fresh U-2 flight, crossed the intercept zone of a SAM. The rocket was launched, met its target, and the major died for his country in a blaze of exploding fuel. No one would ever know whether the firing crew was Russian or Cuban, whether the shot was accidental, locally ordered, or in response to commands from Moscow. But a Soviet weapon had downed an unarmed American plane. "We are in an entirely new ball game," said an ExCom member. . . . Decisions came swiftly. The next morning the SAM sites would be taken out, followed by an attack on the missiles Monday, an invasion Tuesday. The hard-liners were in charge.

Scali was summoned and sent to see Fomin again to see if the downing of the U-2 was a new kind of message, and to let it be known that it was intolerable. He made the date, raged to the Russian about the "double cross." Why did the terms change? And why was an American plane with neither bombs nor guns destroyed? Scali watched surprise cross the other man's face. "Oh, no!" said Fomin.

And while all this had been happening, there had been the nearest of brushes with disaster. A U-2 had taken off from Alaska on a polar flight to check for atmospheric radiation from possible Soviet nuclear test blasts (despite a Kennedy order barring all such flights for the moment). The pilot got lost briefly and headed into Soviet airspace, thereby putting an unidentified invading blip on Soviet air defense radar screens. They had to decide in minutes whether or not to retaliate. By enormous good fortune, the American suddenly found his bearings and streaked out of the danger zone. Later Kennedy was told the story. He shook his head. "There is always some son of a bitch who doesn't get the word."

Evening approached . . . War was again only hours away. . . . All that remained was to reject the new Russian note, and alert troop-carrier and other invasion units. But Kennedy held out for a last shot at peace. He would send one more unarmed U-2 over Cuba in the morning. If a SAM fired at it, then and only then would the bombing begin. "It isn't the first step that concerns me," he said, "but both sides escalating to the fourth and fifth step—and we don't go to the sixth because there's no one around to do so." . . . He had been reading Barbara Tuchman's The Guns of August, which relates how war came in 1914 because of breakdowns in communication, official stubbornness, loss of control, and resignation to the "inevitable" by so-called statesmen. Afterward, he would say that he didn't want survivors, if any, to write a book about this moment called The Missiles of October.

What should be the reply to the latest Soviet ultimatum? . . . Robert Kennedy came up with a brilliant notion. Ignore it. Simply accept the terms of Khrushchev's first letter, in a comparable spirit. Dizzy with fatigue, he and Sorensen drafted a response. It said that instructions would go out to American representatives at the UN to work out a "permanent solution to the Cuba problem along the lines suggested in your letter of October 26."

Then, during a break for a hasty meal (from 7:30 to 9 P.M.), Robert Kennedy met Russian Ambassador Anatoly Dobrynin at the Justice Department to hand him the note. He was blunt and direct. He noted the continuing work on the Russian missiles, the downing of the U-2. American patience was running out, he said. Time was running out. Dobrynin asked: What about the Turkish missiles? Kennedy would later summarize his answer in this way. There could be no deal under pressure, he said. In any case the decision would have to be made by NATO. However, President Kennedy had been "anxious to remove those missiles from Turkey and Italy for a long time." It is "our judgment," said Kennedy, that "within a short time after this crisis [is] over, those missiles [will] be gone, four or five months." That was the word that Dobrynin passed back to Moscow, and Khrushchev—and consequently historians—was left to ponder whether it was an official offer, or purely the personal speculation of a man who happened to be the brother of the President of the United States.

ExCom's final session was brief. No more could be done. Peace rested, for now, on the button-pushing fingers of the SAM officers in Cuba.

Robert Kennedy, exhausted, slept hard on his Virginia estate, but awoke with characteristic Sunday morning energy and family feeling, ready to take his children to a horse show. While he was there, he was called to the phone. It was Dean Rusk speaking. A new message had been received from Khrushchev. By processes still locked in Soviet files, he had come to a decision. The missiles would be dismantled and taken home.

John F. Kennedy countered with a relaxation of all pressure. The U-2 flights were canceled, the blockade lifted. Orders were given to officials not to crow or put Khrushchev in an awkward position. Even SGA—the special anti-Castro task force—was eventually disbanded. In a few weeks, the Soviet bases disappeared, over Castro's bitter objections. Next, the Ilyushin medium bombers were brought back to Russia. Photographs verified it all.

Three months later, the American missiles were taken out of Turkey and Italy.

Who had won? Did Kennedy "pay" too much? Was Khrushchev forced to eat crow by a firm American stand? Did either man overreact? Or did they each know wisely when not to push that final, fatal inch? Historians are still arguing about it.

IN RELIEF, THE COUNTRY SUSTAINED Kennedy with a strong Democratic vote in the elections. With the start of his third year as President, there was a sudden rush of unaccustomed warmth in Soviet-American relations. It was as if the leaders of both nations had become more reflective and more responsible. The clearest sign of this was the way in which they dealt with the nuclear testing issue.

Since September of 1961 both sides had been conducting numerous experimental explosions to improve their weapons systems. The Russians had set off one atmospheric monster blast with the force of 58 million tons of TNT, nearly three hundred times as powerful as the weapon that had seared Hiroshima. The pollution of earth, water, air, crops, and livestock from the fallout of such airborne "shots" was causing worldwide concern. Both nations, from a sense of their own safety needs, moved some tests underground. Moreover, Kennedy launched efforts to limit or end the tests through agreement in the Geneva disarmament conferences that had limped along since the late 1950s. But they faltered for two reasons. One was that the newest members of the "nuclear club," France and China, would not discuss the subject. They were far behind and believed they needed the tests. The other was that the Russians clung to their refusal to permit "on-site" inspections within the U.S.S.R., to verify compliance with any test ban. Only underground testing was at issue. Tests in the seas or in the air could now be detected by instruments placed outside a nation's borders. But the seismic tremors of underground blasts could be passed off as earthquakes by a nation that chose to cheat.

In December 1962, Khrushchev moved to break the deadlock. "It seems to me, Mr. President," he wrote, "that the time has come to put an end once and for all to nuclear tests." For this "noble and humane goal," the Soviet Union would be ready to accept three annual inspections.

Kennedy responded positively, but came under heavy pressure from his own nuclear "establishment." Its prominent members included most former service chiefs, the former AEC chairman, Lewis Strauss, Dr. Edward Teller, the "father of the hydrogen bomb," and powerful Senators like Illinois Republican Everett Dirksen and Georgia Democrat Richard Russell, chairman of the Senate Armed Services Committee. Kennedy was compelled to demand more inspections to prevent Soviet duplicity, and the movement toward a ban stalled. But during April and May of 1963 Great Britain, now also with nuclear-bomb-making capability, proposed a top level meeting of Soviet, American, and British negotiators.

Kennedy sought to prepare American opinion to accept the idea, especially in a speech at Washington's American University on June 10, 1963. It was an astonishing call for a rollback of Cold War feelings. "Some say," the President told his Commencement Day audience, "that it is useless to speak of world peace or world disarmament . . . until the leaders of the Soviet Union adopt a more enlightened attitude. . . . I also believe we must reexamine our own attitude . . . for our attitude is as essential as theirs. We are both caught up in a vicious and dangerous cycle in which suspicion on one side breeds suspicion on the other, and new weapons beget counterweapons." He continued:

> Let us not be blind to our differences, but let us also direct attention to our common interests and to the means by which those differences can be resolved. And if we cannot end now our differences, at least we can help make the world safe for diversity. For, in the final analysis, our most basic common link is that we all inhabit this small planet. We all breathe the same air. We all cherish our children's future. And we are all mortal.

The next month he sent the peripatetic, indestructible Averell Harriman to Moscow to join Gromyko and Britain's Lord Hailsham in treaty talks.

Khrushchev pragmatically broke the deadlock over inspection by simply proposing to ignore it and settle for what could be achieved, a limited test ban treaty covering space, the oceans, and the atmosphere. On July 25, 1963, the three negotiators signed the Treaty of Moscow, embodying his idea. In presenting the pact to the Senate, Kennedy said it was "particularly for our children and grandchildren, and they have no lobby here in Washington." But the treaty's opponents had a powerful lobby, and in the end Kennedy had to agree to safeguards proposed by the military-industrial complex in order to win ratification. These included the promise to continue "aggressive" underground testing, to maintain nuclear research programs, to be ready to resume airborne tests quickly if they should be "deemed essential to the national security," and to spend freely on intelligence. In a sense the treaty was approved with crossed fingers. Yet after 336 nuclear explosions in eighteen years there was a halt. In Sorensen's words, "the genie was at least temporarily back in the bottle."

A sudden breakthrough succeeded this event. There was the installation of a "hot line" between Kremlin and White House to prevent accidental war, and the first major sale of U.S. grain to the U.S.S.R. since the Cold War had begun. In addition, there was joint Soviet and American support for a resolution by the UN General

Assembly calling on both nations not to place nuclear devices in outer space. Khrushchev was seeking even more easement of tension, floating the idea of a nonaggression treaty between NATO and Warsaw Pact nations, if only because he himself was beginning to worry more about war with China than with the West.

On the anniversary of the Cuban missile crisis the new spirit was palpable. It was easy, long afterward, to think that if John Kennedy's Administration had endured beyond November 1963, there might have been still more days of thaw ahead.

Yet there was another side. Halfway around the world, Kennedy was continuing his battle against what he saw as a Communist thrust disguised as a "war of national liberation." Saving Vietnam was still on his mind. The full story of Kennedy and Vietnam can only be understood in the context of an overall survey of the American misadventure there. But it can be said that during those sunny hours of accommodation while the test ban was forged, Kennedy was sinking deeper into a dilemma from which he could not escape without reworking all of his conceptions of the realities of Southeast Asia.

All through his Administration his counselors on Vietnam asked for an increased American advisory "presence," and more U. S. aerial and logistical support. And he provided it, lured by the argument that, in time, and with enough aid to Diem, the Viet Cong would be beaten. Between the beginning of 1962 and the summer of 1963, the number of United States training and support personnel attached to the South Vietnamese army rose to 12,000. They were allowed to enter combat with their units. United States air personnel were empowered to attack Viet Cong strongholds. Support was increasingly given to programs that were gradually shifting the burden of the war to American shoulders. And this was all done in secret. And in vain, for Diem and his brother, Ngo Dinh Nhu, continued to be visibly unpopular with large masses of their own people.

Yet when a number of American voices suggested that perhaps the United States would do better to abandon ship and leave the Vietnamese to settle what seemed to be their own civil conflict, Kennedy stuck to his guns, to the definition of the war as a Communist "invasion," to the domino theory. In a July 25 press conference, he said: "In my opinion, for us to withdraw from the effort would mean a collapse, not only of Vietnam but of Southeast Asia. So we are going to stay there."

The commitment of advisers went up to 25,000, of whom, by October 1963, some 47 had been killed. The Administration kept prodding Diem to institute reforms. Finally, after many secret cables, internal battles among U.S. officials in Washington and

Saigon, and Byzantine maneuvers, some of Diem's own officers were encouraged to revolt against him in the expectation of getting American support. On November 1, 1963, their uprising occurred. The next day, Diem and Ngo were captured and shot.

What Kennedy would have done next was never to be known. Almost exactly three weeks later he, too, was murdered by gunfire in Dallas.

The Kennedy Presidency, begun in hope, had ended in unanticipated violence. The contrast between high dreams and brutal deeds had run through his years in office—the brinksmanship and the test-ban treaty, the arms race and the Peace Corps, the fine rhetoric and the manipulative policies in Vietnam. Kennedy was both a molder and a prisoner of the Cold War's history, perhaps wanting to end it but powerless to escape from it. He left behind an America that would become even more deeply enmeshed in these painful contradictions.

Chapter 10

THE QUAGMIRE
1964-1972

DURING THEIR TALK IN PARIS on the last day of May 1961, General de Gaulle proffered to John F. Kennedy some sage advice about the area where France had accumulated painful expertise. "You Americans wanted, yesterday, to take our place in Indochina," he said. "You want to assume a succession to rekindle a war that we ended. I predict to you that you will, step by step, be sucked into a bottomless military and political quagmire despite the losses and expenditures that you may squander."

In his memoirs, the general added this sad observation: "Kennedy is listening to me, but events will show that I did not convince him."

As, indeed, he did not. Out of that failure came an unrelenting American march into the predicted quagmire. Out of it came dire events that would extend beyond Kennedy's lifetime, destroy the Presidency of his successor, and scar America's psyche, probably for generations.

Deep historical paradoxes surrounded the tragedy. Major American intervention in Vietnam began early in 1965, the centennial year of the Civil War's conclusion. That war was now a common treasury of national memories; North and South alike had joined in celebrating the anniversaries of its battles. More importantly, a rush of conscience seemed to affect the nation, so that in 1963, the hundredth anniversary of the Emancipation Proclamation, there was massive support for a gigantic civil rights march on Washington. In 1964 and 1965 Congress enacted (at a Southern President's bidding) strong laws guaranteeing the political and social rights promised to black Americans in the 14th and 15th Amendments. At last, it seemed, both sections and races were truly one. The Civil War was finally liquidated.

And in the next three years unity crumbled. The country suffered a new divisiveness, born of Vietnam. Race riots exploded in major cities. Lyndon Johnson could not offer himself again as a candidate for the White House, could not even travel in public without provoking major antiwar demonstrations, could not sit at the convention of the Democratic Party that nominated Hubert Humphrey in 1968. That gathering was held in a Chicago hall ringed with barbed wire and troops. In the streets outside, young Americans chanted obscenities, waved "enemy" flags, threw garbage at the police—and were in turn charged, beaten, and teargassed as a horrified nation watched on its television screens. Three years had taken the country from mellowness to madness.

War, the traditional unifier of a national society, was tearing America apart. And there was another anomaly. America's Vietnam plunge was the direct fruit of Cold War assumptions—a move to keep the dominoes from toppling in crucial Southeast Asia. But while the war was on, relations between the United States and the U.S.S.R. were more amicable than they had been since the 1945 handclasps along the Elbe. The two giants signed a treaty against the proliferation of nuclear weapons; they entered into discussions on the limitation of strategic armaments; they broadened their cultural, scientific, and trade exchanges. In 1967, Soviet Premier Alexei Kosygin (who had replaced Khrushchev in late 1964) met briefly with President Johnson at Glassboro, New Jersey, and shouted to goggling crowds: "I want friendship with the American people."

But most importantly, these gestures were made while the United States was intensifying an air and land war against North Vietnam, a Soviet ally and client, with no fear of provoking a major confrontation with Moscow. A tacit understanding seemed to bind the two capitals in an agreement to limit the conflict to the Indochinese peninsula. Some popular histories of the 1970s, in fact, would more or less assume that the Cold War had ended around 1963.

If so, how did one explain its horrendous legacy in Vietnam? Perhaps it was the result of a mad momentum that swept mighty peoples along on historical currents that, once in motion, could not be mastered. Certainly there was little logic or clarity to the war years. Their echoes, in fact, remain confusing, haunting, and alive.

VIETNAM WAS ALWAYS PERCEIVED through distorting lenses by official Washington. Kennedy's various special emissaries to Saigon presented hastily gathered impressions, carefully shaped by Americans in that capital who had a vested interest in positive reports. The two leading U.S. officials on the scene early in 1963 were Ambassador Frederick Nolting and General Paul D. Harkins, chief of the military mission. They were, respectively, a career diplomat, fresh from European experience and a spit-and-polish professional soldier who said on arrival that he wanted only optimists on his staff.

Yet the actual situation was full of ambiguities stemming from Vietnamese history and culture, subjects of which the American experts in Saigon were largely innocent. In South Vietnam alone there was deep conflict between Catholics and Buddhists; between Vietnamese generals and officials trained by the French and imbued with a Parisian outlook, and those seeking a return to Vietnamese traditions; between peasants and landlords, mountain tribes and coastal villagers, descendants of various linguistic and ethnic groups at loggerheads for centuries past.

Vietnamese farmers were not easily fitted into rational plans for counterinsurgency. They clung to their ancestral gravesites and resisted forced resettlement to strategic hamlets. They saw the flow of battle as ruled by the "mandate of Heaven." There was an incalculable gulf between Americans who measured the progress of the war with computers and Vietnamese village chiefs who consulted astrologers.

Communism might well have alienated many of the South Vietnamese, but the Viet Cong had managed to identify itself with Vietnamese nationalism more than with Marxism. Official United States doctrine saw the National Liberation Front, North Vietnam, China, and the U.S.S.R. as part of a web of world Communist governments. But the NLF was an umbrella group of anti-Diem forces, though dominated by the Viet Cong—i.e., the Vietnamese Communists. China and Vietnam had been enemies for a thousand years, even though Peking gave Ho Chi Minh some help, for reasons of its own. And while Moscow likewise supplied some aid to Hanoi, North Vietnam appeared less dependent on Russia than South Vietnam did on the United States—at least in some Vietnamese eyes. In any case, Vietnamese politics on both sides of the dividing 17th parallel defied neat categorization. The incontestable difference was that by 1963 the Viet Cong was winning its battles against the South Vietnamese army and widening its control of the provinces.

Perhaps no one leader in Saigon could have mastered the situation and infused his ranks with unity and combativeness, but Diem was especially disastrous. He severely repressed opponents, thereby widening the fissures in his country. He played favorites, took bribes from generals and provincial governors in return for their appointments, accepted rake-offs from contractors, and allowed a good deal of American aid in cash and supplies to disappear into the pockets of his friends or into the black market—hardly a way to build loyalty or morale.

In the end, Diem's failings seemed to simplify the issue. It took a long time for honest reports on how badly he was doing to reach Washington. When the bad news was no longer suppressible, however, it simply led the Kennedy entourage to encourage the coup that slew Diem and his brother, Ngo Dinh Nhu. The Administration hoped that a change of cast would improve the script.

It actually had no such happy effect. Diem and Nhu had eliminated many strong and able men who might have been rivals, and in the year and a half following their deaths in November 1963, the armed forces installed and ousted at least three leaders. By June 1965, the premiership had fallen to an Air Force commander, Marshal Nguyen Cao Ky, a youthful, sporty, moustached figure who had fought for the French and Bao Dai against the Viet Minh, and who, in a press interview in 1964, declared: "I have only one hero—Hitler. . . . We need four or five Hitlers in Vietnam."

The reshuffling of command in Saigon during 1964 was therefore an interim period in which a completely new assessment of the conflict was possible; new lines of policy could be explored without the burden of previous commitments. It was also a year of changing of the guard in Washington, as Johnson took over the Presidency, won reelection overwhelmingly in his own right, and set his future course. It was a year—the last one—of relatively free choice about Vietnam.

The point of departure for any new program was a simple reality: What had been tried so far was not good enough. The optimistic phrases were still on tap for the headline writers—statements such as Defense Secretary Robert McNamara's 1962 boast that "every quantitative measurement we have shows we're winning the war," or Secretary of State Dean Rusk's early 1963 assurance that the Saigonese forces were "turning an important corner." But classified documents bore a gloomier viewpoint. The Kennedy team's disillusionment with Diem had stemmed from the clear recognition that the war was being lost under his direction. More than a year after Diem had been ousted, General Maxwell Taylor (who by then was the ambassador to Saigon) summed up the grim facts in a paper that admitted that there was "no national tendency toward team play or mutual loyalty among many of the leaders and political groups within South Vietnam," whereas, by contrast, "the ability of the Viet Cong continuously to rebuild their units was one of the mysteries of this guerrilla war." Not only did the VC units have "the recuperative powers of the phoenix, but they have an amazing ability to maintain morale."

If such was the case, what could be done? One alternative was to cut losses and get out; in September of 1963 John F. Kennedy said to some of his close associates that he wished gradually to wind down the Vietnam involvement regardless of consequences, but that it was unthinkable until after the 1964 election. Perhaps a hint of that possible intention was implicit in a public statement that ultimately the war was a Vietnamese responsibility: "They are the ones who have to win it or lose it." But Kennedy's official position remained prudently hard-line.

The choice other than disengagement was to increase the ante and put more military pressure on the enemy. The Joint Chiefs and some hawkish members of the Administration were already recommending such a course in January 1964 to the newly installed President Johnson. Their preferred instrument was airpower, in which American superiority was unquestioned. But airpower's primary value would not be against the invisible and scattered Viet Cong, but against North Vietnam. In order to justify its application there, a new evaluation of the failures of Saigon was necessary. The strength of the Viet Cong was no longer seen as due to popular disaffection for Diem or those after Diem. Rather, it was because reinforcements from the north were streaming down the trails through the jungles—including those of "neutral" Laos and Cambodia. Hanoi was the villain, and the war against it had to be intensified, as the South Vietnamese government was beginning to insist.

Such appraisals actually began to be implemented that very month through a program known as 34A, a series of U.S.-supported commando raids on North Vietnam for sabotage, psychological warfare, and intelligence-gathering purposes. In addition, American and Thai pilots, flying propeller-driven fighter-bombers with Royal Laotian Air Force markings, bombed North Vietnamese and Pathet Lao troops in Laos, while regular U.S. Air Force craft conducted photo reconnaissance. McNamara approved this covert air war, and also ordered preliminary studies and preparations for an open bombing campaign against the North.

The proposed action would carry long-range consequences, however. For one thing, the United States would be bombing a nation with which it had no direct quarrel—a sticky diplomatic point. To win popular support for the bombing, the public characterization of the war would be changed. South Vietnam, instead of being the target of an insurgency, would become a "peaceful nation," attacked by its neighbor. A civil war would be transformed into an invasion, and the propaganda line would allow of no ambiguities, thereby hardening positions and reducing the chances of negotiation. In addition, aerial warfare would be costly and would create hostages to fortune in the form of American air bases requiring protection against Viet Cong attacks, which Americans would have to furnish if the South Vietnamese were not up to the job. A momentum would be created, in which a new input of American power would generate the need for still more American commitment, and the war would begin to take on a red, white, and blue cast.

These, then, were Johnson's choices. To get in deeper, with risks. Or to get out. The case against getting out, however, was powerful. It defied the Cold War axiom, by now time-hallowed, that to abandon an anti-Communist ally for any reason would demonstrate a fatal weakness of will that would open the entire world to further Soviet or Chinese aggressions. Few public figures, in 1964, would risk political suicide by challenging that view. Few would then contend that nationalism, the true revolutionary force at work in Indochina, could possibly guarantee Ho Chi Minh's resistance to Moscow and Peking pressures better than American bombs could.

At the same time, there was a practical argument against a heavier involvement—the example of Korea, where the United States had been caught in a land war on an Asian peninsula, unable to match manpower with the enemy or to exploit fully its own technological assets. Lyndon Johnson, a master politician, knew that the Democrats had been punished for that misfortune in 1952. But he also knew that they had likewise suffered at the polls for what was perceived as their inaction on China in the late 1940s. If the prospect of an entrapment and stalemate in Indochina was politically (and militarily) nightmarish, so was that of letting Indochina "fall" to the Reds. "I am not going to lose Vietnam," Johnson had said almost immediately after taking office. "I am not going to be the President who saw Southeast Asia go the way China went."

What could he do to avoid the horns of the dilemma? Simple. He would win. It took him a year to make up his mind, but by early 1965 he came to believe that he could achieve what he was to urge on a group of soldiers to whom he gave a pep talk, that is, "bring home the coonskin."

McNamara and most of the generals offered Johnson a technocratic victory. There need be no confrontation between divisions as in Korea, they said. This would be an antiguerrilla operation. Defoliants would deny the Viet Cong cover; the regrouping of the populace would deprive them of support. Helicopters could swiftly shuttle soldiers to threatened points. Helicopter "gunships" and napalm-dropping tactical aircraft could make any battlefield an untenable hell for the VC. McNamara loved to deal with this technician's war in the cool precision of statistics—so many weapons and troops invested, so many hamlets secured, so many Viet Cong eliminated. The "body count" became a yardstick of success. One could even develop figures on the various "kill ratios" of dead to wounded, firepower to total casualties, dollars to dead enemies.

And if North Vietnam continued to replace those dead Viet Cong? That was where strategic bombing came in. Limited but punishing raids would force Ho to come to terms, drop the demand for a unified Vietnam, or at the very least settle for a coalition in Saigon including anti-Communists. But the force used would be carefully doled out—never so much as to frighten the Soviets or Chinese into action.

These were typical of the "hard-nosed" calculations made by the degree-laden experts—the arithmetic edging Johnson toward a wider war. He could win, "the best and the brightest" were saying, if he enlarged his bet. And of all Presidents inclined by temperament to accept that advice, Lyndon Baines Johnson was the likeliest.

He was an unusual man, powerful, manipulative, gigantically energetic, crude, earthy, born to lead—yet also beset by hidden anxieties and insecurities, almost pathetically hungry for approval. Books would be written about the tragedy of his public life, which both peaked and collapsed within a few years in the 1960s. Johnson entered politics, from rural Texas, in the age of Franklin D. Roosevelt, and absorbed fully the notion that a beneficent federal government could interpose society's collected power on behalf of the downtrodden and so lift them to self-sufficiency. Over time, he accumulated a profound knowledge of how to achieve his goals within the American political system, especially in its fullest flower on Capitol Hill. As Senate majority leader in the Eisenhower era, Johnson had specialized in getting legislation enacted, welding coalitions through a combination of cajolery and pressure on key lawmakers, a process described by his opponents as "arm-twisting," and by Johnson himself as a simple application of the biblical verse, "Come, let us reason together." He gave the job total concentration and exhausting quantities of work, enough to give him a major heart attack in 1955. (Another would kill him in 1973.) He brought into the twentieth century many of the coarse yet idealistic traits of the disappearing American frontier.

He had felt out of things in the Kennedy White House, dominated as it was by Easterners and Phi Beta Kappa-flaunting Ivy League graduates—"the professors," as he called them. On acceding to power in November of 1963 it became his ambition to emerge as President in his own right and put his brand on American history. This he would do by securing enactment of laws to create what he called a Great Society—compassionate, egalitarian, forward-looking, as he saw it. Its elements would include a "war on poverty," a vigorous endorsement of the civil rights crusade, an array of public works, massive aid to education, urban renewal, job-creating programs for youth, all the shining targets of a generation of liberalism. And he would, by late 1965, impressively create much of the design and include in it a landslide 1964 election win over the conservative Republican candidate, Barry Goldwater.

Vietnam did not fit into the scheme. It was marginal, an inherited problem that he would solve as he wound up and improved on the Kennedy agenda. It could not be ignored. For one thing, Johnson's own view of the war was totally conventional. "It's just perverted history to claim that it's civil war," he told a young writer after it was all over, "just pure bad history manufactured by the Harvards. . . . There was no insurrection before the Communists decided to take part." He believed that "the minute we look soft, the would-be aggressors will go wild. We'll lose all of Asia and then Europe and be an island by ourselves."

But in addition he thought that failure to win in Vietnam would cripple him in Congress, thwart his program, sacrifice the future to the conservative hard-liners. "If I don't go in now," he was reported to have said in the 1964-65 winter of decision, "and they show later I should have gone, then they'll be all over me in Congress. They won't be talking about my civil rights bill, or education or beautification. No sir, they'll push Vietnam up my ass every time. Vietnam. Vietnam. Vietnam." In his own eyes he was a moderate, choosing, through controlled escalation, the middle road between appeasement and total war. In a relatively short time he could do what was necessary. As a master dealer, after the bombing—the arm-twisting—he would offer inducements that would bring Hanoi around like a reluctant Senate committee chairman. In his words it would go like a "filibuster—enormous resistance at first, then a steady whittling away, then Ho hurrying to get it over with."

Johnson's tilt toward escalation began as early as the summer of 1964. The "security" fetish, his style of keeping a free hand by divulging as little as possible until decisions were made, plus the needs of the presidential campaign (in which he was running as a man of peace against Goldwater, who demanded vigorous action against North Vietnam), all combined to keep White House deliberations clandestine. Yet Johnson wanted congressional authorization for the expanded war he was considering, and he secured it in the Gulf of Tonkin resolution, a delegation of war-making power that stemmed from a controversial episode.

At 8:30 P.M. on August 4, the television networks were alerted that the President would shortly go on the air with a major announcement. Soon afterward, Johnson faced his fellow Americans with grave news. Earlier that day, two American destroyers on a routine patrol in international waters had been fired on by North Vietnamese torpedo boats, and had engaged them in combat. To deter any further such outrages, Johnson said, he had ordered a firm reprisal. Even as he spoke, American aircraft from nearby carriers were bombing four North Vietnamese naval bases and a great oil depot. The raid was reportedly so successful that later, privately, Johnson was exultant.

Next day he asked Congress to pass a special resolution. After a preamble characterizing the attacks as "part of a deliberate and systematic campaign of aggression that the Communist regime in North Vietnam has been waging against its neighbors," it authorized the President to "take all necessary measures to repel any armed attack against the forces of the United States," and also to "prevent further aggression" and assist any member of the Southeast Asia Treaty Organization "in defense of its freedom."

What the President did not tell Capitol Hill, or the television audience, was that the Tonkin Gulf incident grew out of the 34A harassment operation. On July 31, South Vietnamese destroyers had carried out a raid on several North Vietnamese ports. On the following day two U.S. destroyers, the *Maddox* and the *C. Turner Joy* (by a historical coincidence named for the first chief U.S. truce negotiator in Korea), had come within a few miles of the North Vietnamese coast. They carried special devices with which to pinpoint, for future reference, the location of "enemy" radar installations. The North Vietnamese assumed (as radio intercepts showed) that the two American vessels were part of South Vietnam's striking force. On August 2 they sent out three boats to take on the destroyers, which sank one of them. Then, on the night of the 4th—early in the morning, Washington time—there was another confusing melee, in which the *Turner Joy* and the *Maddox* reported apparent attacks from uncertain numbers of unidentified ships, at whom they returned fire with unconfirmable results, the "battle" depicted by Johnson as a defense of freedom of the seas.

In Congress, only Oregon's maverick Senator Wayne Morse had misgivings about the facts of the case, but in quick, secret hearings McNamara tried to wave them away, denying all U.S. knowledge of, much less cooperation in, 34A operations. And there was heavy pressure against probing too deeply into what had happened. The prevailing sentiment was summed up by one of Morse's colleagues: "Hell, Wayne, you can't get in a fight with the President at a time when the flags are waving." Nevertheless, Morse remained unconvinced, but only Alaska's Senator Ernest Gruening joined him in voting against the resolution. So Johnson went to the Democratic convention with a blank check for a wider war in his pocket. Thereafter events proceeded on a fateful timetable.

In November, the Viet Cong attacked American planes parked at an airfield in Bienhoa. This led to pressure from the Joint Chiefs of staff for a "prompt and strong response." Johnson, however, allowed only "low-risk" attacks on infiltration routes through Laos. Then, in February, the Viet Cong struck at the U.S. military advisers' compound at Pleiku. Invisible warriors appeared from nowhere to lob mortar shells and grenades into the barracks and motor pools, then vanished into the night. Eight Americans died, sixty were wounded, and that ended the hesitation. Here was, in McNamara's words, a "clear challenge," a test of will. We could not allow the North Vietnamese to be mistaken abour our intention to stay the course. The President ordered an immediate fifty-plane air strike, and began Operation Rolling Thunder, the sustained bombardment of North Vietnam. Two Marine battalions were ordered to protect the airfields from which the campaign would proceed.

From that point it was natural to argue the precise mode of using the American soldiers. General Westmoreland, the chief American officer in Vietnam, felt that the troops should play an active role; they should move out into the countryside in "search and destroy" missions against Viet Cong bases and engage North Vietnamese "main force" units. Ambassador Taylor believed that such a role would inevitably demand more and more manpower, and he proposed that the U.S. simply guarantee "enclaves" in South Vietnam. The Westmoreland strategy, however, implicitly promised a final victory and was the one selected.

And so began a terrible three years.

The Americans discovered, as had the French, that the Viet Cong was not an ordinary army, with vulnerable spots like headquarters and depots. It was a handful of mercury. It rolled back into "pacified" villages as soon as the U.S. troops left. Its supply trains might consist of civilians, carrying shells one at a time through hand-dug tunnels. Even the regular North Vietnamese units fed into the South were uncannily apt at camouflaging their trucks and artillery, surviving strafing and napalm runs, and replacing their casualties.

For the American infantrymen—the "grunts," as they called themselves—the Viet Cong, or "Victor Charley," or simply "Charley," made the war a nightmare. Here was an enemy without uniforms, indistinguishable from civilians. Innocent-looking Vietnamese teen-agers might dash suicidally from a hut (or a "hootch") lobbing grenades concealed in their clothes, or firing from rifles plucked from under a mattress. Booby traps were concealed in wells, cooking pots, chicken coops. It was tempting, therefore, to kill or herd into camps any Vietnamese in sight, and burn all buildings. The horror was compounded rather than lessened by the fact that it was a war without parades—a war in which the young soldiers could carry tape recorders, screeching rock music, into combat, in which they could control the constant fear and isolation with readily available marijuana and other drugs, making of battle (for some, at least) a freaked-out "trip" into hell.

The more deeply involved the United States became, the less inclined the Saigon government was to fight. Saigon was filled with black marketeers—South Vietnamese and American officials, contractors, and deal-makers doing business as usual in elegant restaurants, while the streets swarmed with refugees, Vietnamese draft-dodgers, whores, beggars, and an occasional bomb-throwing terrorist. In 1967 Marshal Ky yielded to the regime of General Nguyen Van Thieu, elected under tight army control; in 1971 Thieu would run unopposed. Yet the United States could not abandon Saigon without profound loss of face. The client controlled the patron.

It was a bizarre struggle, in which correspondents could drive or helicopter into the countryside, film or watch an engagement, come home, change clothes, open a cold beer, and report it all—uncensored—to the people at home. Americans, gathered around their television sets, saw unforgettable scenes from this "living-room war"—bound and frail-looking Viet Cong captives, equipment-burdened Americans setting fire with PX cigarette lighters to hootches, screaming wounded being lifted into choppers, piles of anonymous dead that were the stuff of body counts, sweating men pinned down in tall grass by fire from invisible machine guns, black-and-red billowing explosions of a tactical air strike on the enemy.

They watched it go on. And on. Unendingly. Bombing raids extended to oil depots and refineries, dams, railyards, power stations—but Hanoi got replacements for material losses from the Soviet Union, shook off civilian casualties, and hung on. General Westmoreland wanted enough troops to raise the level to 194,000 by the end of 1964, to 443,000 by the end of 1966, and to 542,000 by the end of 1967. The Joint Chiefs talked about possibly invading Laos, Cambodia, or North Vietnam itself. The last measure was sure to demand many more men, require a formal call-up of reserves, and perhaps bring in the Chinese.

Johnson had not planned it that way. He had expected to wind up the war in a year or a year and a half, and to do it without official mobilization or new taxes or a cutback in the Great Society. And he had failed. He had trusted the hard-liners, and not the few insiders, like Under Secretary of State George Ball, who had warned of the trap in 1965. Now he had to face the unfaceable. Vietnam was a poisoned potion he had swallowed. Throughout the country, the war was becoming a symbol for aspects of American society that had

long gone unquestioned, but were now losing support. The emphasis
on winning, for one thing. The certainty that material prosperity
could be exported to "backward" countries and would unerringly
improve them. The willingness to use force for good ends, or in
effect to send out both missionaries and gunboats. These ideas were
under harsh scrutiny, especially by the elite young who were just
reaching political consciousness. They saw America the beautiful as
America the bully in Southeast Asia. Thanks to Vietnam, Cold War
America was coming apart.

BACK IN THE 1950s, reacting to the frustrations of the Korean War,
Americans had seemed to make a fetish of conformity. In
contrast 1965—the year in which the United States took over the
main burden of ground fighting in Vietnam—seemed to end the
period of consensus. More and more Americans—primarily young
Americans—began to question the essential purity of the nation's
international behavior, the benefits of a consumer-oriented economy, the values of striving for upward mobility. By the end of the
1960s these truisms were under furious attack. The critics might
have represented only a minority view, hugely amplified by the
media, but they had to be taken seriously since they had a major
influence on public behavior.

The civil rights movement was an example. Up to 1965 its leaders
had been able to appeal to traditional American beliefs. Even
peaceful civil disobedience was meant only to "shame" the white
majority into acting in accordance with its democratic and Christian
heritage, already embodied in the Declaration of Independence and
the Constitution.

But by 1965 the movement changed direction. Rebellious young
blacks—and "blacks" was now the word preferred to "Negroes"—in
the Student Nonviolent Coordinating Committee (SNCC) and the
Congress of Racial Equality (CORE) wrested attention from Martin
Luther King's Southern Christian Leadership Conference. They
protested the slow pace of change. They demanded rather than
petitioned, their slogan being an appeal to a vaguely defined "black
power." When reproached for abandoning nonviolence, Stokely
Carmichael, of SNCC, said that violence was as American as cherry
pie, part of a "racist" and "oppressive" U.S. history.

Violence came to America's growing urban ghettos in 1965, first in
a riot in the black district of Los Angeles known as Watts, where
hundreds of blacks threw rocks through windows, torched buildings,
and allegedly chanted "burn, baby, burn." Soon there were other
"long, hot summers," and comparable upheavals in Philadelphia,
Rochester, Chicago, Newark, Detroit. All of the torment, the
shouting, the crash of glass, the screams of sirens, the explosion of

police and National Guard tear gas bombs, appeared on the ultimate theater of violence, the evening television newscasts. The riots—despite conservative fears to the contrary—were largely sponta-neous, confined to black neighborhoods, and victimizing mostly black citizens. They were outbursts of rage at deep-seated problems of economic deprivation. But above all, they were carried on or defended by men and women, black and white, who saw the ghettoes as a more urgent problem than any created by the Viet Cong, and for whom the war in Vietnam was at best a diversion from their priorities, at worst one more outrage by white Americans against nonwhite Asians.

There were other questionings of the American way of life. A 1962 bestseller, *Silent Spring*, by Rachel Carson, worried about the destructive impact of industrial effluents and agricultural pesticides on the environment. Nonstrident though it was, the book became the Bible of an environmentalist movement that asked whether or not unchecked industrialization was carelessly tearing apart the fragile balance of nature. By a natural extension, the hitherto unchallenged national goal of constant growth—vital for both the prophets of affluence and those of equality—was thrown into question. It was significant that the best-known symbol of wealth, the Detroit-made car, came under attack in a series of books that condemned it as wasteful, polluting, and dangerous. The first volume on the subject, Ralph Nader's *Unsafe at Any Speed*, appeared in 1965.

Various Nader disciples went on to criticize the basic quality of the goods mass-produced by American corporations. And while "consumerism"—the education of buyers to beware—began to grow, Betty Friedan's 1963 book, *The Feminine Mystique*, was read and discussed everywhere, it seemed. It bitterly challenged the notion, fundamental in suburbia, that a woman found her deepest fulfillment in motherhood and homemaking. Other changes rede-fined the possibilities of life for women. New birth control devices offered them greater decision-making power about having babies and having sex. New fashions such as miniskirts and bikinis freed them from the sheltering but smothering confines of maidenly modesty, and suggested that they might be adventurous and take their place as equals in the work force, in the professions, in the family itself. This new feminism, like consumerism, and like the "black power" movement, found many concerns more urgent to it than the anti-Communist crusade. And it wasted little admiration on the American past.

Striking transformations were sweeping the world of the young, the sons and daughters of the well-off and successful involved in what was labeled a "counterculture." New voices spoke irreverent messages into their willing ears. In the early Sixties they listened to the good-humored mockery and sentimental ballads of the Beatles; by 1968 they flocked in hundreds of thousands to hear "rock"—a driving, repetitive, orgiastic music whose chief performers made Elvis Presley seem a quaint figure of antiquity.

Suddenly, on the campuses of liberal-arts colleges of long renown, the "far out" was "in." Trend-setting students took as role models the "hippies," the cult of "flower children" who dressed in costumes that emphasized both originality and aboriginality: beads, headbands, long hair, bare feet, tattered jeans. It was "hip" to seek the peace and tranquility induced by smoking marijuana (or taking other drugs), and to flee the ugliness of the acquisitive "rat race" that constituted life among the "squares." It was "beautiful" to forego traditional individualism in favor of some loosely defined communal existence in which the word "love" was bandied about freely. A successful show, *Hair*, put it all together by describing itself as a "tribal, love, rock musical," and made money by helping to teach the despicable nature of the pursuit of money.

How far the counterculture penetrated into schools of business administration and engineering, the citadels of "squareness," was unclear, but it was the campus rebels rather than the "go-along" types who held the attention of the media. Through demonstrations and sit-ins, techniques borrowed from older radical movements, they forced many college administrators virtually to abandon any pretense of control over the students' private lives, and sometimes to institute new and "relevant" academic programs, such as Black Studies, or to permit previously forbidden kinds of political activity on campus. Such actions were often incomprehensible to parents and professors—the term "generation gap" was expressive—and totally stunned many lower-middle-class Americans who saw college as a golden opportunity for which students should be, if anything, submissively grateful.

Above all things, the "turned-on" young rejected the war. Like the new crusaders for equality and for a reshuffling of American priorities, they saw the Vietnam intervention as the epitome of what they most disliked—the use of raw power on "innocent" people. Student antiwar protesters were rarely Marxists, despite conservative efforts to prove them so. A major campus antiwar organization, Students for a Democratic Society (SDS), was more nihilistic than Bolshevik. It represented a "new left," which the disciplined and humorless Communists of the 1940s or the progress-worshiping and rational Socialists of an earlier era found self-indulgent. SDS, in turn, would have had little use for the sexual and artistic puritanism of the Politburo.

Student antiwar activism was in part romantic. The youth culture, that strange blend of commercialized nonsense and high aspiration, saw the Viet Cong soldier as the embodiment of man against machine, of indigenous culture against imperialism, as a true believer in black pajamas fighting tanks and bombers with barehands. American "with it" youth also considered the army the epitome of authoritarianism. They loved books like Joseph Heller's Catch 22, whose antihero, Yossarian, simply wanted to escape from his World War II bomber squadron. They sang along with Bob Dylan, an imitator of the folksy radical, Woody Guthrie, and laughed, when allowed, at the jokes of entertainer Lenny Bruce, who drowned patriotism and religion in obscenities.

So the campuses were natural centers for antiwar protest. It was there that many academics could find a platform for presenting the antiwar objections that were no longer being heard within the government, because those who voiced them were sidetracked or fired. It was there that "evils" like the Reserve Officer Training Corps or research for military purposes could be safely attacked within the framework of university self-government. And it was there, among sympathetic professors and administrators, that the students had a perfect theater to act out their discontent with the war.

At first the student anti-Vietnam movement turned away more people than it won over. Many Americans saw the antiwar students as part of a distasteful group of fornicators, potheads, and foulmouthed freaks. In the same fashion, there were extreme antiwar speakers who denounced even responsible Americans, with doubts about the war but a sense of duty to support it, as the kind of people who had, in the name of profit and God, plundered Mexico, enslaved the Africans, and wiped out the Indians. Such accusations often got more play in the headlines than the conservative statements of traditional pacifist organizations that had been against the war from its start.

Hence, during 1966 and 1967, arguments over the war were loud but not enlightening. Obscenity became the commonplace of dialogue; Washington officials—including the President—could not visit campuses without provoking literal riots. As in certain other polarizing episodes of the past, like the Sacco-Vanzetti case of the 1920s, the facts were lost amid the declamations about honor, duty, peace, militarism, and freedom. The debate was almost more cultural than political, [which was perhaps why it did not generate a new McCarthyism.] But whereas in the 1950s the country had been suspicious and divided, by 1967 it was outraged and divided.

And then came 1968, and the beginnings of an unexpected transformation. Suddenly, in that year, painful truths about Vietnam began to come to light, and they fed a body of moderate antiwar sentiment that had been slowly growing amid the cacophony. The most convincing antiwar arguments had been appearing every week in the lengthening casualty lists. Local television stations would often roll the names of the dead of their region over scenes of waving flags, white crosses, dirge-playing bands. The weekly totals were beginning to reach the five-hundred-and-over level as 1967 ended, and those long, unheralded processions of coffins unloaded from incoming transports brought the agony home as nothing had yet done. Ordinary Americans, unshaken in their patriotism, began to wonder if the deaths abroad and the turmoil at home were not, after all, too high a price for a victory that never seemed to materialize. Once that doubt was implanted, they were willing to listen at last to the doubters. And once the façade of deceit behind which the war was conducted was fractured, a majority of them were shocked out of their willingness to underwrite any further intervention. It was a slow process, but it was greatly accelerated on January 31, 1968, with the Tet offensive.

TET WAS THE NAME of the Vietnamese lunar New Year, and to celebrate it in 1968, the Viet Cong struck hard, simultaneously, and in huge force all across South Vietnam. At least thirty cities were hit, among them Saigon itself, where a small VC squad even managed to seize part of the compound housing the U.S. embassy. A month of bitter, bloody fighting followed. At its end, the places seized by the Viet Cong were all retaken, and the body count ran into thousands (including South Vietnamese soldiers and civilians). General Westmoreland proclaimed the episode a famous victory. The Viet Cong, he said, had failed in a last, desperate bid to topple the Saigon government and was fatally devastated by its casualties.

But Westmoreland's assurances did nothing to change the fact that Tet was a fatal psychological shock to the pro-war forces in the United States. Public opinion had, for a long time, accepted government assurances that the Viet Cong was dwindling, gasping as the bombs choked off the flow of aid from the North, ready for the final American knockout punch. Tet mocked all these boasts. The Viet Cong had mounted an operation that took planning, logistical buildup, and concealment that would have been impossible without popular support. Clearly it was alive and well. The national reaction was summed up in the reported reaction of newscaster Walter Cronkite, reading the first press association bulletins on the uprising: "What the hell is going on? I thought we were winning the war."

Moreover, there was a growing American revulsion at the nightly carnival of death and fire served up from Vietnam in the name of protecting "freedom." An American colonel earned a fugitive renown, and greatly strengthened the peace forces, when he explained why his men shelled a village to rubble in order to oust its Communist occupiers: "We had to destroy it in order to save it." It seemed a metaphor for the entire war. A searing photo from the period of the Tet offensive became an indelible part of the memories of the 1960s—a Saigon official firing a bullet through the head of a man, hands tied behind him, described—without further evidence—as a terrorist. This vied for the honor of most disillusioning shot of the war with the picture of a screaming, naked ten-year-old girl, her clothes burned off by napalm. And in March of 1968 the public did not yet know that a U.S. infantry company, helicoptered into the little village of My Lai, simply and summarily shot more than a hundred civilians, women and children included, on the orders of Lieutenant William Calley. (When the story broke a year later and Calley was court-martialed, he described the murders as "no big deal," which was in fact the way the war had conditioned most of the troops to regard the killing of Asians.) Belatedly, news of the My Lai massacre buried a bit deeper the idea that the Vietnam War was a high-minded adventure.

Tet and the events surrounding it brought much of the country, as well as Lyndon Johnson, to the point of saying "Enough!" Westmoreland, in February, asked for another 206,000 men, but the President refused. The times were changing. Hawks were leaving the nest. McNamara, disillusioned with the war, had been moved to the World Bank, and his replacement at Defense, Clark Clifford, was counseling the President to reduce the bombing and to try to woo Hanoi and the National Liberation Front to the conference table. Earlier efforts, by neutrals, to arrange negotiations had always gone sour. Somehow, one party was never ready to listen when the other was talking, or signals were missed. But now there was an urgency about starting talks, a new intensity.

Brushfires of revolt flickered in Johnson's own political camp. A group of antiwar Democrats had nominated a peace candidate to run against him in the New Hampshire primary. The man was Minnesota's liberal Senator Eugene McCarthy, an unusual politician, a self-confessed part-time poet, a Catholic intellectual who had spent some time in a monastery, an occasional teacher of political science, and overall a quirky, humorous, sarcastic individualist who did not generally seem comfortable in politics. Yet McCarthy, who seemed to be the very last person who could successfully win votes from an incumbent President in an intra-party fight, had struck a nerve when he announced his intention to campaign for a "rational and political solution to this war." Aided by a youthful army, a "children's crusade" of doorbell-ringing college-age volunteers, he won an amazing 42.4 percent of New Hampshire's Democratic vote, and twenty delegates. This was not political insurgency; it was revolt. What was more, polls showed that McCarthy was going to beat his opening performance in the upcoming Wisconsin primary.

Lyndon Johnson pondered the figures and his own inmost feelings. Then, on the evening of March 31, he went on the air with a twofold surrender. First he announced a partial unconditional bombing halt in all areas north of the 20th parallel (where most of North Vietnam's cities were contained), and said he hoped it would encourage Hanoi to discuss mutual troop withdrawals. And then, coming to his last page of script, he faced the camera and announced: "I shall not seek, and I will not accept, the nomination of my party for another term as your President."

The speech was historic. The war was far from over, but the illusion that a limited application of American power could defeat Ho Chi Minh was dispelled. In clinging to it for three years, Lyndon Johnson had sacrificed the Great Society and his own political future, started a runaway inflation, involved the government in a number of deceptions, and polarized the nation. The effect of these disasters would continue for years, consuming other lives and careers, but Johnson was the first and chief victim.

From there, events occurred in fast-moving succession. General Westmoreland was called home to become Chief of Staff and was replaced by General Creighton Abrams. The bombing halt resulted, in May, in Hanoi's agreement to talk. Parleys began in Paris but were inconclusive and frustrating, primarily because Johnson was still not free or willing to accept a political resolution of the war that involved abandoning Thieu. But Thieu would not deal with the NLF, and North Vietnam would not withdraw until the NLF was at the very least admitted to a coalition government in Saigon, and so there was an unbroken deadlock. Johnson, incapable of either repudiating or terminating the war, was stripped of his beloved "options." Even the experienced Averell Harriman, the perennial negotiator, who became U.S. spokesman in Paris, could not produce an answer.

McCarthy's New Hampshire victory had encouraged Robert Kennedy to make a bid for the nomination as a second antiwar candidate. When Johnson withdrew, Vice President Hubert Humphrey entered the lists as his presumptive successor, and was instantly trapped in ambivalence about the war. He could not join McCarthy and Kennedy in criticizing Johnson's policies, yet every effort he made to defend even a limited continuation of them alienated the rising antiwar sentiment. While the campaign warmed up, two shocking events took place. On April 4, Martin Luther King, Jr., was shot by an assassin in Memphis, sparking several days of riots and arson in Washington itself. Then, on June 5, after winning the California primary—the last step on the way to what seemed assured nomination—Robert F. Kennedy was gunned down in a Los Angeles hotel kitchen. The two murders did not appear to be linked to the fact that both men had become converts to the antiwar cause. Yet they underscored a frightening impression that passions were running amok—that the political atmosphere of America was tainted by the smoke from Southeast Asia's battlefields.

And that rancid aura overhung Chicago as the actual hour of the convention approached. Thousands of demonstrators converged on the city. The convention hall itself, ringed by barbed wire and troops and police (summoned by Mayor Richard Daley in his determination to keep order), rocked with bitter debate. With Kennedy gone, Humphrey was guaranteed the nomination over McCarthy, but the peace delegates battled for a platform calling for an unconditional U.S. end to bombing any part of North Vietnam, followed by speedy withdrawal. They lost out to an Administration-sponsored version that hinged any further bombing halt to the safety of U.S. troops and to the response of Hanoi—that proposed, in short, to continue the use of bombing as a lever in negotiations. It also endorsed further aid to South Vietnam's armies.

Shouts, chants, and insults were exchanged. Newsmen on the convention floor were occasionally roughed up by security guards. And on nomination night itself the demonstrators, frustrated by Daley's success at keeping them largely out of the sight of the delegates, gathered near the major downtown hotels. Though they included a cross-section of all the various opponents of the war, cameras and police attention focused on some extremists who taunted the police surrounding them with assorted obscenities and slogans. Overreacting in what an investigative commission was later to call a "police riot," the bluecoats rushed the penned-in crowds, sprayed them with tear gas and Mace, and clubbed whoever got in their way amid jeers and chants of "The whole world is watching!" Among those watching as young men and women were dragged off to police vans were those inside the auditorium (who saw it on television screens) and Hubert Humphrey in his suite overlooking the streets where the attack was under way. The smell of tear gas filled his room as he looked at the set and saw the delegates handing him the prize he had struggled for all his political life—now irretrievably sullied, thanks to Vietnam.

Meanwhile, the Republicans had nominated Richard Nixon. Back from the political dead after his loss to Kennedy in 1960 and a subsequent defeat for governor of California, Nixon sensed the conflicting and ambivalent attitudes of the American public. He recognized the swelling disillusionment with the war. But he also perceived that a large body of U.S. opinion, the so-called silent majority, was not yet ready to "surrender" in Vietnam, and moreover was furious at some of the more extreme manifestations of the counterculture. This backlash was something he could capitalize on brilliantly. For his domestic policy he announced a return to law and order, and the traditional American values of patriotism, religion, and duty—all to be achieved without sacrificing the social gains of the past. And as for the war, he said that it should end on terms that satisfied American honor and commitments. How? Well, he hinted ambiguously, he had a plan but would not divulge it. He insisted that he would not undercut Johnson. Thus he was patriotic, prudent, and antiwar all at the same time, an appearance that he maintained by avoiding debate throughout most of the campaign.

Humphrey struggled with the legacy of Johnson, trying to defend and abandon the war simultaneously. It was an impossible assignment. But he received a boost at the end of October when Johnson ordered the unconditional bombing halt that the doves in Chicago had asked for. Numbers of them then flocked to Humphrey's side, abandoning earlier disgruntled vows to stay at home or work for splinter parties. It was, however, too late. The popular vote was split almost down the middle. The final results were not clear until the morning after Election Day, but Nixon had won. His victory signified that a bare majority of those who voted were eager to get 1968 behind them, and believed that Nixon was the one most likely to achieve that result.

YET NIXON FACED A DILEMMA on taking office, an eruption of the conflict between peace and patriotism that he had muffled during the campaign itself. The NLF and Saigon remained intransigent at the Paris talks, and Nixon would not, any more than Johnson, force Saigon to knuckle under by threatening to leave Thieu in the lurch. Yet Nixon knew that the sorest point with the public was the number of American fatalities. So, in mid-1969, he announced a compromise—a program of gradual withdrawal of U.S. ground forces. At the same time, however, he declared that he would continue strong material support of the South Vietnamese armies, and he made up his mind to resume heavy air operations and gamble that they would win the final decision—despite the discouraging record of the preceding four years. This policy of fighting the war with Saigon's soldiers and American air power was called "Vietnamization," and was part of a newly proclaimed Nixon Doctrine. It promised that Asian anti-Communist governments could count on American armaments to resist aggression, but must furnish their own troops. "Asian boys," as Nixon put it, must man the ramparts of Asia.

Vietnamization had political benefits. The ground-troop withdrawals went slowly at first (at the end of 1970 there were still some

380,000 U.S. troops in Vietnam), but the casualty lists were reduced, and that temporarily defused the worst of the antiwar protests. But the steady bombing of the Viet Cong wrought more havoc in the South Vietnamese countryside, and savagely multiplied the numbers of civilian refugees, cripples, and dead.

Nixon carried on the new policy for a year, fending off criticisms through counterattacks by his sharp-tongued Vice President, Spiro Agnew. But in May of 1970 he overplayed his hand. American military officials had long been troubled by what they believed to be heavy infiltration of neutral Cambodia and Laos by the North Vietnamese, who used trails in the two countries as protected supply and reinforcement routes. There was apparent truth in the charge, though some question about the extent of the benefit reaped by the enemy. All the same, Nixon approved a secret bombing of those countries from bases in South Vietnam and equally "neutral" Thailand. On April 30, he suddenly announced something more drastic, namely a brief American incursion into Cambodia to wipe out what he described as major Communist sanctuaries, headquarters, and supply concentrations. Though Nixon defended his action as necessary to save American lives, and limited it to sixty days and a penetration of no more than twenty-one miles, it was unmistakably a widening of the war. A sense of betrayal sparked a new spasm of resistance among the peace advocates. On the campuses particularly, there was intense resistance; literally hundreds of them were taken over by students and faculty members who announced a strike in protest. On the campus of Kent State University in Ohio, in the heart of middle America, National Guardsmen—themselves the age of the students—were called in to preserve order after persons unknown set fire to an ROTC armory. There was a confrontation with demonstrators, a volley of shots—and four of the students fell dead.

Congress, deeply aroused, repealed the Gulf of Tonkin resolution in June. The Senate even passed an amendment to the annual military appropriation bill to cut off any further funds for operations in Cambodia after July 1. The battle over presidential war-making powers would pit Nixon against Capitol Hill for the rest of his Presidency, but he had enough clout in June 1970 to get the amendment defeated in the House.

Nevertheless, the reaction shook him, and on October 6, 1970, Nixon proposed a cease-fire in place and a general peace conference on Indochina, involving other major powers. This overture did not bring results. It angered Saigon further, and it did little to calm the peace movement, now aroused by the disclosures of My Lai and inflamed anew in the spring of 1971, when a Pentagon defense analyst, Daniel Ellsberg, leaked to the press the documentary study of the whole process of entering the war that McNamara had ordered a few years earlier. These Pentagon Papers, published in the New York Times and Washington Post, fed the disillusionment. Though the Nixon Administration was in no way involved in the story (which covered the years from 1962 to 1966), it went to court in search of an injunction to prevent publication of the papers. This was a protective reaction to defend the classification system, the whole secret machinery of Cold War policy-making vital to any President regardless of party. The Supreme Court, however, on First Amendment grounds, denied the request.

Nonetheless, by mid-1971 the basic elements of the Cold War apparatus were in hot water—the combination of executive power, secrecy, and bipartisanship that had been forged starting in 1947. If it was not to suffer further erosion, the war had to be liquidated in some fashion that was not seen as a surrender to international Communism. A new approach was necessary—something that would change the context of negotiations, and lift the Vietnam question from the level of whether or not American decisions regarding that area helped or hurt the Soviet Union.

Such an approach was possible. The Russians were in a mood for fresh assessments. They, too, were in trouble. They had definitely lost China by 1909, and were badly frightened by Peking's emergence as a nuclear power. They suffered continuing economic distress, and in 1964 Khrushchev had been ousted as a consequence of various shortfalls in Soviet production. In 1967 their Middle Eastern client, Egypt, had been thrashed by Israel in a six-day war. And in 1968, disturbed by liberalization in Czechoslovakia, they had offended the world by a swift invasion, which escaped being a Hungary-style bloodbath only because the Czechs had not openly resisted. For them, too, it seemed a good time to explore new strategies.

Nixon had already suggested a new style of relationship between the superpowers in his inaugural address, which called for "an era of negotiation" to follow the long "period of confrontation" of the past. What did that mean specifically? Would Nixon, the quintessential Cold Warrior, change his ways? Would Washington adopt a new conception of what the Soviet Union represented in the world—one in which accommodation on Vietnam and other matters might be reached in a nonapocalyptic setting?

The specific answers would only come over the course of ensuing years, but the framework was being evolved by Nixon and his National Security Adviser, Henry Kissinger—they would dispute the exact division of credit later—as 1972 opened. It was an election year, a moment of decision for Nixon, and it would open up a wholly new phase of the long Soviet-American relationship (though there had been earlier signals of what was coming, observable to knowing eyes). Almost everyone would be surprised, however—to the delight of Nixon, who enjoyed foreign policy with a theatrical flavor—that the new era would really begin, not in Moscow, but in Peking.

Chapter 11

THE LIMITS OF POWER
1969-1976

I T WAS RICHARD NIXON'S happiest hour. He was smiling, good-humored, expansive. Everything was going superbly. Around him in the Great Hall of the People in Peking sat eight hundred assorted diplomats, technicians, journalists, and guests, happily finishing a Chinese feast.

He was doing everything right; his usual preparatory diligence was paying off. The small gesture of learning to eat with chopsticks And the bright idea of having had his experts dig out a poem by Chairman Mao that he, Nixon, could quote in response to a welcoming toast: "So many deeds cry out to be done, and always urgently. . . . Seize the day, seize the hour."

So here was the hour seized, witnessed by more people than any comparable occasion in history, thanks, in Nixon's words, to "the wonder of telecommunications." It was intoxicating to a political man who loved the spotlight and was facing an election in the coming autumn. Enthused beyond the power to sit still, he lifted his goblet of mao tai, and walked around the hall clinking glasses with the smiling Communist officials.

It was Monday, February 21, 1972, the end of a long day that had begun with the presidential plane, the *Spirit of '76*, touching down at Peking's airport. Premier Chou En-lai had been there with an honor guard. He had been formally correct, not overcordial—until he caught sight of the rotund, curly-headed figure of Henry Kissinger, the President's Assistant for National Security Affairs. "Ah, old friend," he said. But for the deplaning U.S. party there had been no children presenting bouquets, no demonstrations and banners. It would not do just yet for the People's Republic to honor the imperialists too demonstratively.

Yet that mood had changed almost as soon as President and Mrs. Nixon had been driven to the guest compound. There was an immediate call. Would the President and Dr. Kissinger wish to have a meeting with Chairman Mao? Of course, although the President arrived for the meeting a few minutes late, perhaps his own form of diplomatic response to the cool airport reception.

The session with Mao had been cordial. Dressed in a simple gray tunic and trousers, the seventy-eight-year-old leader was a piece of living history. In his book-crowded study with windows facing a frozen garden, he seemed to Kissinger to be "at the center of wherever he stood." He spoke with apparent spontaneity, but every point he made was an item in the agenda of talks that would involve Nixon, Chou, Kissinger, Secretary of State William Rogers, and China's Foreign Minister Chi Peng-fei, like Rogers a man for working out details.

The Monday night banquet climaxed a day of growing warmth, and the cordiality would thereafter not slacken for a week. On Tuesday the People's Daily carried favorable stories and pictures of China's deified leader shaking hands with the Americans—a positive signal. The official talks began next day, February 22, Washington's birthday, and went on steadily amid more entertainment and sightseeing. Nixon visited the Great Wall, the tombs of the Ming emperors, and on Friday morning the Forbidden City. There he was accompanied by Field Marshal Yeh Chien-yeng. A light overnight snowfall had blanketed the grounds. Said Yeh: "The snow has whitewashed the world."

The snow could not quite whitewash reality. On the last night in Peking guests and hosts alike got little sleep as they struggled to write a communiqué that would sum up where the two sides stood after their conversations. In the end, no amount of toasting and gymnastics and Ping-Pong exhibits would wipe out fundamental differences. They agreed on a joint statement with separate paragraphs expressing each nation's view on the issues. When it finally emerged, at a Sunday news conference in Shanghai on the President's way home, it was full of formulas that each side could interpret as it wished, touching on Vietnam, Korea, Japan, India, and the most crucial issue of all, Taiwan. Peking stated that the island was a province of China, that its "liberation" was purely "an internal affair," and that all American forces there must withdraw. The United States "agreed" that Taiwan was part of one China, that the Chinese must settle its future themselves, and that the withdrawal of U.S. forces in the area was an "ultimate objective"—statements that did no harm to existing treaties with Chiang Kai-shek's regime.

Both Peking and Washington agreed to exchange negotiators, if not actual ambassadors, at an early date. And both politely and untruthfully said that their reconciliation was not directed against the Soviet Union.

After the session with the press and Nixon's promise to build "a bridge across 16,000 miles and twenty-two years of hostility" came an exchange of gifts. From Nixon a set of American-made porcelain swans, worth a quarter of a million dollars. From the Chinese two giant pandas, Hsing-Hsing and Ling-Ling.

Was it peace? Or excellent theater? Or both?

Certainly it was astonishing. Here, in the heart of the world's second-mightiest Communist state, was a smiling Richard Nixon, the one-time pursuer of Alger Hiss, the Vice President who would have sent U.S. troops to Dienbienphu in 1954. With him was Henry Kissinger, the German-born refugee, intellectual, and Harvard scholar, suddenly raised to star billing in the Administration—the same Kissinger who had said, ten years earlier, that Communist peace feelers should be regarded warily, since Communists advocate peace "not for its own sake, but because the West is said to have grown so weak that it will go to perdition without a last, convulsive upheaval."

Vietnam and other vicissitudes of the 1960s had changed the minds of both men, just as the split with Moscow had created fresh attitudes in Peking.

The vastly dissimilar Nixon and Kissinger were joined together in a moment in history because they shared a vision of the world and their place in it. The well-staged quest for a "generation of peace" might be Nixon's pet project, but the execution depended heavily on the skills and drives of his National Security Adviser.

THE ANNOUNCEMENT HAD COME from Nixon's transition team office in December 1968, and it surprised almost everyone. Henry Alfred Kissinger was to be the new President's Assistant for National Security Affairs. As news-watchers well knew, however, Kissinger was closely associated with Nixon's longtime past rival for the Republican nomination, Nelson Rockefeller. Yet here he was, receiving a plum of a post that was of critical importance.

The National Security Adviser could do much to control what foreign policy and defense issues reached the presidential eye, and in what shape. That did not happen when Eisenhower and Dulles were at the top of the pyramid. But it was potentially possible for a strong-minded Adviser, working from within the White House, to wrestle initiative away from a less forceful Secretary of State. The Secretary, too, was a presidential counselor, like all Cabinet members, but he had to run his own department, now a gorged bureaucratic monster struggling daily to digest enormous quantities of problems and information. And, like the other Cabinet officers, the Secretary had to deal with lobbyists, congressmen, and special political constituencies. The National Security Adviser needed only to deal with the President, and only on crucial matters.

McGeorge Bundy and Walt Whitman Rostow had exerted important influence on Kennedy and Johnson. And there was an even bigger role in store for any successor of theirs who could build a close rapport with the Chief Executive, could master the office infighting within the White House "family," and could cultivate his own informants and publicizers among the capital city's influential journalists.

Henry Kissinger could do that brilliantly. He was a child of twentieth-century upheaval, a ten-year-old Jewish schoolboy in Fürth, Germany, when Hitler came to power. His schoolteacher father endured the slowly tightening noose of Nazism for five years (while little "Heinz" and his brother Walter were beaten up by Aryan classmates), and then fled to the United States. Heinz, transformed to Henry, finished high school, entered the army to become a translator-interrogator in 1943, and did a postwar stint in military government. Then, a blazing passage through Harvard on scholarship, B.A. summa cum laude in 1950, Ph.D. in 1954. His thesis was later published as *A World Restored*, an admiring look at Castlereagh, Metternich, and the other tough, conservative states-men who had made a peace in Europe in 1815 that lasted for a century.

Kissinger stayed on as a teacher and consultant at Harvard, as the Cold War changed it and other universities from ivied treasuries of gentlemanly values and inherited wisdom to "think tanks" at government disposal. His 1957 book, *Nuclear Weapons and Foreign Policy*, preached stock Cold War doctrine, but held that limited nuclear war was better than "massive retaliation." He became known, and advised the Rockefeller Brothers Fund, the Psychologi-cal Strategy Board of the NSC, and other study groups. His popular seminars were attended by bright young future foreign ministers from countries all over the world. By 1964 he was published, promoted, established—a "defense intellectual." At a Christmastime cocktail party in 1967, he met Richard Nixon.

By then the emerging outline of his philosophy was clear. The bipolar Soviet-American rivalry was inherently unstable and dan-gerous. What the world needed was order and legitimacy—a set of "basic arrangements" accepted by all the major powers, "who must remain in equilibrium with each other." It was not enough merely to prevent the spread of Communism. There had to be a "moral consensus" to make "a pluralistic world creative rather than destructive." As an example of what that meant he advocated "regional groupings, supported by the United States," able to "take over major responsibilities for their immediate area."

Kissinger was not utopian. "The iron law of history," he insisted, was that "no longing is completely fulfilled." The Soviet Union could neither be defeated totally nor wooed into good behavior by a show of kindness. Instead, the United States must devise an overall picture of how it wished Moscow to behave in international society, and balance all parts of its own foreign policy to achieve that result. This was the foundation of "linkage"—making arms reduction, for example, conditional on Soviet restraint in areas like the Middle East.

Kissinger admired the patient and far-seeing pragmatism of elder statesmen like de Gaulle or West Germany's Konrad Adenauer. He deplored the improvisatory character of American foreign policy, its tendency to swing wildly in response to crises. "Until we've answered . . . long-range questions," he said, "we can't make the tactical decisions."

Certain predilections were woven into that view. It was important to show steady toughness of will, for one thing. Likewise, to keep domestic politics and politicians as far away from influencing foreign policy as possible. And, too, to seek stability in long-term arrangements by reliance on autocratic regimes that were not easily blown over by gusts of religious, social, or nationalistic passion. Reproached for such undemocratic leanings, Kissinger would argue that the ultimate morality lay in preserving the peace and avoiding incineration.

Richard Nixon liked those ideas, too. That was why he plucked Kissinger from Rockefeller's ranks. And Kissinger, in the national spotlight, began to perform brilliantly for him. He reorganized the NSC supporting staff so that it ran like a crack team, with Kissinger the coach and star. (Among his young aides was a military deputy, Colonel Alexander Haig.) He poured up to nineteen daily hours of dedicated energy into his work. And he sold the results to the press effectively. In an Administration not distinguished for its intellectual sheen, Kissinger was impressively articulate, accessible, and funny.

It was true that he suffered from a well-known egocentrism. Once, when he was advising Rockefeller, someone had ordered one of his memoranda rewritten. "When Nelson buys a Picasso," Kissinger grumbled, "he does not hire four house painters to improve it." But he made fun of his own vanity. Asked if he preferred to be called "Doctor" or "Mister," he said in his heavy accent that he was not fussy; "Your Excellency" would do well enough. Or he would tell reporters: "There cannot be a crisis next week. My schedule is already full." He enjoyed as an ironic joke a society-column reputation as a swinger who attended events and parties with a succession of desirable women, and he easily charmed academics and columnists of all political persuasions. He was, in fact, such good copy that he could make trouble for himself with other White House staffers, especially the two top Nixon assistants, H.R. Haldeman and John Ehrlichman, whose job it was to see that no member of the Administration team outshone the President. There was, around the White House, "a certain wariness about him and the whole empire he [was] building."

But Richard Nixon—at least in 1969—was not perturbed. He knew that Kissinger's basic loyalty to the office itself was immense. That was exactly what Nixon, a man morbidly sensitive to fancied disloyalty, liked. His own public career was haunted by his sense of having to struggle against unfair rejection. In the Hiss case he imagined himself as locked in a lonely outsider's battle with liberal snobs who never forgave him for being right. In 1962 he wrote that there was "a residue of hatred and hostility towards me—not only among Communists but also among substantial segments of the press and intellectual community." In that same year he lost a bid for the governorship of California, and angrily told reporters at a postelection press conference: "You won't have Nixon to kick around anymore." He was, he announced, through with politics.

He was not. He returned from the dead, carefully working the Republican grass roots, faithfully supporting local candidates, wooing delegates at political banquets, and convincing many observers that there was a "new Nixon." Perhaps there was. His ideas seemed to change in the hard school of the 1960s. In a 1967 article in *Foreign Affairs* he telegraphed two new positions. He said we could not "afford to leave China forever outside the family of nations . . . in angry isolation," and that "the role of the United States as a policeman is likely to be limited in the future." On taking office he unveiled a conciliatory attitude in an Inaugural Address reminiscent of Kennedy's eight years earlier:

> Let us take as our goal: Where peace is unknown, make it welcome; where peace is fragile, make it strong; where peace is temporary, make it permanent. . . . After a period of confrontation, we are entering an era of negotiation. . . . With those who are willing to join, let us cooperate to reduce the burden of arms, to strengthen the structure of peace, to lift up the poor and the hungry.

The phrases rang marvelously. His past Red-hunting record freed him to utter them without vulnerability to charges of softness. In Clark Clifford's words, he was "the first American President . . . who didn't have to worry about Richard Nixon."

But in truth Richard Nixon was not free of inner compulsions, such as the desire to personalize the structure of peace through incessant summit diplomacy. Nixon would travel more than any

President had ever done, visiting thirty-one countries and territories, flying almost 148,000 miles in the presidential jet. He would also receive a long series of visiting heads of state in Washington. His restlessness was epic. When not flying abroad he shuttled between Camp David and his homes in Key Biscayne, Florida, and San Clemente, California. He functioned best when he could create an atmosphere of urgency; it was a giveaway to his character that he entitled his political autobiography *Six Crises*. He personalized the Presidency with fierce intensity. Often he saw maneuvers of other nations as attempts to challenge his manhood, victimize him again. He responded by sudden spurts of toughness, to show that, much as he wanted to be liked, he would not be pushed around.

He drew vast sustenance from his self-identification with "America" and the Presidency, both institutions of unlimited power to his mind. Endowed with their magic, he believed he would fashion an American-shaped peace, through his dealings with world leaders. Foreign policy became the centerpiece of his Presidency because it best served his needs. At least, that is, foreign policy that lent itself to drama. He was bored with routine problems that had diplomatic repercussions, like the fate of the dollar or oil reserves.

This was the man who found Kissinger useful. Kissinger's ideas of worldwide "deals" fitted the Nixonian conception of peacemaking. Kissinger's pragmatism suited Nixon's urge to show firmness, to be tough even when the liberals howled. And there was a symbiosis that went beyond doctrines. Both men distrusted bureaucracy, whose policies, in Kissinger's words, were the "lowest common denominator." Both were obsessive about secrecy, and unashamedly deceitful. Kissinger enjoyed hoodwinking the press by being in Paris or Peking when he was supposedly elsewhere, and the President cheerfully helped in the game. And when Nixon demanded wiretaps of top NSC aides in order to stop leaks, Kissinger (despite later claims to the contrary) apparently went along readily. Finally, each filled a vital gap in the other's abilities. Kissinger had no gift for American politics; he needed to serve a President who could manipulate the electorate into supporting his policies. Nixon benefited from Kissinger's good press contacts since his own were disastrous.

And so they worked together. Kissinger, who had the presidential ear for up to several hours daily, became, as *Time* magazine said, a "combination of professor-in-residence, secret agent, ultimate advance man and philosopher-prince." In 1971, after some talk of Kissinger's leaving, Nixon wrote him: "Frankly, I cannot imagine what the government would be like without you." So the two, in 1969, started swiftly on an ambitious agenda.

At its head stood the crucial item on which all else hinged, namely resolving the issue of Vietnam. Everything else, to some extent, was tangled in that knot.

THERE WAS A PROBLEM of distinguishing style from substance in the Nixon-Kissinger foreign policy, and nowhere were the ambiguities better illustrated than in the tortuous path toward an exit from Vietnam. For not only did the President continue simultaneously to reduce the American ground commitment while stepping up the air war, but he pursued the negotiations begun in 1968, and added both clandestine parleys and secret fighting. The public war, like the public peace negotiations, was particularly orchestrated to get maximum political leverage in the United States. The hidden operations were to send messages to Hanoi.

Nor did the confusion end there. Within the new foreign policy framework it was important to move toward harmony with both the U.S.S.R. and China. To do so meant abandoning the John Foster Dulles view that merely to negotiate with Communists gave them undeserved respectability. Yet while preparing public opinion for summitry in Peking and Moscow, Nixon proclaimed his old anti-Communist doctrines to defend his actions in Vietnam. He was, he insisted, supporting the right of South Vietnam's people to resist the forcible imposition of Communist slavery; his language was that of the "old Nixon."

To complete the puzzle, the behavior of the Chinese and Russians was far from uncomplicated. By 1969 each feared the other; each had reason to accept the new American cordiality. But each also had to offer support to North Vietnam in order to appear the chief guardian of small "socialist" countries. Mao and Soviet boss Leonid Brezhnev, therefore, wanted to get Nixon out of Vietnam without either humiliating him or forsaking their fellow Communists in Hanoi.

The very first National Security Study Memorandum requested in 1969 by Kissinger—NSSM-1—dealt with alternatives in Vietnam, and set forth the bleak perspectives that governed the events of the next four years. Stripped to essentials, it said that almost all the experts agreed that Thieu could not possibly win the war without a massive escalation of the U.S. ground effort. Even a stepped-up aerial war, the consensus ran (disputed here by the Pentagon), could not prevent the indefinite continuation of Hanoi's aid to the Viet Cong. So if the United States would not increase its investment in Thieu's victory, then it must either abandon him altogether or try to promote a political solution.

Nixon chose a middle course consistent with political necessities and his own temperament. A confessed defeat that Nixon could not accept either personally or officially was out of the question.

Kissinger, too, believed that simply to leave Thieu to his fate would destroy American credibility, the cornerstone of the great-power arrangements he contemplated. Yet both men knew that the pressure from the American Congress and public to bring the troops home had become irresistible. There seemed little doubt that a majority of the nation was sick of the war or, at least, of Americans dying in Vietnam.

Nixon's solution, therefore, as stated earlier, was to end American deaths, gradually, by a phased program of U.S. troop reductions, and at the same time to get Hanoi to agree to a simultaneous withdrawal and a deal with Thieu. To bring this about he would strengthen Thieu as much as possible in anticipation of the final U.S. departure, and punish Hanoi from the air and in other ways to induce Ho Chi Minh to make concessions and end the war quickly.

Perhaps Nixon was persuaded by the military that Thieu could be braced enough, and Hanoi hurt enough, to force a settlement in which the South Vietnamese president could survive. Kissinger was apparently sure from the start that without U.S. troops in force at his back, Thieu would topple eventually, but he hoped, as he wrote early in 1969 in *Foreign Affairs*, that a "decent interval" might ensue between American departure and Saigon's collapse so that the two events might not seem connected. Both Kissinger and Nixon underestimated Hanoi's durability and Thieu's limitations; what they managed to achieve was simply a prolongation of the torture.

Nevertheless, pursuing his aims, Nixon went on national television on May 14, 1969, to offer his peace plan. Simply put, it was that all foreign troops in South Vietnam should be withdrawn, after which there would be an internationally supervised cease-fire, followed by elections. It was an offer sure to be refused. The basic Hanoi argument had been, since 1954, that all Vietnam was a single country. The North Vietnamese did not think of themselves as outsiders, or even acknowledge the presence of their forces south of the 17th parallel.

What Nixon did not say on that May evening was that the United States was already ending the second month of an expanded, secret war in Indochina. B-52s were already bombing Cambodian jungle trails through which North Vietnam's infiltration routes ran. CIA-led Laotians were conducting operations against suspected North Vietnamese and other Communist forces in their country. American aircraft were flying photographic missions over North Vietnam and hitting antiaircraft batteries that tried to interfere—the official term was "protective reaction strikes." And other U.S. planes were plastering Viet Cong concentrations in the South, wreaking heavy damage on the countryside. An elaborate system of falsified reports hid the Cambodian and Laotian sorties from scrutiny.

One of the alleged reasons for the secrecy was to protect Cambodia's roly-poly, jazz-loving, amiable Prince Norodom Sihanouk, a man trying futilely to preserve his country's neutrality. Sihanouk knew of the North Vietnamese presence within his boundaries, but he could do little to prevent it. In the same way, given the circumstances, he had no choice but to accept the U.S. bombardments without protest, urging only that care be taken not to kill any Cambodians, an impossible assignment. What he hoped to avoid was making Cambodia a full-scale war zone.

As the first anniversary of Nixon's election neared, and phased troop withdrawals were under way, the President tried almost obsessively to end the Vietnam war on terms satisfactory to him. He sent a secret letter to Ho Chi Minh urging "an early resolution of this tragic war." He authorized Kissinger to begin secret meetings in Paris with Xuan Thuy, North Vietnam's official delegate to the stalled four-party conference there. Meanwhile, however, Kissinger was studying other military options, saying that he refused "to believe that a little fourth-rate power like North Vietnam doesn't have a breaking point."

Nixon played one other card that October. He ordered the U.S. chargé d'affaires in Warsaw, Walter Stoessel, to seek out discreetly the Chinese ambassador to Poland and say that the United States stood ready to send a senior official to the Chinese capital to discuss future relations.

In November, Nixon publicly reiterated his May proposals. This time it would not be Ho pondering them. The Vietnamese patriarch died on September 2, 1969, just after answering Nixon's secret letter by saying that America's "war of aggression" must be called off before reaching a "correct solution" to the Vietnamese problem. But Nixon, in his address to the nation, once again insisted that he would not take the "easy way" of total and immediate withdrawal, thereby leading to the "first defeat in our nation's history." He appealed for support in his course of gradual U.S. troop reduction and the "Vietnamization" of the fighting to the "great silent majority of my fellow Americans."

The next high point in the saga came in the spring of 1970. During a visit by Sihanouk to Peking in March (ostensibly to get its help in asking the North Vietnamese to leave Cambodia alone), his strongly anti-Communist prime minister, Lon Nol, led a coup against him and deposed him. Lon Nol's forces were immediately plunged into heavy fighting with the Khmer Rouge, the Cambodian Communists, who probably had North Vietnamese aid. The Joint Chiefs feared that the unforeseen revolt might end in actually kicking Cambodia more firmly into the Communist camp, should Lon Nol's enemies overwhelm him. They urged more bombing, a quick transfusion of aid to him, and an attack on North Vietnam's "sanctuaries" along the border.

Nixon responded to the idea well. On April 20 he announced new U.S. troop withdrawals, but within another few days consented to an enlargement of the war that was supposedly winding down. He knew that he was courting public outrage, but he felt once more that he was being tested, both by the North Vietnamese who still stubbornly resisted his terms and by the "peaceniks" at home. "Ike lost Cuba," he reportedly told his staff, "but I won't lose Cambodia." On the night of April 25, 1970, just before the final decision, he braced his nerve with a Saturday night Potomac River cruise on the presidential yacht *Sequoia*, during which he watched the movie *Patton*, a film biography of his hero.

At 9 P.M. on April 30 Nixon went on television again (as always, on short notice), backed by a large map of Indochina. Still concealing the year-long U.S. bombardment of Cambodia, he insisted that U.S. policy had been "to scrupulously respect the neutrality of the Cambodian people," whereas North Vietnam had filled the border area with "major base camps, training sites, logistics facilities, weapons and ammunition factories, airstrips and prisoner-of-war compounds," as well as a Pentagon-like headquarters, the Central Office for South Vietnam, or COSVN. (None of these establishments was ever found during the subsequent two months.) In order, therefore, to protect American troops still in Vietnam, Nixon explained, there would be a joint South Vietnamese and American "incursion"—a twenty-mile-deep, sixty-day-long penetration of Cambodia with the objective of "cleaning out major North Vietnamese and Vietcong occupied territories . . . which serve as bases for attacks."

The invasion of Cambodia paralyzed peace efforts for much of the remainder of 1970. The Chinese broke off the Warsaw discussions, and the secret meetings of Kissinger and Xuan Thuy were also suspended until late in the year. By then they had reached an impasse. The United States was receding from its insistence on mutual troop withdrawal by itself and North Vietnam, but was now demanding the return of its prisoners-of-war—mostly shot-down aircrews—as a precondition to its own final departure. The North Vietnamese continued to demand a political solution, to wit, the end of the Thieu rule, before anything else. There the sides were to rest for nearly two years more.

The fall elections of 1970 came and found America still deep in what was now considered, to his dismay, Nixon's war—and 1971 was to bring further demonstration that it was a hopeless conflict. In February, with American air support, a South Vietnamese force undertook an invasion of Laos, and was swiftly routed by North Vietnamese there. To the gallery of unforgettable American newspaper photos a new set was added: frightened ARVN soldiers clinging desperately to the skids of already-full helicopters taking off in retreat. Then, that very summer of 1971, President Thieu, running for reelection, imposed so many restraints on the opposition candidates that either in prudence or disgust they all withdrew, making the election a one-man farce. The two events together badly undercut the propaganda claims for the success of "Vietnamization" and the prospects of democracy in Saigon.

Under the circumstances, Nixon and Kissinger welcomed a breakthrough in relations with China. In December 1971, Mao had given an interview to a journalist, Edgar Snow, to whom he confided that although Nixon was a "rightist," he was the man with the power to deal with certain problems between China and America, and that he, Mao, "would be happy to talk with him either as a tourist or as President."

Next came a curious episode known as Ping-Pong diplomacy. In April 1971, a Red Chinese and an American team were both playing in an international Ping-Pong tournament in Nagoya, Japan. At its end, the Chinese invited the Americans to compete in Peking the next month. They did and were soundly beaten at the table, but nonetheless received a kind welcome from Chou En-lai. This was a second signal that all was forgiven as far as Cambodia was concerned; Nixon's message through Warsaw, along with his very visible relaxation of certain controls on trade with and travel to the People's Republic, had borne fruit. Soon there was an invitation through neutral Pakistan to send a high-level emissary to the Chinese capital, and Nixon unsurprisingly chose to dispatch Kissinger.

The trip itself had been handled amid the cloak-and-dagger trappings that the National Security Adviser and the President loved. Early in July Kissinger made very visible public appearances in Saigon, then New Delhi, and finally Islamabad, Pakistan's capital—ostensibly on a routine base-touching trip to the East. But in Islamabad he suddenly became "indisposed" and was whisked off to a mountain resort (it was said) to recover, leaving canceled a state dinner for ninety people. The precautions went so far as to having the dinner cooked, in case nosy newsmen called to ask the unsuspecting chef for the menu. Actually, at 2:30 A.M. on July 9, Kissinger was driven to the Rawalpindi airport and put aboard a Pakistani commercial airliner parked in an isolated area of the field. Two Chinese navigators, especially flown in, and the Pakistani crew only learned at the last moment the identity of their special passenger.

The Kissinger trip to Peking cleared the air between the two countries. He and Chou hit it off well. Chou in effect confessed that China—isolated, at odds with her former Russian helpers, torn up by the "cultural revolution," and in great economic distress—would welcome a United States link. She asked only that Washington accept the future of Taiwan as an essentially Chinese issue. Kissinger, in turn, made it clear that American politics dictated some kind of U.S. support for the Taiwan government (such as pro forma resistance to its expulsion from the UN, which took place that fall) for at least a while. But, he said, the new United States view of the world visualized the People's Republic as one of the five great pillars of international order, the others being itself, Western Europe, the U.S.S.R., and Japan. After these points were established, the Nixon visit of the following spring was arranged. Kissinger flew back to Islamabad secretly, returned to the public eye, and continued to Washington, and on July 15 Nixon hugely enjoyed another short-notice television spectacular, informing the public of the historic meeting and of his pending trip to Peking on a "journey for peace, not just for our generation, but for future generations on this earth we share together."

That set the stage for the Vietnam affair to reach its climax and resolution in 1972.

It was North Vietnam that forced the issue on the battlefield. On April 1, a month after Nixon's visit to China, Hanoi's forces struck across the demilitarized zone (the DMZ), with twelve divisions of their own plus six Viet Cong divisions—the entire force bolstered by Soviet-made tanks and artillery. Within two weeks they had smashed their way deep into two key provinces and were threatening Hue and Saigon. Nixon's response was to decry this new invasion and begin a massive bombing of North Vietnamese targets with nearly a thousand planes. But any further escalation, such as bombing Hanoi or mining the vital port of Haiphong, posed a hard problem. It had been arranged that the President should visit Moscow in May. Following the trip to Peking it would be the climax of the year of détente, which was also an election year. A really major blow against North Vietnamese cities might provoke Moscow to cancel the summit in a depressing reenactment of what happened after the U-2 episode of 1960. Yet something had to be done to stop the complete unraveling of Thieu's forces. Nixon gambled—and won. Hanoi and Haiphong were bombed on April 15 and 16, and mines sown on May 8. But the Moscow invitation remained in force. And Peking, too, sent a signal. Its Ping-Pong team, then on tour in the United States, was permitted to make an all-smiles visit to the White House.

These developments kicked off the crucial final months of

dealings, marked by the sending of various covert messages in the Cold War's special language. Moscow and Peking continued to supply Hanoi, but made it clear that they were willing to see North Vietnam take a savage beating from the U.S. rather than forsake détente. Therefore, North Vietnam would have to soften its position somewhat. The United States, meanwhile, knew once and for all that Thieu could never be made truly independent, and that even all-out logistical support for him was a dead end. He would have to be forced into some kind of face-saving arrangement that allowed the Americans to collect their prisoners and go home, to the last uniformed man.

In August, Kissinger journeyed again to Saigon to tell Thieu that he was going to have to do some accommodating of his own. Meanwhile, both Russia and China had given similar advice to Hanoi. By the end of summer, all the "clients"—the Viet Cong, the Hanoi government, and Thieu—had gotten the appropriate hints from the principals that the flow of outside backing was not limitless. And dealings thereby reached a new level of earnestness. Kissinger began to meet again in September, in Paris, with Le Duc Tho, a member of Hanoi's Politburo. On October 8, Tho offered a deadlock-breaking plan that became the substance of the final agreement: a cease-fire, U.S. withdrawal, the return of American POWs, and the unity of North and South Vietnam to be acknowledged, though a National Council of Reconciliation and Concord would run South Vietnam, along with Thieu, until election time.

The North Vietnamese said that they wanted it all settled by October 31. They understood American politics well enough to know that Nixon desperately desired a peace announcement before Election Day, and they wanted to deal with him while he was still under that pressure. As it happened, they failed. When the then-U.S. ambassador to Saigon, Ellsworth Bunker, informed Thieu of the plan on October 19, Thieu reacted like a "trapped tiger." Nixon was not yet ready to draw the tiger's teeth. What he did was to arrange for a press conference by Kissinger, on October 26, at which the National Security Adviser said that some details remained unsettled, but he could safely report: "Peace is at hand." Twelve days later, Nixon buried the peace candidate of the Democrats, Senator George McGovern of South Dakota, in an electoral landslide, winning forty-nine of the fifty states.

But Vietnam's agony was not over. The North Vietnamese, possibly in answer to Thieu's reservations, raised some new ones of their own. They said, for example, that return of American POWs would be conditional on Thieu's freeing his political detainees. Argument on this and other matters continued until late in November, when Hanoi suddenly broke off the talks.

Then, on December 18, ten grim days began. First of all, there was a massive airlift of supplies to Thieu. And secondly, while denouncing Hanoi's sudden "reneging" on the tentative agreement, Nixon ordered heavy B-52 strikes on Hanoi. There was an outburst of both domestic and world outrage against these Christmas-week assaults, which had dubious military value, killed over two thousand civilians, leveled a hospital, and cost the U.S. somewhere between 15 and 35 B-52s (depending on whose estimates of the number shot down were more accurate).

After nearly two weeks of the so-called carpet-bombing, however, the North Vietnamese agreed to new meetings on January 8, 1973. Nixon was later to claim that this vindicated his action and brought Hanoi back to the table to make important concessions. But the final changes in the actual text were minor; some details were deliberately fuzzed. The presence of the North Vietnamese armies in the South was not officially recognized, and the fate of the political prisoners of Saigon was left to further negotiation. Neither side could introduce new weapons but could replace any that were "worn out, damaged, or destroyed"—all potentially ambiguous terms. The demilitarized zone was clearly identified as a temporary barrier, not a political boundary. And so on. In effect, Hanoi was left to deal with Thieu later. The United States would get its "decent interval" for complete withdrawal. And in a final sweetener, never implemented, Hanoi was supposed to receive some kind of financial and material help from the United States in "healing the wounds of war" and in the "postwar reconstruction of the Democratic Republic of Vietnam and throughout Indochina." All parties would respect the neutrality of Laos and Cambodia—a stipulation immediately ignored by everyone.

And so it ended. The prisoners of war came home to televised, tearful brief glory at the end of March 1973, and the last American soldier departed South Vietnam on the 27th of that month. Both Viet Cong and Saigon troops continued to hit at each other and seize positions, ignoring the Indonesian, Canadian, Polish, and Hungarian observers on the International Control Commission monitoring the cease-fire. In the first three weeks of February, 213,000 South Vietnamese civilians were rendered homeless. Kissinger made a February visit to Hanoi. Thieu was officially received at San Clemente—but not in Washington, where he might have had to face possible demonstrators. The ground fighting in Cambodia thundered on, and so did increasingly heavy U.S. bombing. All the same, the façade of peace had been erected.

There was not much in the situation to cause anyone to smile, but Kissinger contributed a touch of possibly inappropriate humor. When asked what he had been doing at the moment the official documents were signed in Paris on January 27, Kissinger reported from Washington that he had been "making love, not war."

IF THE TRIP TO PEKING was the chief jewel in Richard Nixon's crown in 1972, the second was his other "journey for peace" to Moscow. And the most glittering facet of that May mission was the Strategic Arms Limitation Treaty of 1972, or SALT I, as it came to be called when a second (though, by 1984, still-unratified) pact succeeded it in 1979.

Arms control talks had been going on fitfully with various interruptions since 1959. They had been aborted most recently in August of 1968 when Russia had sent tanks into Czechoslovakia to undo a sudden liberalization of the regime of Communist Anton Dubček, which the Soviets had found threatening. The Czechs, as noted earlier, accepted the inevitable, so that the invasion was bloodless—but it rankled in world opinion. Nonetheless, Nixon suggested renewal of the arms talks in 1969, for both countries were aware of the perils posed by their growing, sophisticated nuclear stockpiles.

No longer were there "missile gaps" that could be measured in a few hundred rockets. On the contrary, by the early 1970s each side already was aiming thousands of nuclear warheads at the other. The Defense Department had calculated that if only one hundred U.S. megaton "devices" landed on their assigned targets in the U.S.S.R., some 37 million Russians would die and 59 percent of that nation's industrial capacity would be destroyed. If three hundred warheads reached their impact areas, the deaths would rise to 96 million, the destruction to 77 percent. Both sides were rich in "overkill." Both sought to increase the accuracy and defensibility of their super-weapons.

An arcane vocabulary emerged from the ranks of nuclear strategists: "credible deterrent," "counterforce," "first-strike," "hard targets," "throw weight," MIRV, ICBM, ABM. These deceptively bland and bureaucratic terms hid the appalling realities of the subject and made seemingly rational discussion possible. A primer of nuclear war, however, revealed a world of bizarre assumptions and science fiction made palpable. Nuclear warheads were carried by "delivery vehicles"—aircraft or missiles. The powerful land-based ICBMs were housed in underground silos—detectable by cameras in orbiting satellites—or in submarines, where they were both mobile and invisible, but smaller. The development of Multiple Independent Re-entry Vehicles (MIRVs) in the early Seventies allowed more than one warhead to be placed in each missile. Thus a single ICBM launched from Utah, for example, might carry enough punch to devastate four, five, or more Siberian cities. And vice-versa.

U.S. and Soviet planners long operated on the theory that their purpose was not to win a nuclear exchange but to prevent one by making it clear that if the enemy launched a first strike, it would suffer a horrible counterstrike. Each side targeted the other's major cities, and what kept them both on good behavior (or deterred them) was the prospect of mutual assured destruction (MAD).

Yet there were always tempting possibilities of victory. One side—call it A—might adopt a "counterforce" policy; that is, aim weapons at B's launching sites. That could signal a possible intention to "take out" the enemy weapons and prevent the counterstrike. B might defend against this by "hardening" its silos or by developing an antiballistic-missile system (ABM) to destroy the incoming "vehicles" or by putting more warheads in submarines or aircraft. (Planes, subs, and silos formed a "triad" of nuclear power.) But these purely defensive measures could frighten A deeply. What if B provoked A to launch its entire arsenal, and then, with some or all of its own missiles intact (and millions of its people dead), rained retaliation on the now-helpless A? Such "scenarios" were constantly being tested and evaluated; always, for the planner representing his country in war games, the inconceivable question loomed: "Can I be in a situation where the enemy has nuclear weapons still available and I have none?" And always the answer was to guard against that disaster by building bigger, newer systems to redress the balance. So the piles of weapons grew, the danger of accidental "launches" increased, and billions in wealth were drawn from peacetime economies. The world's peril was acute when there were only two members of the "nuclear club." The entry of others generated even more brain-numbing possibilities of Armageddon.

It was knowledge of the ruinous risks and costs imposed by the mad competition that brought both sides to concurrence on the need for limitation. Limitation was not a total answer. It ignored "theater weapons," small nuclear warheads carried by NATO and Warsaw Pact forces, and it also overlooked the conventional weapons race on land and sea. Nor did it reduce the burden of arms by proposing the destruction of a single existing weapon, though each side might agree not to build a particular system in return for some concession by the other. (The lost system thereby became a "bargaining chip.") All that SALT treaties could do was to bring the opponents into some kind of strategic balance so that neither should lie awake nights fearing that the other had gained the fatal edge and was planning a preemptive strike.

Even that "simple" task bristled with complex issues. What weapons should be included? How did one match the different capacities of different weapons—huge Soviet missiles that could carry more and bigger warheads versus smaller but better-guided U.S. rockets? How did one equate the killing power of each country's various old and new fleets of airplanes and submarines?

To solve these conundrums took time, and so when Nixon reached Moscow on May 22, there had already been many months of meetings between arms-control technicians of both nations, each set of experts flanked by wary military planners watching for giveaways. They had hammered out rough agreements that Kissinger, Gromyko, and their staffs, in round-the-clock final bargaining sessions, could put in final form during a hectic week full of the pomp of summitry. Finally, on Friday the 26th Nixon stood before a microphone in an Intourist hotel, and announced that SALT I had been signed and was to run for five years.

The numbers did not really matter. To take only one example, they allowed each side to have 2,400 delivery vehicles of which 1,320 could be multiple. Whole paragraphs of such provisions did not change the fact that the United States and the U.S.S.R. still had enough warheads aimed at each other to uncap an inferno far beyond human imagination. But a symbolic step had been taken.

SALT I—ratified by the Senate the next year—was the capstone of the 1972 visit. Yet it was only one of a broad cluster of agreements reached by the United States and Russia between 1971 and 1973. Both powers were in a mood to deal. The Soviet leadership, beset by a faltering economy and restless satellite states, yearned for technological and material assistance, plus international respectability. The United States, still burdened by Vietnam, was also in a mood for accommodation. A shrinking dollar and an unfavorable trade balance sharpened the appetites of the government and of private businessmen for profitable new ventures. And finally, a revivified Western Europe was in a position to serve as mediator and balance wheel between the superpowers. The road to détente was opened in 1970 by West German Chancellor Willy Brandt, who signed treaties with the Soviet Union, the German Democratic Republic, and Poland, recognizing the post-1945 frontiers and thereby accepting the de facto partition of Germany and its territorial losses in World War II. In return, the Russians guaranteed permanent access to West Berlin. The issue that had brought Europe to the knife-edge of war in 1948 and 1961 was closed.

U.S.-Soviet agreements, then, bloomed like a hundred flowers during Nixon's trip and Brezhnev's return visit to the United States in 1973. American businessmen were invited to taste Russia's huge industrial and consumer markets. The things they sold were as simple as Pepsi-Cola and as industrially crucial as metallurgic furnaces and ammonia plants, computers and machine tools, electronic gear and mining equipment. Once again, as in past eras,

Russia helped itself by importations of Western technology.

And from America they also bought indispensable foodstuffs. In 1972 alone, following a disastrous home harvest, they purchased 19 million tons of wheat, corn, and soybeans. They did so in a transaction that was kept quiet, so that they got grain at a low insider's price of under two dollars a bushel, aided by a Commodity Credit Corporation loan of half the $1.2 billion total price. Only a handful of trading companies was let in on the action (and subsidized for selling below world-market figures). Once the sale was completed and publicized, the price of wheat shot to over five dollars a bushel. U.S. consumers were gouged and outraged—so were farmers not cut in on the deal—and inevitably the whole affair was denounced as "the great grain robbery."

An American who had, like Rip Van Winkle, been asleep since the early 1950s would indeed have rubbed his eyes in the détente atmosphere of June 1973. Brezhnev was entertained at Camp David and at San Clemente, and declared, in a press conference, that the Cold War was over. Still more agreements were announced—for air travel between the two nations; for sharing of information on earthquakes, the seabed, air pollution, outer space; for peaceful development of atomic energy; for cultural exchanges; for a linkup of the U.S. and Soviet space capsules, Apollo and Soyuz, on a 1975 mission; for "urgent consultations" if war threatened; and for parleys to slow the conventional arms race in Europe. And as the most confounding signs of the time to both Marxist and capitalist dogmatists, there were even agreements opening up office space in Moscow for Occidental Petroleum, International Harvester, General Electric, and Chase Manhattan Bank.

It seemed almost supernatural—and was a little deceptive. The few months following Brezhnev's visit quickly showed how difficult it was to control the unstable world.

At the heart of the problems that began to accumulate around détente was the fact that Richard Nixon, détente's chief salesman, was in deep trouble at home. The steadily unfolding Watergate scandal produced new ramifications each day. What began as a "third-rate burglary" of Democratic National Headquarters in Washington mushroomed into revelations of a swarm of ugly activities: wiretaps, break-ins, and other operations of so-called plumbers to plug information leaks and harass "enemies." All were managed by high White House staffers and financed by a slush fund of millions, some of it contributed by lobbies and corporations that expected and got special favors in return. All were covered up by a clique of Nixon subordinates who were trying to "stonewall" the developing investigations by Congress, the Department of Justice, and a specially appointed prosecutor. In the prying, such embarrassments as the secret bombing of Cambodia came to light. There was, as Nixon had been warned by one of his associates, a cancer growing on the Presidency—and therefore on presidential leadership and public confidence in it.

A Congress angry at Nixon and his abuses of power retaliated. First, it imposed a deadline on the use of funds for bombing Cambodia, to take effect August 15, 1973. Next it drafted a War Powers Act, designed to restore its own constitutional prerogatives. The President, under the proposed legislation, had to notify Congress, within forty-eight hours, of any military operation he commenced, giving his reasons for it. At the end of sixty days he had to terminate the action unless the legislature approved it. The measure—passed in October over Nixon's veto—was seen as reducing the chances of war by curbing an overzealous Chief Executive.

Kissinger became Secretary of State in August 1973. His prestige was still high, and Nixon hoped that some of it would rub off on his tarnished Administration. That same autumn, Kissinger was awarded the Nobel Peace Prize, along with Hanoi's Le Duc Tho, for settling the Vietnam War. (Tho refused his, but Kissinger accepted, leading someone to observe that the proportions were right: half a prize for half a peace.)

October also brought more strains on the new cordiality toward Moscow. On the 6th, Egyptian and Syrian troops roared across their borders with Israel in a surprise attack that launched the Yom Kippur War, named for the Jewish holiday on which the blow fell. Six years earlier, in the Six Day War, Israeli armies had repelled a similar thrust and destroyed the Soviet-equipped armies that launched it. This time, however, the tables seemed, at first, to be turned; the Egyptians and Syrians caught the Israelis by surprise and forced them back with heavy initial casualties.

The assault both startled and rankled Kissinger. Although, to Washington's deep satisfaction, Egypt's new leader, Anwar Sadat, had expelled most of his Soviet advisers in 1972, he still had a few (as did the Syrians), so that Brezhnev had clearly known of the coming blow and had neither tried to halt it nor warned the United States. Yet a 12-point declaration of principles signed at the end of the 1972 summit had asserted that Washington and Moscow had a responsibility to "do everything in their power so that conflicts or situations will not arise which would serve to increase international tensions." And Nixon and Brezhnev, in 1973, had also agreed to promote "the quickest possible settlement in the Middle East." Certainly the U.S.S.R. had violated that understanding in principle if nothing else.

Kissinger did not choose, however, the route of an open breach with the Russians. Instead, the United States undertook a quick airlift of supplies to the Israelis. Israel's armies thereupon stabilized their position on the Syrian border, and, in a daring counterattack, crossed the Suez Canal and invaded Egypt. By the third week of the war the entire Egyptian Third Army was surrounded in the Sinai Peninsula and Cairo itself was threatened. Now it was the Soviets' turn to rush supplies for Egypt to the fighting zones, while Nixon and Kissinger put the U.S. Mediterranean fleet, plus an airborne division, on alert.

But at root neither power wanted their new relationship to die amid blood and fire in the desert. Each supported a cease-fire, and Kissinger was able to talk the onrushing Israelis into accepting one. Then, in an exhausting series of visits to the Mideast, and shuttlings among Cairo, Damascus, and Tel Aviv, he managed to get the armies disengaged and a truce accepted. Yet this triumph of personal diplomacy with proud and stubborn leaders like Israel's Golda Meir, Sadat, and Syria's Hafez Assad, while enhancing Kissinger's well-cultivated reputation for wizardry, left the basic problem of reaching a permanent Middle East peace unsolved. The area was still a booby trap for the stability Kissinger cherished.

The Yom Kippur War proved that the U.S.S.R. was not yet immune to a touch of adventurism by proxy. But Kissinger was in no position to moralize. Only a month earlier a military coup had overthrown Chile's freely elected leftist president, Salvador Allende. For two years previously, the United States had covertly encouraged that result by financing strikes, protests, and anti-Allende newspapers and candidates (while openly using its influence in the Export-Import Bank and World Bank to cancel or sharply restrict loans to Chile). Allende's crime appeared to be his acknowledged Marxism and his nationalizing of U.S. copper properties. The destabilization of his government was a throwback to the era of ousting Arbenz and Mossadegh. Détente sometimes seemed to fulfill Ambrose Bierce's cynical definition of peace as "an interval of cheating between two periods of fighting."

The Yom Kippur War produced, as a side effect, another blow to American self-confidence in a difficult post-Vietnam era. Angry at U.S. support of Israel, the oil-producing Arab states that dominated a cartel known as the Organization of Petroleum Exporting Countries (OPEC) imposed a boycott on shipments of petroleum to the United States, and threatened to do likewise to Western Europe and Japan. Suddenly Americans, locked into long, combative, wearying lines at gas stations, and facing severe electric power cuts (because most generators were oil-fired), realized how energy-dependent they had become. After a hard winter, the truce ended the embargo and eased the grip on the American jugular, but the basic problem would not go away.

October 1973 also brought the resignation of Vice President Spiro Agnew, who faced trial for accepting illegal payments from contractors while he was governor of Maryland. The "Saturday Night Massacre," in which Nixon fired special Watergate prosecutor Archibald Cox, also took place that month. The resulting "firestorm" of public protest launched impeachment hearings in Congress. The Nixon Administration was plainly doomed.

During the spring and summer of 1974 the noose tightened around the beleaguered President. In a last bid to gild his tenure with foreign policy achievements, Nixon journeyed, in June, to the Middle East and in July to Moscow, where he signed a limited underground nuclear test-ban treaty. But he was unwell with phlebitis in Egypt (where Sadat turned out huge crowds for him) and distraught in the U.S.S.R., haunted by the fast-approaching inevitable. On August 8, faced with certain impeachment and trial in the Senate, Nixon resigned. Vice President Gerald R. Ford, named by him to replace Agnew the preceding autumn, took over.

Henry Kissinger—to whom, as the senior Cabinet official, the President's letter of resignation was sent—remained where he was. Yet things would not be the same with the famous team separated. Kissinger, too, would, in the long run, feel the impact of Watergate.

KISSINGER'S POWER HAD RESTED both on his own reputation and on the ability of the executive branch to conduct foreign policy independently—a prerogative almost unchallenged since 1940. Yet his Superman costume began to fray even before Nixon left office, and the new backlash of congressional assertiveness struck at the roots of his influence. The Watergate investigations revealed his role in White House wiretaps and in the secret war in Indochina. And, as a foretaste of coming events, in that summer of 1974 Turkish paratroops suddenly dropped onto Cyprus, where Greek and Turkish settlers were locked in dispute over control of their island's government. An irritated Congress, remembering that weapons supplied to NATO members were not to be used for aggressive action, cut Turkey off from further arms shipments. In retaliation, Turkey said it would close down American military installations within its borders. Kissinger pleaded for the legislators to change their minds; the bases, he said, were badly needed for intelligence gathering and other activities. But to no avail. The ban continued, and Turkey (for the time being) threw the Americans out.

Then, in September, the frustrated Secretary journeyed with President Ford to Vladivostok, there to reach a tentative agreement on further strategic arms limits. He returned to find some

congressmen worrying about a possible U.S. loss of "strategic
superiority." "What in the name of God," he asked in reasonable
exasperation, "is strategic superiority?" The tough questioning
illustrated that a strange alliance was forming against him: hard-
liners in the Republican Party, who yearned for Dulles-era
simplicities; Pentagon lobbyists who distrusted arms limitation;
liberals upset by Kissinger's coziness with Soviet totalitarianism;
and former "doves" nursing long memories of the Christmas
bombings of Hanoi.

In 1975 Kissinger's opponents gained strength. A special Senate
committee on intelligence activities, chaired by Idaho's liberal
Senator Frank Church, exposed various CIA dirty tricks, including
its (and Kissinger's) share in undermining Chile's government. And
then the inevitable happened. Kissinger's Indochina peace fell
apart. The Khmer Rouge took the Cambodian capital of Pnom Penh
in mid-April, while the North Vietnamese thrust out of their truce
lines and, on April 29, occupied Saigon at last. Transport planes took
off around the clock from Tan Son Nhut air base until almost the
last minute, evacuating U.S. civilians and at least some of the South
Vietnamese who had entrusted their lives to American protection.
And, on the final day, helicopters from nearby carriers darted over
the mobbed, panicky streets and landed atop the U.S. embassy to
take out the last officials, while crowds fought and clawed in the
offices below, trying to attain the roof and safety. In gunfire and
screams the American adventure in Vietnam ended.

But all was not quite over; there was a sudden, dramatic
after-explosion. On the morning of May 12, a freighter under U.S.
colors, the *Mayaguez*, on its way toward Singapore, passed through
waters claimed by Vietnam, Cambodia, and Thailand. It was halted
by Cambodian gunboats. Its crew of thirty-nine was taken, first to
the island of Koh Tang on their ship, and then, in fishing boats, to
the Cambodian mainland.

The news of this "piracy" reached Ford and Kissinger in the small
hours of the 13th and provoked instant response. In their minds was
the sad example of the *Pueblo*, an electronic intelligence-gathering
vessel of the U.S. Navy, captured by North Koreans under similar
circumstances in January 1968. Its crew was detained under harsh
conditions for a year, and only released after an official U.S.
apology for spying. Ford did not want another *Pueblo* incident, and
Kissinger did not want Cambodia's new masters assuming that the
United States was now utterly toothless. The two reached a quick
decision. Before nightfall Marine helicopters were landing troops on
Koh Tang in the face of heavy fire, and bombers roared over the
mainland to pound a Cambodian air base and oil depot into smoking
pyres.

This response triggered martial pride that had been forgotten in the immediately preceding years. "I'm very proud to be an American today," said the new Vice President, Nelson Rockefeller. And Barry Goldwater, who had seized the 1964 Republican nomination from Rockefeller, was equally enthusiastic. Without Ford's muscular reflex, he said, "every little half-assed nation would be taking a shot at us."

The only trouble was that no one had bothered to check diplomatic channels to find out if the Cambodians were simply mistaken, or at least open to reasonable persuasion. The fact was that on learning of the U.S. attack on Koh Tang, they promptly notified Washington, through neutral channels, that they would return both ship and crew. The message got to Ford and Kissinger three hours before the mainland bombing raid was slated. Yet the air strike went on nonetheless, even as the crewmen were being brought back to their ship. They were actually visible to U.S. pilots making strafing runs on Koh Tang, and frantically waved white tee-shirts in the air to identify themselves and avoid being sunk by their rescuers. Once the crew members were returned, the Marines evacuated the island, but not until the heavy fighting had cost them five dead, sixteen missing, and approximately eighty wounded. The operation was, in the words of the Tokyo newspaper *Yomiuri Shimbun*, "like using a cannon to shoot a chicken."

Yet the *Mayaguez* rescue, momentarily satisfying to many, did not arrest the general U.S. will to disengage. That was proven when, in midsummer of 1975, Kissinger once more sought congressional authorization to prop up an anti-Communist regime, this time in Africa. The scene was the Portuguese colony of Angola, which Lisbon was about to free. Three African factions were fighting for dominance. One of them, the Popular Movement for the Liberation of Angola (MPLA), had Soviet backing. Eleven thousand Cubans also came to join its forces. Whether Castro sent them at Moscow's command or with its consent was vague. But it did not matter. Though Kissinger asked for aid to the anti-MPLA forces, Congress once again defeated his proposed appropriations. It saw no vital U.S. interest at stake, and was not seeking another overseas adventure. By February 1976 the MPLA was supreme in Angola. The Soviet Union, which had "lost" Algeria and Ghana in the 1960s through the replacement of friendly rulers by hostile ones, had scored a small comeback.

Yet these signs of the continuation of the old rivalry were overshadowed, in July 1975, by what was probably the climactic hour of détente, a supersummit involving not only Ford and Brezhnev, but the heads of every major European nation as well.

The gathering was the windup of a long Conference on Security and Cooperation in Europe, and the leaders were meeting to sign a thirty-thousand-word declaration that was, in effect, the nearest possible thing to a general peace treaty of World War II. It was held in neutral Finland, amid pomp such as Europe had not seen since the Congress of Vienna met on similar business in 1815. Every European government except Albania's was represented, as well as the United States and Canada. Helsinki's hotels struggled to keep 2,500 rooms for staff members, technicians, and dignitaries like Ford, Brezhnev, and Tito appropriately housed and fed.

Nearly three years of preliminary negotiation were embodied in a series of agreements that, for the sake of clarity and order, were grouped in what the negotiators somewhat inelegantly called three "baskets."

Basket One dealt with frontiers and with "general confidence-building measures." All the signatories accepted the principle that existing frontiers should not be violated (but might be changed by "peaceful persuasion"). This effectively legitimized the borders established by Soviet arms in 1945. It was, said exiled Soviet dissident and novelist Aleksandr Solzhenitsyn, "the funeral of Eastern Europe." But there was also a pledge of "nonintervention in the internal affairs" of the signatories, and this could have been considered a reproach to the Russians for their invasions of Hungary and Czechoslovakia, and a repudiation of the Brezhnev Doctrine (announced at the time of the Czech incursion) that the U.S.S.R. would intervene in any country where "socialism" was endangered. Unfortunately, it was also used by the Russians to challenge some of the provisions of the human rights agreements of Basket Three.

Basket Two was generally easy to accept. It contained agreements for the exchange of technical and scientific data, and for better liaison between such bodies as the European Economic Community and its East European counterpart, the Council for Mutual Economic Assistance, or COMECON.

Basket Three, however, roused contention. Its language was worked out carefully to oblige Western desires for greater democratization within the Soviet Union and its subject states, while not doing too much violence to the Russians' insistence that such things were domestic matters. The Basket Three statements, therefore, expressed pious hopes for the free movement of ideas and people within and across frontiers, but in ambiguous, committeelike words. The signers pledged themselves to "appropriate measures" for increased contacts. They would "look favorably" on granting visas for the reunification of families. They would encourage the "improvement of working conditions for journalists," and "access to an exchange of oral, filmed, and broadcast information." In practical terms this meant that the Soviet Union would permit some European papers to appear on a few select Moscow newsstands. Or that they might yield a few more exit visas to the thousands of Soviet Jews who desired to emigrate.

Despite their vagueness, the Helsinki agreements were willingly signed by Ford, who was in a happy frame of mind. Though he had recently committed a blunder in refusing to offend the Russians by receiving Solzhenitsyn at the White House, he was still generally popular in the United States and was well received on a ten-day swing through Europe that preceded the grand conference. His known good nature tended to nullify the effects of some of his worst actions, and in a sense he rose to a high level of statesmanship in his final statement on signing. He knew that the accords were vulnerable, and that the Soviet Union got legitimization of its world status in return for the woolliest promises of liberalization. Yet he said that history would judge the gathering "not by what we say here today, but what we do tomorrow; not by the promises we make, but by the promises we keep."

It was a good point. The Helsinki accords could only be assessed by the future, but the reassuring array of Soviet-American pacts, especially those on arms limitation, offered promise that there would actually be a future.

Not everyone would have seen it that way. There were those who still saw the bear as most dangerous when he stood with open arms. Yet that summer of 1975, just thirty years after V-E Day, seemed to herald a momentary renaissance of the hopes of that brave beginning when toasts still celebrated the common valor of all the Axis' enemies, and when only two or three atom bombs existed in the world, still unknown and unused. The fact that détente happened to reach its crest after a string of U.S. setbacks was unfortunate, but did not detract from the value of reconciliation.

Yet was Helsinki's brightness the glow of sunset or sunrise over détente? The ambivalence that lingered in the American mind—the old ambivalence that ran back to 1917—was still there. Were the Russians potential friends or natural enemies? Voyagers toward an alternative future or sinister plotters? Partners and customers or imperialists in idealists' clothing? What changes would time work in them?

Détente alone could not answer such questions, but it offered time to weigh them. Kissinger and Nixon's worst enemies could not deny that. Even Solzhenitsyn, while deploring Helsinki and almost everything done by the West in what he considered its steady retreat before the Soviet barbarians, said: "Is détente needed or not? . . . Not only is it needed, it's as necessary as air. It's the only way of saving the earth."

Chapter 12

THE PERILOUS SEESAW
1977-THE PRESENT

J IMMY CARTER—HE DISDAINED the use of his full name, James Earl, Jr.—walked up Pennsylvania Avenue to the White House after his swearing-in. It was his way of setting a tone. In a sense, he took his example from another Southern President, Thomas Jefferson, who had also disdained pomp and clip-clopped alone on horseback to his inaugural oath-taking. But Jefferson had been a freethinking intellectual, a slave-holding planter-aristocrat. Carter was of a different Southern tradition, Baptist and populist. He wanted others to believe that he himself was as homespun in essence as the ordinary American people. He promised them, the morning after his election, a government that would mirror their own innate goodness.

Foreign diplomats and capital press pundits were puzzled by this opening gambit. What kind of foreign policy would such a man create? How would the ship of state be navigated by a self-proclaimed Washington outsider, who had ridden to victory on the tide of popular disillusionment with the federal government? A man who had no discernible attitude profile on foreign affairs, had made no speeches and cast no votes on diplomatic issues. No President since the Cold War had begun was so innocent of experience in and with the world beyond the seas.

In Carter's case the problem was compounded by inconsistencies. For all of his posing as a "peanut farmer" and a solid citizen of little Plains, Georgia (Sunday school teacher, Lions Club, membership on school and planning boards), he was actually a well-educated, complex, and ambitious figure. He had gone from high school briefly to Georgia Tech, and then to Annapolis in 1943. He was graduated in the top tenth of his class. Five years later he was part of the Navy's nuclear submarine development program. He confessed later to a long-term hope to run the Navy eventually, but duty brought him home to take over the family business, as eldest son, when his father died in 1953.

Driving, planning, investing, he swelled the seven-hundred-acre farm to six times that size, broadened its spin-off operations in making and marketing peanut oil and fertilizers, mechanized and modernized, and burst out of Plains in less than ten years. He ran for the state legislature in 1962. In 1970 he became governor of Georgia. He was a mixture of Old and New South, a streamlined administrator, a late but sincere convert to desegregation who made important minority appointments and beefed up urban social services, but a man who still spoke in the slow, soft tones of hot and lazy afternoons spent sipping Coca-Cola. He was a weekday technocrat, and a Sunday "born-again" churchgoing neighbor. He kept company sparingly, mainly with his wife and immediate family, and with fellow Georgians like banker Bert Lance, lawyer Griffin Bell, young political science whiz kids like Jody Powell and Hamilton Jordan. And yet he was tapped, in 1973, for membership in a prestigious organization created by banker David Rockefeller. Called the Trilateral Commission, it was a working group of executives drawn from the management elites of the United States, Canada, Europe, and Japan. Its purpose was to consider long-range ways of promoting "orderly" economic development throughout the world. It was the Seventies' counterpart of the groups that had once supported the Marshall Plan and foreign aid.

In 1976 Carter marched doggedly to the presidential nomination, primary by primary and caucus by caucus, and then to a slim victory over Gerald Ford, who was burdened with a general public irritation at the paradox of a sluggish economy in the midst of rising inflation. Along the way, Carter gave few cues as to his future foreign policies. He spoke of ending Vietnam-era tensions through an amnesty for draft-resisters. He told a *New York Times* reporter in June 1976 that future issues of war and peace would be "more a function of economic and social problems than of . . . military security." And in his inaugural in January 1977 he seemed to vote solidly for goodwill and high ideals. He spoke of moving toward an "ultimate goal—the elimination of all nuclear weapons from this earth," and he said, too, that the United States would support "the basic right of every human to be free of poverty, hunger, disease, and political repression."

They were fine words, like the fine Carter smile that already delighted cartoonists. But making policies to flesh them out took more than goodwill. Experienced hands could have told Carter that foreign policy was formed in conflict. It was the fruit of infighting among presidential advisers, bureaucrats, and lobbies—high-minded and self-interested alike. It could not simply be announced from anyone's pulpit; it needed to be constantly fine-tuned and sold. And even when a foreign policy consensus was reached within the Administration and then with Congress and the voters, it had to be floated among allies. Finally, it was subjected to the tests of constant challenge, sometimes by the U.S.S.R., and sometimes by wholly unexpected developments on a globe beyond control.

Jimmy Carter, a man of slide rule and prayer book, learned these facts by hard experience. His world stewardship constantly ran into gales, often changed direction, and in the long run shifted generally from détente toward a harder line, mirroring, as it did so, America's shifting mood in an unruly and fearful time.

IT ALL BEGAN BRAVELY ENOUGH, but the clash between ideal and reality appeared almost in the first euphoric moments after the election victory. Carter proudly announced that in forming his Cabinet he would avoid naming the conventional figures who moved in and out of high Washington posts like clockwork figures each time a new Administration's hour struck. But he then chose a Secretary of State from the very heart of the veteran foreign relations and defense establishment. Cyrus Vance was a low-keyed, affluent, West Virginia-born lawyer. He came into public service via prep school, Yale (where he was graduated in 1939, a classmate of McGeorge Bundy), wartime Navy duty in the Pacific, and several years of Wall Street legal service. He arrived in Washington with the New Frontier, first as counsel for Senate committees on space, aeronautics, and defense, then as Secretary of the Army in 1962. People liked "Cy" Vance for his "honesty [and] quiet, steadfast courage of his convictions." He was a fact-oriented, instinctive conciliator, the man sent to investigate insurrections in Panama, the Dominican Republic, or Detroit—the one to negotiate among Turks and Cypriots, or with representatives of Saigon and the Viet Cong in Paris in 1968. He disliked abrasive tactics. They were not the style of a director of Pan Am and IBM, a member of the Trilateral Commission and the Council on Foreign Relations, a gentlemanly tennis player.

By the time he joined Carter's supporters in 1976, Vance had committed himself down the line to détente, SALT, human rights. He found a kindred spirit in the new ambassador to the UN, Andrew Young, another of Carter's Georgian friends, and a onetime stalwart in Martin Luther King, Jr.'s Southern Christian Leadership Conference. Young's was the new—and black—face in the top foreign policy crowd, his presence a portent of Carter's intent to woo the liberated states of Africa.

The Special Assistant for National Security Affairs, Zbigniew Brzezinski, was also new to Washington but was not unknown to powerbrokers. He, like Henry Kissinger, was a defense intellectual. He had, in fact, been Kissinger's Harvard faculty colleague in the 1950s. There were other parallels, too. Both men were foreign-born and spoke accented English. Both were refugees, but Brzezinski was a victim of Stalin rather than Hitler. His father was a Polish diplomat who had been on assignment in Canada, where he stayed when the Reds swept into complete control in Warsaw in 1946. Son Zbigniew, educated in Canadian Roman Catholic schools, found his way to Harvard, a research fellowship, and a doctorate. His thesis: "The Permanent Purge: Politics in Soviet Totalitarianism."

The year 1960 brought Brzezinski to Columbia as a specialist in public law and East European affairs. His books and articles argued that new technological forces would, in time, loosen the grip of old and rigid ideologies like Soviet-style Communism. In the interim, the U.S.S.R. must be confronted with a firm no to any adventurism it undertook as it struggled to support its fading power by conquest.

Though Brzezinski appeared more spiny and hawkish than Vance, the two men seemed to have little overt conflict at first. It was Brzezinski's initial wish to maintain a low profile; he had no immediate urge to be a carbon copy of Kissinger, and in any case he was not nearly as close to Carter as Kissinger had been to Nixon. Nor was Cyrus Vance as easily effaced as William Rogers.

So the Carter "national security" performance began with a more seasoned cast than advertised, and the President learned at once how hard it was to please the critics. His nominee for head of the Arms Control and Disarmament Agency, Paul Warnke, was assailed by conservatives during confirmation hearings as an alleged believer in "unilateral disarmament." Though he was approved, it was only by an 18-vote Senate margin (58–40), short of the two-thirds he would need to confirm any new SALT agreement.

Next the President, possibly to set himself off from Ford, who had blundered in not receiving Solzhenitsyn, wrote a warm reply to an open letter from Andrei Sakharov, a distinguished Soviet physicist and dissident. Sakharov had urged more pressure by the United States on Moscow to live up to the Helsinki accords. The results of the Carter letter were a testy statement from the Kremlin and more crackdowns on Soviet dissidents that spring—plus the cancellation of television time for the U.S. ambassador to the U.S.S.R. to make a brief Fourth of July speech to the Russian people.

Meanwhile, Carter had announced that the United States would consider any government's sensitivity to human rights as an important element in determining future relations with it. This stung the self-esteem of right-wing regimes with which America had significant dealings, such as those in South Korea, the Philippines, Indonesia, and Chile. After outraged reactions from their capitals, the State Department was forced to admit publicly that the United States would not exert human rights pressures at the cost of weakening alliances. In fact, effective action on the subject was not easy. Communist states could dismiss U.S. "meddling," and America's friendly clients could only be urged so far without alienating or weakening them.

Carter pushed on with developing his pacific image. In an obvious gesture of hemispheric reconciliation, he strove for ratification of a treaty negotiated under President Johnson, whereby Panama would get full sovereignty over the U.S. Canal Zone after the year 2000. Despite heavy Senate opposition, he won (with a vote to spare) in April 1978.

Carter also seemed eager to slow the arms race. He held back authorization to develop the B-1, a new manned bomber desired by the Air Force, and also denied permission to develop the neutron bomb, a weapon designed to make nuclear war more conceivable by reducing heat and blast effects so that, while radiation would wreak terrible damage on enemy personnel, military objectives themselves would not be obliterated. Some commentators wryly said that the neutron bomb was therefore a perfect weapon for a capitalist (or at any rate a materialist) society—it showed a proper respect for property.

And in 1978 Carter savored the triumph of his life, and his Administration, when fortune and two Middle Eastern statesmen handed him the chance to be midwife to peace between Egypt and Israel.

For three years following the truce in the Yom Kippur War the situation had remained essentially deadlocked. The basic problem was on the west bank of the Jordan River, seized by Israel in the 1967 war. In that year the area, part of the Kingdom of Jordan, became merely an Israeli-occupied territory, to be bargained over in a peace conference that unfortunately never came about because no Arab state would deal with Tel Aviv. By 1977, however, the West Bank—now capitalized, an entity of its own—had taken on huge emotional importance. There was a new Israeli Prime Minister, Menachem Begin, a conservative with strong support from religious parties who insisted that the area was part of the ancient Hebraic kingdom, and should be permanently annexed. And at the same time a new generation of Palestinian Arabs had grown to adulthood and was increasingly swayed by the arguments of the Palestine Liberation Organization, led by Yasir Arafat. Arafat proclaimed that the West Bank, and in fact all of Israel's territory, was the Palestinians' homeland, and that it must be freed from the "Zionists" and made into a new Arab state.

The PLO, like other small and determined groups without a legal military apparatus, was trying to achieve its goal by terror. Through the bombing of public places, the shelling of innocent civilians, the hijacking of airliners, and the kidnapping of diplomats and other hostages, it aimed to dramatize the injustices the Palestinians claimed to be suffering, to make the world pay heed and yield concessions. (The PLO was thus part of a new, disquieting element in world politics. It was one among a number of terrorist "liberation" organizations, all composed of young zealots extravagantly willing to kill and to die, all somehow able to acquire weapons and hiding places, and all impossible to control by normal diplomatic processes.)

The West Bank situation seemed, therefore, beyond resolution in 1977, particularly with the PLO and the Israelis each convinced that the other side consisted of murderers with whom there could be no discussion. But there was a possible door to peace ajar in the less explosive area of the occupied Sinai desert. In October, Egypt's Prime Minister Anwar Sadat boldly pushed it open. A man with an apparently deep eagerness to make his mark in history and on the Arab world, and to lift the economic burden of war-readiness from his struggling country, Sadat stunningly announced that the policy of nonrecognition of Israel was nonproductive, and that he would, if necessary, even visit Israel in the quest for a solution to the impasse.

The Israelis, however much surprised, accepted the proposed breakthrough, which offered them important advantages too. Sadat got his invitation to visit Begin, and on November 19 he addressed the Knesset (the Israeli parliament). After a brief minisummit whirl, the two nations, enemies for nearly thirty years, agreed to begin talks at the ministerial level, looking toward a treaty.

The United States watched with delight. A peaceful Middle East that offered no options for Soviet intervention, and that forced no uncomfortable choices between Jew and Arab, was something almost impossibly good to hope for. And in fact it proved almost impossible to bring off. Sadat, in order to avoid total isolation from his Arab neighbors, had to insist that his peace offer was conditional upon Israel's renunciation of the West Bank to some kind of Palestinian entity. Begin rejected this. Nor was Israel in a hurry to abandon its defense installations, oil fields, and settlements in the Sinai. Talks broke down; there were angry words by both Sadat and Begin for the evening telecasts in the United States, and by the summer of 1978 the peace process had shuddered and stalled.

It was at that point that Carter stepped in as mediator. He invited both men to join him in face-to-face meetings at Camp David to see if, with American good offices, harmony might be restored. Possibly because neither Sadat nor Begin wanted the onus of rejecting the offer, they both accepted.

So, from September 5 to 17, 1978, in the hideaway in the Catoctin Mountains that had become a second seat of American government, an extraordinary conclave took place. The highest officials of three governments worked ceaselessly amid the scenic pleasures of an Appalachian autumn. Rustic cabins became offices. Brzezinski and Hamilton Jordan shared one (named "Witch Hazel") with each other and with piles of papers. Vance trundled the long distances between residences in a golf cart, while other dignitaries wobbled on bicycles. Everyone became increasingly sleepy as each meeting of the heads of state was followed by all-night conferences and drafting sessions with aides. But there were moments of relaxation: tennis doubles (Carter and Vice President Mondale against Vance and Brzezinski) and evening movies, including The Sting, An Unmarried Woman, and The Spy Who Loved Me. Likewise there were moments particularly appropriate for the camera, such as the celebrations of occasions for Muslim, Jewish, and Christian prayer by the devout trio of leaders. In its way, it was Carter's version of Nixonian summitry.

And, incredibly, it worked. As the days went by, it became clear that the fundamental issues like the future of the West Bank or sovereignty over Jerusalem were beyond real agreement. But the Americans pushed Begin and Sadat together on the Sinai. And beyond the specifics of promising Begin compensatory air bases and peacekeeping garrisons, there was the intangible force of Carter's evident interest and concern. No American President, said Begin gratefully, "has ever so involved himself in our problems."

Finally it was done. Begin, Sadat, and Carter, all smiles for the cameras, announced that they would initiate a "peace process" in which it was hoped that other states might later join. Sadat got a vague Begin commitment to seek "autonomy" for West Bank Arabs and to impose a temporary moratorium on Jewish settlements there, plus a firm understanding that the Sinai would be returned. Begin got the certainty of a peace treaty within the ensuing year. It was nebulous, but heartening. The three embraced again and again for the media, and even appeared jointly before the Congress of the United States to announce the "spirit of Camp David." Not since Theodore Roosevelt mediated the end of the Russo-Japanese War in 1905 had the United States and its President played so direct a role in turning swords into ploughshares.

It was Carter's hour to enjoy, even though all the other Arab states, plus the PLO—and the Russians—promptly denounced and spurned any part in the Camp David accords. Moreover, the peacemaking momentum of the event carried him on into 1979 as a seeker of concord. In January of that year patient work by Vance and others resulted in the "normalization" of relations with Peking, and the preparations for the first formal exchange of ambassadors. (The consequent de-recognition of Taiwan as "China" provoked a brief and ineffectual legal challenge by Senator Barry Goldwater.) Meanwhile, Vance pressed on with the effort to get a new SALT treaty, and finally had one for a waving, grinning Carter and Brezhnev to sign in Vienna in June.

SALT II was not as far-reaching as its predecessor. Like SALT I, it shelved some problems in order to get agreement on others. The Soviet "Backfire" bomber was excluded from the treaty—but so were U.S. aircraft in Europe that could carry nuclear warheads. The Soviet Union was "allowed" to maintain a slight lead in heavy missiles, and the United States agreed to a two-year delay in deploying "cruise missiles," those low-flying air- or sea-launched bombs that could slip under Soviet radar and land warheads within fifty feet of a target. But to offset the delay in exploiting this technological advantage, the United States could begin work on the MX and modernize its submarine-borne missile arsenal. In all, SALT II continued to present a grisly arithmetic of death-dealing power, though critics and defenders debated about who had the advantage when the columns were added up.

When he laid the agreement before the Senate in the autumn, Carter stood as he still wished to be seen, the champion of nonviolent benevolence in the world's various trouble spots. Then, in one disastrous year, Carter's attempted structure of peace—like his political future—was shattered.

TO BEGIN WITH, SALT II intensified a long campaign of harassment against arms limitation. Antitreaty lobbies such as the Committee on the Present Danger—formed in 1976 and numbering in its ranks such seasoned hawks as James Schlesinger and Paul Nitze, and such newcomers as Norman Podhoretz, editor of *Commentary* magazine—launched (along with the American Security Council and the American Conservative Union) a well-financed campaign to convince voters that the Russians were in a mad race to achieve strategic superiority, and that the SALT deals denied the United States its technological edge, gave the Russians catch-up time, and lulled America into complacency. This viewpoint, in the words of New York's Senator Daniel P. Moynihan, rapidly went "from heresy to respectability if not orthodoxy." Though Carter had campaigned on the promise of a cut in defense spending, his Administration was forced even before SALT II's signing to make some concessions to this outcry. In December of 1977, Secretary of Defense Harold Brown, speaking to the National Security Industrial Association, a trade council of defense contractors, declared: "We will not be outgunned. We will not be bullied. We will not be coerced." Six months later Carter himself, addressing the Annapolis graduating class, denounced the U.S.S.R.'s buildup of arms as "excessive far beyond any legitimate requirements." (The problem in the entire debate, however, was just who determined each nation's "legitimate requirements.") By 1978's end, the proposed Carter budget for the next fiscal year (1979-80) said nothing of arms cuts.

In areas other than armaments, too, the fabric of détente was unraveling. Africa was an example. In May 1978, rebels from the province of Shaba in Zaire (the former Congo) launched an attack on the anti-Communist government of Prime Minister Joseph Mobutu. Mobutu succeeded in getting French and Belgian troops committed to help him handle the rebels, and the Carter Administration furnished the air transports to bring in the European soldiers, plus $17.5 million in economic aid to Mobutu. This move delighted Brzezinski, eager to counter what he saw as the American "defeat" in Angola. When Soviet Foreign Minister Gromyko told Carter that the Russians had no hand in the uprising, Brzezinski said it was "one of the most mendacious performances I've ever witnessed."

But volatile Africa simmered on, a cauldron stirred by many meddling hands. In 1977 Ethiopia, which had thrown out its Emperor Haile Selaoolo in 1074 and all U.S. advisors two years later, was attacked by Somalia, on its southern border. Somalia had been a Russian client, but was one of those African countries like Ghana, Algeria, and Egypt that had turned against the Soviets. A number of Cuban technicians and troops was now sent to Ethiopia's aid and turned the tide. The United States did not make any countermove because most black African states saw Somalia as the aggressor. Then, in February 1979, North and South Yemen, two tiny states on the southern edge of the Arabian Peninsula, fell to warring with each other. North Yemen, considered pro-Western, got a large quantity of American-made arms through Saudi Arabia, while Castro sent seven hundred advisers to South Yemen. After some inconclusive fighting, however, the two Yemens signed a truce, and later North Yemen turned to Moscow for more aid.

In all of this it was hard to read a consistent pattern, but Carter's political opponents charged him with laxity in the face of Communist designs on the "Horn of Africa" that pointed to the Arabian Sea, the Persian Gulf, and the routes plied by tankers laden with Middle Eastern oil. Under such pressure, the State Department edged toward an African policy more concerned with meeting "Soviet expansionism"—which suggested closer ties with the two strongly conservative white regimes remaining on the continent, those of Rhodesia and South Africa. A voice against this trend was lost in the summer of 1979 when Andrew Young had to resign for making informal, clandestine contacts with PLO representatives in violation of official American policy.

In the fall of 1979 the Carter line was perceptibly hardening everywhere under the political pressure. An example was the President's firm—if not very specific or meaningful—public statement in September that the presence of a Soviet combat brigade stationed in Cuba since 1962 and suddenly rediscovered was "unacceptable." In the new, official U.S. viewpoint the Soviets were "acting up," rushing to lead the world in arms, getting tougher with dissidents, probing in Africa.

But the Soviet Union had its own view of things. It saw the United States courting China, denouncing the arms control it had once sought, and scare-mongering in the Caribbean. It was confusing, said one Soviet spokesman to a *Time* magazine reporter: "The present leadership in Washington has never adopted one line to which we could adjust or respond." The root question, for both countries, seemed to be embodied in the title given by the reporter to his article: "Whatever Happened to Détente?"

Whatever the answer might have been, two events in the final weeks of 1979 now blew apart what little was left of détente.

ON OCTOBER 19, A GULFSTREAM II JET landed at New York's LaGuardia Airport, and a five-car motorcade whisked a Very Important Person to a private seventeenth-floor hospital suite on Manhattan's East Side. The VIP was the former Shah of Iran, whose throne the CIA had preserved back in 1953, and who had since fallen on hard times. For a long period he had benefited from the Cold War, being showered with U.S. military hardware—especially under the Nixon Doctrine—as America's strong friend in the Persian Gulf region. Sustained by that and by oil revenues, the Shah pushed on with the modernization of his country, on his terms. Whatever he may have achieved in building showplaces, he ignored growing problems of rural poverty, urban overcrowding, unemployment (including idleness among university-educated youth without technical or managerial jobs that they felt were due them), and resentment by a large number of fundamentalist Islamic clergymen who believed that the Shah was leading the nation away from its faith in Allah and taking it down the "devilish" road of Westernism. The Shah's response to criticism in his later years had been to intensify the abuses of his secret police, SAVAK. Widespread arrests and torture begot more unrest, which was used to justify further repression in a fatal cycle.

As 1978 drew to a close, U.S. diplomatic sources knew that the Shah was in trouble. Demonstrations against him were growing, he had no real backing in the Majlis, the Iranian parliament, and even the army could not be counted on. Carter showed no disposition for special measures to support him; the folly of propping up an unpopular puppet was one of the lessons of Vietnam. The Carter Administration expected to be able to work with whoever would emerge from an Iranian revolution. Events proved this to be a wildly wrong guess.

On January 16, 1979, the Shah left Teheran for an extended "vacation" in Egypt; later he would flee to luxury hideaways in Mexico and the Bahamas. The civilian government that succeeded him promptly invited home the Ayatollah Ruhollah Khomeini, an exiled holy man of enormous popularity with the Iranian masses. He flew back from Paris and into mob scenes of frenzied acclamation. The politicians who had sought popularity by repatriating him got an unpleasant shock. It was clear that he could command the allegiance of the crowd on behalf of any person or cause he chose; he could make or break leaders; he was the de facto government. U.S. diplomats were shaken. "Whoever took religion seriously?" mused a bewildered American.

Khomeini's revolution spelled trouble for Washington. He was virulently anti-American—America was the "great Satan" behind the wicked Shah—and he was easily able to exploit popular rage against the ex-monarch. It was clear that if the Shah ever sought refuge in the United States, Americans in Iran would be the targets of violence. For that reason, Carter backed away after an initial invitation, and said that he would not admit the Shah—whose unappetizing human-rights record he disliked—to the United States. As Carter recalled it for a reporter in 1981, his attitude was: "Blank the Shah!" (And "blank" was the word he used to the reporter.) "Blank the Shah! I'm not going to welcome him here when he has other places to go where he'll be safe." But there was pressure on him from David Rockefeller, from Kissinger, from the aging John J. McCloy and others, to change his mind. The basis of their case was twofold: image and prestige. The United States should not callously abandon an old ally and friend, or weakly permit others to dictate its policies on asylum.

Then, Carter later insisted, a wholly new element was injected. The Shah was suffering, it was revealed, from lymphoma, a form of cancer, and Carter was absolutely assured by doctors that his life could only be saved by immediate treatment, available nowhere but at New York Hospital. Under those circumstances he said yes. On the 18th of October, the American mission to Teheran informed Prime Minister Mehdi Bazargan that the Shah would arrive in the United States the next day. The Iranian offered to protect the embassy, which was therefore not evacuated—but he warned: "You're opening a Pandora's box."

On the 20th the Shah underwent surgery for removal of his gallbladder, which the disease had affected. For the next two weeks street mobs swarmed in Teheran, shouting anti-American slogans. On November 4, a crowd of some four hundred "students" rushed the embassy, snipped the chains in front of the iron gates to the compound, and poured in. The small Marine guard was ordered not to fire and imperil lives needlessly. Clerks and officials were seized while frantically trying to shred documents, rounded up, blind-folded, and paraded for photographers. The militants carried banners saying, among other things: "Khomeini struggles, Carter trembles."

Whatever their original intention had been, they quickly formu-lated a demand: The Shah must be returned or the hostages would be held indefinitely, or even tried as U.S. spies. The imprisonment of the diplomats was a violation of courtesies and traditions universally respected from biblical times, but the militants held the trump cards. The Iranian government could not or would not oust them without the Ayatollah's approval, and the Ayatollah withheld it. And the militants also controlled the lives of the hostages, thereby underscoring the bizarre dilemmas of power in an age of terrorism. Some high American officials called for an ultimatum, a threat of blockade or bombs, a "reassertion of American will," in the words of Henry Kissinger, lest the United States appear, as Nixon once described it, "a pitiful, helpless giant." But Carter, at this time, was having a recurring nightmare in which the militants assassinated one hostage each sunrise until he capitulated. He did not want to sacrifice the captives' lives. Moreover, a move too violent might bring the Russians crashing in to "rescue" their small neighbor—or might overturn Khomeini but bring something worse in his wake.

That left nothing but excruciatingly tiring negotiations and chessboard moves, while the 1980 presidential campaign began. Iran was a short-term asset for Carter, and a long-term disaster. In the short run the country rallied behind him, but eventually it punished him for its frustration. Week after week liberation would seem imminent, then presumed "deals" would collapse. The President froze Iran's assets in U.S. banks, though Khomeini ignored that pressure and said he would leave the question to the new Majlis to be elected, a process that would take months. UN commissions came to Teheran and went home empty-handed. Vance and Hamilton Jordan slipped quietly in and out of Paris— Jordan sometimes in moustache and dark glasses—to meet with the Iranian foreign minister in secret. And every night, relentless newscasts in the U.S. counted the days of captivity and interviewed hostages' families, and fed the sense—renewed just five years after Saigon had fallen—of the United States being impotent, out of control of events, unable even to punish the posturing youths whom they saw hurling stones and jeering at the American flag.

Then, when the Iranian crisis had been tearing at American feelings for about six weeks, the Soviet Union proceeded to lacerate them with a thrust into Afghanistan.

This mountainous buffer state between Pakistan and the U.S.S.R. (a nineteenth-century battleground for czarist and British troops and tough native riflemen) was already in the Red orbit. Its 1979 ruler, Hafizullah Amin, was a Communist who himself had earlier overthrown another Communist strongman. But apparently, in Soviet eyes, Amin did not act vigorously enough in suppressing an uprising of Muslim tribesmen. Perhaps the U.S.S.R. feared that the contagion of rebellion (and Khomeini) would infect its own large Muslim populace in Central Asia. Perhaps, like the United States with Diem fourteen years earlier, it wanted to replace an ineffective dependent strong man with one better able to control things—only to find that it still needed to brace him with troops of its own. The reason is still unclear, but whatever it was, on Christmas Day, Soviet planes began unloading tanks and troops at Kabul's airport. The Russians claimed that Amin had invited them in, under a mutual defense treaty, to help put down "terrorists." But within days, Amin was killed and replaced with Babrak Karmal. By January 1, 1980, there were fifty thousand armed Russians in Afghanistan.

Jimmy Carter seemed almost grateful for the chance to explode. He vented on Moscow and on détente the verbal assaults that he had withheld from the Ayatollah for the hostages' sake. He denounced the "callous violation of international law," the "deliberate effort of a powerful, atheistic government to subjugate an independent Islamic people." In a private briefing for senior congressional figures, he called the invasion "the greatest threat to peace since the Second World War."

And he did more than talk. He ordered the Sixth Fleet to eastern Mediterranean bases, alerted U.S. units in Turkey, stepped up diplomatic discussions to secure rights to naval bases in East Africa, and called for a crash program to create a Rapid Deployment Force for action in the Persian Gulf. He sent Defense Secretary Harold Brown to talk with China about possible weapons deals, and also offered increased armaments to Pakistan. To an ABC correspondent he said: "My opinion of the Russians has changed more drastically in the last week than . . . the previous two-and-a-half years." And, finally, he canceled U.S. participation in the 1980 Moscow Olympics, embargoed further shipments of grain and high-technology materials to the U.S.S.R., and decided that it was expedient at the moment to withdraw the SALT II agreement from the Senate's ratification deliberations. "Good God," said an unnamed Administration official to a news gatherer, "this is Cold War in the most classic, extreme form."

But none of it had much practical effect. Richard Helms, onetime ambassador to Teheran and former CIA head, put it clearly. For Russia it was "no gamble at all. What are we going to do about it? We have no forces there. . . . What can we do for the time being but remonstrate?"

The Russians stayed in Afghanistan. The main beneficiary of the new militancy was Brzezinski, who now began to emerge into the limelight more, and whose growing quarrels with Vance surfaced. Brzezinski had always held that the Soviets needed frequent raps on the knuckles to convince them of things. Vance remained convinced that diplomacy was the essential key to world order. That point of view clashed with Brzezinski's philosophical idea that "in life you must take risks." He had a touch of flamboyance; in China, a rumor ran, he had once climbed the Great Wall shouting, "Last one to the top gets to fight the Russians in Ethiopia." In Pakistan early in 1980 he posed for a picture in which he seemed to be brandishing a rifle in the direction of Kabul.

In the post-Afghanistan atmosphere Vance's position was weakening. It finally collapsed on an April day in Washington when Carter, under steady political pressure to be decisive, agreed to an attempted rescue mission for the hostages in Iran. The plan was adopted at an NSC meeting from which the vacationing Secretary of State was absent. It sounded James Bondish. Six Hercules C-130 transports would fly from secret allied bases to join eight helicopters from the carrier *Nimitz* at a secret desert landing strip in northern Iran, once used by SAVAK. They would set up a base. Then commandos would helicopter to Teheran's outskirts where they would be met by Iranians recruited by the CIA and provided with trucks with Iranian Army markings. In these they could get past the embassy guards, free the American prisoners, radio in helicopters, and be ferried back for evacuation in the C-130s. If necessary they could fight their way to a nearby soccer stadium for the helicopter airlift.

Carter said the plan was "the best we could evolve." When Vance got wind of it, he opposed it as passionately as Brzezinski supported it. It would most likely get the hostages killed, Vance said, along with soldiers and civilians on both sides, or it might topple the government of Abolhasan Bani-Sadr, who wanted to settle the crisis, or it might result in the arrest of the two hundred Americans still at large around Iran.

In vain. The wheels ground on. On the night of April 24 the "birds" took off for the rendezvous at Desert One, and Cyrus Vance wrote out his resignation, which he dutifully would not make public until after the mission, no matter how it turned out. It turned out terribly. Three helicopters were disabled with mechanical failures during the five-hundred mile flight, forcing the commanding officer to decide on aborting the mission. During refueling for the return flight, a helicopter crashed into a transport, an orange balloon of flame exploded in the harsh dawn, and eight men died. There was not even time to wait for the wreckage to cool so as to extract the bodies. The rescuers took off at 4:30 A.M., leaving the carcasses of the ruined aircraft—and their hopes—on the sand.

Vance was replaced by Senator Edmund Muskie of Maine. Muskie, who had been vice-presidential candidate in 1968 and an active contender for the nomination in 1972, was far from a pushover. But given his newness to his post, it seemed that the dominant foreign affairs voice would now belong to Brzezinski.

It did not really matter. Few initiatives were left to the Administration, now branded, rightly or wrongly, as visibly inept. Carter remained on the defensive until November, assailed skillfully by Ronald Reagan, the Republican nominee, whose charges echoed the line of the Committee on the Present Danger. There actually was an arms race, said Reagan in one of his repeated lines that drew laughter and applause, but only the Russians were running. Fighting off such assaults, Carter asked for supplementary billions for the Pentagon, announced the conclusion of an agreement with NATO to station nearly six hundred medium-range Minuteman and Pershing missiles in Europe during the early 1980s, and issued Presidential Directive 59, which called for a change in nuclear strategy. Under it, more American warheads would be aimed at Soviet launching sites.

The only favorable breaks for the President that summer were slow in developing. The Shah had left the country in December of 1979 for refuge in Panama, then in Egypt. On July 27 he died there. The issue of his return was, therefore, moot. The Iranians could back away from it if they chose. The new Majlis was finally elected and the hostage issue was no longer politically useful to the Ayatollah. And, on September 22, Iraq attacked Iran, which thereupon found itself needing military supplies, money, and support. Bearding the Americans was now merely a distraction.

It was, therefore, a simple matter of bazaar haggling. There were no direct talks between Washington and Teheran, and nothing was resolved before the American election day. But the Algerians offered to be middlemen, and as 1980 waned, Deputy Secretary of State Warren Christopher flew back and forth across the Atlantic, chaffering in billions and in fifty-two lives.

The final deal was, in effect, that the United States should return Iranian assets of $8 billion (some $5 billion of which went to pay off their debts to American banks), and they should let the prisoners go free. The United States made no apologies for past misconduct, and handed over no ransom that did not originally belong to Iran. Patience had finally paid off.

But it did not reward Jimmy Carter politically; it was too late for that. The final haggling was with a lame-duck Administration, for on November 4 Reagan had swept the election, carrying all but six states. Between that date and mid-January, Christopher continued to plug toward the final package of complicated legal and financial transactions. He was helped somewhat by Reagan, whose tough public statements made it plain to Teheran that they would get no better deal by waiting for him.

Before dawn on January 20, Carter and his aides, with the final documents signed, raised a champagne toast "To Freedom!" in the Oval Office. But the hostages did not file aboard their planes until 12:35 P.M. that day. Ronald Reagan had been President for half an hour.

The captives returned home to an explosion of public rejoicing that suggested the depth of the nation's need for heroes, for compensation to ease the psychic pain of the ordeal. In the jubilation there were no recriminating glances backward, but no sense either of the episode's mark on the future. It was not clear what Americans thought they had learned—how well they understood the depth of Iranian grievances, the meaning of Iran's revolution as a portent, or the new demonstration of the limits on American power.

A PPROXIMATELY ONE WEEK after Inauguration Day, a moment of either low comedy or high significance was enacted at the State Department's underground parking lot. The limousine of Soviet Ambassador Anatoly Dobrynin approached by a privately used back entrance. This privilege of special admission was long-standing. Its purpose was to allow the ambassador to come and go without attracting inconvenient press attention and rumors of crisis. But this time the chauffeur was told that he would have access thenceforward only via the main driveway, shared by the rest of the world's diplomats, from Algeria to Zambia.

Was this symbolic? Would almost twenty years of thaw end, not with vetoes in the Security Council, but in a garage?

Such a message was in keeping with the self-portrait that Reagan had sketched as a campaigner; for all his relaxed personal style he seemed not only implacably anti-Russian, but trigger-happy to a degree that stirred apprehension. He professed skepticism of any agreement with the Soviets, who, he would say on one occasion, "reserve unto themselves the right to commit any crime, to lie, to cheat." "Let us not delude ourselves," he told an interviewer. "The Soviet Union underlies all the unrest that is going on. If they weren't engaged in this game of dominoes, there wouldn't be any hot spots in the world."

Reagan's choice for Secretary of State, retired General Alexander Haig, seemed at first to be trying to exceed his commander-in-chief in the tough talk department. Haig belonged to a new breed of top officers who knew "politics, international affairs, and people." He came out of West Point in 1944, some two-thirds of the way down his class list (214 of 310), but all the same his career had been an impressive one. He was a good detail man, and knew how to cultivate the right subjects and associates. Washington friends introduced him to Kissinger, who made him a military deputy on the NSC. There he impressed Nixon, who passed over 240 senior generals to promote him from two to four stars. Haig moved into the role of White House coordinator in the last year of the collapsing Nixon Administration.

Paradoxically, Haig had trouble in his confirmation hearings because he was so close to Kissinger. But his early pronouncements left no question of where he stood on the source of the world's villainies. The U.S.S.R., he said, was guilty of "training, funding, and equipping international terrorism." And, in a bizarre syntax that baffled and amused the press as it had not been since Dwight Eisenhower's press conferences, he said that arms talks must wait upon Moscow's "reining in of what has been a hemorrhaging of risk-taking." He warned the Kremlin that, in the Mideast for example, "a change of the status quo would be met with the full range of power assets."

Haig, moreover, made an issue, in his first month in office, of the future of El Salvador, a tiny Central American country of four and a half million, like many of its kind possessing a landed oligarchy, a civilian president, and a military junta that actually did the ruling. It was beset with an insurrection that Haig promptly proclaimed to be in fact a Communist guerrilla takeover attempt, armed and financed by the U.S.S.R. and Cuba. Charging that the 1979 overthrow of Nicaraguan dictator Anastasio Somoza had also been their handiwork, he said: "Next is El Salvador, to be followed by Honduras and Guatemala. . . . A hit list, if you will." Then he issued a policy decision that was, for many, a nervous reminder of Vietnam days. U.S. military aid and advisers would be sent to President José Napoleón Duarte's government, whose army was already killing large numbers of allegedly rebellious civilians.

At home, Haig supported the call for a crash American arms buildup, to cost almost a trillion dollars over five years, starting with a 1981-82 military budget of nearly $136 billion. In June 1981 he made a trip to the Pacific area, and one of the things that emerged from it was a definite U.S. commitment of future arms sales to China. When worker unrest shook Poland's Communist regime in 1981, Haig declared: "I think we are witnessing a historic unraveling of Marxist-Leninism in the Soviet model." Meanwhile the President, in a commencement address, was also describing Communism as "a sad, bizarre chapter" in human history, which might now be at "the beginning of the end."

But as it turned out, it was Haig who was at the beginning of the end. His style made him a target not only for Reagan's opponents, but for those within Administration councils who found him too much the Kissinger disciple beneath the rhetoric—or perhaps too personally ambitious. He did not take kindly to being kept away from the President or overridden in decisions by the White House inner council. A war went on between some presidential advisers and Haig, punctuated by leaks to the press and occasional Haig threats to resign. In June of 1982, Reagan accepted one of those threats. Haig departed and was succeeded by George P. Shultz, a former dean of the School of Business of the University of Chicago, who had been Secretary of the Treasury under Nixon. Known for his economic conservatism, Shultz had no discernible track record in foreign policy.

The bureaucratic significance of this shift at the helm of State from a soldier to a business expert was unclear. It was not a victory for the National Security Adviser's office. Reagan's first choice for that post, Richard Allen, was relatively obscure and remained so until forced out of office for not reporting a gift he had accepted from a Japanese businessman. The successor was an equally unnoted man, Judge William Clark. And in October of 1983, Clark was named Secretary of the Interior and replaced by Robert C. McFarlane, who also rarely made the headlines. The President clearly preferred that media attention not be focused on any of his principal security advisers, whether Shultz, McFarlane, or Secretary of Defense Caspar Weinberger. Like his often-stated hero and model, FDR, he himself would be the central public figure in enunciating foreign policy.

So far as the actual conduct of foreign affairs went, the Shultz regime seemed to continue the general tone of militancy that had thus far been the Administration's hallmark. In four distinct areas of policy-making—the western hemisphere, the Middle East, Europe, and arms control—a taste for confrontation was in evidence. It pleased the President's conservative supporters, and it dismayed his opponents who preferred a more cautious approach, because the President was masterly at evoking patriotic themes to generate popular support for risky initiatives and putting the best possible face on their outcomes.

In Central America the Reagan team continued to ask for—and get—increasing amounts of money for military aid to the government of El Salvador, as the war against the guerrillas dragged on unsuccessfully. The funds did not come without a struggle. Congress—and especially the Democratic-controlled House—kept insisting that certifiable progress in improving human rights be made, and there was special concern over the failure of the government to rein in the so-called death squads, directed by right-wing army officers, that intimidated liberal dissenters. But Reagan spokesmen insisted that El Salvador was on the road to democracy and needed armed protection as it made its way. They proudly hailed an election held in March of 1982, even though it was boycotted by the insurgents (who feared betrayal if they laid down their arms to take part in it), and even though it left the balance of power with the extreme conservatives. And in March of 1984 they were arguing that another soon-to-be-held election was further proof of their case, as they increased the military aid request from the $64 million of fiscal 1984.

But sending advisers to El Salvador was only part of the Reagan Central American policy. Extensive U.S. military and naval maneuvers were held in 1983 and early 1984 in Caribbean waters and in "cooperation" with the armies of El Salvador's neighbors, Honduras and Guatemala. Nor was that all. The President continued to insist that the insurgents in El Salvador were being armed by Nicaragua. So he authorized equipment, training, and support (funneled through the CIA) for an anti-Sandinista army of Nicaraguan exiles that conducted operations against the Managua government from sanctuaries in American-dominated neighbor states. Supporting these "contras," the Administration held, was not an attempt to overthrow the Sandinistas by force, something prohibited by the Organization of American States' charter. It was simply a way of putting pressure on Managua to stop exporting revolution—a hint that two could play the game of subversion, and a hint meant to be heard in Havana as well as Managua.

But there was an even stronger "hint" yet to come. The President had long complained that the little independent island nation of Grenada, under a new, left-wing Prime Minister, Maurice Bishop, was possibly about to become a Soviet-Cuban base. In mid-October of 1983, a junta calling itself the People's Revolutionary Army staged a coup and murdered Bishop and three of his ministers. Promptly, on October 25, U.S. air and seaborne forces invaded Grenada.

Even as the paratroopers were landing, the United States offered two public explanations for its act. One was that the unstable situation threatened the lives of U.S. civilians, especially of several hundred American students at a medical college on the island. The other was that two nearby small Caribbean nations, Jamaica and Barbados, had asked the United States to step in, fearing that in the turmoil Cuba might seize Grenada. And in fact, once ashore, the Americans found themselves in combat not only with some Grenadans (the country had no army), but with several hundred Cubans, who were building an airstrip on the island and were also armed reservists.

After the island was secured Reagan, on national television, said that this justified his action. The airstrip, he contended, was clearly designed for military purposes, and large stocks of Soviet-made weapons had been discovered. We had gotten there "just in time." Not only were the students grateful (they appeared in newscasts happily kissing American soil after being airlifted out), but the Grenadans themselves welcomed their liberation from "Marxist thugs." These statements could not be independently verified until two or three days after the occupation, since the media had been barred from the operation. But they appear to have convinced a majority of Americans, to judge by public opinion polls, even though they were regarded with some skepticism by other world leaders, including Britain's staunchly conservative and pro-Reagan Prime Minister, Margaret Thatcher. But the underlying message was not so much to world opinion as it was to Castro and the Sandinistas, telling them that the United States was ready to use force in pursuit of its objectives.

Nonetheless, in that autumn of 1983, a year before the next U.S. election, the President perceived a need to defuse a growing criticism of his Central American course. He resorted to a device that had worked for him on other occasions, naming a special, bipartisan, blue-ribbon commission to "investigate" the entire Caribbean situation and present him with a report by the following spring. To its chair he named Henry Kissinger. The report emerged in February of 1984. It contained no surprises. It agreed that long-run social and economic reforms were needed to bring true stability to the region, and proposed an aid package of $8.5 billion over the succeeding three years. But it also endorsed the view that the Soviet Union and Cuba presented a clear and present danger to the hemisphere, and were the hidden forces behind Nicaragua and the El Salvadoran rebels. Therefore, to permit a "Marxist" victory in El Salvador would be a disastrous demonstration of American weakness, inviting further conquests. And so, the report concluded, there was need for a "significantly larger program of military assistance."

Meantime, there was the intractable Middle East. The Reagan Administration had begun by exploring new approaches to the

Israeli-Palestinian conflict, hoping somehow to achieve what had eluded all previous administrations, namely to keep Israel secure and satisfied and at the same time woo the Arab states. But from mid-1982 onwards, Mideast policy was completely dominated by the continuing and escalating crisis in Lebanon.

The underlying problem was that for years no single force among Lebanon's Christian and Moslem factions was able to take and maintain power, and no accommodation among the contending groups could be reached. The result was that private militias carried on constant warfare with each other, producing an appalling toll of civilian casualties. To complicate matters further, Syrian troops occupied the northern part of the little country, and the PLO had established de facto control in the southern portion, facing the Israeli border. From there (ignoring and ignored by a UN peacekeeping force) it carried on harassing attacks on Israeli settlements—until June of 1982.

In that month the Israeli government decided to expel the PLO from Lebanon, and in doing so, opened a Pandora's box. Israeli invaders drove the PLO back into Beirut, which was then pounded by Israeli planes. But to spare further noncombatant deaths, the Israelis were persuaded to let the PLO fighters evacuate the city peacefully, and to withdraw their own forces from Beirut itself, though not from southern Lebanon. The maintenance of order in the city would be left to an international contingent.

That contingent included United States Marines. But the story did not end there.

A new Lebanese government was formed, under a Christian leader, Amin Gemayel. Its army swiftly came under attack by hostile militia, including Shiite Moslems—who, it was charged, were being egged on by Syria. And Syria was a Soviet client.

During 1983, Reagan and Shultz followed a twofold path with regard to Lebanon. They attempted to produce agreements among the contending Lebanese factions, and also to get Syria and Israel to agree to a mutual withdrawal of forces. And they also called for strengthening and reinforcement of the U.S. Marine (and naval) presence in the Beirut area, and seemed to be gradually changing the nature of the mission. Instead of merely being neutral peacekeepers, it sometimes seemed—to judge by Administration rhetoric—the Marines were to provide stability until the Gemayel government consolidated its control. To many congressmen this sounded onimously like the support of one side, and not necessarily the strongest side, in a civil war—echoing Vietnam. It could be an invitation to attack. And the echoes grew louder. When there actually were some sniper attacks, the Marines and their supporting warships were authorized to return fire in order to protect themselves. How far would such "protection" go? How deeply would it involve Americans in combat with Lebanese Moslems? Or Syrians? Or Soviet advisers to Syrians? Clear answers were not forthcoming. Congress and the President quarreled over whether or not the War Powers Act applied to the situation—and came to an inconclusive stalemate that gave the President a full year and a half to keep the Marines in place, even though he insisted that he needed no sanction at all.

Then, in the final months of 1983, the situation was partly resolved by a rapid sequence of events. On October 23, 1983—the week of the Grenada invasion, as it happened—a truck loaded with explosives crashed through a security post and exploded inside the Marine barracks. Two hundred and forty-one sleeping Marines died. (A simultaneous attack killed over seventy French soldiers, also part of the international detachment, which likewise contained Italian and British units.) A wave of negative public opinion swirled around the President's Middle East policy. At first he tried to brave the storm—beefing up American naval forces, citing once again the need to stay the course against the Soviet threat, and promising to find and punish the terrorists responsible for all assaults against Americans. There were further attacks on Marines, more casualties—and retaliatory U.S. air strikes and naval gunfire. (One black American pilot, shot down and captured, was released through the intercession of Democratic presidential contender Jesse Jackson.)

But the underlying fact was that the Gemayel forces were losing their hold in the Beirut area. By the middle of February 1984, Moslem militiamen were clearly established in control; the Americans were totally vulnerable and had no Lebanese government presence to support. The British and Italians pulled out; the French opened negotiations looking to the same end. And the President withdrew the Marines to aircraft carriers offshore, announcing that the United States was not abandoning its position, but merely redeploying its forces.

In one sense, it was a Syrian victory; Gemayel was forced to call for a new round of talks with his Damascus-backed enemies, and to repudiate an earlier troop withdrawal agreement with the Jerusalem government that would have made Lebanon the second Arab state to recognize Israel's existence. Israel had failed to pacify Lebanon and make it a protectorate. The United States had likewise come to grief in its attempt to create, in months, a settlement that had eluded diplomats for generations.

But in another sense, the President had been saved from making heavier commitments and incurring further political embarrassments at home. And while the employment of American armed forces (however unclear their mission) had failed, Reagan had once more demonstrated his unhesitating reliance on force when he thought it useful.

In Europe, Reagan, Shultz, and Weinberger pushed ahead with plans (begun during Carter's term) to start the deployment of U.S. medium-range nuclear missiles by the end of 1983. Though there were widespread protests from European disarmament groups, consent had been won from all the NATO governments involved by the end of 1983, and the emplacement of the weapons began. There were other stresses between the United States and her European allies, primarily over trade and monetary matters, but they did not become truly critical. Part of the reason was that there were certain bedrock realities to the situation in Europe that remained unchanged as NATO approached its thirty-fifth birthday, and events of the early 1980s in Poland demonstrated them all too graphically.

The first of these was that while European neutralists deplored what they saw as excessive militancy by both Washington and Moscow, Moscow had a disconcerting way of behaving more frighteningly. In the summer of 1980, a strong Polish trade union movement known as Solidarity, under the leadership of Lech Walesa, an eloquent, dynamic shipyard worker, had emerged as a strong unifying force among all those who were dissatisfied with Poland's Communist Party dictatorship. Strikes and peaceful protests forced a number of democratic reforms on the Warsaw government. But in December of 1981, clearly acting under Soviet pressure, Poland's Red rulers declared martial law, outlawed Solidarity, and arrested Walesa among many other dissident leaders. (He was released after about a year.) Few actions could have done more to buttress the arguments of those in the West who claimed that Europeans really had to choose between forces favoring freedom and those endorsing tyranny.

The other fundamental truth uncovered by the suppression of Solidarity was twofold. Heavy as was the Soviet hand, it was still exercised only in those neighboring countries that had been in the Russian orbit since 1945. And in effect, little could be done about it. The Reagan Administration joined other Americans in deploring and criticizing the crackdown, and undertook limited sanctions against both Poland and the U.S.S.R. But in fact Poland was as far beyond effective U.S. help as Grenada was beyond Russia's.

Finally, there was the matter of arms control. The Reagan commitment to it had never been strong, inasmuch as the whole thrust of Reagan's 1980 campaign had been that the Russians had cynically used arms reduction and limitation talks as a smokescreen while rushing ahead with their own massive buildup. So within the new Administration, the U.S. Arms Control and Disarmament Agency did not enjoy a high priority on funds or personnel. Its well-known hawkish head, Eugene V. Rostow, was dismissed in the spring of 1983, and there was a brief headline flap when the President appointed, as deputy director, an inexperienced negotiator who had earlier indicated considerable doubt about the value of the entire arms limitation process.

The Soviet Union seemed likewise little inclined to take risks on behalf of arms reduction, and once more played into the hands of the more militant elements in the United States by hardheadedness. Leonid Brezhnev (who had signed the SALT treaties) died early in 1983, and was replaced by Yuri Andropov, who appeared to be less accommodating. Andropov threatened that if the United States went ahead with its plan for deployment of Pershing missiles in Europe, the Russians would forthwith walk out of all arms reduction talks. When this failed to produce any change in the Americans' execution of their plans, the threat was carried out, thus severing one of the few precious lines of communication between the two powers. During the months preceding the walkout, both sides offered proposals that they were reasonably certain the other party would not match. These tenders were therefore primarily for propaganda purposes. The Russians made a "no-first-use-of-nuclear-weapons" promise that they knew the Americans would reject because NATO was inferior to the East European bloc in conventional weapons. The Americans, in turn, promised that if the Russians dismantled all of their nuclear weapons aimed at European targets, they would take all U.S. "nukes" out of Europe—knowing full well that the Russians would refuse the deal if it did not include French and British missiles.

And while arms limitation and reduction talks languished, the arms race itself went on. Reagan, after a long battle, secured congressional approval to start MX production, with an understanding that there would be a new "basing mode." The missiles would be placed in existing silos. (Since one of the constant complaints of the Reagan team before the election was the vulnerability of those silos, this made bewilderingly little sense.) Eventually more mobile, smaller, and therefore more easily protected missiles would be built to replace them. A political compromise, not a military one. Reagan also pushed ahead with plans for the B-1 bomber, nerve gas production, stronger and better Tridents, and antisatellite space weapons, and won approval for all but the last-named, insisting all along that he was only "rearming" America.

In February of 1984, there was talk of the possible revival of Soviet-American arms talks, or even of a summit meeting. One of the reasons was that Yuri Andropov died, and was succeeded by

Konstantin Chernenko. Like most high-ranking Politburo members, he was something of a mystery, and it was thought that he might be inclined to a newer and more conciliatory approach. And on the other side, it was possible that with the U.S. election drawing near, candidate-for-reelection Reagan might find it useful to defuse his warlike image by a parley with the Russians.

But such talk was only speculative as March of 1984 began. The snows of winter might melt in the Urals and in the Rockies, but not necessarily in the foreign offices of the giant nations. The basic trend was clear and unmistakable. Going into the middle third of the 1980s, the thermometer of Soviet-American mutual feelings was still far down at the icy levels of the 1950s.

Did that foreshadow a revival of the Cold War in Dullesian terms? Not entirely, perhaps. Would the children born in Eisenhower's day, who had grown to maturity under the shadow of the two great rivals, go to the brink again? Probably not in the same way. Every epoch is different, and much had changed since the world was divided between Stalin's Russia and post-V-E Day America.

The nuclear superpowers now threatened themselves and the world as no one ever had before, with at least 9,000 American and 7,000 Soviet warheads ready to fire, each one far more powerful than the Hiroshima and Nagasaki bombs. A single Trident submarine skipper would soon be able to push the launch button on 24 missiles, each with 14 warheads, and thus rain the equivalent of 100,000 tons of TNT on each of 336 separate targets. Such weapons technology posed a threat in which traditional talk of "protecting" nations and their values through war defied reason. Perhaps such knowledge would restrain future missile crises, like that of 1962.

But on the other hand, the number of members of the "nuclear club" was growing. It was known that countries like Pakistan and India and perhaps others could soon join France, Britain, China—and, it was widely suspected, Israel and South Africa—as possessors of nuclear bombs. The world was reminded of this when, on June 5, 1981, Israeli fighter bombers destroyed the Osirak nuclear reactor near Baghdad, Iraq. Prime Minister Begin claimed that it was an act of self-defense—that he had information that the facility was on the verge of producing bombs that would be used against Israel.

Even without nuclear technology, once-backward nations had awesome and expensive arsenals of their own. The United States alone had sold $100 million worth of arms, ranging from rifles to radar-carrying spy planes, to an array of countries since 1945. The U.S.S.R. probably had done likewise. These heavily armed small nations were capable of attacking each other more readily than major powers, who had more at risk. And this perilous irresponsibility was even more true of terrorists.

There were other unpleasant, destabilizing surprises in the world for the U.S. and the U.S.S.R. Both nations, for all their differences, were based on Western revolutions that had placed heavy faith in science, reason, and history. Both, therefore, were surprised by how strongly traditional religious passions, as shown in Iran, could challenge the appeal of both Marxism and democracy. "Weak" and once-colonial nations could be driven to unpredictable actions by old faiths, ethnic rivalries, insoluble food shortages, or other things not encompassed in either the Communist or capitalist blueprint of the world. And as for sophisticated, modernizing, emergent non-Western nations like China and Japan, they, too, might seek pathways to the future independent of any other cultures.

The superpowers were not in full control of events. They were not even in full control of their own systems. For the U.S.S.R., the doomed Polish insurgency only called attention to past rebellions in the satellites, and to critical shortages and economic failures and loud dissents within the huge, polyglot Russian empire itself. It might be true that the Politburo's aging leadership belonged to a dying breed.

But the United States, while its problems were of no such magnitude, also had internal crises to manage. Conservatives and liberals might disagree on the causes and the remedies, but both identified the same persistent problems: inflation, unemployment, an aging industrial plant, decaying cities, energy dependence and energy waste, slow growth, a lack of social consensus on basic values, rigid and noninnovative bureaucratic structures everywhere. All modern industrial nations were facing comparable conundrums, swinging between political parties in search of a solution.

With such a welter of problems the contest for mastery of the world's future between the ideologies espoused by Moscow and Washington—the issue of who would be Number One—could become an irrelevancy.

Or the Soviet-American conflict could go on, and get out of hand, and leave the world merely a cinder.

No one could foresee the long run. Great rivalries and great dangers had existed before. Soothsayers had predicted the world's end in the year 1000. Instead, the world got the age of the cathedrals. Christians and Muslims warred from the seventh to the seventeenth centuries as if one or the other must come to rule the world, but at the battle's hottest, when the Turks were at the gates of Vienna, the Renaissance was in flower. Catholics and Protestants, and the young modern nations of the world—France, Spain, England, and Holland—were at each other's throats in the very decades when a New World unfolded before explorers' eyes.

The age of the jet, the computer, television, the moonwalk, organ transplants, and antibiotics might generate new adventures for a restless humankind. It might just be that no previous moment in eternity endowed people with so much power for good or evil.

That would make ours a very special age. Human recorded history alone is some six thousand years long, so that the single generation of the Cold War was, historically speaking, the mere blink of an eye. Was it a wink opening on new vistas? Or on the final pages of the human saga? The answer might well be up to those who succeed that generation—the heirs to an experience unique in the whole march of the past—to decide.

REFLECTIONS
OF A HISTORIAN

And so we have had nearly forty years of it. Forty years of "war" where the shooting is only intermittent and never directly between Russian and American soldiers, "war" where the fingers never dare to squeeze—or to let go of—the nuclear trigger. Forty years of "peace" that is neither tranquil nor assured, of "peace" under arms, "peace" burdened by suspicion and fear, "peace" in which the language of diplomacy is indistinguishable from the language of conflict. What have those years done to us as a people? How has life on the brink made us different?

For a start, it would be hard to overstate the degree to which the Cold War has changed the constitutional framework of the American government. It has accelerated almost beyond measurement the concentration of power in the executive branch at the expense of congressional power. It has increased the sheer size and weight of the federal establishment to a point where the needle runs off the scale. And it has drastically limited the concept of government by an *informed* citizenry.

Consider, first, the Presidency itself. At the very beginning of the Cold War, there were critics who held that the issue of presidential personality was important in launching the conflict. Scrappy little Harry Truman, they argued, got us into arguments with Stalin that a more flexible and pragmatic FDR would somehow have avoided.

Although in the long run such a view oversimplifies history, it is still true that individual presidential decisions have been at the core of every new Cold War development. Given that, it's fair to say that to a greater degree than ever before, our immediate national course has been set in part by the style and attitude of the man in the White House. What are his own views of Communism? Does he see it as a malign shadow over the entire globe, or simply one among several possible varieties of local tyranny? Does he take an active interest in the making of foreign policy? How secure does he feel in dealing with foreign leaders? Does he see himself as an adroit negotiator? Does he fear or welcome being "tested" at summit meetings? And at home, how much power does he exert over his own staff and Cabinet? Does he control the flow of information and initiate actions, or does he merely follow the lead of the strongest faction within his inner circle of advisers? And finally, how adroit is he at "selling" a position to congressional leaders and the public? At dealing with the press? Can he stick to decisions in the face of popular pressure?

Presidential Cold War leadership depends on some combination of these personal factors. Since Truman's day, the seven men on whose desk the buck stops have veered between belligerence and accommodation not only in response to outside pressures—including, of course, Soviet behavior—but within the framework of their own self-perception. Eisenhower had vast assets. He was popular, he had enjoyed good wartime contacts with the Russians, he did not have to defer to the military experts. As a result he could genially and confidently reconcile apparent impossibilities. He could work with John Foster Dulles, the architect of brinkmanship and heresy-hunting, and he could then, almost without skipping a beat, initiate the first real thaw in the Cold War.

John F. Kennedy fought to prove, by toughness, that his relative youth did not make him a pushover. Yet after coming closest to the brink, he reached for accommodation at least partly to sustain his image of coolness and "hard-nosed" liberalism.

The tragedy of Lyndon Johnson and Vietnam had at least one of its roots in the President's inner turmoil. Johnson took us deeper into the quagmire partly because he could not stand the thought of losing any battle whatever and partly because domestic politics were his prime theater, and he therefore deferred uncharacteristically—and disastrously, as it turned out—to his principal foreign policy and military advisers.

Following him came the complex figure of Richard Nixon, who rose to power by denouncing the "softness" of others on Communism, and who dreaded giving the impression of personal weakness. But Nixon also yearned to go down in history as a peacemaker, and boasted inordinately of his capacity for dealing on a personal level with other world figures. Out of these competing ego needs arose a President who could be toasted in Peking and Moscow while conducting a war against a Soviet ally situated on China's border!

Gerald Ford had no special urge to be a maker of diplomacy, and seemed to carry out without quarrel whatever decisions his national security staff reached. Jimmy Carter never seemed fully at home in the world of foreign affairs except when he was able to play the congenial role of peacemaker between Egypt and Israel. He came into office promising to avoid reflexive and fearful anti-Communism. But when the Soviet Union invaded Afghanistan, he was swept along in the tide of revulsion, indulging in rhetorical excesses that seemed characteristic of much of his vacillating official behavior. Moreover, a natural aloofness and self-righteousness kept him from developing a strong base of support in Congress or with the public. So when the Iranian hostage crisis broke, he was never able to defend his actions effectively. The result was a public bitterness that both defeated Carter and sowed a crop of jingoism that Ronald Reagan harvested.

As for Reagan himself, the final verdict is not yet in.

But whatever may be the inner wellsprings of presidential behavior and however constrained he may be by factors outside his own will, the unchangeable fact is that it is the President who presents the agenda, takes the initiative, makes the earliest riposte to situations. It can hardly be otherwise in an age of instant communication and overnight crisis. Yet when the writers of the Constitution made the Chief Executive the commander-in-chief and diplomat-in-chief, so that he might act with "energy, secrecy, and dispatch," they were thinking of a world governed by patterns as formal as an eighteenth-century garden. Before the President acted militarily, Congress would declare war. After he had taken action in foreign affairs, Congress would ratify and fund his undertakings.

But the Cold War has not been played by rules. Wars are neither declared nor, in some cases (like Korea), officially won or lost. Truman ordered the Berlin airlift and the dispatch of American troops to South Korea without, or in advance of, congressional approval. Kennedy launched the Bay of Pigs operation and managed the Cuban missile crisis without authorization from Capitol Hill. Johnson did go to Congress to secure the Gulf of Tonkin resolution. But by then, thousands of American advisers were already in Vietnam without official legislative sanction, and what Johnson got, in fact, was a blank check allowing him to use whatever means he chose to protect them. Nixon bombed Cambodia in secret for over a year. Congress ultimately reacted with the War Powers Act of 1973. But it has been resisted by every President since, is untested in the courts, and is exercised only reluctantly and gingerly. The latest example took place in the autumn of 1983 when Congress authorized Reagan to keep Marines in Lebanon for up to eighteen months, and the President accepted without acknowledging the validity of the Act.

The Cold War has been a major force in the "imperial" reshaping of the Presidency.

But if today's constitutional restraints on the President himself are frail, they are even weaker on the intelligence and defense "establishments" that the years of Cold War have created. Their growth is a prime example of the runaway momentum that growing institutions can generate—like an avalanche started by dislodging a single rock. When the Central Intelligence Agency was created, it seemed only sensible to unify the overlapping intelligence-gathering agencies of the individual armed services. And the "operational" mandate of the Agency—the secret dirty tricks—could be defended as a response to the unusual nature of the Cold War. After all, these methods had been safely and effectively used by the OSS during World War II.

Who would have foreseen that by 1953, when it was only six years old, the CIA would help restore the Shah of Iran to his throne? Or, a year later, engineer a change of government in Guatemala? Who could have predicted that it would have a minuscule "air force" of U-2 spy planes by 1960, or accumulate a guerrilla army and a mini-navy to invade Cuba in 1961? Who would have suspected that it would have a hand in assassinating the Congolese leader Patrice Lumumba, in attempting to murder Castro, or in "destabilizing" the government of Salvadore Allende in Chile, which led to his death? And who would have thought that its secret propaganda funds would find their way into the budgets of American unions and universities? Or that a President would use it, as the Watergate investigations revealed, to spy on and harass domestic political enemies?

There was a post-Vietnam reaction against the CIA in the 1970s, and especially against its exercise of domestic surveillance. But efforts to tighten congressional oversight have been only episodic. As 1983 ended, the Agency was busily conducting an unofficial war in Nicaragua, and who knows what unrevealed operations were in progress. There was no serious proposal afoot to restrict or publicize the CIA's budget. In some form or another, it seems a permanent part of the institutional landscape.

The same can be said of the other elements of the security machinery emplaced between 1945 and 1948: the Pentagon, with its vast budgets, large parts of which are inaccessible to general congressional scrutiny because their technical opacity discourages the lawmakers, or because they are shielded by classification; the classification system itself, only slightly dented by the Freedom of Information Act; the gigantic contracts for procurement and research, which have interlocked corporations, universities, and the armed forces in an amalgam that we loosely style "the military-industrial complex." Even the office of National Security Adviser— originally thought of simply as an informational link among the

White House, the Pentagon, and the State Department—became, in the hands of a brilliant bureaucratic fighter like Henry Kissinger, a policy-making force in itself.

All of these were seen as simple necessities in the 1940s. All of them are here to stay for the foreseeable future because, rightly or wrongly, and despite all criticisms, they are still successfully portrayed as indispensable to the national security. And all of them are, to say the least, extremely hard to reconcile with the concept of limited, accountable (and frugal) government that is the supposed bedrock of American liberty. These paradoxes all stem from the central paradox of the "war" that is neither war nor peace.

The curbs on executive and military power in our democracy have not been exclusively constitutional. Traditionally, the party system guarantees that a critical eye will always be focused on the Administration in power. But tradition dictated with equal force that in time of war, politics stopped at the water's edge. The trouble was that the old dictum did not foresee a time when a state of "war" would be almost permanent. When the formerly isolationist Republican Senator Arthur Vandenberg was won over in the late 1940s to support of the Truman Doctrine, and when Senator Robert A. Taft lost out to Eisenhower in 1952, it marked the effective end of an era when powerful voices spoke out against far-reaching global involvement. Neither of the major parties, while out of power, has gone to the voters in an election year with a platform strongly denouncing the other as too aggressive, too prone to see Communist influence at work in the world, too lavish with defense expenditures. On the contrary, the usual line is that the incumbents have done too little for national defense.

The basic premise of the Cold War—the need for a strong, worldwide, and permanent response to the Soviet threat—is de facto, beyond debate between most Republicans and Democrats. That means that it is almost completely immune to public evaluation. For a number of reasons, particularly the growth of costly television campaigning, minor parties that might raise such unpopular questions attract almost no attention. What is more, this unwillingness to contest the foundations of foreign policy affects the entire political forum, because "domestic" and "foreign" policies can no longer be easily separated. They overlap in such areas as civil liberties, trade, and especially public expenditure. So the Cold War reinforces a strong national tendency toward consensus politics and makes it almost unshakeable. Only during the Vietnam War did dissent break through, and even then it did not capture either party.

But the attenuation of political debate does not merely touch

Republicans and Democrats. The ongoing Cold War has affected that political culture that cuts across, or stands outside of, major party lines. Both Republicans and Democrats could once be divided loosely into "liberal" and "conservative" camps. And there was always a minor constellation of "radical" parties. All three groups have suffered serious identity confusion.

It was the liberals, in the contemporary American sense of adherents of the New Deal, who had the hardest time accommodating old principles to new realities. Tolerance of all viewpoints was supposed to be a liberal hallmark. But once the premise was accepted that domestic Communists were enemies of democracy, it was necessary to "expose" and "neutralize" them in liberal organizations, and to support legislative and executive antisubversive action. It sometimes took considerable and convoluted explanation to distinguish these procedures from old-fashioned right-wing Red-baiting. It also rendered liberals vulnerable to ridicule by conservatives, who could charge that liberalism was at last belatedly and dimly seeing the light. Moreover, one thing led to another. Liberals, responding to Cold War pressures, next had to swallow unpalatable peacetime doses of two more cures for American "weakness" that they had traditionally opposed—to wit, heavy military expenditures and secrecy in government.

In the 1950s liberals still believed they could have it both ways. That prosperous decade convinced them that they could continue to strengthen enlightened capitalism at home and also present it abroad as an irresistible alternative to Communism. But that logic required large amounts of both economic aid and military assistance to help stabilize foreign governments—which, outside of Western Europe, were rarely democratic governments—against "Communist-led insurgency." And in the bitter 1960s liberals discovered, first, that the nation could not afford both guns and butter, the Great Society and the Cold War; and, second, that among the competing religious and political faiths in the client states, democratic values often ran far back in the pack.

And so, expansionist and utopian illusions that stretched back to Woodrow Wilson's 1919-style progressivism took a severe beating. Liberalism lost both its vitality and its long dominance in American political thought.

Conservatives were able, in the early 1980s, to capitalize on liberal frustration, but they faced their own contradictions. Their staple of argument since the 1940s has been the twofold need to check the monstrous and invasive growth and cost of government and to restore constitutional first principles. But conservatives found that it was impossible to conduct the Cold War with the vigor they desired unless they gigantically enlarged the armed forces and stepped up the powers of the intelligence agencies, both of which are part of government. And, too, they found that the process required expenditures and deficits on a scale that made the New Dealers look miserly by contrast. From time to time voters have overlooked these inconsistencies as they have elected conservatives to office, but from the point of view of American political thought as a whole, the Cold War has created a sharp break with the past.

Finally, American radical factions outside of mainstream politics also show Cold War shock. The American Communist Party was never a force in elections, but many of its acknowledged members worked energetically in other political movements. That pattern was destroyed in the 1950s and has never been fully restored, even after American Communist leaders emerged from jail and isolation in the 1960s. There is a peculiar psychopolitical result. Almost all Americans today grow up hating and fearing Communism without ever encountering an actual Communist.

The non-Communist left was also caught in a special Cold War vise. American socialism suffered many mid-century blows, including innate factionalism, the appropriation of some of its best ideas by the New Deal, and the failures of particular socialist governments in the world at large. But one of its severest problems was in its Cold War stance. Socialists denounced both the American military-industrial complex *and* the Kremlin for mutual warmongering and contempt for "people's needs." They thereby became entrapped in a lonely, harsh middle ground that made it even harder to convince most Americans that socialism was an acceptable and respectable idea.

But what of native American radicalism? That streak of populism with deep roots in the American heartland and offshoots to right and left as diverse as the IWW, the Nonpartisan League, Huey Long, Father Coughlin, and, finally, George Wallace? It did not escape confusion, either. For the essential ingredients of this anti-urban, anti-intellectual political elixir were isolationism, pacifism, and folksiness; suspicion of big business and big government in cahoots against the little fellow; rejection of foreign entanglements and foreign wars as traps baited by the profit-makers. There was no way in which this tradition could survive in pure form without challenging the Cold War. That was impossible, and the best that someone like Wallace could do was argue that the Russians should be resisted by America without pussyfooting or depending on allies. But Wallace was patently uncomfortable with the need to formulate military or foreign policies, and he chose a peculiar solution in 1968. He chose as his running mate General Curtis LeMay, once Chief of Staff of the Air Force. But air power was the pure embodiment of high-tech weaponry, designed by "pointy heads," built by supercorporations, and requiring a worldwide network of bases in friendly countries. The contradiction was palpable whenever the two men stood together on a platform.

In every segment of the political spectrum, it appeared, carefully thought-out old positions perished and were not replaced—not even by the antiwar movement of the Sixties. The young protestors, however dedicated, never developed a formal set of arguments to rebut the domino theory, and preferred instead to sing that love and peace were better than hatred and war. Experienced political antiwar leaders like Eugene McCarthy or Robert Kennedy, looking for the widest consensus, focused narrowly on extrication from Vietnam without discussing the wider context of the war.

The young rebels—even the most outrageous—occasionally acted as if they would simply ignore the political structures and histories of both the U.S. and the U.S.S.R. as irrelevant. This was a kind of denial that they might have learned, from necessity, as the first generation to grow up under the threat of immediate nuclear extinction. What can one do, in order to go on living, but deny threats that seem irreversible? Some of the ferment of the Sixties survives in the antinuclear movement of the 1980s. But as of now, there is no sustained, organized, broad-based attack on the arms race—no politically strong movement fitted out with a popular rhetoric, legends, symbols, heroes and heroines comparable to those of, say, the abolitionist or women's suffrage crusades—for a major party to consider.

In all of the above there is no intention to suggest that only the Cold War is responsible for the disillusionments, irrationalities, and discouragements of our time. Nor is it to suggest that the Cold War is only the responsibility of one side. Or that it "shouldn't" have happened, which is as meaningless as saying that other historical events like the Reformation or the French Revolution "shouldn't" have happened.

What I do believe, however, is that all of American political culture shares traditions of activism, self-help, faith in the possibility of a better tomorrow. No part of it was prepared for the restrictive, dampening effects of decade after decade of a state-of-war situation. It is a long time to wander in the wilderness.

And what of the great globe itself? What has the Cold War wrought beyond our borders? The ripples of a rivalry between giants extend far. Francis Parkman wrote that it was because of the eighteenth-century war between the Kings of England and France that men scalped one another in North American forests and laid siege to ancient cities in India. So in the same way, the Cold War has been a worldwide historical force as well as a worldwide historical fact.

The rebirth of Western Europe after 1945 is a curious and positive spin-off of the Soviet-American conflict. It was made possible in good measure by American aid, and the American aid (like that to Japan) was forthcoming because of Cold War pressures. The United States did not return to isolationism as in 1919, and instead of a miserable, weak, and embittered Europe producing totalitarian movements, there were economic miracles and healthy democracies on the western side of the Iron Curtain. What is more, in their efforts at recovery, and especially in order to implement the Marshall Plan, the nations of Europe laid the foundation for economic cooperation that brought the centuries-old vision of a "United States of Europe" closer to realization. In a curious way the help we gave was like the space program—something worth doing in its own right, but which was made politically possible only because of American rivalry with the U.S.S.R. In the long saga of that rivalry there are not many happy thoughts to cling to, but this is one of them.

With regard to Asia, what is impressive is how the changes induced by the Cold War have only reinforced certain persistent patterns. The rise of China to the status of a modern, unified power began with the overthrow of the Manchus in 1911. The Communist Revolution of 1949, whatever it may have done or not done to and for the Chinese people, was one step in that episode. And it was a step taken with Soviet help as one of *their* moves in the Cold War. Ten years after 1949, China started to break away from its dependence on Moscow. Meanwhile, there is Japan. On the rise since 1851, it was smashed in 1945, then rebuilt with United States input, and it has now become again a major industrial power, both the ally and competitor of its American mentors. These two nations, China and Japan, in short, could not be kept satellites of the Cold War rivals. They will have much to say about the history of the twenty-first century, and American destiny will quite possibly be involved with theirs to a much greater extent than it will be with Russia's.

We think of ourselves as putting the imprint of modernity on Asia, and it's true, but Asia, in turn, shapes our history. (If you have a taste for historical playfulness, remember that America came into being in the first place because someone was trying to find a shortcut to Asia.) And in fact we may have less power over the future of Asia than we believed at the peak of our post-1945 power. One great story of the twentieth century is that of the swift decolonization of the world since that year. At the beginning of the process, Russia and America alike believed that the new nations would make a choice between "Communism and capitalist democracy," as our propaganda put it, or "socialism and fascist imperialism," as theirs did. But over the last thirty-five years, events have changed all that. A nonaligned bloc of nations, led by India, emerged, determined not to give unqualified loyalty to either camp. And time has shown that there are more than two dominant ideas contending for human minds. Nationalism, race, and religion are not dead. After years of Cold War indoctrination, Americans had trouble understanding that Ho Chi Minh won support from millions of Vietnamese not because he was a Communist—perhaps in spite of it—but because he was perceived as their George Washington. In South Vietnam in 1963, battles beween Buddhist subjects and Catholic rulers made headlines and puzzled readers who could not fit such struggles into accustomed political pigeonholes.

When the Ayatollah Khomeini replaced the Shah, it quickly became clear that he was a zealous Moslem, burning to scourge Iran of the influences of the degenerate modern world (of which the United States was the worst example). He owed more to Mohammed than to Marx. The agony of Lebanon is the latest chapter in a struggle between Christian and Moslem that goes back to the Latin Kingdom set up by the Crusaders in the thirteenth century. Some Israeli annexationists demand the West Bank because it belonged to the pre-Christian biblical kingdoms created by David and Solomon. The struggle of South Africa and its black neighbors may bring Cubans into Angola, but it is a war of blacks and whites as much as of Reds and whites. And some foretell that the climactic struggle of the next era will not be between East and West, but between the starving and the industrialized nations—the South and the North!

Thanks to Soviet-American rivalry, arms have been poured into these areas, so that Druse militiamen, Afghanistani tribal warriors, Central American Indians, Iraquis and Iranians, clothed in modern uniforms and ancient beliefs, make war with lethal new weapons produced in Czechoslovakia or California. To that extent the Cold War, by making Third World violence more efficient, has increased the amount of death in the world, though it can hardly be blamed for the impulse to kill.

The Cold War, therefore, has been an agency in spreading both the benefits and the blights of "civilization." Nineteenth-century evangelicals believed that steam locomotives and printing presses were God's means to convert the heathen. They were right, in part. They only failed to foresee that the people sitting in darkness would imitatively embrace dynamite as well as Bibles, and that the developed nations would vie for the privilege of making the dynamite available.

But the Cold War as a force for modernizing the world is not irresistible. Not only do old faiths persist, but some so-called "weaker" peoples even resist modern war machines. Nineteenth-century European powers controlled subject peoples with handfuls of soldiers, most of them native mercenaries. Yet now, with infinitely more firepower at their disposal, they are often stymied. We and the French learned this in Vietnam; the Russians may be learning it in Afghanistan. How does one "win" against suicidal guerrillas? What good are bombers against enemies that do not have an industrial grid or huge supply dumps to smash? Westerners make war on the premise that if you inflict enough "pain" on the enemy, he will yield somewhere short of total annihilation (though in fact that is not the way the Great Powers behaved in World War I). But what happens when there is no limit to the hurt that zealots are willing to endure?

That leads to a final set of sobering reflections on what some have called a post-historic age—that is, an age that no longer believes in predictable, orderly, forward motion in human affairs. In summarizing these years, I have tried to see the Cold War as if I were turning the insights of history onto a major episode far in the past—such as, for example, the national and religious rivalries of four centuries ago that led to the peopling of the New World. But there is always the discouraging consciousness that this time the story is different, not because the end cannot be foreseen, but because there are moments when it seems to be all too painfully foreseeable. The arms race in today's Soviet-American contest may confirm the notion that technology will destroy the human race faster than it can liberate it from drudgery.

The most depressing of all possible historical statistics is this: On August 6, 1945, there were only two nuclear weapons in the world ready for immediate use. Thirty-nine years later there are in excess of thirty thousand. Each new weapon—the H-bomb, the Poseidon submarine, MIRV, the MX—and each addition to the arsenal of old ones has been defended, as this book shows, with the seemingly unanswerable argument that, terrible as these devices may be, "we" must go ahead with them in order that "they" may not get ahead of us and submit the world to blackmail or be tempted to a first strike. Since we can assume that these propositions are also advanced in the Politburo, the bottom line is that each side is the prisoner of its worst imaginings. If the technicians of one side can conceive of an awful weapon, so can those of the other, so it must be built for protection and "stability." In the end, weapons technology becomes the keeper of the prison house. Those, in fact, who propose the abolition rather than simply the "control" of nuclear weapons are often met with the answer that it's too late; we are powerless; the Bomb cannot be "disinvented." This existential condition, this absurdity whereby the safer we make ourselves through more weapons the more endangered we become, is the most striking of all the paradoxes in this story. Is there a "biological" meaning to the Cold War? Have we reached this point through some kind of evolutionary mechanism, in which our propensity to violence and our technical ingenuity have finally combined to threaten us with extinction as a species?

These grim considerations engulf the idea of "progress" that was central to enlightened thought as recently as in the childhood of our grandparents. Only think! A world in which everyone believed that what was new was better, and that the holding of such a belief was what distinguished civilized from barbarian peoples. The bloodletting of the First World War smashed that view. What was left of it was further pulverized by the Second and its aftermath—the discovery of the death camps. Perhaps in a sense we should view the Cold War as the third war of the century. It is not a direct battlefield confrontation between the principals, but instead it is fought in many theaters in many ways, and over a long period of time. But it presents us with a fresh diet of horrors—the revelation of Stalin's crimes, genocide in Kampuchea. Arrests and torture the world over. Terror inflicted en masse by governments equipped with modern administrative and technical resources—and likewise by the lone terrorist who flings his bomb into a restaurant crowded with holiday diners. All these are exhibits of the spirit of violence and hostility loosed on the world.

Who is to blame, and where are the villains? This book does not attempt to pinpoint any. It acknowledges and regrets that Russian secrecy makes it impossible to represent fully their viewpoint. But what will it matter whose "fault" it was if the day comes when the ground trembles and the final missile rises out of its silo balanced on a pillar of flame? The question left is not: Whose fault? The question is: Is there an exit?

Is there an exit? Must history end in our time? That is not a question that one can answer here. But there is this to consider. Sometimes, one can become overpoweringly gloomy in going over this story because history is, as Clemenceau once said, a series of "depressing repetitions." It seems as if nothing changes. The debate over whether to make the H-bomb, in 1949, is echoed in the debate over whether to place the Pershings in Europe in 1983. For Guatemala in 1954, read El Salvador thirty years later. The Marines in Lebanon in 1983 camped within sight of the beach where other Marines—old enough now to be their fathers—went ashore a full quarter of a century ago. Under Soviet pressure, Solidarity is battered in Poland—and the stones echo with the cries of the dead of Budapest in 1956, the prisoners of Prague in 1968.

Is there an exit?

Perhaps not. But read again, and you will suddenly find some forgotten names. Once, there was fear of a clash in a place called Azerbaijan. Once, fists were shaken over Trieste. Once, there were two little islands called Quemoy and Matsu, flash points that might have ignited the final bomb. Who remembers them now? The symbolic, cruel Wall still divides Berlin—but there has been no crisis there since an agreement of 1971. The world-conquering Russians leave Finland alone; the imperialistic Americans, whatever the current Administration says, have honored the unofficial pledge not to invade Cuba. As the prophets of "deterrence" remind us, the Doomsday Machine's button has not yet been pressed. Each day is another day of life. Another day to act as if we were not the creatures, but the creators, of history.

After they had been in the wilderness for forty years, God said to the Israelites, through Moses: "I have set before you life and death, blessing and cursing; therefore choose life, that both thou and thy seed may live."

So far, in some stumbling fashion, we are still here, and still choosing life.

BIBLIOGRAPHICAL ESSAY

a. *General Observations: The Perils of Cold War Studies*

The following paragraphs are in no sense a complete bibliography of the Cold War or even of this volume, and for every book that is mentioned there are several that I have apologetically left out. It is simply a list of books, and only books, with some identifying annotation, for a nonspecialist reader who wishes to track the story or any part of it further and deeper. It does not include any of the numerous magazine articles used in the preparation of this volume. And it is furthermore confined to those titles likely to be available in a local library of moderate size. Nevertheless, many of the works it cites contain bibliographies of their own, which will open additional doors of investigation.

I think it important, however, that every reader understand the special limitations of writing the Cold War story. First of all, there is the simple matter of difficulty in getting the facts straight. The raw material is incomplete and impure. Diplomatic historians usually begin by working from such primary sources as the official documents generated by governments in the conduct of their foreign policies. Now, the United States has a program of publishing such documents in annual or special compilations under the title of *Foreign Relations of the United States,* followed by a year or some special identifying tag such as *The Conferences at Malta and Yalta 1945.* In theory the record was supposed to be made public reasonably soon after the events it covered. But with the fetish of security that has grown since the early 1950s and the tremendous resistance of the bureaucracy to declassifying confidential papers, the publication program has lagged further and further behind. As of 1977, no papers dated later than 1951 were available, and that twenty-six-year lag has widened since. For example, we know much more about how we got involved in Vietnam than we do about many other post-1960 events simply because Daniel Ellsberg chose "illegally" to go public with many classified documents in *The Pentagon Papers* (Neil Sheehan, ed., 1971).

There are other varieties of government-printed documents, too: the *Public Papers of the Presidents*, for instance, where the full texts of various Executive Orders, speeches, memoranda, and directives can be found and quarried for leads. These are somewhat more up-to-date, but again, the emphasis is on the word "public." They contain nothing of a confidential nature. The Office of the Joint Chiefs of Staff and the Office of the Chief of Military History have both sponsored elaborate historical programs, and volumes are now available on the Korean War, to take one example, that are very helpful. But they also have had to pass the barricades of "official" approval. From time to time the government has also issued special white papers to buttress the argument for some action (one memorable case being the documentation of North Vietnamese infiltration into South Vietnam), but these are, by definition, one-sided. Occasionally one or both houses of Congress have held hearings on some topic related to the Cold War—for example, the 1951 firing of General MacArthur by President Truman—and the published testimony in these is a source of historical material. Yet such volumes are likewise not allowed to contain classified material.

What about the private papers of public officials? Many of these are placed by men and women who served the White House in the presidential libraries—those combined monuments, museums, and archives built, or on the way to being built, for every Chief Executive since FDR. They, too, can provide valuable insights; sometimes they are annotated and excerpts are published independently—as, for example, Robert H. Ferrell, ed., *Off the Record: The Private Papers of Harry S Truman* (1980). But it cannot be overemphasized that whether such unpublished manuscripts remain in private hands, in university libraries, or in public repositories like the Library of Congress, they are not supposed to contain still-classified material, and where they do, such material cannot be used. In addition, many sets of papers are deposited under severe restrictions concerning their use and publication.

It seems almost superfluous to say that, bad as the situation is with regard to U.S. public documents, it is infinitely worse where the U.S.S.R. is concerned. Moscow only rarely publishes diplomatic documents, and then with great circumspection—as, for example, *Correspondence Between the Chairman of the Council of Ministers of the U.S.S.R. and the Presidents of the U.S.A. and the Prime Ministers of Great Britain During the Great Patriotic War of 1941-45* (2 vols., Moscow, 1957). Furthermore, there are no accessible collections of "private" papers of Soviet officials—if, in fact, any of them run the risk of keeping personal files. And researchers into Soviet history are denied access to a third category of materials available to those who study the American side of the Cold War: the uncensored published memoirs of actors in the story, and the works of independent journalists who have spoken with the participants or seen events firsthand.

That being the case, it is almost impossible to know what really went on in the Politburo during any episode of the Cold War. There are scholars who do the best they can to interpret Soviet foreign policy-making by gathering information from various "open" sources. They read *Pravda, Izvestia,* and other Soviet press organs. They look for patterns in the economic and social data released in official Russian publications. They weigh the reports of foreign journalists friendly to the U.S.S.R. against the letters and writings of dissidents or exiles and the revelations of Western reporters and diplomats who have spent time in the Soviet Union and then come home to tell what the Russian censors forbade—as, for example, Harrison Salisbury in *Journey for Our Times* (1982). Nevertheless, even the most objective Sovietologists will admit that they work in a regrettable twilight.

But the problem for the general reader does not end there. The responsible scholar burrows into the material described above, cuts himself out a carefully limited "turf," and tries to digest a small bite. Take, for example, Akira Iriye, ed., *The Origins of the Cold War in Asia* (1977), or Bruce Kuniholm, *The Origins of the Cold War in the Middle East* (1980), or Vojtech Mastny, *Russia's Road to the Cold War* (1979), or a book that is even more tightly focused, Robert L. Messer, *The End of an Alliance: James F. Byrnes, Roosevelt, Truman, and the Origins of the Cold War* (1982). Such narrow monographic studies are the building blocks of broader narratives (and I hereby express my gratitude for them). But they are often far too detailed for the general reader. They are aimed at other scholars.

And often aimed with hostile intent! That is an additional problem for the general reader. The scholars themselves can and do differ passionately about the interpretation of their evidence, as I shall indicate below, and while a nonspecialist can usually count on their "data" being accurate, he or she cannot at all be certain that their conclusions are based only on a disinterested zeal for truth. People who deal with Cold War history are caught in its magnetic field.

So the final word of caution to the reader is this: Be tentative in judgment. Practically no one is fully informed or fully detached.

The bibliography below does not make great use of specialized studies, which are not usually available to the general public. Instead there is heavy emphasis on memoirs, journalistic accounts, and broad surveys, which tend to preserve the human juices of the tale even though they may be somewhat self-serving or stint on detail.

b. General Works

The most recent overall professional survey is Walter La Feber, *America, Russia and the Cold War* (4th ed., 1980), which has a thorough bibliography. La Feber, who teaches at Cornell, is critical of many American claims and assumptions, but in my view is basically factual and even-handed. In a more essayistic and interpretive vein is Adam Ulam, *The Rivals: America and Russia Since World War II* (1971). Ulam, a Harvard-based specialist in Soviet history and a biographer of Stalin, has a firmly negative view of Soviet aims and tactics. But he does not see their leaders as supernaturally wicked or unswervingly dedicated to world conquest, and is not unwilling to find fault with American policy, though he spends considerable energy quarreling with the "revisionist" historians (of whom more in a moment), whose slant is generally anti-Washington. Ulam has also written the most accessible history of recent Soviet foreign policy: *Expansion and Coexistence: Soviet Foreign Policy, 1917-1973* (2nd ed., 1974).

Carl Solberg's *Riding High: America and the Cold War* (1973) is the only previous work that tried to integrate U.S. domestic and diplomatic history for the Cold War years and did so in a popular style that came naturally to a former editor and writer for *Time*. Another highly readable overview is Richard Barnet, *The Giants* (1977). This is not so much a history of the Cold War as a thought-provoking examination of the two superpowers some thirty years after it began. Some will find it objectionable because Barnet does not emphasize a "moral" contrast between the Russian and American "systems."

c. The Early Period: 1945-1953

It is in works that go back to the origins of the Cold War that the lines of division among historians are sharply drawn, because the issue becomes, in effect, "Who was at fault? Who started it all?" Loosely speaking, there are those who fully endorse what became the official American viewpoint as described in this book—namely, that the United States, eager to return to the paths of peace, was forced to rearm itself and the "free world" because the Soviet Union showed a clear intention to overpower Europe and perhaps the rest of the world by force and subversion. (This proposition, asserted with theological intensity, is still the mainstay of conservative thought on what America's world policies should be today.) At the other pole, so to speak, was the basic argument of Henry Wallace and his Progressive Party in 1948. It held that the U.S.S.R. had legitimate security needs and understandable anxieties after years of being a pariah nation and then suffering Hitler's devastating invasion, and that a more tolerant and flexible U.S. attitude— less dominated by the automatic anti-Communism of the business community—would have averted the Cold War.

The orthodox view dominated the field at first. But in the 1960s, especially in the critical atmosphere of the Vietnam era, the dissenting, or "revisionist," outlook was embodied in a number of studies, some of them quite zealously anti-American.

Before citing examples, however, it is best to mention several books of the 1970s that are neither orthodox nor revisionist, but tried to synthesize various viewpoints without imbalance or overall moral judgments. Among these are John L. Gaddis's *Origins of the Cold War* (1972), Daniel Yergin's superbly written *Shattered Peace* (1977), and Thomas G. Paterson's *On Every Front: The Making of the Cold War* (1979). All three are extensively researched, and all make due allowance for miscalculation, prejudice, and even deliberate exaggeration by American leaders and draw to some extent on revisionist assertions. But all are aware that the statesmen of the day—probably on both sides—had less room to maneuver and manipulate and less actual power to control events than propagandists gave them credit for. Paterson's book has an especially good bibliography.

Valuable examples of "orthodox" history are two of several books by Herbert Feis, an impeccable (and exhaustive) scholar who also happened to work for the State Department: *Churchill, Roosevelt and Stalin* (1957) and *From Trust to Terror: The Onset of the Cold War, 1945-50* (1970). A sampling of revisionist writing on the same period would include Denna J. Fleming, *The Cold War and Its Origins* (1961), David Horowitz, *The Free-World Colossus* (1965), Gabriel Kolko, *The Politics of War* (1968), and Gabriel and Joyce Kolko, *The Limits of Power: The World and U.S. Foreign Policy, 1945-1954* (1972). In my view, the revisionists add a useful dimension to the story by making us aware of how such terms as "free world" and "national security" were basically defined by a U.S. leadership that had long worked within or on behalf of American corporations with overseas interests—so that saving the world from Communism in the late 1940s neatly coincided with saving it as a frontier for American capitalism. But the revisionists too glibly ignore provocative or threatening aspects of Soviet behavior. Some of them also write from what they call a Marxist perspective, and argue that "American imperialism" is an inevitable

late stage of capitalist growth and decay. This kind of abstract
theorizing about historical "laws" does not take into account, it
seems to me, the degree of complexity in history.

Books keep appearing on various subtopics within the broad
category of the onset of the Cold War, often providing new
arguments or updating old ones. On the question of the early history
of nuclear weapons, for example, there is solid material in the first
volume of the official history of the Atomic Energy Commission by
Richard G. Hewlett and Oscar Anderson, *The New World,
1939-1946* (1962), and also in a recent work, Gregg Herken's *The
Winning Weapon: The Atomic Bomb in the Cold War, 1945-50*
(1980), which deals with America's very high (and frustrated)
expectations of diplomatic invincibility thanks to its exclusive
possession of the A-bomb. In the controversial arena of the
loyalty-security programs and the McCarthy era, a book that is
critical of the "witch-hunts" but solidly factual is David Caute, *The
Great Fear* (1978). The use and misuse of history for Cold War
purposes is very well covered in Athan Theoharis, *The Yalta Myths*
(1970). A recent biography of Senator McCarthy by David M.
Oshinski, *Conspiracy So Immense: The World of Joe McCarthy*
(1983), tries to put the man and the period named for him in some
kind of perspective. It is no easy chore. Two relatively recent books
take a fresh look at the Hiss and Rosenberg cases and, contrary to
what many liberals have thought for years, believe that these
"victims" were at least partially guilty as charged. They are: Allen
Weinstein, *Perjury: The Hiss-Chambers Case* (1978), and Ronald
Radosh and Joyce Milton, *The Rosenberg File* (1983).

Old controversies, like old soldiers, never die. The wisdom of
what we did and did not do in Korea, 1950-53, is still on the agenda
of debate. William Manchester's *American Caesar: Douglas MacArthur, 1880-1964* (1978) colorfully (but fairly) presents the General's
view of that war and how he would have won it if left alone by the
White House and the Joint Chiefs of Staff. But Omar Bradley's
autobiography, *A General's Life*, written with Clay Blair (1983), tells
a different tale, as does General Matthew B. Ridgway (who
succeeded MacArthur) in *The Korean War* (1967).

Truman's was the key Presidency of the Cold War—perhaps of
the century—so it is natural that biographies and autobiographies of
the man from Independence are a major source of Cold War
information. Most useful to me were two volumes by Robert J.
Donovan, *Conflict and Crisis* (1977), which covers Truman's first
term, and *Tumultuous Years* (1982), which deals with the second.
They combine Donovan's journalistic experience with careful
documentary research. Truman wrote his own memoirs, too, which
are worth consulting. The trouble with them is that, like all

presidential memoirs, they are largely drained of uncertainty and passion, and, needless to say, prove—with the aid of documents carefully dug up and culled by researchers—how wrong were the President's foes. Truman's recollections are in two volumes: *Years of Decision* (1955) and *Years of Trial and Hope* (1956). There is more of "give-'em-hell Harry" in Merle Miller, *Plain Speaking: An Oral Biography of Harry S Truman* (1974), but the problem is that Truman's tape-recorded recollections many years later are self-censored, and therefore often at considerable variance with the earlier documentary record. That is a general problem in "oral history."

Next come the memoirs of other public figures—often good reading but only when bearing in mind that those who rise to high office rarely, in the words of the humorist Finley Peter Dunne ("Mr. Dooley"), "bear a grudge against themselves." There is Dean Acheson, *Present at the Creation* (1969), George F. Kennan, *Memoirs, 1920-1950* (1967), James F. Byrnes, *Speaking Frankly* (1947) and *All in One Lifetime* (1958), Charles Bohlen, *Witness to History, 1929-69* (1973), Walter Bedell Smith, *My Three Years in Moscow* (1950), and Lucius Clay, *Decision in Germany* (1950). Because Acheson, Kennan, and Bohlen are thoroughly literate, their memoirs sound less like the special pleading that in fact they are. There are also valuable insights into the extreme Cold War mind-set in Walter Millis, ed., *The Forrestal Diaries* (1951).

Finally, there are two journalistic memoirs that will repay the curious reader fond of intimate and gossipy details: Cyrus L. Sulzberger, *A Long Row of Candles* (1969), and Arthur Krock, *Memoirs: Sixty Years on the Firing Line* (1968).

d. The Eisenhower Years: 1953-60

Eisenhower's memoirs are useful, subject to the reservations mentioned earlier. They are in two volumes: *Mandate for Change* (1963) and *Waging Peace* (1965). A lively insider's view is provided in Emmett Hughes, *The Ordeal of Power* (1963), by a newspaperman who became one of Ike's speechwriters but later left the Administration. Of biographies that deal with Eisenhower's Presidency, Peter Lyon, *Eisenhower* (19TK), is critical but full of useful information. As for the controversial John Foster Dulles, there is much that is worthwhile in Townsend Hoopes, *The Devil and John Foster Dulles* (1973), but anyone curious to know more about Dulles will do well to look at Ronald W. Pruessen, *John Foster Dulles: The Road to Power* (1982), which only goes to 1952 but will soon be followed by a second volume. Pruessen, who is sympathetic to revisionist thinking, nonetheless finds Dulles more than a compulsive moralist obsessed with the Red menace. He may have been that, but he also had a sophisticated comprehension of the international networks of modern economic and diplomatic power, and it is the odd combination of this twentieth-century globalism with old-rugged-cross righteousness that makes the man so intriguing.

e. The Kennedy and Johnson Years

Two biographies by White House staffers present the Kennedy Presidency sympathetically; they are Theodore Sorensen, *Kennedy* (1965), and Arthur M. Schlesinger, Jr., *A Thousand Days* (1965). A more disapproving, though not totally negative appraisal is to be found in Richard J. Walton, *Cold War and Counter-Revolution* (1972). Walton's wariness about high-minded invocations of the cause of "world freedom" is attested to in an earlier work, *Henry Wallace, Harry Truman and the Cold War* (1976).

As for specific episodes of the Kennedy regime, Peter Wyden's *The Bay of Pigs* (1979) is a thoroughgoing account of that sad chapter. The Cuban missile crisis is handled in two books: Elie Abel's *The Missile Crisis* (1966) and David Detzer's later *The Brink: The Cuban Missile Crisis* (1979). Robert F. Kennedy wrote his own story of that agonizing crunch in *Thirteen Days: A Memoir of the Cuban Missile Crisis* (1969), and there is more on his role in all aspects of Kennedy foreign policy-making in Arthur M. Schlesinger, Jr., *Robert F. Kennedy and His Times* (1978).

Literature on Vietnam abounds, all of it a minefield. To touch only on highlights, I think the best place to start is with the Pentagon Papers, cited earlier. In my opinion David Halberstam's *The Best and the Brightest* (1972) is excellent, though there are defenders of Johnson who will disagree. George Ball, in *The Past Has Another Pattern* (1982), his autobiography, provides the perspective of a sympathetic insider who opposed the deepening involvement and finally had to quit. Townsend Hoopes, in *The Limits of Intervention* (1973), also throws light on the political infighting in Washington and Saigon that so affected the outcome. As for the torments of Lyndon B. Johnson, whom Vietnam destroyed, some of them are poignantly revealed in Doris Kearns's extraordinary portrait, *Lyndon B. Johnson and the American Dream* (1976). Vietnam literature continues to appear, as wounds still fester. A compilation of views is presented in Guenter Lewy, *America in Vietnam* (1978). Stanley Karnow's *Vietnam, a History,* prepared to accompany his PBS television series on the war, appeared too late for me to use, but seems to be excellent, and is balanced. However, we are still far too close to those divisive years for any truly comprehensive and sympathetic understanding of them, so all works on the subject should be read with great caution.

f. From Nixon and Détente to Reagan and Confrontation

The closer one gets to the present, the more diffcult it becomes to find works that are detached or complete. Not enough has been revealed; not enough has been settled. Much of the information I used for the most recent years comes from magazine articles, and any good journalist will admit how ephemeral are his creations. The reader's watchword should again be: Proceed with Caution.

For the Nixon and Ford period, Nixon tells his side of the story in *RN: The Memoirs of Richard Nixon* (1978), and Henry Kissinger has also published memoirs under the title *The White House Years* (1979). Against their versions of events are arrayed Tad Szulc, *The Illusion of Peace: Foreign Policy in the Nixon Years* (1978), whose title more or less suggests the basic viewpoint, and Seymour Hersh, *Kissinger: The Price of Power* (1983), a stinging critique that has provoked some gratified and some angry reviews and rejoinders. A friendlier, but not totally admiring biography of Kissinger is to be found in Marvin and Bernard Kalb, *Kissinger* (1974).

An interesting academic overview of the period of the 1960s and 1970s is provided in Stanley Hoffman, *Primacy of World Order: American Foreign Policy Since the Cold War* (1978). In view of very recent events the words "since the Cold War" sound strange, but 1978 was a year just about the last one—of détente and hope.

A good story that highlights the complexities of arms reduction talks is John Newhouse, *Cold Dawn: The Story of SALT* (1973). Current (1984) works on the nuclear weapons competition fall into the category of advocacy rather than history.

The Carter Presidency is still controversial, as is well illustrated by two books on Iran. Barry Rubin, in *Paved with Good Intentions: The American Experience in Iran* (1980), suggests that our fatal flirtation with the Shah, and Carter's refusal to repudiate him cleanly until too late in the game, begot the hostage crisis. Michael Ledeen and William H. Lewis's *Debacle: The American Failure in Iran* (1981) looks at the same record and concludes that it was an error not to give the Shah even more support when his regime was threatened, since he was, from the standpoint of America's interests, the best available choice.

Carter has published the first volume of his memoirs, *Keeping Faith: Memories of a President* (1982), and his aide, Hamilton Jordan, has told the Carter side of the hostage negotiations in *Crisis: The Last Year of the Carter Presidency* (1982).

As for Reagan, at least one book-length critique of his Central American policy has appeared, Walter La Feber's *Inevitable Revolutions: The United States in Central America* (1983). And as of this moment, the first inside-the-Administration memoir is out. This is ex-Secretary of State Haig's *Caveat: Realism, Reagan and*

Foreign Policy (1984), a Haig's-eye view of what he aspired to do
and who did him in. There will undoubtedly be more such volumes
to come.

INDEX